SNACKS

A Canadian Food History

SNACKS

JANIS THIESSEN

Snacks: A Canadian Food History

21 20 19 18 17 1 2 3 4 5

University of Manitoba Press
Winnipeg, Manitoba, Canada
Treaty 1 Territory
uofmpress.ca

Cataloguing data available from Library and Archives Canada
ISBN 978-0-88755-799-6 (PAPER)
ISBN 978-0-88755-529-9 (PDF)
ISBN 978-0-88755-527-5 (EPUB)

Cover design by David Drummond
Interior design by Jess Koroscil

Printed in Canada

The University of Manitoba Press acknowledges the financial support for its publication program provided by the Government of Canada through the Canada Book Fund, the Canada Council for the Arts, the Manitoba Department of Sport, Culture, and Heritage, the Manitoba Arts Council, and the Manitoba Book Publishing Tax Credit.

Funded by the Government of Canada | Canada

for Tim,
whose idea this was

CONTENTS

INTRODUCTION

"There is a certain amount of comfort in a bag of chips or a chocolate bar."

——— ANONYMOUS OLD DUTCH EMPLOYEE ———

Snack foods are simultaneously loved and reviled. Many of us eat them—and in great quantity. But we are told they are not healthy, either physically or morally. Snacks are filled with sugar or fat or salt, each of which—rightly or wrongly—has been linked in popular discourse with a host of diseases: hypertension, diabetes, bad cholesterol, and (the most recent, and seemingly most pressing, concern) obesity.[1] Our moral health is threatened by snacks as well. We are warned that we have replaced the cooking of raw ingredients in our homes—and the consumption of the resulting meals at a table surrounded by family and friends—with the hasty and lonely consumption, in cars and on the go, of processed food substitutes filled with chemicals and produced by faceless, industrial entities.

When I was growing up, snacks were always available in my parents' home. There were cases of Pic-a-Pop stacked beside the furnace in the basement: bottles of orange, root beer, and (my father's favourite) black cherry soda. The glass bottles fit neatly into the bright orange plastic cases provided by the Winnipeg bottling company, which would pay a deposit for their return. Beside these basement Pic-a-Pop cases were accompanying stacks of boxes of Old Dutch potato chips, primarily salt and vinegar flavour. In the pantry and kitchen, my parents stocked boxes of Cracker Jack, the occasional box of Lucky Elephant popcorn (which was coated in neon pink candy), Eat-More and Kit Kat chocolate bars, and Nutty Club pearled peanuts (with their bumpy coating of red candy). The freezer contained boxes of Mackintosh's Toffee; my father preferred his toffee rock-hard and would smash it into eatable bits with his fist. The refrigerator held bags of Paulins Puffs, the chocolate-covered marshmallow cookie with a graham wafer base topped with jam: my parents liked the crack of the cold chocolate as they bit into the cookie. We got Wagon Wheels in our school lunch boxes and ate a cookie or two after our breakfast in the morning (our mother said it was important to start the day with something sweet). And buried in the bottom of my mother's sewing machine cabinet was a secret stash of candy, accessible only to her.

Snacks were much less available to my father during his own childhood. Born in 1925, he had vivid memories of the traditional brown-paper lunch bag his church distributed to children at Christmas, filled with roasted peanuts in the shell, a few pieces of hard candy, and one precious Christmas orange. During prairie summers, he would catch gophers for the government bounty of five cents per tail, spending the money on Pepsi. Decades later, he could still sing the old jingle, "Pepsi Cola hits the spot! Twelve full ounces, that's a lot. Twice as much for a nickel, too. Pepsi Cola is the drink for you." But, despite this comparative paucity of snacks, his childhood diet was not necessarily healthier than mine. Typical meals included strips of deep-fried dough (known among Russian Mennonites as *rollkuchen*), salted and served with watermelon; bread spread with rendered pork fat (also known as crackles or *jreewe*); or *plauten pie*—a shallow apple pie baked on a cookie sheet (eaten as an entrée, not as a dessert).

Snack Food or Junk Food?

My father's Russian Mennonite childhood diet had much in common with that of journalist Michael Pollan's mother. Pollan says she "grew up in the 1930s and 1940s eating a lot of traditional Jewish-American fare, typical of families who recently emigrated from Russia or Eastern Europe: stuffed cabbage, organ meats, cheese blintzes, kreplach, knishes stuffed with potato or chicken liver, and vegetables that often were cooked in rendered chicken or duck fat."[2] Pollan has become famous for his three food rules: "Eat food. Not too much. Mostly plants."[3] Doing so will reduce your risk of obesity and improve your health, he claims. By contrast, Michelle Allison, who blogs as the "Fat Nutritionist," asserts: "Eat food. Stuff you like. As much as you want."[4]

Pollan has elaborated on his food rules, declaring, "Don't eat anything your great-grandmother wouldn't recognize as food."[5] He notes, "If your great-grandmother was a terrible cook or eater, you can substitute someone else's grandmother—a Sicilian or French one works particularly well."[6] Pollan has been criticized for the ahistorical, classist, romantic vagueness of this advice. Food historian Rachel Laudan, for example, notes that "our grannies were born sometime from 1880 to 1970. . . These grannies all came into a world in which they could count on at least some industrial foods. . . . [E]ntire populations in the richer parts of the world today eat as well as, actually better than the greatest emperors of the past."[7] She observes that Pollan's rules "had already been advocated by Rousseau in the middle of the eighteenth century."[8] Outlining the history of the development of industrial agriculture and its dramatic transformation of "coarse, limited diets, periodic hunger, malnutrition, and famine," she declares that "artisanal versus industrial does not map on to good versus bad food."[9] Thus, "the modern romantic tradition, which runs from [British cookery author] Elizabeth David through admirers such as [American restaurateur] Alice Waters and [American cookbook author] Paula Wolfert, to [journalists] Michael Pollan and Mark Bittman paint the use of modern science and technology in food as inappropriate, distasteful, and dangerous. I think it's essential."[10]

A quarter century before Pollan's critique and Laudan's defence of industrial food, anthropologist Sidney Mintz outlined the severe limitations of the pre-industrial diet and the historical dominance of sugar in the European working-class diet in his landmark book, *Sweetness and Power*. Mintz's careful historical work revealed the impoverishment of the great-grandmothers' diets that Pollan so casually lauded. The late nineteenth-century workers' diet was "unhealthy and uneconomical,"[11] "both calorically and nutritively inadequate and monotonous."[12] Bread and beer were the staples,[13] and what little protein was available was reserved for the male head of the household.[14] Sugared tea for the industrial working class became not a luxury but a necessity, a cheap and fast way of adding essential calories to an insufficient diet.[15] Pollan's food rules, which emphasize education and personal choice, are revealed to be inadequate and impossible by Mintz's historical approach to the subject of sugar. He says, "The changing nature of the industrial workday, the cheap calories (both in cost and in resource use) provided by sucrose, and the special-interest groups intent on pushing its consumption make such cumulative pressure difficult to resist on an individual or a group educational basis. . . . Diet is remade because the entire productive character of societies is recast and, with it, the very nature of time, of work, and of leisure."[16]

Mintz, Pollan, and Laudan have brought the history of food to the attention of the general public; yet, food history is a fairly recent field of academic study. Though undertheorized at this early stage, it shows signs of providing productive insights into such broad areas as migration studies, labour history, sensory history, and the history of capitalism. Taste, according to historians Gerald Fitzgerald and Gabriella Petrick, is "both something an individual possesses and something negotiated between individuals or groups"; it is "a dialectic relationship between producers and consumers."[17] It is a physiological phenomenon associated with eating, yet also is defined as a determinant of social class. Pierre Bourdieu's *Distinction*, Mintz's *Sweetness and Power*, and Carolyn Korsmeyer's *The Taste Culture Reader* have emerged as key texts in the study of taste and its intersection with class.[18] Contemporary criticism of snack (or junk) food consumption has ties to class as well.

Public discourse on snack food shows similarities to that on alcohol, tobacco, and drugs. Nancy Reagan's dictum "just say no" to drugs, for example, is echoed in Pollan's and *New York Times* columnist Mark Bittman's pleas to individuals to make food choices that do not include processed foods.[19] By contrast, *New York Times* reporter Michael Moss, in his discussions of junk food, uses the language of addiction, which in some ways displaces responsibility from the individual consumer to the broader political-economic system (while still ignoring the role of the worker in this process).[20] Food historian Sara Davis, for example, argues that the language of addiction is a frame similar to the "demon drink" metaphor used by the earlier temperance movement: "Teetotallers had legitimate concerns about the effect of alcohol on physical and behavioural health, but their frame for this substance and its effects was one of possession: *demon drink*. . . . When an appealing, catchy frame gets louder than the actual exchange of information, it drowns out reality-based problem-solving."[21] Morality is often tied to what one chooses to manufacture or consume, but Davis cautions that food of all kinds is "morally neutral." The temperance movement was often about the social control and moral judgement of the lower classes by their "betters." In the same way, popular discussion of snack foods is too often about control and judgement of others. Davis says, "When we talk about the junk food habits of Other People in a way that depicts these Other People as thoughtless, addicted eating machines, that's dehumanizing. And elitist. Because let's be honest, when we worry about the junk food habits of Other People, we usually mean Fat People or Poor People or High School Kids, right? And it suits us to think of these groups of people as being unable to make decisions for themselves, just as it suits us to jokingly cast our own entirely human desires as uncontrollable urges."[22] We need to look past this binary of "choice" and "addiction" to the lived experiences of eaters. This lived sensory experience reveals that people have chosen to eat snack foods for a variety of reasons including taste, which is shaped not just by the physiological experience of eating but also by collective memory. The labour process that results in these products, however, is acknowledged by consumers (and, too often, also by scholars) only in a superficial manner.

Telling the Story of Snack Foods

This book tells the story of independent Canadian snack food manufacturing firms—their owners, managers, workers, and consumers—in the twentieth and twenty-first centuries. A business, labour, and social history, this book examines the production, promotion, and consumption of snack foods. Industrial capitalism after the Second World War transformed Canadian society, as the manufacturing of non-essential products escalated, and postwar prosperity and increasing working hours transformed snack foods from 'treats' to replacement or supplementary 'meals.' In an article for *Food, Culture & Society*, Katherine Turner explains that the transformation was assisted by the fact that "a worker's time could be better spent earning wages than producing cooked food at home."[23] This process was hastened in the 1970s and 1980s as real wages stagnated and food access in poorer neighbourhoods became more limited. As a consequence, according to food scholar Marion Chan, in Canada, "the snack meal is now second only to dinner."[24] The average Canadian ate more than 300 between-meal snacks (including snacks of fruit and vegetables) in 2010.[25] The Canadian snack food industry is a small part of the nation's food industry, constituting only 3.1 percent of employment and 1.1 percent of manufacturing plants in the sector in 2009.[26] It is nonetheless an important player, employing more than 7,500 workers in approximately 100 factories with combined annual revenue of $2.5 billion.[27] The majority of these factories are located in Ontario, with Quebec and western Canada as residence to most of the remainder. Many of these manufacturers underwent consolidation in the 1980s and 1990s, so that the largest four companies now produce 82 percent of snack foods in Canada.[28] The industry is often blamed for obesity, though Canadian caloric intake has been decreasing in recent years.[29]

The stories of several Canadian independent manufacturers of snack foods are highlighted in this book: potato chip makers Old Dutch, Hardbite, and Covered Bridge; Cheezie manufacturer W.T. Hawkins; chocolate makers Paulins, Moirs, and Ganong; and candy makers Robertson's, Cavalier, Purity, Browning Harvey, and Scott-Bathgate (Nutty Club). Source material includes private company documents, archives, newspapers, trade journals, and labour union records, as well as sixty-one oral history interviews conducted with business owners, managers, workers, union leaders, and snack food consumers.

These sixty-one interviews were conducted using the four-stage life history method recommended by oral historian Alexander von Plato.[30] In the first stage, participants were asked to tell the story of their life. The second stage asked participants to clarify any aspects of the life story that were unclear. The third stage was an open-ended conversation with participants regarding their experiences and memories of Canadian snack food manufacturing and consumption. The fourth stage (which von Plato calls the "challenge" stage) asked participants to respond to popular perceptions that snack foods are responsible for obesity.

The "life story" question of the first stage of the interview did not restrict the interview participant to discussion of their life as related to snack foods. The broad request to "tell me your life story" allowed participants to determine the level of detail they wished to share. Some simply provided a resumé of their life (birthplace, schooling, spouse and children, workplaces). Others, however, took this opportunity to share more detailed and more personal stories. Leaving the question open-ended enabled participants to introduce subjects that mattered to them, and which could be insightful for the research. It was also one way of sharing control of the interview.

Questions asked at the second stage of the interview were solely for clarification of aspects of a participant's life story (e.g., *Where* was that factory you said you worked at when you were twenty-five?). Questions at the third stage of the interview were determined by two factors: what the participant chose to share during the first (life story) stage, and what was relevant to their connection to snack food manufacturing and/or consumption. Such questions included: What are your earliest memories of eating prepackaged salty snacks? What memories do you have of your parents' eating or serving such snacks? How has your taste in snack foods changed over time? What were the most significant changes in the history of the company you own or for which you work? How have your company's products and their advertising changed over time? What is a typical workday for you? How has your work changed over time? What gave you the most satisfaction in your work? What did you learn from your work experiences? Were you ever frustrated by, or did you experience, any conflict on the job? How was that conflict resolved? How did you feel about, and what was your involvement in, various events, such as changes in company ownership or product lines?

Interviews lasted from one to two hours and were recorded in digital audio. Those interviewed were given the option of remaining anonymous; six of the sixty-one interviewed opted to do so. Of these sixty-one total interviews, forty-seven (forty-four named and three anonymous) were particularly detailed; these are the ones that were used in the writing of this book. Interviews were deposited at the Oral History Centre at the University of Winnipeg, provided participants gave consent to do so, and subject to whatever restrictions they chose to impose.

Companies discussed in the following chapters were chosen with an eye to longevity, significance, and accessibility. With one exception (Chapter 3), I focus on some of the oldest companies in Canada. Most of these businesses were founded in what were then the largest urban centres in Canada (such as Winnipeg, 'gateway' to western Canada), as well as some of the longest-established settler environs (such as Ontario and the Maritimes). Some—though not all—of the companies discussed eventually spread across the country, either through establishing additional production facilities or increasing product distribution or both. Companies were also chosen because they left an extensive and accessible archival record (e.g., Moirs), were willing to share source material (e.g., W.T. Hawkins), or contributed something unique to the story of Canadian snack foods (e.g., Hardbite).

Readers may wonder why some of their favourite snacks are omitted. The book focuses on independent businesses, which are often understudied—a consequence of the difficulty of accessing privately held records. Such companies are often small and family owned, and their stories are relatively unknown. Many manufacturers of popular Canadian snacks no longer exist as independent or Canadian businesses, and thus do not fall into the parameters set on the research for this book. These are often businesses that were bought up by competitors during the consolidation of the industry that happened in the 1980s. For example, Lowney Cherry Blossoms, a chocolate-covered cherry, is now manufactured not by Lowney but by Hershey. Independent manufacturer Allan Candy was similarly purchased by Hershey.[31] Neilson's Jersey Milk chocolate bar, invented by a Canadian dairy, is now produced by the chocolate giant Cadbury.[32] Other treats popular in Canada were, in fact, not Canadian but British or American products; for example, Mackintosh's Toffee, my father's favourite, was a British invention and is now owned by Nestlé.[33]

Some of the independent businesses discussed here are quite large; thus, the question may arise as to how significant is the distinction between corporate giants and independents. Two of the largest firms discussed in this book are Old Dutch (with 1,300 employees, 500 of them in Canada) and Ganong (with 350 employees).[34] In terms of size, there are major differences between Old Dutch and PepsiCo (makers of Frito-Lay chips), and between Ganong and Mondelēz International (makers of Cadbury chocolates). PepsiCo has more than 250,000 employees, while Mondelēz has more than 100,000; both spend approximately $2 billion annually on advertising their products.[35] Old Dutch, by contrast, spends less than $10 million on advertising.[36] The research and development departments at Canadian independent companies are small—in some cases, non-existent—unlike those at the food giants. And yet—as David Monod reminds us in his history of Canadian retailers[37]—it is corporate giants that set the industry standards that smaller enterprises often then must emulate.

Writing about Snack Foods

In the last decade, Canadian food history has emerged as an area of serious academic study. Nathalie Cooke's *What's to Eat? Entrées in Canadian Food History* was the first edited collection in the field, appearing in 2009.[38] A more wide-ranging collection, edited by Franca Iacovetta, Valerie Korinek, and Marlene Epp, is *Edible Histories, Cultural Politics: Towards a Canadian Food History*. Cooke's contributors largely focus on types of food (tourtière, turkey, Red Fife wheat) and cookbooks. The editors of *Edible Histories*, by contrast, argue that "the history of food is also about the history of power, or cultural politics that are classed, raced, sexed, and crossed with lines of authority, struggle, subservience, survival, and daily life."[39] This collection thus reflects the field's shift in emphasis to "something beyond food itself that is revealed through looking through the lens of food."[40]

Monographs in Canadian food history remain rare, though several contributions in particular are worth noting. Tanya Basok's *Tortillas and Tomatoes* is an exceptional example of a work in food history that uncovers the significance of migrant agricultural labour to food production in Canada.[41] Ian Mosby draws attention to the role of the state in shaping Canadians' food consumption, including through the rise of nutritional science and the production of the *Canada Food Guide*.[42] A history of alcohol by Craig Heron studies labour and the state as well as definitions of masculinity, while Steve Penfold's history of the doughnut examines the development of franchising in Canada.[43] Some interesting works in Indigenous and so-called ethnic food history blend history with literary studies in innovative ways.[44] These examples reveal the diversity of interests of Canadian food historians, incorporating histories of society, business, labour, science, the state, ethnicity, and gender.

As for the history of snack foods, little serious work on the topic has been published. David Carr's *Candymaking in Canada* offers much detail but little analysis of the industry.[45] Dirk Burhans's *Crunch! A History of the Great American Potato Chip* and Andrew F. Smith's *Popped Culture: A Social History of Popcorn in America* each focus on only one type of snack food, and only in the United States. More recently, Michael Moss's *Salt Sugar Fat: How the Food Giants Hooked Us* has received widespread attention. Moss, however, does not consider workers or the labour process, and focuses his attention on huge multinationals. As a consequence, the majority of North American snack food manufacturers—smaller, independent, and often family owned—are ignored. This book, by contrast, tells the story of many of these smaller firms and their workers.

Perhaps the most popular author on food issues is journalist Michael Pollan, whose numerous books on the subject are *New York Times* bestsellers. He blames cheap industrial food (such as junk or snack food)[46] for causing obesity, together with corn ("the keystone species of the industrial food chain, and so in turn of the modern diet")[47] and carbohydrates.[48] His eater's manuals and manifestos declare that most new grocery store items are not food but "edible foodlike substances. They're highly processed concoctions designed by food scientists, consisting mostly of ingredients derived from corn and soy that no normal person keeps in the pantry, and they contain chemical additives with which the human body has not been long acquainted."[49] Pollan asserts that one should "eat only foods that have been cooked by humans. If you're going to let others cook for you, you're much better off if they are other humans, rather than corporations"[50]—a suggestion that dismisses the human labour involved in making snack foods and other prepared foods. What is a potato chip fryer operator like Covered Bridge's Thomas Broad, for example, supposed to conclude regarding the value of his or her work in such circumstances?[51]

Labour is still too often ignored or misrepresented by food scholars. In their introduction to a special issue of *Labor* on food studies, editors Susan Levine and Steve Striffler declare that more labour histories of the food industry are needed, of "not only farm workers and migrant labor or meat-packing and poultry plants but the giant food processing, distribution, and retail industries that took form during the twentieth century."[52] Sarah Besky and Sandy Brown note that scholars lag behind the general public in connecting food and labour. Public support for the Fight for Fifteen (an international campaign for a fifteen dollars per hour minimum wage), for example, "has not translated into increased attention to waged labor in the burgeoning interdisciplinary field of food studies."[53] Unwaged food-related labour, meanwhile, is often misrepresented. Too many contemporary food activists, Tracey Deutsch notes, perceive the "unpaid and time-intensive labor of food procurers" through a lens of patriarchy.[54] As a consequence, they perceive the shift to processed food as a consequence of "women's poor choices."[55] The result is a neo-liberal emphasis on individual rather than structural changes as the solutions to contemporary food crises.

Pollan is, for many scholars, the epitome of this patriarchal, neo-liberal approach to food studies. He tells his readers, "Eat all the junk food you want as long as you cook it yourself."[56] He declares that people should be willing to pay more for their food (dismissing those who are unable to do so),[57] to eat only when hungry (minimizing food's role in social customs and celebrations), and to avoid eating for "entertainment," as doing so is a "costly anti-depressant."[58] Snacking is condemned as a meal replacement that contributes more calories to one's diet,[59] as the cause of obesity,[60] and as the consequence of the "outsourcing of our food preparation to corporations."[61]

I do not take Pollan's ahistorical, nostalgic position that processed, prepackaged food is inherently bad. My stance has been shaped in part by historian Rachel Laudan's *Gastronomica* article, "A Plea for Culinary Modernism: Why We Should Love New, Fast, Processed Food,"[62] which reveals the way in which the modern food industry (while undoubtedly flawed) has brought unprecedented variety to the Western diet and dramatically reduced hunger and many nutrition-related diseases.[63] The rejection of industrialized food, or what Laudan terms "culinary Luddism," is "a moral and political crusade."[64] It is a crusade that ignores history, taking a nostalgic view of the past as some ideal of good nutrition.[65] But nostalgia cannot "wish away the fact that our ancestors lived mean, short lives, constantly afflicted with diseases, many of which can be directly attributed to what they did and did not eat."[66] Industrialized food allowed for better nutrition and gave people "choices other than hard agricultural labor" and hours of food preparation.[67] Insisting that North Americans eschew processed foods for home cooking, as Pollan does, is a form of class arrogance. Laudan says, "If we urge the Mexican to stay at her metate, the farmer to stay at his olive press, the housewife to stay at her stove instead of going to McDonald's, all so that we may eat handmade tortillas, traditionally pressed olive oil, and home-cooked meals, we are assuming the mantle of the aristocrats of old. We are reducing the options of others as we attempt to impose our elite culinary preferences on the rest of the population."[68] Laudan urges us to reject nostalgia, and instead embrace "an ethos that comes to terms with contemporary, industrialized food, not one that dismisses it, an ethos that opens choices for everyone, not one that closes them for many so that a few may enjoy their labor, and an ethos that does not prejudge, but decides case by case when natural is preferable to processed, fresh to preserved, old to new, slow to fast, artisanal to industrial."[69]

Arguments for home cooking in lieu of snacking also demonstrate gender bias. Journalist Emily Matchar, for example, critiques Pollan for presenting sexist, classist, and body-shaming arguments.[70] Citing the example of Julia Child's mother, who had paid domestic help in the 1920s, journalist Tom

Philpott points out that "people with sufficient means have long been able to opt out of cooking."[71] This point is made as well by food historian Sara Davis: "There's a lot of unacknowledged privilege at work when food activists insist that the endgame should be more people cooking more meals at home."[72] Sociologists Sarah Bowen, Sinikka Elliott, and Joslyn Brenton, in their study of 150 mothers, conclude, "The idea that home cooking is inherently ideal reflects an elite foodie standpoint. Romantic depictions of cooking assume that everyone has a home, that family members are home eating at the same time, and that kitchens and dining spaces are equipped and safe."[73] Laudan credits processed food with reducing the labour involved in food preparation, a task that historically has been that of women. In an article in *Washingtonian Magazine*, Todd Kliman observes, "That we can talk about 'a cake made from scratch' when the butter, sugar, and flour that go into it are highly processed shows how we have lost awareness of the energy that formerly went into food preparation."[74] The notion that people in the contemporary Western world have moved away from some ideal past when families ate together and children knew how to cook is one of the myths debunked by Danish scholars Boris Andersen and Morten Hedegaard Larsen. While acknowledging that the present food system needs improvement, they argue that such change should occur "without resorting to an overt idealization of our foods and food habits of the 'good old days,' while also steering clear of the many myths concerning the supposed decline of our present food culture."[75]

The problem, then, is not the existence of snack foods. Rather, it is a system that makes snack foods more accessible and more filling than other foods for too many people who do not have the means to engage in the individual consumption patterns of the elite. As restaurant worker activist Saru Jayaraman observes, "Every book you read by a food luminary—every one—talks about how the problem is corporate control over the food system. . . . But the solutions are always, 'Go to the farmers' market.' 'Buy an heirloom tomato.' 'Buy organic.' It's always very individual and consumptive. It's not about targeting these corporations and loosening their control over our democracy, which is at the root of everything."[76] My discussion in the following pages of the history of Canadian independent snack food producers reveals that there exist alternatives to Big Food (the corporate food parallel of Big Tobacco), though the consolidation of the industry is evidence of the difficulties of sustaining those alternatives. Laudan notes that her agenda is "to restore some sense of the benefits of modern food so that we do not waste time and energy trying to turn back the clock but can continue to improve our food system and disseminate those improvements as widely as possible."[77] Sharing the stories of the businesses and workers in this book, then, adds a necessary counterpoint to the voices of those who would argue that snack food producers all conform to the model described by Michael Moss (which focuses on large multinationals) and who view consumers of snacks as poor decision makers.

Just as home cooking is incorrectly viewed as the solution to the perceived problem of snack foods, obesity—often described in terms of an "epidemic"—is blamed on snack foods as well. This latter argument has all the appearance of common sense, yet scholars demonstrate that concerns about body fat are complicated, sometimes misplaced, and often entwined with our understandings of class.[78] Historian Harvey Levenstein records that obesity is a concern primarily "among poorer Americans, especially African-Americans and Hispanics, who were developing diabetes and other obesity-related diseases at alarming rates."[79] Fat taxes (that is, taxes on fatty foods) have been considered as a way to redress the presumed subsequent demands on the health-care system by those who are overweight. "This approach," Levenstein writes, "seemed to echo the anti-smoking crusade, which sought to tax and discomfit smokers for their own and the public good. The most striking parallel with smoking, though, lay in regard to class."[80] The middle and upper classes, most of whom no longer smoke, found it easy to enact legislation against smoking: "As with smoking, it was the poor who were thought to be the most unconcerned with the health consequences of their actions. . . . Rarely was it pointed out that fatty and sugar-rich diets were much more economical for the poor than ones based on fresh fruit and vegetables."[81] Levenstein calls attention to the moralistic, class-rooted nature of the discourse on obesity,[82] while fat studies scholar Natalie Boero comments on the culture of "mother blame"—and particularly blame of working mothers—that resides behind concerns about childhood obesity.[83] Sociologist

Julie Guthman, meanwhile, argues that cheap processed food and obesity are consequences of capitalism: "not only does [processed food's production] involve the super-exploitation of the labor force, but [its consumption] also provides an outlet for surplus food. Insofar as this surplus manifests in more body mass, the contradiction is (temporarily) resolved in the body."[84]

The moral judgement of working-class people (particularly women) in much of the popular discourse on snack foods is not new, historians remind us. Kathryn Hughes observes that early nineteenth-century authors like William Cobbett produced cookbooks and household guides that were "aimed at stopping the working classes from squandering money in the pie shop."[85] Even chef Jamie Oliver's campaigns for school lunches, Hughes says, are "less about getting nutritious food inside people than to teach them a lesson. Learning how to make and eat slow food is to develop a capacity for delayed gratification that, in turn, fits both maker and consumer for life under capitalism."[86] Journalist David Freedman declares that many of the recipes promoted by those in "the wholesome-food movement are, in any case, as caloric and obesogenic as anything served in a Burger King."[87] Pollan's "eater's manifesto," then, is "relevant mostly to the privileged healthy."[88] Workers, Hughes reminds us, do not all have the time or the equipment or the accommodations to make "slow food" from scratch. She says, "Far from being the refuseniks of capitalism, unable to master its first principle of delayed gratification, the people who rely on fast food outlets [and, I would add, those who enjoy snack foods] are its honourable foot soldiers. We should salute them."[89]

Popularity of Snack Foods

Growing concern about the effects of snack food consumption on diabetes and childhood obesity make the subject of the history of the Canadian snack food industry an important and interesting one for many people. The stories of the businesses in this book challenge the biases and assumptions within current conversations regarding snack foods in light of the history of their production and enjoyment. There is no doubt that North Americans love their salty snacks. Americans ate 9.8 kilograms of salty snacks per person in 1999; Canadians consumed half as much: 4.9 kilograms per person.[90] Explanations for the difference in consumption patterns between the two countries are difficult to find. It may be that the eating habits learned when consuming the comparatively larger portions in American restaurants, in relation to the portions in Canadian restaurants, are carrying over to Americans' snacking habits.[91]

Snack food is a subset of industrial food, defined by Gabriella Petrick in her chapter "Industrial Food" in the *Oxford Handbook of Food History* as the "foods that are mass produced in a factory setting and require no or very little cooking to make them edible" and that are the products of "the Cold War and the Baby Boom Generation."[92] The industrial food system emerged in part as a result of technological developments that included refrigeration; mechanization of harvesting, milling, baking, and meat slaughtering; mass distribution; and plastic packaging. The reasons for the shifts in consumption of various foods—particularly for the increased consumption of industrial food—are much more difficult to determine and explain.[93] Social changes, in addition to these technological changes, probably also contributed to the rise of industrial food. Longer working hours and fewer stay-at-home parents, as real wages stagnated in the 1970s, may have contributed to greater consumption of portable convenience foods that could serve as meal substitutes.[94]

Though regional differences in snack food consumption are documented, explanations for these differences are thin on the ground. North Americans like salty snacks; Europeans prefer confectionery; Central and South Americans prefer cookies and cakes; Asians favour dairy-based snacks like yogourt, cheese, and ice cream.[95] Within Canada, foods like chips, chocolate, and candy are much less popular as a snack than fruit or yogourt.[96] Differences within Canada exist as well: Atlantic Canadians and those living on the prairies and in British Columbia are more likely than other Canadians to consume snacks.[97]

The popularity of salty snacks, and their use as meal supplements or replacements, has led to critiques of them as contributors to obesity and general poor health. Manufacturers of potato chips—one of the most popular salty snacks—tend to object to the characterization of their product as "junk food." Old Dutch Foods, for example, has asserted in a pamphlet in the past that "potato chips aren't junk food at all!"[98] Former Old Dutch plant manager Martial Boulet declares, "I can't see where there could be junk in them. There are potatoes. They use canola oil."[99] An anonymous industry expert similarly asserts, "I've tried to get that [junk food idea] out of everybody's head. It's a potato, c'mon."[100] At 150 calories per twenty-eight grams, chips are, Old Dutch once claimed, "an appropriate snack for pre-teens & teenagers, since they tend to burn up calories faster than adults."[101] Chips, the company declared, "contain more nutrition and essential vitamins than many staple food products which are consumed in the average daily diet, including bread."[102] Promotional material from the company's archives note that potato chips contain more potassium per ounce than apples or oranges, and as much fibre "as four slices of cracked-wheat bread"; an ounce of potato chips provides the same amount of calories and carbohydrates as a cup of milk, but more than three and a half times as much calcium and six times as much iron.[103] In the past, Old Dutch has argued that their chips were healthier than those of their competitors: fried in cholesterol-free sunflower oil,[104] Old Dutch chips have nine grams of fat per twenty-eight grams of chips rather than the industry standard of ten, and less salt than the typical chip: 160 milligrams of sodium per twenty-eight grams (the same as a slice of white bread) versus the industry average of 175 milligrams—less sodium than a similarly sized portion of Rice Krispies or hot dogs. Old Dutch claimed their original and ripple potato chips had 50 percent less saturated fat than that of competitors Ruffles or Lay's.[105] Ken Dick, Saskatoon manager of Old Dutch, observed in the 1970s that the company's products had more protein than fish sticks, and argued it was "wrong to label foods with that kind of nutritional value 'junk.'"[106] Former company president Vernon Aanenson took a position that is common in the industry: "No matter what you eat [it] is fattening, if you eat enough of it."[107]

Nutritionists and others have argued that the problem with chips and similar snacks is their nutritional value compared with other foods. The problem is not those who eat snacks responsibly, they argue, but that children, for example, according to a 1976 *Winnipeg Free Press* article, "have them for breakfast or replace a nutritious type of food with them."[108] Others claim that with no trans fats and with less sodium than a plain twelve-grain bagel from Tim Hortons, Old Dutch chips are not as bad as other options mistakenly viewed as healthy.[109] Sociologist Anthony Winson condemns these chips and bagels as "nutrient-poor products" or "pseudo-foods."[110] He defines pseudo-foods as "a wide spectrum of nutrient-poor edible commodities that are typically high in sugar, fat, and salt—as well as in the often prodigious calories they provide—and low in key nutrients such as proteins, minerals, and vitamins." Pseudo-foods are not limited to foods typically considered to be junk, but also include products such as breakfast cereals, fruit juices, and some restaurant meals.[111] These products are "adulterated" with salt, sugar, and fat, and designed to "addict" those who consume them.[112] The language of addiction, as we have seen, is problematic. Neither is it clear where and why Winson sets his boundaries. What is the minimum percentage of nutrients a food must possess for him to consider it actual—and not pseudo—food? And is there no place in his world for foods whose purpose is to provide pleasure rather than—or in addition to—sustenance?

The views of those like Winson have led to efforts to control consumption of snack foods. Such efforts have included banning these foods from school cafeterias—an approach not always well received by those with happy memories of eating these products as occasional snacks rather than meal replacements. The author of a letter to the editor of the *Winnipeg Free Press,* for example, reflected nostalgically, "At camp I couldn't wait to buy some Old Dutch ripple chips and beef jerky at the tuck shop with my allowance. And look at me, I'm not obese."[113] Steven Aanenson, president of Old Dutch Foods, observes that potato chips have been in existence for more than a century, yet concerns about obesity are fairly recent. Per capita consumption of potato chips has not significantly increased in the last half century, he asserts. He notes that he himself eats more chips than the average person, but he also exercises regularly. Obesity is a complex issue, and cannot be blamed on any specific food, though Aanenson comments that he does not hear anyone attacking the ice cream industry.[114]

——— • ———

The Canadian snack food industry is not a monolithic entity. Historically, it has been comprised of a variety of business models, ranging from thousands of people working in technologically advanced factories, to small, seasonal operations employing a handful of people working on ancient equipment in backyard machine sheds. Some companies have been highly innovative, expanding product lines and establishing additional production facilities in neighbouring provinces. Others produce only one item, and take measures to ensure that their company does not grow beyond its current size.

The stories of those who founded, managed, and worked at these companies are told over the next seven chapters. The first three chapters are on potato chips: Chapter 1 outlines the history of Old Dutch potato chips, and Chapter 2 focuses on growers of chipping potatoes. Chapter 3 examines niche rivals to Old Dutch: the Covered Bridge and Hardbite potato chip companies. The history of W.T. Hawkins and their sole product, Cheezies, is the subject of Chapter 4. Chocolate makers Paulins, Moirs, and Ganong are examined in Chapter 5; only Ganong has been able to continue in business to this day. Chapter 6 looks at Robertson's Candy, Cavalier Candies, Purity Factories, Browning Harvey, and Scott-Bathgate's Nutty Club, most of which have survived the consolidation of the candy industry in Canada. The final chapter focuses on the child consumer of snacks, sharing the stories of western Canadians who were contestants on *Kids Bids,* a game show sponsored by Old Dutch.

This book is a rare contribution to the field of food studies in its use of oral history to give serious attention to the role of labour in food production. The majority of studies of work in food history draw exclusively on written sources. According to Máirtin Mac Con Iomaire, in his article "Culinary Voices" for *Oral History* magazine, "The voices and life experiences of most food workers (both domestic and professional) are hidden, apart from the minority who wrote cookbooks or memoirs."[115] The sixty oral history interviews conducted in the research for this book thus constitute an important resource. Commenting on my earlier published research on Canadian snack food manufacturer W.T. Hawkins, the British Library's Polly Russell suggests that it is the first research in more than thirty years to examine "changes in food production systems . . . from the perspective of food producers."[116] Clearly, much more such work, foregrounding the stories of workers, is needed.

Snack foods are both comfort foods and foods eaten in social settings. They are frequently consumed at celebrations, large and small, ranging from family birthday parties to movie nights with friends. They can be little rewards to the self for surviving a tough day at work, or small indulgences to be enjoyed when money is tight. If there is indeed "a certain amount of comfort in a bag of chips or a chocolate bar,"[117] as an Old Dutch employee avers, then we would do well to know more about these products, their makers, and their consumers before we try to take that comfort away. Examining the production and consumption of Canadian snack foods from an historical standpoint, it is hoped, will provide greater understanding of—if not sympathy for—those who take such comfort.

1

OLD DUTCH POTATO CHIPS

A Canadian Company?

"If you're going to eat chips, eat Old Dutch. Think globally, eat chips locally."

—— ACE BURPEE, WINNIPEG FREE PRESS, 2009 ——

Old Dutch Foods is a manufacturer of potato chips with production and distribution across Canada. Many western Canadians believe the company to be a Winnipeg business, though they are owned by a family in Minnesota. An American company, Old Dutch Foods Incorporated, was founded first. The company's homepage stated, "Since 1934 we've delivered the finest snacks, fresh from the heart of the Upper Midwest. We make them close by so they're guaranteed fresh."[1] The Canadian company, Old Dutch Foods Limited, was founded later as a separate company in Winnipeg, albeit under the same ownership. Their website claims, "It all started in Winnipeg in 1954—most Winnipeggers didn't even realize that the Old Dutch brand was their own."[2] Does it matter to Canadians if snack foods are manufactured in Canada by Canadian companies owned by Canadians? What, exactly, does it mean for a snack food to be "Canadian"?

Scholars, journalists, and politicians alike have long debated the perceived importance of Canadian ownership of businesses—in other words, the significance of economic nationalism. Thomas Naylor's 1975 classic, *The History of Canadian Business,* provides a careful analysis and critique of the changing percentage of foreign ownership in various sectors of the Canadian economy.[3] In his excellent introduction to the Carleton Library edition of Naylor's work, political economist Mel Watkins notes that, more recently, the focus of Canadians has shifted from foreign ownership to corporate globalization, though, ten years ago, it was primarily non-academics who were discussing these issues.[4]

Symbolic forms of economic nationalism—that is, the use of nationalist myths and symbols to brand a company and sell products—also have a long history in Canada. Paula Hastings demonstrates that, as early as the late nineteenth century, manufacturers were more potent purveyors of English Canadian nationalism than were politicians, intellectuals, or cultural events.[5] A century later, the connection between marketing and nationalism was strengthened in the wake of the 1988 Free Trade Agreement between the United States and Canada.[6] Given Canadians' increasing access to American consumer goods, Catherine Carstairs explains, consumer nationalism in Canada tends to emphasize Canada-branded rather than made-in-Canada goods.[7] Taking a social (rather than economic) history approach, Patrick Cormack and James Cosgrave argue that companies like Tim Hortons have promoted themselves as "the cultural site for the articulation of Canadian values."[8] Old Dutch potato chips, then, must be seen in the context of these larger debates about what constitutes Canadian identity in the business realm.

The consideration of Old Dutch raises questions as well about whether there is value in distinguishing between large businesses (defined by Innovation, Science, and Economic Development Canada as those with more than 500 employees)[9] and multinationals. Multinationals and large corporations have come under increasing criticism.[10] Once a company like Old Dutch reaches a certain size, do they conduct business any differently from large global conglomerates? Are their practices any more generous, any more informed by local conditions?

Origins

Old Dutch potato chips trace their origin back to 1934, when Carl J. Marx founded the Old Dutch Products Company in St. Paul, Minnesota. According to Peter Carlyle-Gordge, in a *Winnipeg Free Press* article, he chose the name "Old Dutch" because "he associated the Dutch with long-standing cleanliness and quality."[11] Marx prepared chips in his own home: he fried them himself, enlisted the aid of a woman to package the chips, and distributed them to area businesses in his passenger car. By 1937, the business had expanded, and Marx was able to relocate to 412 South Third Street, Minneapolis, where he employed twenty-five workers.[12] The company was negatively affected by rationing in the Second World War. Shortly after the war, Marx changed the business name to Old Dutch Foods, since "Old Dutch Products" was too often confused with the popular Old Dutch Cleanser. In 1951, Marx's health was in decline, so he sold the company to Vernon Aanenson, a certified public accountant, and Arthur C. Eggert, Aanenson's business partner, for approximately $200,000.[13] Aanenson later described how he came to acquire the forty-employee business: "I was having lunch at the Covered Wagon restaurant with an acquaintance, when a fellow by the name of Charlie Skinner came up to me and said he heard that I was looking to acquire a business. I said, 'maybe.' That's when he told me that the owner of a potato chip company, Karl [Carl] Marx was his name, was looking to sell his company. On August 1, 1951, I got into the potato chip business."[14]

Old Dutch Foods expanded under the new ownership. A year after purchasing the business from Marx, Aanenson and Eggert bought the potato chip division of the Potato Products Company of East Grand Forks, Minnesota, which sold chips under the Scotts brand.[15] In 1954 or 1955, Old Dutch was approached by L&M Distributing, a candy and tobacco company in Winnipeg operated by Joe Lamonica and Vern Miranda, who asked to distribute chips in that city. For a time, L&M used Miranda's mother-in-law's basement as their warehouse.[16] Four years later, the popularity of Old Dutch chips in Winnipeg was such that it made more sense to open a factory there rather than deliver chips from Minnesota. The Winnipeg plant opened in 1959, and in 1965[17] Vernon Aanenson became sole owner of the company, which he incorporated in the United States as Old Dutch Foods Incorporated and in Canada as Old Dutch Foods Limited.[18] That same year, the American factory moved from downtown Minneapolis to the suburb of Roseville. A second Canadian factory opened in Calgary in 1970.[19]

With the death of Vernon Aanenson in 1998, management and ownership of the company was left in the hands of his sons, Steven (Steve) as president and chief executive officer, and Eric as vice-president and chief operations officer. Both sons had earned physics degrees from the University of Minnesota; Eric had worked on lasers at Lockheed, and Steve had worked in the aerospace industry at Ball Corporation. Eric, in particular, was pleased to shift to a management position at Old Dutch. As reported by Bernard Pacyniak in an article in *Snack Food*, Eric had experienced "growing dissatisfaction with the rampant bureaucracy prevalent at Lockheed."[20] At the turn of the millennium, Old Dutch had approximately 1,300 employees and a quarter of a billion dollars in sales; 500 of these employees were in Canada (180 of them in Manitoba) and most of the sales (more than $140 million) were made in Canada.[21] The company was named one of *Manitoba Business* magazine's Top 100 businesses in 2005.[22]

The company's Canadian and U.S. websites both emphasize the national and regional identity of Old Dutch: the U.S. website promotes the company as Midwestern; the Canadian website pushes the Winnipeg connection.[23] The U.S. corporate head office is in Saint Paul, and American manufacturing plants are located in Roseville and Minneapolis. The Canadian head office (which is also the accounting office) is in Winnipeg; the Canadian sales and marketing office is in Calgary. The business expanded into eastern Canada in 2007 through the acquisition of Humpty Dumpty Snack Foods. As a consequence, the company's Canadian manufacturing plants now extend across the country: in Airdrie and Calgary, Alberta; Winnipeg, Manitoba; and Hartland, New Brunswick.[24] This nationwide distribution is the culmination of a long-held dream: Vernon Aanenson stated in 1959 that he expected "to distribute Old Dutch products across all of Canada eventually."[25] The company attributes their success to a distribution system of branch offices that also contain warehouse facilities, thus ensuring rapid delivery to retailers well before expiry of the products' ninety-day shelf life.[26]

Figure 1. Old Dutch delivery van, Roseville, Minnesota, 2013.

OLD DUTCH PARTY SPREAD

1 pt. cottage cheese
Sprinkling of chives (cut in)
Sprinkling of celery seed
3 tbs. mayonnaise
2 7-oz. pkgs. Old Dutch Potato Chips

Beat thoroughly until light and fluffy. Sprinkle paprika over the top and serve [illegible] Old Dutch Potato Chips.

OLD DUTCH HAWAIIAN APPETIZER

1 ripe, mashed avocado season well with lemon juice, salt and pepper
2 pkgs. cream cheese
2 7-oz. pkgs. Old Dutch Potato Chips

Beat cheese and avocado together until fluffy. Serve in small pottery bowl, surrounded by Old Dutch Potato Chips.

OLD DUTCH SNAPPY SPREAD

1 cup cottage cheese
¼ lb. Roquefort cheese
2 pkgs. Philadelphia Cream cheese
1 clove garlic (minced very fine)
⅓ cups chile sauce
½ cup mayonnaise
2 7-oz. pkgs. Old Dutch Potato Chips

Thoroughly beat together until fluffy. Ice until thoroughly chilled. Serve spread on Old Dutch Potato Chips.

Figures 2–3. Old Dutch Foods recipe book, c.1951.

The size and scale of Old Dutch undoubtedly require a degree of professional management. The company is nonetheless distinguishable in this respect from global corporations like Frito-Lay, reported by Andrew Smith in *The Business of Food* to be the "largest snack food conglomerate in the world."[27] The company has a very flat management structure with few layers, both in Canada and in the United States. Management discussions tend to be informal, involving whomever is necessary, rather than conducted as formal board of director meetings.[28]

Taste

Potato chips, when first commercially produced in the early twentieth century, were unflavoured—just thin slices of potato, fried and salted. By the 1950s, flavoured potato chips had been introduced. In 1959, half the potato chips produced in the Old Dutch plant in Winnipeg were flavoured.[29] Old Dutch made only six types of potato chips back then: barbecue, hickory-smoked, pizza, onion and garlic, ripple, and plain (unflavoured). Seasoning was sprinkled on "in powder form after the chip has been fried"—a labour-intensive practice, according to a *Minneapolis Star* article.[30] The company claims to be the first to introduce the popular sour cream and onion flavour, which they developed with Minnesota's North Star Dairy in 1968. Old Dutch also claims to be the first in Canada to offer the salt and vinegar flavour.[31] By the 1970s, Old Dutch offered the additional flavours of barbecue and onion and garlic, as well as new cuts of potato chips such as shoestring.[32] A decade later, new products included popcorn twists, "Cheez Corn," and sour cream and onion–flavoured rings.[33] The onion and garlic flavour was discontinued in 1996, to be replaced by "all dressed" ripple chips and a new French onion flavour.[34] Such experimentation with, and improvement upon, flavours was ongoing—not always to the satisfaction of all customers, some of whom had developed strong preferences for particular Old Dutch products. The onion and garlic flavour was brought back into production, since its removal from the product line "caused such an uproar" among customers.[35] An online petition was launched in 2009 to "bring back the original flavor of Old Dutch

BBQ potato chips" after the flavour was changed to a "bold" barbecue by the company.[36] Customer Al Basler asserted, "I have been buying Old Dutch BBQ chips since I was 7 years old. That is over 47 years. I will not buy any more Old Dutch chips until you bring back the original BBQ flavor. The new 'bold' is crap and is not a worthy substitute. . . . How dare you get rid of a necessary lifelong favorite snack."[37]

Such replacements of flavours are necessary, however. "Dogs"—flavours that sell in low volume—must be removed from the product line, because Old Dutch has limited space on store shelves.[38] In addition, flavour preferences tend to be region-specific: Canadians prefer stronger and more diverse flavours, as well as anything vinegar-based (such as ketchup,[39] dill, and barbecue), compared with Americans' preferences. These differences may be the result of the British tradition in Canada of using vinegar on french fries, a practice not common in the United States. By contrast, Midwestern Americans tend to prefer sour cream and onion as well as cheese flavours, possibly as a result of the region's Scandinavian heritage, though barbecue is also popular.[40]

A long-standing feature of Old Dutch chips that some fans claim affects their flavour is in danger of disappearing as a result of improvements in technology. When stored or harvested below ten degrees Celsius, potato starch turns into sugar; the result, when these potatoes are processed, is brown chips.[41] There are those who have a preference for these darker chips: "Pale chips have no character. The brown versions have an extra caramelly almost-burnt-but-not-quite edge that gives their pale cousins a proper beatdown," claims one blogger.[42] Old Dutch themselves promote these "defects" as desirable qualities: their website explains, "Sometimes you will notice green edges or brown potato chips. These unique attributes are what makes our potatoes one-of-a-kind and hard to duplicate by any of our competitors."[43] But, with the introduction of optical scanners in the 1990s, most of the darker chips on the production line are detected and removed before being packaged.[44] "That's the industry standard—the whiter, the better. . . . A little bit of brown has a lot more flavour, but it is the industry standard," says an industry expert.[45] Since the 1950s, other flaws in chip production have been avoided through a careful process of quality control. In the 1950s, bad chips could result from too much humidity, or from temperature changes that render the oil in which they are fried rancid. Old Dutch's lab chemists test the oil multiple times daily, as well as performing checks for moisture and sugar content of potatoes.[46]

Other consumer preferences include purchasing Old Dutch chips in boxes rather than bags. These "twin pack" boxes contain two bags of chips, so consumers do not have to open one large bag and chips stay fresher. With improvements in bag packaging, these boxes are no longer as necessary. Filling the bags with nitrogen prior to their being sealed delays oxidation of the chips. In earlier years, the bags were made from glassine (a type of grease-resistant paper); when the temperature dropped below minus thirty degrees Celsius (not uncommon in a Winnipeg winter!), the bags would break. Contemporary chip bags are of more stable construction. But consumer nostalgia means that Old Dutch continues to package chips in boxes as well as bags, despite boxes' being more expensive to produce.[47]

Other innovations in Old Dutch potato chips have been the result of consumer demand for healthier and more flavourful snacks. Old Dutch introduced baked (rather than fried) potato chips, reduced the sodium in their chips, and introduced natural (rather than artificial) seasonings (including reduced sulfites and monosodium glutamate).[48] Not all Old Dutch employees are fans of the baked chips, describing them as tasting "like cardboard."[49] And not all flavours have been improved in these ways: it has not been possible to adjust the sodium level or remove the artificial colouring in the ketchup flavour, in particular, without changing its taste significantly.[50] New flavours and textures were introduced to appeal to generational and regional differences in taste. An article in the *National Post* stated, "Teenagers go for intense flavours like Doritos.[51] Adults gravitate to sour cream and BBQ flavours. Canadians in general like salt and vinegar flavours, and ketchup flavour is particularly popular in Manitoba. Those two flavours nonetheless are duds south of the border."[52] Kettle-cooked chips (marketed as Dutch Crunch) and intensely flavoured chips (marketed as Rave) were designed to appeal to teenagers and to those who liked artisanal chips. Bob Shumka, Old

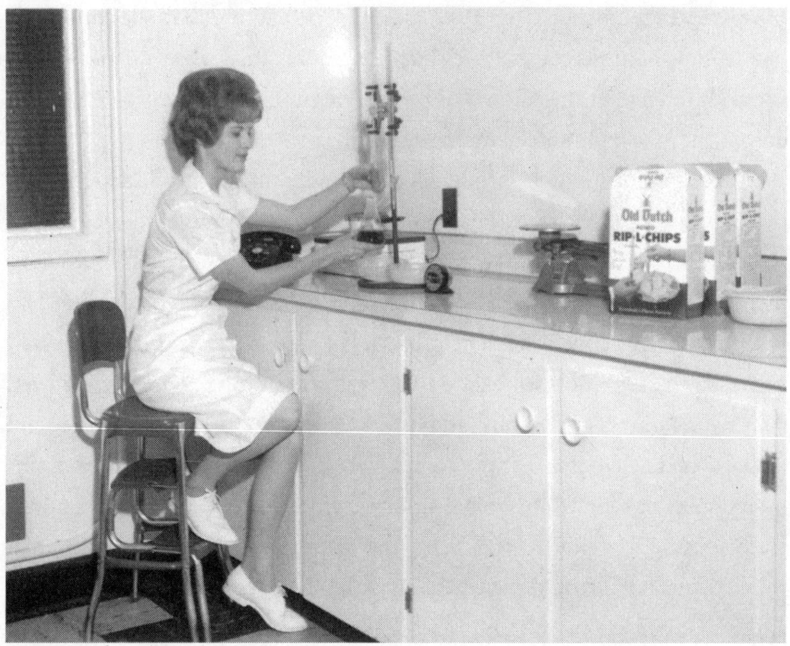

Figure 4. Old Dutch Quality Control Lab, Minneapolis, 1964.

Dutch general sales manager, explained: "In launching Rave, our teen-oriented potato chip line, we ensured that it had a high, high spice level. . . . We heard that the kids were licking the flavors off first, then eating the chip. In our salt and vinegar variety, there's so much extra salt that your eyes water when you open the bag. But the kids love it, because it's their product."[53] Rave was eventually discontinued. But another new flavour, dill pickle, became the third most popular Old Dutch flavour, popular in both western Canada and in the Maritimes.[54]

The history of segmented marketing, as studied by scholars Lizabeth Cohen and Harvey Levenstein, appears to have shaped Old Dutch as much by accident as design. Levenstein explains that crossover or mass marketing was replaced in the 1980s by segmented marketing, in which different products are targeted to specific generations or ethnicities.[55] Cohen demonstrates that market segmentation was a consequence of American postwar prosperity in the period from 1945 to 1975.[56] "What resulted," she concludes, "was a new commercial culture that reified—at times even exaggerated—social difference in the pursuit of profits, often reincorporating disaffected groups into the commercial marketplace."[57]

These innovations in product development and in production at Old Dutch were matched by similar processes at global brands like Lay's, but there are key differences. Major multinationals have research and development departments populated by scientists provided with extensive budgets.[58] At Old Dutch, by contrast, science plays less of a role: chemists monitor quality rather than promote innovation, for example. Company president Steven Aanenson's university training in physics and mathematics has been useful at Old Dutch. He notes that the company had "fairly crude systems in terms of applying flavour" until he personally introduced a quantitative analysis system using a digital scale.[59] Sales and gut-level knowledge, rather than market research, drove decisions about what flavours to produce in Canada and the United States.[60] Ketchup and salt and vinegar flavours were marketed for years in both countries, but were ultimately popular only in Canada. An attempt to market salt and vinegar chips in the United States as a boutique product, selling it in fancier grocery stores in a Canadian-labelled box with French text, fell flat. Sour cream and cheese flavours were seen as sure winners in Minnesota, by contrast.

Processing

Once the potatoes arrive at an Old Dutch processing plant, they undergo a complicated and highly automated production process. Winnipeg's Old Dutch factory—the first Old Dutch plant in Canada—was "said to be the most modern potato chip factory in the world" when it was first constructed, according to a *Minneapolis Star* article.[61] Its newer iteration, located in the Inkster Industrial Park, is even more of a marvel. Here, 453,500 kilograms of potatoes are processed into 136,100 kilograms of forty different varieties of chips every week.[62] Its chip fryer is capable of cooking 1,725 kilograms of chips per hour.[63] Increased automation in that plant has reduced its workforce dramatically. While eighty-five workers were on the factory floor in 2004, twice as many were employed there in 1978 when the plant was new; automation has meant fewer workers are needed.[64] The Winnipeg plant produces 7,000 cases of chips per day from 56,700 kilograms of potatoes and 5,000 kilograms of vegetable oil.[65] Chips are produced up to sixteen hours each day; every night, the equipment is thoroughly cleaned. A cleaning crew of fifteen people starts their work at 9:30 p.m., ending eight hours later. Cleaning crew worker Stephanie Deluso commented, "We always joke around here, and it just doesn't seem as bad [to be working night shifts] just 'cause there are other people with us that are going through the same thing."[66] She usually goes to bed at 7:00 or 8:00 a.m. (11:30 a.m. at the latest), and wakes up at about 5:00 p.m. (8:30 p.m. at the latest). Sanitation supervisor Chad Baxter noted, "It would be harder for sanitation to come in during the day because none of the production workers would want to work at nights, so they [sanitation workers] kind of get the short end of it, if you want to put it that way."[67]

The plant uses some highly specialized equipment. An optical sorter—the BEST Genius machine—checks the visual quality of chips produced. Information is recorded regarding the colour brightness of the chips and the size of any defects. Winnipeg plant manager Bill Bashucky explained, "It can tell, numerically, anything over this certain size you want to reject it. Anything darker than this colour, reject it. . . . It compares the [chip] to the computerized parameters and if it's outside the parameters, an air blast knocks it right out before it gets to the other side of the conveyor."[68] Until the 1970s, the removal of defective potato chips from the line was done by hand: up to twenty people (mostly women) had the task of manually sorting chips. The BEST Genius was installed in 2010 and is capable of evaluating 1,450 kilograms of chips per hour.[69]

The processing of chips is a highly mechanized and coordinated system at the Old Dutch factories. Semi-trailers are removed from their trucks and lifted high into the air by Vanmark hydraulic truck dumpers to unload 30,000 kilograms of potatoes at a time into one of several storage bins in the plant.[70] (Before such mechanization, workers would unload forty-five-kilogram

Old Dutch
Flavorized
POTATO CHIPS
ONE FULL POUND

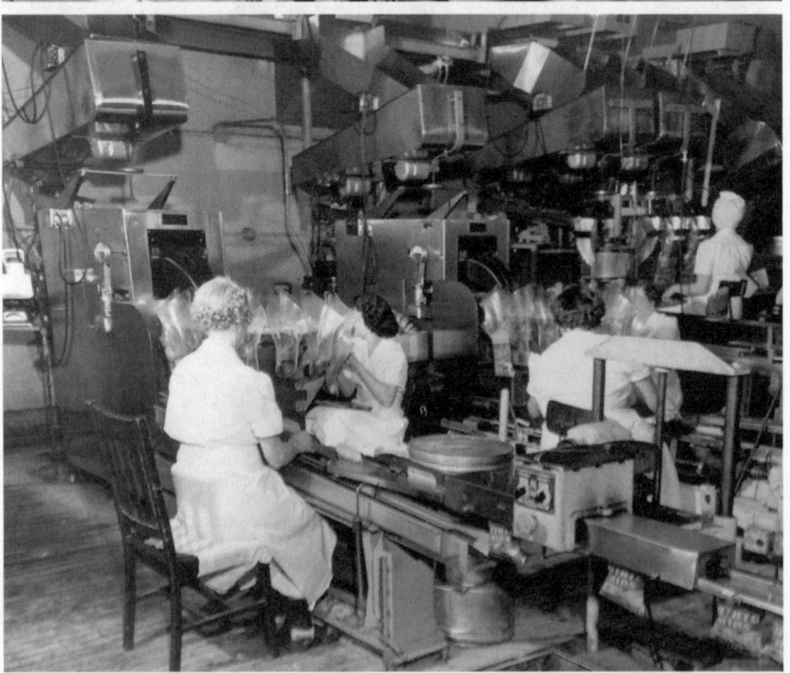

Figures 5–8. Old Dutch Foods factory, downtown Minneapolis, 1953.

bags of potatoes by hand.) The potatoes are taken from these bins, washed in a "gentle flume system by Starr Inc.," and sent in overhead tubes to another room for further processing. Potato starch is removed from the washing process's waste water; in Winnipeg, this by-product is sent to Manitoba Starch Products for further processing.[71] In an adjacent room, tanker cars enter on railroad siding to unload Canadian-grown and -processed canola oil.[72] Cleaned potatoes arrive in a separate manufacturing room, where those that are too large are chopped into smaller pieces by a machine known as a halver. A Vanmark abrasion peeler removes the potatoes' peel. Optical sensors detect which potatoes are incompletely or improperly peeled; these are diverted to another conveyor belt to return to the peeler. The cleaned and peeled potatoes are fed into an Urschel slicer, which uses blades set into a spinning circular ring; potatoes are pushed to the inner edge of the ring by centrifugal force and so are sliced. The thickness of slices can be controlled by repositioning the blades; potatoes must be sliced thicker or thinner, depending on how the particular variety of potato holds moisture.[73] If the potatoes are to be made into kettle chips, then these slices are sent to a kettle; here, the oil temperature is automatically controlled and there are mechanical stirrers to keep the chips separated while cooking. Regular potato chips are produced somewhat differently: the sliced potatoes are washed to remove excess starch and then sent to a completely enclosed fryer. Cooked chips that are defective (too dark) are detected by Optisort optical scanners[74] and individually removed by blasts of air—a task that earlier had been done by hand—while travelling down the Asecco vibrating conveying system to the next stage in the production process. These defective chips are crushed and taken away daily by local farmers for animal feed. Cooked chips are dried by air and lightly salted, and then travel on massive overhead conveyors to the seasoning and packaging area.[75]

The Winnipeg plant contains thirteen packaging lines, allowing the production of thirteen different flavours at a time; three lines are allocated for kettle chips, and the rest for regular potato chips.[76] Located high above the mechanical packing equipment are tumblers that are used to add the flavouring to the chips. According to an article in *Chipper/Snacker*, these tumblers

Figure 9. Old Dutch Foods factory, Winnipeg, mid-1960s.

were "designed by Finn Henrikssen, plant manager at Old Dutch's St. Paul plant, with the assistance of Darrel Skogen."[77] These flavouring drums are enclosed by plastic to prevent cross-contamination of seasoning, so that consumers with milk or wheat allergies can be assured of careful ingredient control.[78] Chips travel vertically down from the tumbler into a series of pocket weighers; a computer weighs each pocket and chooses a combination to empty into a chip bag that results in the correct package weight with minimal overage. The packaging machine then fills the bag with nitrogen to protect chip freshness before sealing the package. Filled chip bags are sent to another machine for boxing. (When production began in the 1950s, however, these tasks were all done by hand.)[79] Computerized equipment detects whether chip bags are properly sealed by applying light pressure to them and checking for air leaks; defects are automatically diverted from the line.

Bagged chips are then sent to boxers and inspected by x-ray for possible foreign bodies.[80] The product is tracked by scanners all down the production line so that the company can identify the exact origin of the potatoes (as well as seasonings) in any given bag of chips, thus making specific product recalls possible, if necessary.[81]

Shipping is a less mechanized, very physical job, despite the fact that boxes of chips are light. Old Dutch operates their own shipping fleet.[82] When chips are packed onto trucks and trailers for shipping, no pallets or forklifts are used. This work is very hot in summer and very cold in winter. As shop steward at the Winnipeg facility, Jean Pierre Petit was able to secure heaters for employees in the shipping area who pack trailers in winter. Management was initially resistant to the idea, as they were worried that condensation would result, which would soak the chips and render them unsaleable. Ultimately, these fears proved unfounded.[83]

Old Dutch manufactures their tortilla chips and other corn products at a facility in Airdrie, Alberta, which received a 4,645-square-metre expansion in 2000.[84] Corn silo capacity is automatically measured and linked to computers at the company's headquarters in Minnesota. To make tortilla chips, 815 kilograms of corn are delivered to one of two simmer kettles. The corn is cooked for fifteen to twenty minutes at a temperature ranging between ninety and ninety-four degrees Celsius. A lime slurry used to be added by hand, but now is pumped in automatically. The cooked corn is sent to a cooling tank, then pumped into a dozen soaking tanks for eight to twelve hours, after which it is sent to a separator to remove waste water. (The waste water is further separated into water to be sent to the sewer system, and solids to be used as livestock feed.)[85] The cooked corn is washed, sent to a grinding mill, rolled into dough by large machines, and cut into chips by a die stamper. A single-pass oven cooks the chips; their moisture is equalized in a special machine, and they are fried in a 50–50 canola-sunflower mix. After seasoning in a tumbler, they are weighed and packaged. Some 1,725 to 1,905 kilograms of corn are processed in this way every hour.[86]

Labour

Old Dutch has had two serious labour conflicts in its history: a strike at Winnipeg's factory in 1973, three months after workers there joined a union; and an eight-month lockout and strike at Calgary's factory in 2009.[87] Winnipeg plant workers joined Local 520 of the Canadian Food and Allied Workers in 1973. They went on strike shortly afterward, protesting wages (which were reputed to be not much above minimum wage) and working conditions at the factory. They were supported by members of the Manitoba Action Committee on the Status of Women, the Manitoba Federation of Labour, and the Winnipeg Labour Council, who walked the picket line and called for a boycott of Old Dutch products.[88] In 2009, contract negotiations broke down with United Food and Commercial Workers (UFCW) Local 401 in Calgary; the Old Dutch workers' collective agreement had been expired for a year.[89] Old Dutch marketing director Scott Kelemen told the press, "We need a resolution to our offer, so our position is to take a lockout to try to get things rolling."[90] Company president Steve Aanenson told me that the difficulty was that the Calgary local had merged with a larger, more militant local and wanted a union shop; Old Dutch had never had a union shop in Alberta.[91] United Food and Commercial Workers representatives noted that the main issue was "a company policy that allows employees to opt out of joining the union and paying dues, even though the UFCW acts on behalf of all staff."[92] (At the time, Alberta was one of a minority of provinces that did not have the Rand Formula as part of its labour law.)[93] The union argued that Old Dutch management were taking advantage of the economic crisis of 2008–09 "to put the squeeze on its workers—even when the company is profitable."[94] They called for a national boycott of Old Dutch products and the private-label brands the company produced (President's Choice, No Name, Great Value, Compliments, and Safeway Blue Bags).[95] The Alberta Labour Relations Board was asked to determine whether management had been bargaining in good faith. The board ruled that the company and the union should resume collective bargaining on the basis of the Rand Formula, determining that Alberta's labour code was unconstitutional and giving the Alberta government one year to revise it.[96] After a 228-day strike and lockout, a new four-year collective agreement was ratified in December 2009 that included union security, and UFCW's boycott ended.[97] Steve Aanenson said that management was "just devastated" by the decision and felt they had been "thrown under the bus" by the province.[98] Aanenson noted that with Alberta's boom-and-bust cycle (due to its dependency on the oil economy), it was difficult to attract and retain workers during boom times; turnover could be as high as 300 percent. With any group of people, some would be pro- and others anti-union; requiring Old Dutch to be "open shop" would limit the company's ability to hire in boom times, Aanenson explained.[99]

United Food and Commercial Workers representative J.P. Petit, who is a former employee and shop steward at the Winnipeg plant, notes that Old Dutch is "a pretty good company to work for . . . they do try to work with the union rather than against them."[100] He describes staff–management relationships as positive, noting that many employees have worked at the company for decades. Disagreements, when they exist, tend to be between employees more often than between employees and management. The shipping and receiving department at the Winnipeg plant, for example, employs only a dozen workers; it is thus "easy to get on each others' nerves" after a while.[101] He says the wage at the Winnipeg plant "isn't the greatest wage but [it] isn't the worst . . . along with the benefits, it's not bad. Over the years, we've always had pretty consistent pay increases to keep up with the times." Benefits include a dental plan, vision care, a health spending account, and a pension plan. The lowest-paid job is packaging chip bags into boxes. Those who work as line operators on the bagging machines receive higher pay. Forklift operators also earn slightly higher wages, as do those who recycle burnt chips. Fryer operators receive the highest pay: when Petit left the company in 2012, shippers/receivers earned seventeen dollars per hour, while fryers earned approximately twenty-two dollars and packers earned sixteen dollars. The absence of paid sick days remains a sticking point for the union at the Winnipeg plant: management allows three lates or absences per quarter year without the employee's needing to provide justification. After more than three days' absence per quarter, employees are required to apply for short-term disability.[102]

Old Dutch's Winnipeg plant is a gendered and ethnicized workspace, though this is slowly changing as a consequence of increased automation. The majority of the workforce is female. There are few women employed in shipping and receiving, in part because of the physical nature of the work. The production and packaging lines, as well as inspection and the laboratory, tend to employ primarily women.[103] Former plant manager Martial Boulet offered an explanation that leaned heavily on gender stereotypes: "A guy wouldn't last long packing chips. I don't think that would be interesting enough for a guy. Plus, it is not a hard job. You keep changing them around so they do not always do the same job. The women seem to like it. And it gives some work to another gender [women]. But, there are some women in the high office, too."[104] Linemen and maintenance workers tend to be males. Interestingly, the cleaning crew used to consist mostly of men, in part because these night shifts involved higher pay; this, too, is slowly changing. Many of the workers at the Winnipeg plant are Portuguese; almost half are Filipina/Filipino.[105]

Bebe Maqsood, an immigrant from Guyana, was employed as a packer at Old Dutch for a decade beginning in the mid-1970s. She reminisced about the convivial atmosphere that existed among workers at the plant back then. There was, she said, a "Code of Ethics of the unmarried staff—nobody would go out with each other. If you did, you were out [of the group]."[106] She recalled that she and her co-workers were "all great friends. . . . We would go out and party; we had a good time; we go to each other's houses. . . . You could always come to them, day or night. You never take a bus—somebody will give you a ride. . . . They were just nice people . . . and everyone looked out for one another."[107]

Maqsood's experience was not unique: former plant manager Martial Boulet recalled that Old Dutch organized Christmas parties, dances, and a social club at their Winnipeg and Alberta factories. The company hired a bus for Calgary workers to play hockey against Old Dutch warehouse workers in Edmonton: play got too rough, though, so they resorted to curling and bowling instead.[108] Maqsood recalled that not even the UFCW strike at the

Winnipeg plant in the 1970s could dampen this genial atmosphere: "Afterward, everybody made up and it was okay," she asserted.

Promotion

Old Dutch engaged in a variety of advertising strategies during their first two decades of operation. The first Canadian advertisement for their potato chips appeared in the *Winnipeg Free Press* in December 1954: a 170-gram package of chips could be purchased in grocery stores for only thirty-nine cents.[109] The first mention of the company's famous Twin Pack (two bags of chips packaged in one cardboard box) appeared two years later.[110] The chips were promoted as "ideal for TV snacks" in 1957, and, the following year, the company was the main sponsor of the Saturday "Western Hour" at Winnipeg's Starland movie theatre.[111] For the first fifteen years of their history, Old Dutch spent an annual average of $214,000 in Canada on advertising ($177,000 in the United States).[112] The company hired an ad agency to write jingles about their potato chips:[113]

> Old Dutch Potato Chips
> Old Dutch, the snappy chips
> Crispy, crunchy, light and snappy—
> Old Dutch potato chips.
>
> Old Dutch the crispiest—
> Old Dutch the tastiest—
> Crispy, crunchy, light and snappy—
> Old Dutch potato chips.[114]

The "Old Dutch Potato Chip girl" dressed in traditional Dutch costume to promote the product. A columnist for the *Chicago Tribune* recalled these early advertisements: "My first television love was the Old Dutch Potato Chip girl. She used to dance provocatively to the anthem of the Old Dutch Potato Chip Co., long blond hair swaying wildly in time to the saxophone music, toothsome smile luring us to thoughts ranging far above Old Dutch Potato Chips . . . if they were to monitor the American male during the [1970s] Flex Balsam and Protein Shampoo ads they would record tingles that have not been charted since the Old Dutch Potato Chip population boom in the early 1960s."[115]

By the late 1970s, however, Old Dutch opted not to spend heavily on advertising—a decision they reversed in the 1990s. Fred Prediger, Old Dutch plant manager in Calgary, declared "the Old Dutch marketing philosophy is to spend money on good equipment to produce the best quality product rather than lots of money on promotions."[116] Marketing expenses as a percentage of sales at the company doubled to almost 4 percent in 1990 in response to increased competition from other chip producers. According to an article in the *Wall Street Journal*, "Because chips are easy to make and account for the largest segment of the [snack foods] industry, the new competitors are focusing their efforts there. The competition is especially keen in the fast-growing 'kettle-cooked' market for extra crunchy chips."[117] The *Winnipeg Free Press* reported that Winnipeg bronzer Lou Wolfe was hired by Old Dutch to gild "100 potato chips in 24-karat gold to be used as promotional incentives."[118] New television commercials aired, with a new jingle:

> The Old Dutch snack in the windmill pack,
> The taste just keeps you coming back.
> Crunch a snack made the Old Dutch way,
> Find the flavour that you crave today,
> Try them all and you're sure to say:
> It's the Old Dutch snack in the windmill pack.
> The taste just keeps you coming back
> To the Old Dutch snack in the windmill pack.[119]

By the turn of the millennium, Old Dutch was engaged in "a more aggressive sales and marketing campaign," reported an article in *Snack Food & Wholesale Bakery*, introducing a new, larger 340-gram bag "as a means of increasing consumption trends in salty snacks."[120] Product placements in the movies *Fargo, Grumpier Old Men,* and *Michael,* and in an episode of the television show *The Office,* further promoted the company.[121] Such marketing efforts were minimal, however, compared with those of competitor Frito-Lay. Winnipeg plant manager Bill Bashucky said, "They [Frito-Lay] have very deep pockets . . . so they spend a wad on advertising. Old Dutch is a small player. . . . Doesn't have the wherewithal to spend that kind of money on media and print advertising. Word of mouth and quality of the product is our advertising."[122]

Though advertising campaigns ebbed and waned, the classic design of the Old Dutch packaging never changed. The company logo remains a detailed artistic rendering of a windmill, designed by wildlife artist Les Kouba.[123] And the packaging retains its iconic stripes and caricature drawings that identify flavours. A *National Post* article described the packaging: "Fringed in red and yellow, the [Dutch] bags and boxes features the words Bar-B-Q spelt out with fiery logs;[124] anthropomorphic onions dancing with garlic bulbs when they are not tangoing with sour cream containers; a salt shaker putting his arms around his buddy vinegar and singing with such vigour about their tasty union that seasoning sprays out of their heads. [Competitor] Humpty Dumpty's dapper eggman has nothing on these guys."[125]

Community involvement and donations were other ways of advertising the company. Indigenous young people near St. Ambroise, Manitoba, built their first hockey rink with the assistance of Old Dutch in 1961.[126] The Flin Flon Trout Festival's Mermaid Queen and the Miss Manitoba competitions had contestants sponsored by Old Dutch in the early 1960s.[127] That decade also saw the company sponsor Polo Park shopping centre's annual Hallowe'en party, the Holland Festival, the annual Royal Canadian Mounted Police provincial skeet-shooting championship, colouring contests for fire-prevention awareness, Red River Exhibition floats, movie showings, outings for Pan-Am Games athletes, and fundraisers for injured Winnipeg Blue Bomber football player Jack Delveaux.[128] In the 1980s, Old Dutch sponsored Family Fun Day on the Paddlewheel Queen riverboat, and hosted children at their Winnipeg factory for a guest lecture by the John Howard Society.[129] A decade later, the City of Winnipeg Parks and Recreation department advertised tours of the Old Dutch plant.[130]

Figure 10. Old Dutch Foods sponsored horse races at Assiniboia Downs, Winnipeg, 1965.
Figure 11. Old Dutch Foods grocery display featuring the "Old Dutch girl," Vancouver, 1959.

Sports teams and sporting events—whether for their own employees or for Winnipeg community members—were heavily sponsored by Old Dutch, including bowling teams (such as the Old Dutch Bac'n Puffs), fastball teams, and football teams (a children's team was called the Old Dutch Crunchers).[131] Vern Aanenson, his sons, and his company's management team enjoyed hunting, fishing, and skeet shooting in Manitoba, as well as presenting prizes for horse racing at the province's Assiniboia Downs racetrack.[132] Since 1958, their regular attendance at, and sponsorship of, Manitoba horse racing resulted in the seventh race's being named the Old Dutch Food Purse.[133] They were regular guests at Jimmy Robinson's duck lodge, established in 1958 on the Delta Marsh near St. Ambroise, Manitoba, where Old Dutch sponsored a trophy for a cribbage tournament.[134] Vern Aanenson was a strong supporter of Ducks Unlimited (a wetlands and waterfowl conservation organization), and was a lifetime member of the Manitoba Wildlife Federation.[135]

This sort of community and charitable involvement on the part of Old Dutch does not differ from the practices of most other major companies. Owners and management at Loewen Windows, Friesen Printers, and Palliser Furniture, for example, participated in local sporting and social events, as well as church and charitable religious activities.[136] Doing so not only allowed them to promote the company as benevolent, it broadened their sphere of influence in the community and reinforced their authority with their workers. Such charitable actions have long been part of traditional paternalist business practices in North America, as Joan Sangster, Joy Parr, and other historians have noted.[137]

Growth and Expansion

Reflecting on the company's tremendous growth, Vern Aanenson declared in 1993, "I don't think an Old Dutch would happen again. I don't think it could be done."[138] He observed that the North American snack food industry was dominated not by family-owned companies like his own, but by multinationals that also produced soft drinks, beer, tobacco, and soap. With the consolidation of grocery stores, independent manufacturers could not compete with these conglomerates for shelf space.[139] Vern Aanenson's son Steve, the current president of the company, agrees with this assessment: his father used to be able to secure sales of Old Dutch by taking people fishing and hunting (which he enjoyed). Such an approach is no longer possible; most grocery chains prohibit employees from accepting payment in kind.[140] When the Aanenson family purchased Old Dutch in 1955, sales totalled $1.5 million; a decade later, they had risen to $20 million.[141] Sales rose to $80 million in Canada (and $40 million in the United States) in 1983. By the mid-1990s, 65 percent of salted snacks purchased in western Canada were made by Old Dutch (sales were $160 million in 1996).[142] In the new millennium, Old Dutch sales were an astounding $250 million. This figure was miniscule in comparison with that of Frito-Lay, their main competitor, whose sales totalled $2.32 billion.[143] This dramatic difference was responsible for the failure of Old Dutch to market their chips in the newly built hockey stadium when the National Hockey League franchise returned to Winnipeg: to sell a possible $30,000 worth of chips, the company was asked to pay $350,000 to secure the franchise. The franchise went to Frito-Lay instead: Old Dutch director of purchasing and logistics David Oye said, "They just have a lot more power . . . [Old Dutch is trying to] hold their own against a huge multinational."[144] Frito-Lay dominated the western Canadian market in the early twenty-first century, reducing Old Dutch's share to one-third.[145]

The company's first efforts to expand into the eastern Canadian market, in the early 1990s, were unsuccessful.[146] Hostess Frito-Lay had the majority of that market share, and took pains to prevent Old Dutch from making any inroads. They purchased all the Old Dutch products available in a number of stores to keep them out of the hands of customers and made deals with retailers to prevent them from stocking Old Dutch again.[147] Toronto corner store owner Anna Choi, for example, reported that she had refused to sell her stock of Old Dutch chips to Hostess, and was told they would sell their Hostess chips to her competitors at a lower price as a consequence.[148] Toronto Shoppers Drug Mart manager Ken Callaghan sold his stock of Old Dutch chips to Hostess and agreed not to stock Old Dutch for some months in exchange for some free Hostess chips to sell in his store.[149] Old Dutch's

Toronto branch manager, Frank Scanlon, commented on Hostess's purchase of Old Dutch chips: "I'd love to know what they're doing with it. . . . For all I know maybe they're eating it themselves and enjoying it—they're having some good chips for a change."[150]

The town council in Winkler, Manitoba, in the heart of the potato-production area that provided the crop to Old Dutch's Winnipeg plant, contemplated taking legal action against Hostess Frito-Lay. Winkler mayor Henry Wiebe commented, "I think council is going to be very interested in doing something about it, because the potato production industry is very important around here."[151] Manitoba Member of Parliament Rey Pagtakhan, whose riding of Winnipeg North included the Old Dutch factory, suggested that Manitobans boycott Hostess.[152] Winkler town council ultimately decided not to intervene in the Toronto "potato chip wars," as growers in the area assured the mayor that their contracts were not threatened by the struggle for market share in Ontario.[153] The *Winnipeg Free Press* was less supportive of Old Dutch than these politicians, suggesting that Old Dutch should be left to their own devices: "Before the federal competition watchdog, the provincial government and the federal Liberal caucus all make pronouncements on the legality and/or morality of Hostess tactics in the mother of all potato chip battles, they should just let Old Dutch get on with its business of breaking into a new market."[154]

Nonetheless, politicians continued to press for intervention. Officials from the federal Bureau of Competition requested a policy meeting with members of management from Old Dutch, to consider the launching of a formal inquiry into the competitive practices of Hostess.[155] Steve Aanenson reported that "out of the 500 or so independent accounts in the Toronto area, Old Dutch's customers had experienced some form of especially competitive pressure from Hostess Frito-Lay in 82 of them." Meanwhile, MP Rey Pagtakhan researched "possible legislative or government action on behalf of Old Dutch."[156] He also wrote a letter to the editor of the *Free Press*, criticizing their stance on the issue. He noted the newspaper's editorial had "advised people like me, who had called for the [Bureau of Competition] to intervene, to stay out of the business of the market place, and to let the potato chip

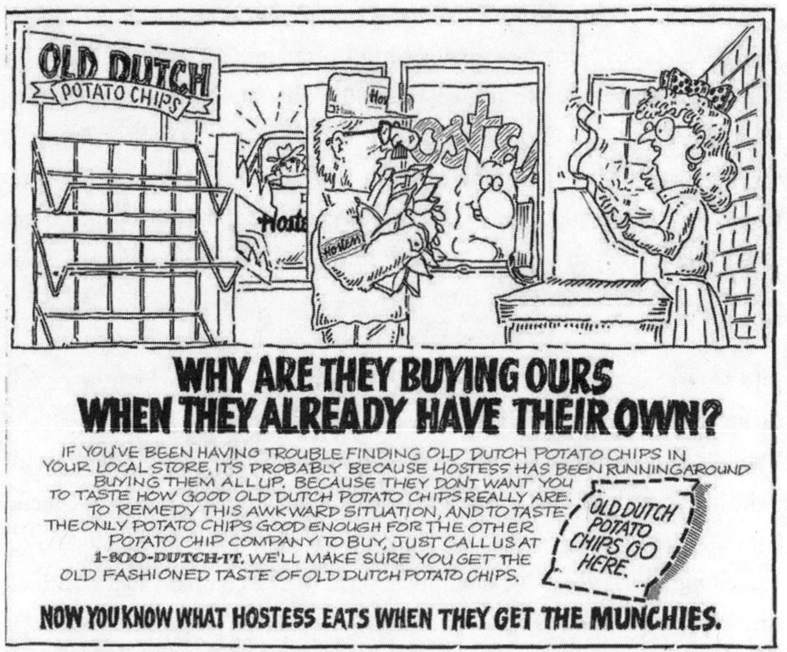

Figure 12. Old Dutch Foods vintage print advertisement, n.d.

giants fend for themselves. . . . The *Free Press* editorial suggested businesses in glass factories should not throw stones, that Old Dutch had taken away volume discounts from a Winnipeg store for advertising Hostess."[157]

Pagtakhan declared he did not believe that Old Dutch engaged in the kind of dubious business practices conducted by Hostess: "I have been told by Old Dutch that they don't condone this type of behavior and work to keep their business practices fair—not impotent, but fair." He asserted that he did not regret approaching the Bureau of Competition.[158] The bureau itself, however, eventually dropped the issue, stating that the incidents with Hostess were isolated. Nonetheless, Old Dutch continued "to face obstacles getting competitively established in the potentially lucrative southern Ontario market." Aanenson asserted that, in an effort to keep Old Dutch out of Ontario, Hostess was undercutting its own profit margins.[159]

Old Dutch has expanded in part by purchasing smaller competitors. In 1981, they bought Happy's Potato Chip Company of Minnesota when its founding owner chose to retire.[160] In 2000, they bought the brand name, rights, and distribution for Nalley's (a British Columbia brand).[161] The largest chip company taken over by Old Dutch was Humpty Dumpty—a buyout that was initiated by Humpty themselves. Before the 1980s, Old Dutch dominated the market in western Canada; in the east, Humpty Dumpty Snack Foods was the chip maker of choice.[162]

Founded in 1947 by Dorothy and Phil Cole, Humpty Dumpty was split into separately owned Canadian and American divisions when the couple divorced. The Canadian division declared bankruptcy in the mid-1990s.[163] Both divisions were purchased shortly thereafter by Small Fry Snack Foods (which was itself formed in the 1980s when Gerald Schmalz purchased and consolidated several smaller Canadian chip companies).[164] Small Fry renamed themselves Humpty Dumpty in 2000.[165] The company had a difficult time competing after 1989, when American-based Frito-Lay purchased Canadian-owned Hostess.[166] Frito-Lay, a much larger company operating on both sides of the Canada–U.S. border, had significantly lower delivery costs due to their higher volume production. Owned by PepsiCo, the company had six production facilities in Canada and 4,000 employees. As the grocery industry underwent consolidation in the 1980s, retailers bought from fewer suppliers. Hostess Frito-Lay was able to offer more incentives to retailers to carry their chips than was Humpty Dumpty. In addition, Humpty Dumpty faced supply problems as provincial marketing boards made shipping potatoes between provinces challenging.[167] The result was that, by the turn of the millennium, Hostess Frito-Lay had 60 percent market share in Canada.[168]

Unable to compete in eastern Canada, in 2005, Humpty Dumpty approached their western Canadian equivalent, Old Dutch, to ask them to purchase 20 percent of their company. Humpty Dumpty shareholders objected, however, and more than half the members of their board of directors were replaced. The objections were that the stock was being sold at too low a price and that the existing board was comprised of people too closely connected to Chief Executive Officer Gerald Schmalz.[169] A year later, a new arrangement was made (with a new chief executive officer at Humpty Dumpty), and Old Dutch took over the eastern chip maker.[170] The result was the first national chip company in Canada in a half century, although one that was less than half as large as Hostess Frito-Lay.[171] The deal probably saved Humpty Dumpty from bankruptcy, and helped Old Dutch as well. Old Dutch had one-third market share in western Canada; company president Steve Aanenson noted, "It's getting more and more difficult to operate as a regional company."[172]

The takeover had its difficulties. For a few years, Old Dutch sold chips in eastern Canada under the Humpty Dumpty label—albeit modified versions of the original products. After a year, however, they also marketed Old Dutch brand chips in the East.[173] Humpty Dumpty's market share had declined to only 10 percent, so they were replaced with the Old Dutch label in 2008.[174] And not all the former Humpty Dumpty factories could be saved. The plant in Lachine, Quebec, closed in 2013; 216 people lost their jobs as a result.[175] The factory had been built in 1964 and could not be modernized. Quebec's minister of industrial policy did not blame Old Dutch for the closure, declaring that too many factories in the province were not modernized, and that the government was "considering introducing measures that will encourage companies to spend more money on renovations."[176]

While the Quebec plant was closed, the New Brunswick plant acquired through the purchase of Humpty Dumpty was expanded. The New Brunswick government, unlike that of Quebec, offered incentives to improve manufacturing facilities. The *Globe and Mail* reported that a $15 million loan was provided to Old Dutch for "a new packaging line, new equipment and more warehouse space in Hartland."[177] This expansion meant the addition of forty new employees to the 128 already working at the plant. In addition, it meant the doubling of potato contracts in the region. New Brunswick potato farmers had been hard hit by the decision of McCain Foods to reduce potato sourcing in the province by 20 percent in response to a higher U.S. dollar and lower demand for their fries.[178] They welcomed the opportunity to sell to Old Dutch.

The expansion of Old Dutch to become a national company would have pleased some of the writers at the *National Post*. In 2006, they proposed that a modern version of Prime Minister John A. Macdonald's National Policy was needed to unite the country: the NCP, or "National Confection Policy," "whereby the crispy resources of the Western provinces will be shared equally with our Eastern brothers and sisters. No longer should Easterners have to secretly order boxes of Old Dutch chips online. No longer should Laureen Harper, the wife of our prime minister for goodness' sake, have to ride her motorcycle all the way to Calgary to get a fix of dill pickle."[179] To those who objected that such an NCP would be centred on an American-owned company, the *National Post* writers countered, "We accept immigrant treats from around the world. Why should it be different for one born in the United States of America? Shame on this kind of anti-American rhetoric!" Equal access to these salty snacks in all parts of the country would result in national harmony: "Every box of Old Dutch Salt 'n' Vinegar features a picture of a salt shaker putting his arm around his buddy vinegar, the two singing with such vigour about their tasty union that seasoning sprays out of their heads. This is how I envision a united Canada, where Old Dutch chips are available everywhere, from the corner stores of Toronto to the dépanneurs of Montreal to the Irving gas stations of New Brunswick."[180] This piece is clearly meant to be humorous, but there is a core of truth nonetheless: Canadians take their snacks seriously, and connect their consumption to their identity.

In addition to such acquisitions, expansion for Old Dutch came, at times, as the result of devastating fires. In 1965, the Old Dutch warehouse in downtown Minneapolis burned down, killing one firefighter; damage was estimated at $75,000.[181] Plans were made to build a new, larger plant at a different location. Three years after the fire, Old Dutch moved from their location in downtown Minneapolis to the suburb of Roseville. The new $1.3 million plant and warehouse occupied 13,935 square metres on a 3.6-hectare site at 2375 Terminal Road. The new site allowed Old Dutch to consolidate their Minnesota operations, which were scattered at four locations in the Twin Cities of Minneapolis/St. Paul.[182]

A series of fires at the Old Dutch facilities in Winnipeg in the 1970s led to relocation in that city as well. Fire destroyed the Old Dutch warehouse on Sargent Avenue in Winnipeg in 1972. The event was an attraction for locals, who, according to a *Winnipeg Free Press* report, gathered like "spectators at a sporting event. . . . The crowd cheered each time a part of the warehouse walls fell in the $325,000 fire."[183] "Whenever part of the wall collapsed, people would yell, 'And the fire wins,' and bits of burning material would float up about 50 feet over the crumbling building."[184] Maintenance man Ruben Riege said the fire began in the bag room that held materials for chip bags. "The fire attracted about 80 spectators, but by 12:30 a.m. only about 15 remained to see the end of the eighty-year-old building. One person said, 'I saw the auto body fire (Pembina Auto Body which burned last week). This is a lot better.'"[185] Three years later, two fires within three days struck the warehouse and plant.[186]

Winnipeg's Old Dutch facilities were relocated to a new industrial park in 1977.[187] Purchasing manager Emily Smith was instrumental in the new plant's beginnings, importing the necessary equipment from the United States.[188] The new building's façade featured some attractive design elements. The *Winnipeg Tribune* described "a combination of gold reflective glass and brown facebrick at the central office block." Practical improvements included "an enclosed semitrailer hoist and dumper, an enclosed railcar loading dock, a high efficiency gas scrubber on the potato chip fryer exhaust, a water treatment system and waste heat recovery systems."[189]

Customer Loyalty

The products of these many factories have earned some very loyal customers over the years. Lois Trast wrote a letter to Old Dutch in 1980, noting that she shipped their chips to her two sons stationed overseas with the American military: "When they come home on leave I always ask if there is anything special they want and they always say, 'Have plenty of Old Dutch potato chips.'"[190] She also packed Old Dutch chips for the daily lunches of her two youngest children, both in elementary school: "every day they have either plain chips or Onion & Garlic for the one and Bar-B-Q for the other in their lunch."[191] A Toronto resident in 2007 posted a request on the Internet with the title "Desperate for Old Dutch Chips," bemoaning the fact that her store no longer stocked the chips and asking for other sources: "I will drive to wherever the chips are."[192] Regan Winters, a native of Saskatoon temporarily displaced to Toronto, observed, "Lays salt 'n vinegar suck compared to Old Dutch. It was a real disappointment the entire time I lived in Toronto."[193] Even Laureen Harper, wife of Canadian prime minister Stephen Harper, claimed to miss "my favourite Old Dutch dill pickle chips. It is the first thing I buy when I head home to Calgary for a visit."[194]

In Winnipeg, Old Dutch chips have long been a requirement for socials (a Prairie classic that combines a fundraising dinner with a community dance, whether organized by individuals or organizations).[195] A Toronto fundraiser in 1985 for Winnipeg's Health Sciences Centre, for example, featured "a buffet of perogies, cabbage roles [*sic*], corned beef, Sal's[196] taste-a-like chili, pickles, cheese, crackers and, of course, Old Dutch potato chips,"[197] reported a *Winnipeg Free Press* article. After the devastating Red River flood of 1997, a fundraising social was held in Calgary where, another *Winnipeg Free Press* article noted, "the classic Winnipeg fare [was] for sale: kielbasa,[198] Old Dutch potato chips and rye bread, washed down with a cup of beer."[199] The Winnipeg organizer of a Toronto fundraiser for the Canadian Museum of Human Rights said she "planned to cram as many bags of Old Dutch chips into her carry-on luggage as possible" before heading to Toronto.[200] The Winnipeg Art Gallery's 2010 fundraiser had "Manitoba Overboard" as its theme, and encouraged participants to "don your best pirate—or Old Dutch potato chip outfit—to get in the nautical or homegrown spirit."[201] Even Winnipeg's mayor and Manitoba's premier were fans of Old Dutch: Glen Murray and Gary Doer met with Manitobans in Ottawa at a reception that featured perogies and Old Dutch potato chips.[202] Winnipeggers define Old Dutch chips as one of the essential components of the "good old Manitoba social": *Winnipeg Free Press* articles describe "social" food as "rye bread, kielbasa, cheese cubes, sweet pickles and Old Dutch chips,"[203] or "Old Dutch potato chips, kolbassa [kielbasa] and Kub [rye] bread."[204] In celebration of its 140 years as a province of Canada, the government of Manitoba planned the "World's Biggest Social" to entice expatriate Winnipeggers back home for the celebrations. Numerous

Winnipeg Free Press reports extol "the weather, the sounds, Old Dutch potato chips, Kub bread, Bothwell[205] cubed cheese . . . they miss the social."[206]

Former and returned Winnipeggers express their cravings for Old Dutch chips; reporter Bartley Kives explained that "ex-Winnipeggers living in Toronto have been known to hoard Old Dutch potato chips."[207] Graca Resendes left Winnipeg for better job prospects in Ontario, but eventually returned to Winnipeg. She said, "After being on your own for so long it's pretty strange to be back. But then again, there's Old Dutch potato chips so I can't complain."[208] Cheryl Krause, a Winnipeg nurse transplanted to Minneapolis, "marked her first anniversary living in Minneapolis . . . and thought longingly about Old Dutch potato chips and kolbassa [kielbasa]."[209] Winnipegger Rick Loewen recalled that, while living in Toronto, he "pine[d] for two things. Old Dutch chips and Sals."[210] Manitoba Opera soprano Andriana Chuchman missed "a lot of the Winnipeg junk food—poutine, Old Dutch chips—and the good Ukrainian food, the kulbasa [kielbasa], the perogies" when she was training in Chicago.[211] A Winnipeg newspaper advised those travelling south during the winter to pack carefully: "If you can't live without Old Dutch Salt 'n Vinegar chips, throw a few bags into your suitcase. The treats you love at home can be hard to find in a Mexican corner store or at the hotel gift shop in Punta Cana."[212] Businesses have emerged to cater to the nostalgic needs of these displaced Winnipeggers. Cam Friesen of Altona, Manitoba, ships Canadian snack foods to Canadians living abroad; a woman in Texas orders Old Dutch chips from him.[213] Jerry Stubbs operates Nostalgia Foods, a company that specializes in shipping Winnipeg food—including Old Dutch chips—around the globe.[214] For a time, even Old Dutch itself shipped chips to those people not able to purchase them in stores. Marketing director Scott Kelemen described the launch of the company's online store in 2004: "Our first order was from Texas last week. Throughout our history, we've had so many people who are Western Canadians and have moved east or south and couldn't find our product. Now we can ship it to them."[215]

Some of these Old Dutch chip aficionados use the product in innovative ways. Midwestern Americans have "a preference for layering Old Dutch chips and ketchup between the baloney and Taystee bread,"[216] reported the

Minneapolis Star Tribune. The concession stand at the hockey arena in Winkler, Manitoba, offers tacos in a bag. *Winnipeg Free Press* reporter Bill Redekop described the treat as "a bag of Old Dutch tacos [chips] cut open sideways, with ground beef, salsa, sour cream, cheese and fresh lettuce tossed on top. You mix it up and walk around eating from the open bag with a plastic fork."[217] Winnipeg chocolatier Constance Popp covers Old Dutch ripple chips with chocolate.[218] Old Dutch Winnipeg plant manager Bill Bashucky recalls his favourite sandwich as a child was Cheez Whiz with crushed Old Dutch onion and garlic chips between slices of toast.[219] Old Dutch themselves encourage using their product as a meal ingredient, publishing recipes on their websites for a chopped salad and a chicken soup that incorporate tortilla chips, a potato-chip-coated salmon appetizer, salmon patties made with dill-flavoured chips, and tuna casserole and meatloaf that contain potato chips.[220]

To return, then, to the questions that opened this chapter: What, if anything, does it mean to "eat local" or "buy Canadian" in the context of Old Dutch? How has Old Dutch used symbolic forms of economic nationalism? Can Old Dutch be seen as a family-owned alternative to large multinationals like Frito-Lay? Or, has their increasing size required them to operate in ways indistinguishable from large global corporations?

The ownership of Old Dutch, in both its Canadian and American forms, is American. As such, they are among those foreign-owned businesses in the Canadian economy that control 18 percent of assets (49 percent of manufacturing assets) and produce 29 percent of revenue (51 percent of manufacturing revenue).[221] Labatt Breweries is another such foreign-owned company, owned by Anheuser-Busch InBev of Belgium. Charlie Angelakos, vice-president of corporate affairs for Labatt Breweries of Canada, argues that it is not the owners but the *workers* who determine whether a company is Canadian. He notes, "Our beer is made with Canadian raw materials by Canadian employees who belong to Canadian unions (some unionized since 1907) and work in breweries in six Canadian cities."[222] Similarly, the majority of Old Dutch's North American production and suppliers are located in Canada.

Old Dutch does share some characteristics with the larger multinational snack food manufacturers that trouble critics. Old Dutch has expanded by taking over smaller businesses, such as Humpty Dumpty. They have introduced significant innovations in product development and in the production process. The latter is highly mechanized, to the point that the product is virtually untouched by human hands. And they advertise their business extensively, including by participating in community and charitable events, in ways that some scholars would deem to be paternalistic.

There are other aspects of Old Dutch's history, however, that defy the characterization of their business as no different from Frito-Lay. Old Dutch has a flat management structure by comparison with the complex hierarchies of large multinationals. They do less research and development. Their takeover of Humpty Dumpty prevented that business from registering for a second bankruptcy and saved the jobs of most of their workers. Old Dutch gave not only employment but also a sense of community to young immigrants to Canada like Bebe Maqsood. United Food and Commercial Workers representative and former shop steward J.P. Petit attests to the generally positive working relationship among the union, the company, and its workers. And Canadian consumers have incorporated Old Dutch chips into their rituals of celebration and community building.

Including their founding owner's years of home-based production, Old Dutch has been making potato chips continuously since 1934—more than eighty years: a long history in the annals of independent businesses. Touring the Winnipeg plant with some Winnipeg Blue Bomber football players in 2009, radio personality Ace Burpee explained why he thinks of Old Dutch as a local business: "All the potatoes that Old Dutch uses here are grown in Manitoba. They use thousands of tons of canola oil . . . all from the Altona [Manitoba] area. The plant still requires a high number of hands-on workers as it is not fully automated like some of its other plants. This means jobs. Lots of 'em."[223] He concluded: "If you're going to eat chips, eat Old Dutch. Think globally, eat chips locally."[224]

2

THE CHANGING CHIP INDUSTRY

Potato Growers and Federated Fine Foods

"In this business you have to be large and give good service and quality to survive."

——— G.H. FAST, QUOTED IN WINNIPEG FREE PRESS, 1968 ———

The history of potato chips in Canada mirrors the history of many other manufacturing industries in this nation: the development of independent businesses, followed by their consolidation into larger (and often foreign-owned) entities. This process in manufacturing firms not related to chip production could also affect the chip industry. The end of sugar manufacturing in Manitoba, for example, resulted in a shift from the growing of sugar beets to chipping potatoes. The increase in the number of producers of chipping potatoes was accompanied by a reduction in the number of potato chip manufacturers.

Canadian suppliers have been intimately tied to producers in the history of potato chips in Canada—far more so than for any other snack food. Potatoes—unlike sugar or cacao—can be grown in Canada. As a consequence, many Canadian potato growers became small-scale producers of potato chips, until much larger American producers supplanted them. Federated Fine Foods—a company begun by potato growers—was thus the only wholly Canadian-owned chip producer in Canada at one point. They found themselves unable to compete when Old Dutch Foods entered the Canadian market. However, government-assisted research, the activities of professional associations, and cooperation within the supply chain allowed potato growers like Kroeker Farms, Haskett Growers, and Southern Potato Company to find success together with Old Dutch.

Small Manufacturers

The potato chip industry used to be populated by hundred of small manufacturers; the cost of freight and the fragility of the product limited their distribution range. For example, Nalley's (based in British Columbia) was a popular brand of potato chips on the west coast of Canada and in the northwestern United States, but virtually unknown outside that region.[1] The situation was similar south of the border: in 1957, some 200 companies made 85 percent of the potato chips in the United States. These companies included Red Dot Foods Incorporated,[2] Williams & Company,[3] Blue Bell Potato Chip Company, Good-ee Potato Chip Company,[4] Goodies Spud Chip Company,[5] Jackson's Incorporated,[6] and Scott Potato Chip Company.[7]

In the 1950s, with postwar prosperity and the creation of a teenager culture, chip manufacturing exploded. An article in the *Northwest* explained the "potato chip business [was not] just a summer industry as it formerly was."[8] Equipment manufacturer O.K. Miller of Chicago claimed that any individual could become an entrepreneur with his home equipment for making potato chips: "I will show you how to turn potatoes into CASH! Start you in a Profitable Potato Chip Business At Home. . . . Even if your community is being supplied with old fashioned chips, I'll show you how to step in and grab the market, rake the profits into your own pocket. You simply manufacture and sell to stores at wholesale—let stores sell for you. I furnish complete plant and exact instructions for making profits the first day."[9] Miller offered equipment that he claimed produced greaseless potato chips at an affordable cost: "And now the complete plant—with my new machine—can be put into your kitchen or basement for less than the down payment on a cheap car."[10]

For a brief period of time, the only wholly Canadian-owned potato chip company in the nation was Federated Fine Foods of Manitoba. Winkler, Manitoba, potato growers who were looking for a market for their potatoes founded the business in 1960. A *Winnipeg Free Press* article reported that the potato growers asked G.H. Fast, general manager of Interprovincial Cooperatives, if his company "was interested in acquiring a chunk of the business and possibly boxing the chips under the Interprovincial brand name."[11] Interprovincial Cooperatives wasn't interested, but Fast was; he already was a part-owner of a radio station in Altona, Manitoba, and thus had experience as an investor. Federated Fine Foods bought an existing business, Hunter Potato Chips, and purchased a factory in Winnipeg. Fast observed, "Our biggest mistake was starting so small. In this business you have to be large and give good service and quality to survive. We should never have started in Winkler. We should have started right here in this [Winnipeg] plant from the beginning."[12]

The success of the company was such that Fast retired from Interprovincial Cooperatives to focus solely on Federated Fine Foods. Four Manitoba potato growers were under contract to the company, two of which were company shareholders. The limited growing season in Manitoba meant that, for two months a year, the company had to import potatoes from California.

By the 1970s, Federated Fine Foods produced Humpty Dumpty, Dutch Maid, Irish, and Hunter brand potato chips, processing one train carload of potatoes daily. Sixty employees produced potato chips in plain, barbecue, onion and garlic, beef, green onion, and roast chicken flavours, as well as popcorn, cheese curls, and pop curls.[13] Overcooked chips rejected as too dark were boxed and sold for a dollar to people in Winkler who preferred their caramel flavour.[14] Griffith Laboratories assisted the company in designing flavourings, which could be a complicated process. Don Kroeker, former chief executive officer of Kroeker Farms, a potato supplier, explained, "Within barbecue, there were a lot of different flavourings, so we had to decide which was the best barbecue flavour or the best onion and garlic."[15] Taste tests were conducted among owners and employees, rather than through broader focus groups. In the spring of 1968, the salt and vinegar flavour was introduced and displaced the company's bestseller: plain potato chips. This flavour was never exported to the United States: a *Winnipeg Free Press* article stated that "Americans don't put vinegar on French fries . . . they use ketchup instead."[16]

Irish Potato Chips, one of the brands produced by Federated Fine Foods, relied almost exclusively on potatoes supplied by Kroeker Farms.[17] At first, the chips were manufactured in a plant set up in the same building that served as Kroeker's potato storage facility. Marketing director Rudy Fast wanted to get the company "off to a really good start" and decided to offer a "two for the price of one" deal to wholesalers. But, as Don Kroeker said, "the error that was made was that it was sold to the wholesalers without any commitment on their part to pass it [the deal] on to retail. So these wholesalers ordered huge quantities and kept our plant very busy, but they were not moving them out fast enough and a big part of that was that many of them were not offering the deal [to customers], so we actually got some back that had been held too long. It cost us an awful lot of money, so it was a really tough start."[18]

After approximately three years, production moved to a new plant in Winnipeg on King Edward Street. Not long after, the company was sold. Kroeker said, "We bit off more than we could chew and we sold it to an Eastern company who, shortly after, closed it off."[19] Irish Potato Chips folded in the early 1950s, when Old Dutch Foods began operating a plant in Winnipeg. With the closure of Irish Potato Chips, Kroeker Farms switched to production for Old Dutch Foods, a move made possible by their participation in the Vegetable Growers Association of Manitoba. The association had a "potato day" at one of their conventions at the University of Manitoba, led by Harold Kutzner of Old Dutch Foods. Kutzner subsequently assisted Kroeker Farms in negotiating a contract with Old Dutch.

Industry Cooperation and Government Support

Old Dutch had long provided educational programs for farmers to improve the quality of potatoes; the growers themselves, under the banner of the Chipping Growers Association of Manitoba, coordinated research with the federal agricultural research station in Morden, Manitoba.[20] Beginning in the 1950s, Old Dutch and the Vegetable Growers Association of Manitoba sponsored "chipping potato seminars" at the University of Manitoba.[21] The guest speaker at one such seminar in the 1970s was Dr. Ora Smith, a former

Cornell University professor and the research director of the Potato Chip Institute International.[22] The *Winnipeg Tribune* reported, "He said the composition of the potato is such that it is still difficult for chippers to maintain a uniform appearance in their product, which gives competing snacks an immediate appearance advantage. . . . By using careful storage and production methods, potato growers can provide chippers with low sugar content and high specific gravity potatoes which produce a better-quality chip."[23]

Uniformity was valued by customers, but difficult to produce from a vegetable whose growing and storage conditions could be so variable. Heavy rains in 1993 delayed the Manitoba potato harvest, for example; as a consequence, forty Old Dutch employees were told to stay home for a day, as there were no potatoes to process.[24] Different sizes of potatoes resulted in different sizes of chips, and bags were packed by weight—but consumers objected to finding fewer, albeit larger, chips in their bags.[25] This size problem is an unavoidable one in the industry, due to the varying sizes of an agricultural product like potatoes.

Nonetheless, there is much that can be standardized and automated about production, even of foodstuffs. The organic materials that are the inputs of food processing are a limiting factor, however. Daniel Sidorick, in his study of vegetable soup production at Campbell, notes that the perishable nature of soup ingredients prevented their stockpiling by the company.[26] Wage-incentive schemes on the vegetable preparation lines were challenging, in part, because of the non-standardized sizes of vegetables.[27] Yet, Campbell tried to control vegetable size as much as possible by developing their own tomato varieties to be raised by farmers under contract, much as Old Dutch experimented with potato varieties and offered chipping seminars.[28] In this respect, then, Old Dutch was no different from other major corporations, shaping and controlling their supply chain.

The plethora of small manufacturers of chips in postwar Canada formed the Canadian Potato Chip Association (CPCA) in 1958 to share information and advocate for their industry.[29] Prior to that year, the members of the CPCA were members of the Potato Chip Institute International. In 1977, the CPCA board of directors included representatives from Yum

Yum Potato Chip Company (based in Quebec), Old Dutch Foods, and Hostess Foods. Committees carried out the work of the CPCA with respect to organizing an annual convention, assisting membership with packaging and labelling regulations, providing advice on environmental issues, and conducting research on potato varieties. The CPCA executive secretary, H.R. (Hank) Taylor, explained in an article in *Chipper/Snacker* that one of the organization's goals was to assist members with the growing government regulation of chip manufacturers: "In the fifties, government involvement in industry wasn't that much. [In the 1970s] government is overly involved in industry."[30] Chips were an important part of the economy, as potatoes were "dollar-wise . . . the largest horticultural crop in Canada" in that decade.[31] In the early 1970s, he said, the Packaging and Labelling Committee was "very active, negotiating with the government in the areas of metrication, bilingualism, claims and proliferation of sizes in the small food products."[32] Chips were the first Canadian food industry to convert from imperial to metric measurements, and the CPCA Environmental Committee worked "with the government to establish industry guidelines for water pollution control."[33]

The CPCA Potato Research Committee contributed funding to research on improvements in storage at federal agricultural research stations located in Kentville, Nova Scotia, and Morden, Manitoba. The Canadian federal government subsidized this research as they wanted to get to a point where it was no longer necessary to import potatoes for the industry. The CPCA negotiated a remission of the duty their members paid when they had to import potatoes (which they did when local potatoes were unavailable during part of the year).[34] The *Chipper/Snacker* article reported that the duty, which was 37.5 cents per hundredweight of potatoes in the late 1970s, was divided in two, "with half returned to the company who bought the potatoes and half allotted for research at the two sites." The Kentville research station studied the aging of potatoes in storage, while the Morden research station studied storage diseases, potato uniformity, and other storage effects.[35]

State support for agricultural development of this sort has a long history in Canada, dating back to the federal government's creation of experimental farms in 1866. Wheat, of course, has always been a crop of interest, but potatoes have also been a focus since 1912.[36] In 1934, federal investment in potato research increased in response to a United States potato breeding program that began in 1929.[37] By the 1950s and 1960s, according to an article in *Acadiensis* by Stephen Turner and Heather Molyneaux, potato researchers' initial focus on the production of disease-resistant varieties was replaced by "commercial, agronomic and industrial considerations."[38] The opening in 1956 of a McCain french fry plant in New Brunswick resulted in major changes in the industry: only 6 percent of New Brunswick potatoes were processed that year; by 1971, the percentage rose to almost 40 percent.[39] According to Turner and Molyneaux, "The McCain presence subjected farmers to the enormous market power of a near monopsony."[40]

Monopsony, the inverse of monopoly, "refers to a single buyer of a good or service." The term was invented by Cambridge scholars Joan Robinson and Bertram L. Hallward in 1932.[41] Monopsony can occur in many areas of the economy, including college athletics, health care, and agriculture.[42] Within agriculture, the typical arrangement involves small farmers selling to large agricultural processors.[43] Roger Blair and Jeffrey Harrison suggest that monopsony might occur in agriculture because it is easier to achieve economies of scale on the processing rather than the production side.[44] Debate over whether such monopsony is good or bad revolves around whether one favours "preserving small economic units" such as farms or the "allocative efficiency and consumer welfare" afforded by centralized purchasing power.[45]

Old Dutch has not had quite the same monopsony effect in western Canada as McCain has had in New Brunswick. Old Dutch works with growers and universities to introduce new varieties in an effort to ensure that local potatoes are available as close to all-year-round as possible. Local potatoes are available until mid-July; Old Dutch then imports potatoes from Oregon until a new local crop is available in August. It is expensive to ship potatoes from the midwestern United States to Manitoba, however, and so profit margins for the company shrink during mid-summer.[46] By the late 1990s, two-thirds of Manitoba potatoes were either destined to become McCain fries or Old Dutch chips, and Manitoba became the second-largest potato producer in the country, after Prince Edward Island.[47] Some twenty-eight producers in the province raise seed potatoes, thirty-seven raise table potatoes, and more than 120 raise processing potatoes.[48] Eighty to 85 percent of Manitoba potato production is used by processors including McCain, Simplot, and Old Dutch.[49]

Potato Farmers

The chipping potatoes for Old Dutch chips in Winnipeg are provided by three southern Manitoba growers: Kroeker Farms, Haskett Growers, and Southern Potato Company.[50] Chipping potatoes are round and white, and (when fried) produce a light-coloured chip without blemishes.[51] In the first years of the Winnipeg plant's operation, boxcar loads of potatoes were delivered from Arizona and California; they tended to be "soupy" by the spring.[52] This problem arose when new potatoes were moved from a hot climate to a colder one in boxcars that were not temperature controlled.[53] Purchasing local chipping potatoes largely solved this problem. Old Dutch president Steve Aanenson declared, "The Red River Valley around Winkler is the most ideal spot in Manitoba for growing chip potatoes. The quality is unsurpassed. We buy 95 percent of our Winnipeg chipping potato stock from around that region."[54] Growers are paid bonuses or given deductions based on the quality of their potato production. Old Dutch works together with these growers and with the Food Science faculties at the University of Guelph and University of New Brunswick (Fredericton) to improve potato quality.

Kroeker Farms began in the 1930s as a family operation, incorporated in 1955, and is now owned by shareholders and managed by non-family members.[55] The decision to move away from family management was made partly in response to the fact that none of the family shareholders live in the region anymore.[56] Don Kroeker said, "We believe that owners living in the community is a good connection for the community. It enhances trust of the community and our company."[57] Originally a corn producer (they built the first corn dryer on the Canadian prairies), Kroeker Farms switched to potatoes in the mid-1940s after a major frost damaged their corn crop. They began farming seed potatoes, then added table, processing, and chipping potatoes. In 2014, they produced just under 405 hectares of chipping potatoes. While they used to grow Kennebec and Irish Cobbler chipping potatoes, they now produce Dakota Pearl, Ivory Crisp, Lady Claire, and Atlantic varieties.[58]

Haskett Growers, another of Old Dutch's potato suppliers, is owned by brothers Larry, Harold, and Marvin Thiessen. They began farming potatoes in 1978; prior to that, they grew sugar beets and edible beans. With the decline of the sugar beet industry in Manitoba in 1996,[59] Haskett Growers purchased a seed potato farm. They later partnered with other potato producers to construct a potato-washing facility. They grow table, seed, and processing potatoes on 1,215 hectares, and produce other crops on an additional 2,025 hectares.[60] One-third of their potato crop is processing potatoes for McCain; one-third is table potatoes for Peak of the Market;[61] the remaining third are seed and chipping potatoes for Old Dutch. Haskett first sold potatoes to Old Dutch in the early 1980s, producing 10,000 hundredweights;[62] in 2014, they supplied Old Dutch with 60,000 hundredweights.[63] Chipping potato varieties are chosen by Old Dutch in part on the basis of when they will mature, so that they do not need to be stored too long before being processed. As well, the company's concern, said an industry expert, "is something that will fry well through the year. Some [varieties] are higher risk as far as storage diseases. That's why sometimes they eliminate them. That's all a part of their selection."[64] Haskett grows three varieties for Old Dutch: Atlantic, Dakota Pearl, and Ivory Crisp.

Southern Potato Company is a fifth-generation family farming business in the Winkler, Manitoba, area.[65] The Kuhl family, owners of Southern, began farming sugar beets in the early 1950s when selling their grain became too difficult. They grew sugar beets for Manitoba Sugar until the mid-1980s,[66] as did many farmers in the Winkler area. When Manitoba Sugar shut down in 1997, there was no other market for sugar beets. The Manitoba Sugar plant was aging, there were few sugar refineries in Canada, and the United States had reduced Canadian access to their sugar market.[67]

The Kuhl family followed the lead of Kroeker Farms and started growing table potatoes in 1960, incorporating that year as Southern Manitoba

Potato Company. The business was helped in the early years by Peter J. Peters ("Potato Pete"), who was hired in 1955 as a potato specialist by the Manitoba Department of Agriculture.[68] Since then, the provincial government has reduced support for experimental agriculture programs, forcing Southern to rely instead on their own knowledge and that of industry experts. In 1978, company president John Kuhl purchased shares from the two siblings with whom he had founded the business to become sole owner. John Kuhl's son Keith became president in 2001, and the company was renamed Southern Potato Company in 2014.[69] The business had begun as a 200-hectare farm, and by 2015 they farmed almost 2,830 hectares, employing fifty people year-round and up to eighty people during the harvest season.[70] When Southern was formed, there were approximately 100 potato growers in Manitoba; today, there are only eight or nine. Farms consolidated to take advantage of the efficiency provided by economies of scale, and members of the next generation decided not to take over their families' farms.

Southern began growing chipping potatoes for Hunter's Potato Chips in 1962 or 1963. Varieties grown at the time included Irish, Kennebec, Orland, Wawanesa, and Warba potatoes.[71] The latter three are no longer acceptable chipping potato varieties, as they produce too dark a chip. Marlon Kuhl, grandson of John Kuhl, said: "You see, in those days, they weren't that fussy as far as color was concerned. . . . Nowadays, when people open a bag of chips, they expect that it is going to be the same every month of the year. If it is plain or ripple, they must be white all the way through and the same consistency and appearance. Those kind of things. Whereas I am assuming that back in those days it wasn't as critical [to consumers]."[72] John Kuhl agreed: "No, people weren't that fussy. I don't know whether the [chip] processors started the demand for a more consistent color. Once they started that, then of course the taste changes and then the general public started to demand it."[73] In the twenty-first century, Southern provides potatoes to Old Dutch—but not the varieties of old. They produce Atlantic potatoes for the month of August, as "they fry right out of the field" and cannot be stored. Dakota Pearl is grown for harvest in September; they can be stored until April or May. Ivory Crisp is stored until June, and Lady Claire can be stored until early August. By sourcing local potatoes year-round, Old Dutch is able to avoid some transportation and import challenges.[74]

Southern's first contract with Hunter's Potato Chips was for 2,000 or 3,000 bags of potatoes. John Kuhl hauled the potatoes, 200 bags at a time, to Hunter's processing plant on Lombard Avenue in Winnipeg. He would unload forty-five-kilogram bags of potatoes by hand from his truck, tossing them down a chute to the plant's basement. After unloading thirty-five bags in this fashion, he would go to the basement and transfer them—again, by hand—to a pallet so they could be moved throughout the plant by a pallet jack. In this way, he would deliver 1,590 kilograms of potatoes using his own strength.[75] Hunter's manufactured only plain potato chips, and the company folded not long after Old Dutch began manufacturing in Winnipeg.

For a time, the three Chorney brothers (Anton R. Chorney, John Chorney, and Joe Chorney)[76] also grew potatoes for Old Dutch. They preferred selling to them rather than to Hunter's, as Old Dutch unloaded the potatoes at their plant themselves. When Southern built a plant to wash their potatoes before shipping them, Old Dutch decided to pay them ten cents more per hundredweight. The Chorney brothers eventually were removed as a supplier for Old Dutch: their unwashed potatoes were often mixed with rocks (a feature of their farmland northeast of Winnipeg), which subsequently damaged the cutting knives at the Old Dutch factory.[77]

Cooperation with Suppliers

Supplier cooperation with manufacturers and with each other has been shown to be significant to business success. Michael Maloni and W.C. Benton, for example, analyze the changing nature of supply chains in the United States. American manufacturers in much of the twentieth century "maintained a distant, competitive supply chain environment with large supplier bases in order to obtain low-cost bids."[78] That has, since the 1980s, been replaced by a "more relational approach by sharing information and cooperatively planning within the chain to position the entire chain as a source of strategic competitive advantage."[79]

Supplier cooperation exists within the chip industry in a way that is simply not possible for candy, chocolate, and Cheezie manufacturers in Canada. The explanation for this may be found in the nature of each snack food's main ingredient: sugar for candy; cacao for chocolate; corn meal for Cheezies. These commodities are produced and traded internationally; potatoes are not, as, according to the Food and Agriculture Organization of the United Nations, they are "a bulky, perishable commodity with high transport costs and limited export potential."[80] Three-quarters of the world's sugar is produced from sugar cane; the rest comes from sugar beets. In 2006, Canada was the thirty-first-largest producer of sugar beets, a much more expensive commodity than sugar cane.[81] As a consequence, sugar beet production in Canada has been in decline since 1951, and 90 percent of Canadian sugar is produced from imported sugar cane.[82] Cacao beans are grown only in Central and South America, Africa, and Indonesia, making it difficult for a Canadian manufacturer to manage their supply chain.[83] Corn is the third most produced cereal crop in Canada (after wheat and canola). Canada's closest neighbour, however, is the largest global producer: the U.S. produces 35 percent of the world's corn. Canada ranks a lowly eleventh in global production.[84] There are far fewer potato growers than corn producers in Canada. Thus, chip manufacturers are able to manage the supply chain—with assistance from a federal government that has been interested in agricultural development for more than a century—to an extent simply not possible in other forms of Canadian snack food production.

The relationship between Southern and Old Dutch is an example of such supplier cooperation. Southern has had contracts with Hostess and Frito-Lay, but stopped selling to them around 2005, preferring the smaller-scale business and positive working relationships provided by Old Dutch. In addition, the Old Dutch plant is only an hour and a half away from their farm, whereas Frito-Lay required them to ship to Alberta (fifteen hours away). Marlon Kuhl said, "When you are that far from a plant, you are always at a disadvantage, so we just looked at our business and the size of the contract and our relationship with Old Dutch and thought that it was important to focus on that. There is so much success and so much history together that we decided that we needed to focus on that and maximize that, and decided that we would discontinue growing potatoes with Frito-Lay."[85]

Despite being independent businesses, Kroeker, Haskett, and Southern work together to produce potatoes for Old Dutch in Winnipeg. If one producer needs to move their potatoes out of storage for any reason, the others will agree to ship that producer's product to Old Dutch first.[86] Kroeker Farms is the largest of the three, and provides the most to Old Dutch. They thus have the greatest number of delivery time periods, so the other two producers, according to an industry expert, "work around them, to an extent."[87] Southern Potato is the second-largest producer, and Haskett is the smallest and most recent producer for Old Dutch. Another form of cooperation is via the Winkler Potato Company, a storage company for chipping potatoes jointly owned by Kroeker Farms and Southern Potato.[88]

These growers rely on a combination of local and Mexican migrant labour to harvest their potatoes. Mexican migrant workers began coming to Canada in 1974 as part of the Canadian Seasonal Agricultural Workers Program (which itself began in 1966).[89] Of the more than 25,000 workers who come to Canada annually as seasonal workers, more than half come from Mexico; the rest, from the Caribbean.[90] In an article in *International Migrant Review*, Kerry Preibisch said that migrant labourers are often preferred in Canadian agriculture because they are "*more willing* to accept the industry's working and living conditions and . . . *less able* to contest them."[91] Located in southern Manitoba, Kroeker, Haskett, and Southern are in the heart of the former Mennonite reserves.[92] Many of the Mexican migrants to this area—up to 400 men every year—are Mennonites, descendants of the Manitoba Mennonites who migrated to Mexico in the 1920s.[93] Their ability to speak Low German with their employers, together with a shared ethno-religious background, is an attraction for these foreign workers.

In addition to labour, the environment is an ongoing challenge to a successful potato harvest. The "base raw material" of potato chips is a living thing and is subject to environmental conditions. Dick McMahon, Old Dutch Foods distribution manager, said that when "somebody else decides what the weather is going to be like," it can create challenges for an industry dependent on a successful harvest.[94] Old Dutch faced such a challenge in the early twenty-first century when a third of the potato crop in Alberta was lost. Both drought and too much rain affect the potato and, subsequently, the quality of potato chips.[95] Haskett and Kroeker use irrigation systems and tiling for drainage in an effort to control growing conditions.[96] They also take measures to control soil erosion and modify soil salinity, such as reducing tillage.[97]

Following a successful harvest, the proper storage of potatoes—controlling for both temperature and humidity—is critical to the quality of the end product. In the late 1970s, Old Dutch built a $1 million potato storage and conditioning facility near Taber, Alberta,[98] capable of storing 7,500 tonnes of potatoes (enough for fifteen weeks of chip production). Storage was leased to five farmers who held contracts with Old Dutch. In Manitoba, by contrast, the growers themselves store the potatoes they produce for Old Dutch; unlike production for McCain or Simplot, Old Dutch does not send field men to check storage conditions in Manitoba: an industry expert said that "it is grower driven."[99] The Alberta conditioning facility ventilates stored potatoes until they cease to sweat. The temperature of the storage bins is then lowered slowly while maintaining 95 percent humidity. Potatoes remain in these environmental conditions until they need to be shipped to the manufacturing plant for processing, at which point the bin temperature is slowly raised.[100] Once shipped to the manufacturing plants, Alberta potatoes undergo quality inspections by Old Dutch quality analysis personnel. Emily Anderson was head of quality analysis at the Roseville, Minnesota, plant in the 1970s. An article in the *Minneapolis Star* reported, "When a lot of potatoes tests up to the standard of Old Dutch, Mrs. Anderson sends the word that lot (or shipment) so and so is ready to be made into potato chips."[101] She would bore holes in samples from each lot of potatoes; the resulting chips from these samples would also have holes in them, making them easy to pick out for quality analysis of colour as well as oil, moisture, and salt content. In Manitoba, much of this testing is presently done in labs at Kroeker Farms.[102]

Another example of supplier cooperation is that Southern is granted considerable independence by Old Dutch. According to Don Kroeker, "As far as production goes, they leave the farming for us and they specialize in chips—baking, selling, distributing, marketing chips."[103] When Old Dutch moved to a new plant in Winnipeg in 1977, they added a lab for quality testing of potatoes. Southern was then required to continually provide samples from various storage bins for testing, which allowed Old Dutch to determine which bins' potatoes to use at any point in time, ensuring that the potatoes were processed at their peak. Potato quality is tested by measuring the sucrose and glucose content, the specific gravity, and the density. All these factors contribute to how well a potato will store and will fry. Cold storage reduces risk of disease, but cold can also increase sugar content, which is undesirable. In the 1970s and 1980s, such testing was done by Southern at the Morden Experimental Station under the direction of B.B. Chubey; with the construction of a lab at Southern in 2010, such testing has been done in-house. Southern's lab allows Manitoba potato growers to support each other. Kroeker said, "Logistically, we are all here in the Winkler area, so we get together and discuss things and if one person has a problem and needs to get a bin off to the plant, then we all kind of work together to accommodate each other. Even at times if one farm is busy and can't keep up hauling the potatoes, we will all help each other with things like that as well. We are operating independently, but we definitely partner together because the ultimate goal is seeing Old Dutch successful through us supplying them potatoes."[104]

This grower cooperation can be traced back to 1964, when Southern joined with Kroeker Farms to form the Winkler Potato Company, which stores potatoes that they grow for Old Dutch Foods.[105] And, as president of the Chipping Potato Growers Association, Marlon Kuhl leads meetings to discuss scheduling of potato delivery and negotiation of contracts with Old Dutch. Their dealings with Old Dutch are mutually beneficial: if the growers overproduce, Old Dutch will purchase potatoes above their contract.[106]

—— • ——

Potato chip manufacturers in North America proliferated in the 1950s. This period of expansion was replaced by consolidation in the 1980s. Federated Fine Foods is an example of one of the hundreds of small, local producers of chips that used to exist in Canada, many of them founded by potato growers. Federated Fine Foods finally succumbed to the competition offered by American-owned Old Dutch when the latter firm entered the Canadian market.

The postwar growth of the chip industry was facilitated by the joining together of manufacturers, farmers, and government to advance snack food manufacturing in Canada. Vegetable growers and chip manufacturers formed their own associations, which worked together to provide education to improve production and offer assistance in navigating increasing government regulation. Government-funded research supported manufacturers in improving their supply chain, contributing to advances in potato varieties and storage methods.

Kroeker Farms, Haskett Growers, and Southern Potato Company began in the early twentieth century as small family farms; they emerged in the 1950s as major agri-businesses, producing potatoes for Old Dutch. Their cooperation with each other, assisted by Old Dutch, played a significant role in the chip manufacturer's success. Old Dutch shaped and controlled their supply chain, working with farmers and researchers to produce potato varieties to their specifications. Farmers in southern Manitoba have found in the company a reliable and supportive purchaser of their potatoes, and a business that grants them considerable autonomy in production. Such cooperation was made possible because of the nature of the key commodity in chip production: the potato.

3

CORPORATE MYTHOLOGY AND CULINARY TOURISM

Hardbite and Covered Bridge Potato Chips

"It's interesting how marketing works."

——— RICKEY YADA, INTERVIEW, 2013 ———

Even as potato growers have diminished in number and grown in size, so have potato chip manufacturers. New players in this market—small, independent companies—needed to differentiate themselves, as they were otherwise unable to compete with Frito-Lay or even Old Dutch, whose entry into the Canadian market led to the demise of Federated Fine Foods' chip production. Hardbite Potato Chips and Covered Bridge Potato Chips have made use of corporate mythology and culinary tourism to carve out a niche for their businesses.[1]

Both Hardbite and Covered Bridge have relied on the mythology of the family farm as a marketing strategy. Hardbite's somewhat convoluted ownership history thus has been recast. Farmer ownership appears to serve as a marketing proxy for the deeply integrated and environmentally sustainable model that the company has built. At Covered Bridge, farmer ownership and food tourism were part of the marketing strategy even before the company began production. Company president Ryan Albright took advantage of proximity to a local tourist attraction, purpose-built the manufacturing facility to attract tourists by the busload, and entered chip manufacturing to make use of his family's own potato production. His promotion of his business as farm-family owned, and his entrepreneurial identification of the business with himself, were ultimately problematic, however. Covered Bridge suffered a lengthy strike and national boycott of their products as a consequence of their investment in their own corporate mythology. Viewing the business as a family and equating their farm origins with independence, the company owner viewed unionization as a personal insult.

Covered Bridge Potato Chips

Like many contemporary snack food manufacturers, Covered Bridge[2] emphasizes the healthy aspects of their products: their chips have no preservatives, no artificial colours, no artificial flavours, and no trans fat, and are gluten free. The business promotes itself with reference to the owner's family's four-generation farm origins in New Brunswick. Covered Bridge is unique in their reliance on the russet potato variety to make their chips, in their use of a local tourist attraction (the world's longest covered bridge) for their corporate identity, and in their willingness to open their production facilities to public view as a tourist attraction in their own right.

Covered Bridge is located just outside Hartland, New Brunswick, home of the world's longest covered bridge. Covered Bridge describes themselves as "an old fashioned kettle chip company with old country taste and tradition."[3] Through promotion to tourists and "unique packaging ideas" (such as selling chips in burlap sacks—another "old-fashioned" touch), the company has been able to cultivate a clientele. Their reliance on kettle-cooked chips (batch cooked at lower temperatures and for longer periods of time than regular chips, resulting in a thicker chip and a harder bite) made from russet potatoes (which produce a darker chip due to their higher sugar content) further distinguishes them from their competitors.[4] The factory, which offers tours, product tastings, and a gift shop, was described in an article in the *National Post* as "an economusée, a sort of living museum of artisanal craftsmanship."[5]

Covered Bridge traces their origins to 2004, when brothers Ryan and Matthew Albright, and cousin Shaun Albright, formed the Carleton County Spud Distributors to sell their (and others') potatoes in Canada and the

United States.[6] The Albright brothers are the fourth generation of a New Brunswick potato farm family; they purchased the family farm in 2006 and founded the chip company that same year.[7] Their vision was to launch a successful potato chip brand and increase tourism to New Brunswick.[8] Prior to the construction of a factory, company president Ryan Albright and two employees cooked chips in his home for a few hours, then loaded the cases into his Toyota Corolla so he could take samples to stores to secure sales.[9] According to Jim Romahn in a *Farm Focus* article, Albright promoted his chips "long before his plant was scheduled to begin production" at trade shows such as the Natural Foods Expo in Boston and the Grocery Innovations Canada show in Toronto.[10]

The first factory-made chips were produced in January 2009.[11] The Atlantic Canada Opportunities Agency provided $528,000 in repayable funding for plant construction, plus an additional $77,150 for marketing to exporters and tour bus operators.[12] An expansion in 2012 was supported by federal and provincial government funding totalling $340,000.[13] In spring 2016, the company underwent its fourth expansion; by then, the number of employees had increased to ninety.[14]

The first employee, Mike McCartney, was hired in 2008, and he was tasked with getting the production line running. McCartney grew up snacking on fruits, vegetables, and crackers: "chips weren't something I would go out and buy."[15] He was working in the food industry when his childhood friend Ryan Albright approached him in 2007 to work at Covered Bridge. The company's initial goal was to make the product clearly distinguishable from typical potato chips, but that presented some challenges. McCartney said,

> The whole idea, from what we initially had planned, was to have a bag that looked full, that was all natural seasonings, a russet potato, a russet burbank potato—because they're a heartier variety that tastes a little bit better—but it also gave us a lot of problems with the machinery, because when you're trying to fill a bag that full, it's harder to seal. An all-natural seasoning is harder to come up with and it's harder to keep your shelf life out

six months. It's harder to get the flavour profile where you want. There's some curves to doing it.[16]

As the first employee, McCartney observed that the business (though still young) has experienced significant changes. "When we first started, it was basically all manually operated. . . . Just a few people, minimal hours, just trying to get things going, and get a few trucks on the road and get a few sales, and start to build and build."[17] He had many responsibilities at first, including shipping and receiving, quality control, maintenance, production, and warehousing. As the company expanded, a marketing manager was hired to take over some of his duties, and he was able to focus on production equipment, mechanics, and warehousing. After two years of operation, the plant expanded from one small production bay with one fryer, one seasoning line, and one bagger to include more fryers and seasoning lines. In 2013, they switched to programmable logic controllers, which allow digital computers to monitor automated machinery. The addition of sweet potato chips to the product line was "a learning curve"[18] for McCartney, requiring much research, including into differences in thickness and cooking temperature. Changes to packaging film barriers, gas-flushing processes, and seasonings have extended their products' shelf life from four months to six months.

A typical day—if there is such—sees McCartney at Covered Bridge doing paperwork, checking the machinery, ordering parts, and making any necessary repairs. Sales at the company increase mid-March until mid-May, peaking at three production shifts totalling 144 hours a week and producing 205 to 225 kilograms of chips per hour. Production decreases toward the end of July, before spiking again briefly in September. Maintenance work increases when production decreases; during peak seasons, McCartney concentrates on training new workers. During the summer, plant tours are offered from 7:00 a.m. to 7:00 p.m. Production is reduced to four days a week the rest of the year, which allows him three days per week for maintenance.[19]

The job gives McCartney some flexibility in his hours, and he enjoys the challenge of the work: "My favourite thing to do is to go out and actually work mechanic stuff on the line. It's not so much the repair and maintenance side of things, but it's go out and when a problem arises where we can't get something to do what we want or we can't find a solution to a problem right away, that's what I like doing the most is going out and finding a solution to a problem that we're having."[20]

McCartney has assisted in the design and construction of some of the equipment at Covered Bridge. He enjoys designing these systems without having to resort to some of the major manufacturers for their large-scale equipment. He received his interprovincial licence for industrial mechanics, is working on securing his welding licence, and would like to obtain an electrical licence as well. "On the other side of the coin," he says, he is "set in my ways and headstrong," as are some other employees. He has learned to "let go of some stuff and embrace other stuff. It's a good company to work for."[21]

Food tourism is a significant part of Covered Bridge's promotional strategy. The factory was purpose-built for tours, with large windows on two walls of the production area that allow tourists to view the manufacturing process. A parking lot accommodates tour buses, whose clientele visit from ten to forty minutes. Students hired as summer workers dress in costume for tour buses: overalls, straw hats, and plaid shirts evoke the farming heritage of the business.[22] In the hallways surrounding the production area, videos are shown of the potato harvest at the Albright farm. Live camera feeds are provided for equipment not readily visible from the windows surrounding the plant. Tourists sample chips hot off the production line and can choose to add any of thirty-five seasonings. An admission fee of three to five dollars is charged for all those over five years of age.

Thomas Broad, fryer operator, is one of the workers whom these tourists observe. He describes the interaction with tourists as one of the highlights of his work: "I enjoy that, it's different. I can't talk to them, but they bang on the window. We get a lot of tourists, a lot of buses, from Japan, Asia, plus regular [North American] tourists every day."[23] Broad interacts with up to 350 tourists per day. He says, "I have had people from all over who want a picture taken with the cook, so I have to come out for photos." He particularly enjoys the reactions of children who tour the plant: "Kids, I like watching kids, I see them in the window just loving it." He acknowledges that, though he finds the work enjoyable, it is also "tiresome, with twelve-hour shifts. I've been here since 6:30 and will be here to 7:30 tonight."

Herr's Potato Chip factory in Nottingham, Pennsylvania, has a marketing strategy similar to that of Covered Bridge: they, too, offer plant tours.[24] Theirs are led not by workers, owners, or students in farmer overalls, but by the company mascot, "Chipper" the chipmunk—"a puppet animated by Jim Henson Puppeteers," according to the company website.[25] A 140-seat movie theatre shows a film about the third-generation family company's history, described by one visitor as "one of the most ideologically charged stories I have ever endured—a squeaky clean version of the Herr family history. The movie is a straight American Horatio Alger, self-made man, story. . . . If the American Dream could be encapsulated in one 15 minute propaganda film, it is offered here to thousands of visitors at the Herr Potato Chip Plant."[26] Clearly, the line between information and propaganda must be carefully navigated for food-tourism marketing strategies to be successful.[27]

Perceptions of the production process at Covered Bridge vary, depending on the narrator. Tourists tend to focus on the technology on display through the large plate-glass windows that surround two sides of the factory (as does the company in their promotional material). Hoppers weigh twenty-seven-kilogram batches of potatoes, washed but skin intact, which are cut by a revolving slicer. The resulting potato slices are transferred to a kettle cooker, where they are constantly and automatically stirred and cooked at 148 degrees Celsius for six minutes. Excess oil is "blown off" by a centrifuge, and the chips travel down a conveyor, where defective chips are removed by hand (unlike at Old Dutch, which uses an optical sorter). Vibrating hoppers deliver the chips to a tumbler where seasoning is added. A second hand picking of defective chips is accompanied by scanning by a metal detector. Then the chips are delivered to a weigh scale that transfers them to a form-fill machine. Bags are filled with nitrogen for preservation before being sealed.[28] This description, based on company promotional material and the account of a typical tourist to the plant, focuses on the product as it moves through the production line.

Employees focus on the labour process in their interviews, emphasizing either teamwork or autonomy, depending on their own job description. One Covered Bridge employee, for example, emphasized the cooperative work of employees. Production departments "hold hands, and it's just like the loop of infinity. If there happens to be a break in one loop, then nothing else happens." A failure at the hopper has consequences down the line for the cutters, the fryers, and the baggers, holding up production. The employee says, "So it's just—everybody holds hands, which is extremely important, the communication, again, that all team members are on board and they're communicating with each other like they need to be."[29]

Thomas Broad, by contrast, spoke of the autonomy he had in his position as fryer operator: "I control all the things for batch times in and out. The supervisor will set lines for a speed to keep up with what I'm running, set tumblers and feeds to match times on my batches so they're not overloading which they used to when we had one fryer, and had a smaller tub to put chips in." With a new and much larger tub, Broad no longer needs to shut the fryer down as often when the tub is full. His specialized job means that he is able to create his own schedule. Despite being scheduled for shorter shifts, he trades hours with another fryer operator so that he has more days off: "I work forty-four hours a week, usually a couple of twelve-hour shifts, so I can get an extra day off to just relax and get away, visit my grandkids. . . . The other fryer operator and I, between the two of us, if I have a short day of five hours then the other operator stays and works and we cover for each other. We work around that way so we can have an extra day off."[30]

Broad was hired at first to work on the production line, but, he said, it was "boring, picking out bad chips. I wanted something different to try." Working as a fryer operator granted him more autonomy and creativity on the job: "On fryers you got to move around; on the grading line, though, you just stand there, your legs get tired, you don't get to move. On fryers, you get to move all the time, from one fryer to another."[31]

In an industry that is highly mechanized, and where the majority of jobs are in packaging, Broad's job is a skilled one. He maintains cutter heads and adjusts them to produce thick-cut or regular chips. "When things go wrong so we get clumps of chips, it's because the cutter heads need adjustment. So you must stop and change them."[32] He monitors moisture, a task that is assisted by technology but requires some operator skill:

> I have a panel to control temperatures up and down to keep moisture between 1.8 and 2.0 so the chips are not too soft or dark. I have to set that, so in the mornings, I fill the fryer and let it heat, put the cutter head in, wait for the fryer to heat up to temperature, then turn on the knobs and buttons and controls and start cooking. I do it by eye; watch the chips and adjust the temperature accordingly and do a sample. A machine does a moisture sample: I crunch chips in a bowl and put them in the machine for reading, and it tells me if I need to go up or down with the temperature. That's how that works; it's pretty neat. I do that every hour so it lets you know if you need to go up or down and I must make the adjustment again. It keeps me busy out there; I like that better than standing in one spot.[33]

The contact of the potatoes with the hot oil drops the temperature down somewhat, before it starts to rise again. Broad says, "You have to wait three to four minutes for the oil to reheat. If you're not watching then you can get dark chips." Varieties in batch size also require attention on his part to make the necessary adjustments: "You can get within two to three pounds; even two pounds makes a difference in temperature. The extra weight drops the temperature and you must wait for it to build."[34]

Though Broad's job is one of the more skilled ones at the plant, he does not have full knowledge of the labour process, and neither are his skills readily transferable to other industries. According to labour historians Craig Heron and Robert Storey, semi-skilled labour emerged as a consequence of the reshaping of labour processes in nineteenth-century Canada in response to the "mechanization, subdivision of labour, and centralization of management."[35] Semi-skilled workers "required less training than the old craft apprenticeships and lacked the all-round knowledge of the whole production process."

They nonetheless had "more responsibility at the centre of the production process than the old-time day-labourers."[36] Some of these semi-skilled workers were able to unionize, and some of their employers were "anxious to reduce [employee] turnover"—thus, deskilling "was not as straightforward a process as many capitalists hoped (and as many theorists have assumed)."[37]

Deskilling in the twentieth century was a similarly complex process, with some skills persisting or intensifying, some new skills being introduced, and some skills disappearing. Heron and Storey emphasize that skill is "more than simply technical competence"; it is also "socially constructed."[38] This is clearly the case at Covered Bridge: the job of fryer operator is the most difficult in the plant and the one that is key to the production process. If, as Heron and Storey argue, "skill is best understood in a specific historical context in which definitions are altered to match the changing dimensions of skilled work and the new characteristics of the skilled worker," then Broad's job is not semi-skilled but skilled.[39] They note the need for historians to understand "workers' own consciousness" in the "process of workplace transformation, in order to understand the dialectic of resistance and consent."[40] Broad's recounting of his personal history reveals that he views himself as a skilled worker.

Broad's first job was with the Canadian Pacific Railway (CPR) and VIA Rail as a locomotive engineer. After an ice jam destroyed the CPR bridge on the Perth–Andover line in the spring of 1987, the CPR abandoned their rural branch lines in New Brunswick. Broad then transferred to London, Ontario. After twenty years with the CPR, he went to work for Noble Metal Processing in Brantford, Ontario, which made automotive parts for General Motors and Chrysler. He had eighteen employees working for him there, whom he trained to use laser welders. Noble Metal closed in 2009, and Broad returned to his hometown in New Brunswick. He interviewed for a job at Covered Bridge, and was hired the next day. He said, "I enjoy this job but wish it paid more, it's not the best I've been paid in the past but it's a job and I like the area here. I'm from Beechwood forty-five minutes away, so I enjoy that. The people here are very outspoken and well liked and we all get along, that makes it easier."[41] His father, whom he described as his best friend, died four years before our interview, and his job as a fryer operator is "something to keep busy and keep my mind off things." The job is more than a simple distraction to him, however. He described in detail the numerous small decisions he has to make on a daily basis:

> You have to be on your toes and keep your eyes open, working with hot oil, and when changing cutter heads. You walk up a ladder to do that and oil gets on things and is slippery, so the floor is sometimes slippery. They've changed the flooring since I started so it's a rougher surface so it's not as slippery and that has helped a lot. You have to have your eyes open at all times when doing that job. When you change cutter heads, they're razor sharp so watch you don't cut hands off or fingers. I've cut my fingers a few times—just nicks, haven't done it for a year and half. You have to be on your toes and your eyes open all the time, play it safe.

Broad noted as well the education and training he received earlier that were transferable to his current position: "I was in a safety course when I was at Noble Metal, and was safety coordinator at that job. I took CPR [cardiopulmonary resuscitation] and first aid through the same company. I took courses with CP Rail as well in Canada and U.S."[42]

Working at Covered Bridge would not be Broad's choice, were other options available to him. He identifies as a train engineer: "That's my job: I miss driving train, but once we lost the bridges I had no choice. I worked twenty years so have a pension, I made sure to get that." Had Noble Metal remained open, he would have stayed there, as his retirement date is nearing. He works at Covered Bridge "to pass the time" until he turns fifty-five, though he may work until he is sixty. "There's a pension plan here, too; every little bit helps," he observes. Though he describes the company as a "good place to work," he is not blind to their shortcomings. "They need to up the wages and get more people to stay. Many leave for that reason because of the wages." Workers move between Covered Bridge and Old Dutch, which has a factory ten minutes away in Hartland. "Old Dutch pays better wages; many from Old Dutch come here because they're unionized and we're not." Broad says, "Several in the last two or three years have come here; I don't know why. I guess they like being in the chip business apparently, or they didn't get along over there because it's a unionized plant and they didn't have the same friendly atmosphere over there. It's a whole different ball game. They like it here better but left the wages there at Old Dutch to come here."[43]

A scant four months after this interview with Thomas Broad, the workers at Covered Bridge unionized. Local 1288P of the United Food and Commercial Workers (UFCW) was certified in early December 2013 to represent all employees, with the exception of the company president, sales and office staff, and management. It appears that the decision to organize stemmed from low wages at the company, as most of the production workers at the plant were reported to make minimum wage.[44] Betty Demerchant was reported as receiving only one ten-cent raise in the five years she worked at Covered Bridge.[45] The starting wage at Covered Bridge was $10.30, while at Old Dutch it was $14.50.[46] The company had funds for four expansions of the business since opening in 2008, but did not similarly invest in raising wages.[47] And production employees were asked to wear shirts that read "I ♥ my job."[48]

To say that collective bargaining did not go smoothly would be an understatement. Bargaining began in January 2014; the two sides went to conciliation in June 2014 and mediation in February 2015. In May, the New Brunswick Labour and Employment Board dismissed an Application to Terminate Bargaining Rights, which the company had filed during the mediation process.[49] Bargaining resumed in the presence of a mediator on 23 June 2015. Company president Ryan Albright asked permission to speak first. He declared, "I will give to my employees the things they are looking for, but never in a union environment where I feel trapped to communicate to my employees on a daily basis for fear of unfair labour practice against myself and the company. For the employees who needed my help personally, I've been there and will not be able to as the union will deem me showing favoritism. . . . The union wants you to feel like they're your friend, they're here for you. It's bullshit."[50]

Albright argued that his provision of a smoking building, optional Blue Cross insurance, and a company gym, together with his plans to provide a larger lunchroom and possibly a profit-sharing program, were evidence of the company's interest in their workers. He concluded: "We've made so many positive changes for the future. We will not take that away and reverse everything by dealing with the negative effect of a union that will hurt all of the employees and careers we have built together. . . . I will give my employees what they want for the increase of wages and the benefits they were looking for, but never ever, ever in a union environment. . . . So I'm done. Carl [Flanagan, UFCW representative], screw you and your fucking Union."[51]

Albright then twice shut down the factory to deliver this same speech to two shifts of production workers, immediately before a scheduled strike vote. The New Brunswick Labour and Employment Board concluded that Albright and Covered Bridge had violated five sections of the Industrial Relations Act.[52] They described Albright's actions as "a direct rather than subtle threat to future employment opportunities and to the sustainability of the enterprise," and directed him to return to negotiations within thirty days.[53] When he did so, he presented a final offer of wages that were lower than what he had offered earlier. The consequence was a strike (begun on 4 January 2016) and a national boycott.[54] Covered Bridge responded to the strike, which they publicly described as "a small bump in the road,"[55] by hiring replacement workers.[56]

The strike ended five months later, in May 2016, with a collective agreement retroactive to January of that year. Wages were increased, an allowance was made for boots and clothing, and provisions for job security and seniority were included. "It took five months to get the deal because the employer did not want to recognize that it was going to be a unionized shop," explained UFCW representative Carl Flanagan.[57] New Brunswick New Democratic Party leader Dominic Cardy argued that the strike was evidence of the need for first contract legislation in the province, which was one of only three in the country that did not have such a law.[58]

The hostility expressed by the company owner during negotiations of this first collective agreement might be explained by Covered Bridge's

Figure 13. Covered Bridge Potato Chips factory, Waterville, New Brunswick, 2013.

Figure 14. Covered Bridge factory, 2013.

corporate identity. The company president was unable to separate his identity from his business, and thus viewed a successful effort to unionize as a personal affront. At Covered Bridge, the company identity is closely tied to the Albright family's farming origins. An article in *Huddle* quotes Albright as saying, "Our goal at Covered Bridge has always been to foster a work environment that has a truly authentic family feel, because it is in fact how we started; as a family."[59] There are some parallels here with historian David Monod's examination of the identity of Canadian shopkeepers in the late nineteenth and early twentieth centuries. Small retailers had a "folkloric image" of shopkeeping, but attributed different meanings to the symbols associated with that image.[60] Property ownership was viewed as a form of independence, and that autonomy led shopkeepers, according to Monod, to "see themselves and their stores as the axle on which society turned and advanced."[61] There was a "symbolic unity of owner and enterprise."[62] These retailers equated their small size with honesty, trust, community, cooperation, and democracy.[63] Covered Bridge draws on the folklore of the family farm for their identity. The symbolic unity of owner and enterprise at Covered Bridge eventually proved problematic. "We try to make working here a lifestyle, and do what we can for our employees," Albright has claimed.[64] The unionization of the employees was thus perceived as a personal insult.

Hardbite Potato Chips

Hardbite Potato Chips is another coastal Canadian chip company with some similarities to Covered Bridge. Hardbite stepped into the void left when Nalley's Canada closed their chip-making facility in Delta, British Columbia, in 1997. Nalley's Canada is owned by Curtice-Burns Foods of Rochester, New York, a subsidiary of Pro-Fac Co-operative.[65] The company sold their chips and snacks division in 1994 to Country Crisp Foods in Utah, but Nalley's British Columbia chip factory was not part of the sale.[66] The 1994 North American Free Trade Agreement made it difficult for Canadians to compete with chip manufacturers on the west coast of the United States, where there were lower labour costs and less stringent environmental laws.[67] A further

Figure 15. Kettle fryer operator, Covered Bridge factory, 2013.

Figure 16. Kettle cooked potato chips, Covered Bridge factory, 2013.

Figure 17. Food tourists seasoning their sample chips after the Covered Bridge factory tour, 2013.

challenge was that local Canadian potato growers were unable to provide sufficient supplies of potatoes to Nalley's for a few successive years.[68]

In the absence of Nalley's, Hardbite Potato Chips became the only chip-producing facility in British Columbia. The company was founded by former Nalley's employees in 1998, and purchased in 2002 by Sepp Amsler of Maple Ridge, British Columbia.[69] Amsler had retired from careers with Sepp's Gourmet Foods and Que Pasa Mexican Foods (makers of tortilla chips) before purchasing Hardbite.[70] He secured sales contracts for Hardbite chips in western Canada, Hong Kong, Japan, and Thailand.[71] The Asian market was chosen "as an alternative to the U.S.," Amsler explained. "It's getting more expensive to export there and there is huge protectionism. In Asia, they love it if you wave the maple leaf around."[72]

Figure 18. Hardbite Potato Chips signage, 2013.

Appearing in 2008 on the Canadian Broadcasting Corporation television program *Dragon's Den*, a reality show that has entrepreneurs make pitches to venture capitalists, Amsler secured a deal, which he later rejected. Robert Herjavec (chief executive officer of the Herjavec Group) and Jim Treliving (T&M Group of Companies) had offered him $350,000 for a 50 percent stake in his chip company. Instead, Amsler found other investors.[73] But, in 2010, Amsler sold the business.

Hardbite launched a major marketing campaign under their new ownership, promoting themselves as connected to farmers. A promotional flyer for the company stated: "Farmer grown, farmer owned, kettle-cooked potato chips. Potato farming is in our roots—so to speak—our family's been doing it since 1920. Today, we don't just grow potatoes for Hardbite Chips, we own the company. From seed to chip—we use the best potatoes, limited ingredients, and we cook in small batch sizes to ensure the highest quality and flavour. Grandpa always said, 'When you do something, do it right.' Pete & Wes, BC Potato Farmers & Potato Chip Lovers."[74]

The folksy reference to grandfathers, the first-name-only owners identified as "potato farmers," and the description of a family farm dating back to 1920 are emotionally evocative but somewhat oversimplified. "Pete" is Peter Schouten, who bought a half interest in the Heppell family farm. "Wes" is Wes Heppell, whose family farm is the one described in the advertising and is incorporated as Heppell Potato Corporation.

Heppell Potato Corporation is a third-generation family farm. Schouten is not a member of the Heppell family, but began working on their farm as a teenager.[75] The Heppell dairy and potato farm began in the 1920s. In 1963, the farm switched to the production of potatoes, vegetables, and turkeys. By 1993, the farm's focus was on potatoes.[76] The company's website states that Heppell's Potato Corporation is "part of a chain of companies, which includes Heppell's maintenance services, Hardbite Chips, Fraser Valley Bio Gas, and Valley Fresh Produce."[77] Fraser Valley Bio Gas recycles the organic chip and oil waste produced by Hardbite into natural gas, which is then used to run Hardbite's fryers.[78]

It was while Schouten was on the board of BC Fresh, a marketing company for British Columbia farmers, that he became acquainted with Hardbite Potato Chips, then owned by Sepp Amsler. He explained, "[BC Fresh] had a customer that was beyond 60 days overdue. He'd been a good customer, so I went to visit him. It was Hardbite." Amsler's health issues and payment problems continued for some time, Schouten recalled, "so I went back and said, 'You should sell me your company.' He said he could never do that. But after a few more days of thinking about it he decided he would. I thought, 'Well, I know how to grow potatoes, I think I can figure out how to make potato chips. I don't know how to market but I know a guy who does and he used to work for Frito-Lay.' So I approached Braden [Douglas]."[79] Braden Douglas, the founder of Crew Marketing Partners (formerly Relevention Marketing), had been previously employed in marketing at Frito-Lay.[80]

Douglas describes himself as "a straight-talking marketing and advertising expert who helps leaders get down to business."[81] His marketing blog describes lessons he has learned in his earlier careers with Proctor & Gamble and Frito-Lay:

> When I worked at Frito-Lay our team created packaging for the World Cup of Hockey (remember that?) and we needed a 'cool factor.' So we signed Martin Brodeur and Ryan Smith to appear on in-store point-of-sale material and packaging. The objective was that fans of these players, or hockey fans in general, would choose to buy our chips because of our association with the celebrities and thus increase sales in the short term, and increase brand loyalty in the long term. For a one-time payment . . . these players did nothing other than provide us with photographs. In fact, we had to superimpose Ryan's head on another hockey player because the photos they supplied didn't quite work on pack. The campaign was a hit and we moved chips baby![82]

Douglas was instrumental in launching the new branding campaign for Hardbite, designing their new website. The provincial government's "Buy Local" program provided the company with $100,000 in funding to promote their brand.[83]

Kirk Homenick, president of Hardbite, described the key aspects of the new branding campaign: "No one was linking chip to grower effectively in Canada. Our owners also own the Heppell Potato Corp., and with the link to their potato farm we have been able to take our products from seed to snack. We also cook all of our chips by hand to give the consumer the very best 'homemade for you' experience in a snack food."[84]

The handmade aspect of the Hardbite brand was emphasized by labelling each bag with the name of the fryer operator who produced its contents. Hardbite's new tagline—"Farmer Grown. Farmer Owned. Handcrafted Potato Chips."—is an interesting one, given that the company's actual ownership is difficult to trace.[85] Promotional material in 2013 listed the ownership as Schouten and Douglas; the corporate website in 2016 features quotes from Schouten alone, who is described as "owner & farmer."[86] The company's directors in 2015, however, included three farmers (Wesley Heppell, Peter Schouten, and George Leroux) and two others (Braden Douglas and Kirk Homenick).[87]

Amsler, too, had promoted the healthy, handmade, and local nature of the chips when he had owned the company: "We are a true kettle operation. We have someone standing there raking the chips all day long so they don't stick, eliminating the need for chemicals to separate them. And because the oil is not overheated, our chips have no trans fats. Everybody says they have no trans fat, but when you overheat the oil—which most chip makers do—you create trans fat.... Everything is local. The potatoes grow across the river from the plant. The boxes are made down the street; the spices around the corner."[88]

Hardbite chips contain no genetically modified organism (GMO) ingredients, no trans fats, no gluten, no monosodium glutamate (MSG), no cholesterol, and no artificial flavours or colours. The chips are available in six flavours: all natural, "smokin' BBQ," rock salt and vinegar, wild onion and yogourt, jalapeno, and Schezwan peppercorn.[89] Jennifer Bain's article for the *National Post* states that, for a time, they also offered a "creamy coconut and curry oriental flavour made with Himalayan crystallized salt."[90] In a competition by the *National Post* for "Canada's Favourite Confection," Hardbite chips placed third, after Nanaimo bars and Nestle's Coffee Crisp chocolate bar. The newspaper described the third-place finish as a "display of corporate pride. . . . We salute this home-grown entrepreneurial spirit and wish their chips all the best."[91]

Marketing Missteps

In a market dominated by American-based multinationals, marketing decisions can be key to ensuring a niche for products like those of Covered Bridge and Hardbite. The strategic decisions to capitalize on the tourist attraction that is the world's longest covered bridge, and to create a tourist attraction of their own through a factory designed as an observation centre and gift shop, have benefited Covered Bridge chips. Hardbite's emphasis on farm-to-chip-bag localism, and the farm heritage of at least some of their directors, also has led to success. Other independent chip manufacturers have made less successful marketing decisions.

Quebec company Yum Yum Chips is a third-generation family business. It was founded by Lionel and Robert Bergeron in 1956, and bought by Paul Jalbert and Louis de Gonzague in 1959.[92] The company's logo, described by one fan as "like a native version of one of the Campbell soup kids,"[93] was discontinued after the 1990 Oka Crisis.[94] In late 2013, Radio CJAD reported, the logo was revived as "a vintage treat for the holidays."[95] Cardboard cut-outs of the logo were distributed to stores, and customers were encouraged to insert their heads into the cutout and take photos of themselves dressed as a stereotype of a Canadian Indigenous person. In the face of protests by Indigenous groups (including a spokesperson for Idle No More Quebec and the grand chief of the Mohawk Council of Kahnawake), the company claimed that their logo was merely "a nod to the founder of the potato chip [Georges Crum], who was native."[96] By 2015, after several adverse reports in national newspapers, the company had abandoned the logo once again.

Figure 19. Vintage bags of Yum Yum potato chips, 2013.

Frito-Lay, too, had an inappropriate mascot for a time. The cartoon character "Frito Bandito" was created in 1967 to sell Fritos corn chips. An article in *Business Insider* reported, "Speaking broken English and robbing unsuspecting bystanders, Frito Bandito was an armed Mexican conman with a dishevelled look and a gold tooth."[97] The Frito Bandito appeared in television commercials, drawn by Tex Avery and voiced by Mel Blanc (of Bugs Bunny fame). After protests from the National Mexican American Anti-Defamation Committee (NMAADC), the mascot was adjusted slightly in 1969: he lost his facial stubble and his gold tooth disappeared. The Frito Bandito came to an end in 1971, only after the NMAADC announced they would file a $610 million lawsuit for defamation.[98] "It casts us as sneaky, untrustworthy thieves, who do not work, who are lazy, irresponsible, and who should be and can be arrested by the superior white man," explained Nick

Reyes, NMAADC executive director.[99] Unlike Yum Yum's efforts, to date, there has been no attempt to resurrect the Frito Bandito.

Viewed in the light of the use of such racist stereotypes, Hardbite's marketing campaign is unproblematic. Does it really matter whether the company is actually owned in its entirety by farmers? The company uses "local ingredients from local growers" and receives support from the British Columbia government's Buy Local program.[100] All waste is directed to Fraser Valley Biogas for use in the production of methane gas and fertilizer. Imperfect vegetables grown on the Heppell farm are sold as so-called ugly produce at lower prices in Loblaws and through Discovery Organics. Vegetables that are even uglier—and thus not saleable—are sold to Enterra Feed Corporation, which uses them in the production of fish or chicken feed.[101] It is this kind of "nose-to-tail eating of the whole farm" that critics of the local food and farm-to-table movements laud.[102] But these details of the business's operation are very difficult to capture in a pithy advertising slogan. "Farmer owned" is, then, not so much a description as a promotional proxy for a variety of sustainable food-production practices.

———— • ————

When products are largely indistinguishable from each other (at base, all chips are simply deep-fried potato slices), marketing can be a significant way to differentiate one's brand from the others available. Food scientist Rickey Yada observes, "It's interesting how marketing works. A potato chip which may just be 'the standard whatever' here, in Hawaii is called 'aloha chips.' But it's no different than the chips that we make here."[103] Martial Boulet, former plant manager for Old Dutch Foods in Calgary, Alberta, made a similar comment. He recalled the variety of potato chips that existed in Canada in the 1960s and 1970s. Red Wagon, for example, was a brand of plain and ripple chips produced briefly by Old Dutch in the early 1960s. Though the packaging was the only difference, many customers were convinced that Red Wagon and Old Dutch chips did not taste the same.[104] In light of their products' similarities to those of the major manufacturers, then, niche producers of potato chips emphasize their company's history and craft ethic. An article in *Bakery and Snacks* by Kacey Culliney states that these "small, boutique snack manufacturers are communicating best and succeeding the most in the healthy snacks category,"[105] since their products "appear safer, healthier and more authentic." According to the article, such niche producers "have a deeply personal story to tell about why they got into the snacks business. These entrepreneurs are passionate about their products and are able to leverage their enthusiasm with consumers."[106]

This passion and deeply personal connection can have its downside. This was evident when production workers at Covered Bridge joined the UFCW. Company president Ryan Albright's identification of the company with himself resulted in his issuing several intemperate statements against unionization. The subsequent boycott and five-month-long strike ended with a first collective agreement with the UFCW, after two years of failed negotiations. In the case of Hardbite, passion could be more powerful than authenticity. Accuracy is not as important as telling a good story, as Roland Barthes has explained: "Men do not have with myth a relationship based on truth but on use."[107] What matters is not whether Hardbite is owned and operated by farmers; it suffices that the corporate image of farm ownership serves to distinguish the company from its competitors, serving as a stand-in for the details of their "nose-to-tail" food-production philosophy.

Small producers like Covered Bridge and Hardbite may never expand to become national (much less international) brands. Nick Leggin, founder of *Potato Chip World,* observes that the chip industry is a difficult business in which to succeed:

> At some point we will lose these older brands—due to the economics or the business model. There are a lot of difficult practicalities to be overcome when considering potato chips. Potatoes are heavy and then you lose all that water volume when you cook them. You gotta store them, make sure they don't spoil, fry them right, and bag them carefully. And you gotta then distribute those. I think that it's really hard to build some

> sort of national brand because there are just so many factors working against you—just the sheer volume of product and the manufacturing and distribution. That's probably why there are so many regional brands and so few national brands. The barriers to entry are so high to be able to do something on that scale.[108]

Marketing, however, may be the biggest challenge for small producers in an environment where multinationals have almost endless funds for national advertising campaigns and for purchasing premium space on grocery store shelves. The use of corporate mythology (emphasizing family, including the family farm) and culinary tourism are novel, though at times problematic, ways for these small producers to differentiate themselves in this competitive business.

4

CHEEZIES

a No-Growth Model

"Big is not always better."

——— KENT HAWKINS, AIR CANADA ENROUTE, 2013 ———

The company W.T. Hawkins is, in many ways, the opposite of Old Dutch, Hardbite, and Covered Bridge potato chip companies. Hawkins is an American company that became Canadian. They make only one product, in only one flavour. They discourage plant tours. They do not advertise and are not on social media. Their corporate history was determined as much by family dynamics as by rational business decisions. And they seemingly have no ambition to expand either their product line or their market share.

The example of Hawkins challenges assumptions about capitalist imperatives like growth and competition, uncovers the significance of family circumstances in shaping the history of a firm, and reveals the role of myth in corporate identity. Still using their original manufacturing equipment, with only minor changes to the packaging equipment over the last half century, the company has not invested in improving productivity. The marital troubles of founder Willard Trice (W.T.) Hawkins seriously affected the scope and direction of the business. Through it all, the company's owners and managers crafted a story of the business that cast historical challenges and limitations instead as strengths and rational choices.

Confections Incorporated

Originally founded in 1948 as a branch plant of a large American snack food company in Chicago with a diverse range of products, Hawkins became an independent Canadian-owned and -operated firm producing a single product.[1] The Chicago parent company was Confections Incorporated, founded by W.T. Hawkins. Few records remain of this company—one whose scope (or hubris?) was so great that their business name ("Confections") and the name of a product line ("Snacks") seemingly did not need further description or embellishment. And yet, this business disappeared by 1960, a casualty of the divorces of the owner.

It is unknown when W.T. Hawkins founded Confections Incorporated of Chicago, but, by the early 1940s, it was one of North America's largest snack food companies.[2] Chicago was a hotbed of snack production at the time: in the 1940s, one-third of America's candy was produced by the 172 confectioners in that city.[3] The business operated at 160 North Loomis Street, sharing space with Champion Bag Company (also owned by W.T.), until 1960.[4] Willard was elected president of the National Popcorn Association in 1946, an acknowledgement of his standing in the industry.[5] Kent Hawkins, W.T.'s grandson, claims that Herman Lay (later to become Frito-Lay) and Gordon Food Services asked to merge their businesses with Confections Incorporated, but W.T. declined because his business was larger than both of theirs at the time.[6]

Willard Hawkins emphasized loyalty to customers and suppliers, particularly after his experiences running his business during the Second World War, with its attendant supply problems. "During the war the selfishness of some manufacturers, the grasping tendencies of some distributors, and the utter unconcern of some retailers toward the consumers emphasized to a far greater degree than ever before, the genuine value of square dealing," he noted in a 1946 newsletter.[7] He described the loyalty of one of the company's distributors, who stuck with Hawkins despite their inability to meet demand during the war: "[Confections Inc.] might have converted their sugar allotments and butter allotments and their packaging allotments to the making of other items which would produce more volume and far greater profits had they chosen to follow the lead of several other short-sighted manufacturers.

Figure 20. Confections Inc., the parent company to W. T. Hawkins, c. 1948–60.

Figure 21. Confections Inc., Chicago, c. 1948–60.

Or they might have sold their entire output to a few big organizations."[8] Because he refused to take advantage of a war situation, Hawkins claimed, the company had retained the loyalty of their business associates and customers. "I appreciate more than I can tell you, the decency and the fineness which was displayed by this Distributor and which has been displayed by all our customers during the past four years."[9]

Confections Incorporated had a detailed training system for their salespeople, known as "route men." The "Division Manager's Manual" observes that "it is very easy for some route men to get into the habit of doing what he pleases. That is, unless our Division Managers train and school these men properly and insist at all times that they do what they are instructed to do."[10] Division managers were expected to train route men in a systematic manner, working beside them until they learned the correct method. According to the manual, route men were encouraged to choose one product each week as a "stampede item" in order to enter a target "store with a 'selling' attitude rather than a 'peddling' impression."[11] Mass displays and weekend sampling were encouraged. A typical route involved 300 to 350 stores, each to be visited weekly, and each averaging five dollars per week in purchases from the company.[12] A memo to distributors from Armand Turpin, general manager, indicated that, in addition to stores, route men were encouraged to tackle "baseball stadiums, park concessions, resorts, beaches, dancing halls and roadstands."[13] Route men were required to complete "route cards" for every customer and file daily reports with the company.[14] New hires, ideally, were to be younger men who could be more readily trained in the company's methods. The "Division Manager's Manual" cautioned that division managers were discouraged from hiring salespeople with previous experience in the bread, pie, or dairy industries, since those businesses "have little merchandising to them and such men get into a habit of just 'peddling.'"[15] New hires were to come, preferably, from major businesses like Colgate, Palmolive-Peet, Lever Brothers, Heinz, and Kraft. Failing that, it was better "to take a complete green horn that has not been subjected to peddling connections. Such a man can be trained to our way of doing things . . . will believe and do what we tell him."[16]

Figure 22. Sales manual for Confections, Inc., c. 1950s.

LET'S FACE FACTS

IT'S easy enough to talk about selling Snacks by the ton. It's another thing to *do* it! It's simple for a fellow to say to himself, "I'm going out and knock 'em dead" . . . but the accomplishment of that resolution calls for *more* than just old-fashioned determination.

Sure, it takes good salesmanship to do the job—but it also takes a thorough understanding of *the way* to make Snacks sell in big volume *in your customers' stores!*

This little 3-minute booklet was prepared to give you the *"know how,"* based on actual RECORDS OF RESULTS made in stores just like those you contact every day. Actual FACTS stripped down to their essence.

It was also designed to furnish you with a *selling tool* that you can actually use when you're calling on your customers.

Take those 3 minutes to read this booklet. And then take it along with you to *use* on your route.

CONFECTIONS, INC.

Selling Fact No. 1 A Woman Enters Your Customer's Store for ONE REASON Only . . . *TO BUY FOOD!*

Let's not kid ourselves. When Mrs. Housewife goes to the Grocer's she goes there to buy meat, vegetables, flour, sugar, lard, and other staple items for her family's meal.

*She **Doesn't** Stop in Just to Buy SNACKS!*

Figure 23. Excerpt from Confections Inc.'s sales manual, c. 1950s.

In exchange for their labours, including during evenings and weekends, successful route men were rewarded. Prizes offered as sales incentives included "chef rotisseries," Dormeyer hand mixers, Westinghouse blankets and toaster ovens, Oneida cutlery sets, jewelled Bulova watches, Waring blenders, and Polaroid cameras.[17] In the late 1940s, salesmen were asked to compose and submit a "simple two line jingle" for a radio advertisement for Confections Incorporated; the top three submissions would win a Cadillac five-passenger sedan, an eighteen-day trip for two to Bermuda, or a diamond ring worth $1,000.[18] The proliferation of television stations across Canada was seen as a boon for the company, a memo to buyers and supervisors reported, as "people are buying and eating more than ever before 'in-between-meal' snacks such as Cheezies, Caramel coated and buttered popcorn."[19] Hawkins encouraged sales supervisors to do what they could to increase potato chip consumption in Canada.[20]

The downfall of Confections Incorporated began shortly after W.T. Hawkins married his third wife, Berenice, in 1950. Three years later, his wife took him and his children to court. Berenice Hawkins sued her stepson, stepdaughter, and stepson-in-law for alienating the affections of her husband, whom she described in her suit as "popcorn king" Willard Trice Hawkins. She requested $400,000 in damages from his children for encouraging her husband to leave her and to hide his whereabouts. Her lawyer claimed that Hawkins was worth more than a million dollars. The *Chicago Daily Tribune* reported, "Almost immediately after the marriage, according to the suit, the defendants became unfriendly to her and began a conspiracy aimed at destroying the marriage and 'obtaining a property settlement on them.'"[21] The children, Berenice claimed, persuaded W.T. to move her from their family home in River Forest, Illinois, to Oak Hill Farm in Wadsworth. The newspaper article said the son then "sought [unsuccessfully] to evict her from the farm, to which the company held title."[22] She asserted that her son-in-law "was given the title of manager of the farm to aid him in evading military draft."[23] Berenice Hawkins attempted to file suit as well for separate maintenance, but deputy sheriffs were unable to locate her husband.[24]

Two months later, Berenice Hawkins demanded an accounting of her husband's assets. She claimed that her husband had fled to Toronto after spending some time in Mexico, transferring "all his property to a holding company in an effort to defraud her." She demanded one-third of his assets, which included Confections Incorporated and Champion Bag Company of Chicago, Aerosmith Incorporated of Washington, and W.T. Hawkins Limited of Tweed, Ontario.[25] A month after filing this demand, Berenice Hawkins was compelled by court order to vacate the sixty-hectare farm with its fourteen-room home in Wadsworth. The farm was taken over by Confections Incorporated, then headed by W.T.'s son Webb.[26] By June of 1954, Berenice and W.T. were divorced. She received a settlement of $105,000, a tenth of the wealth she had claimed W.T. possessed.[27]

By 1960, Confections Incorporated was no more. In addition to the cost of the divorces, the company had apparently been targeted by the Teamsters Union and the Mafia.[28] An article in *Country Roads* reported, "Change suddenly seemed like a good idea. Luckily, Hawkins had already established a much smaller operation in Canada."[29] Confections Incorporated declared bankruptcy and W.T. focused his attention on the Canadian plant he had established in 1949.[30]

The Canadian Cheezie

The most popular product of the Canadian plant was the Cheezie, a uniquely Canadian snack. Cheezies, described on the company's stationery in 1955 as "Cheese Flavored Honeycomb Corn Puffs," are a cheese-coated snack made from extruded corn. The name "Cheezie" itself is trademarked by W.T. Hawkins Limited. While similar snacks are marketed by other companies, Cheezie fans and the Hawkins company themselves argue that the Cheezie is distinctive and superior. In the words of one blogger, "It's difficult to convey to the uninitiated the vastness of the gap that separates Hawkins Cheezies in their assymetrical [*sic*], lumpy, orange-fingered grandeur, from the inferior sort that melts into grainy sludge in your mouth."[31] It is an opinion that is not uncommon among Cheezie fans. A Canadian family living in Guatemala participates in an annual party that offers tastings of various cheese-flavoured extruded snacks. According to a blog post, "25 varieties of cheesies [*sic*] of all forms are venerated, discussed, tasted, judged. Oh, and eaten. . . . Annually, it is Hawkins that takes pride of place among discerning revelers. True, there is the odd party goer who insists on some other brand, like those Hostess puff balls that disintegrate in your mouth like sponge toffee. But dissenters are quickly and drunkenly shouted down by Hawkins loyalists."[32]

One customer suggests microwaving Cheezies for fifteen seconds: "they are delicious!!!"[33] This fondness for warm Cheezies is shared by former Hawkins production manager Geraldine Fobert, who asserts that Cheezie developer Jim Marker preferred them that way, too:

> I can honestly say that, if mom packed lunch, or my sister, you always went to the end of the tumbler [in the production factory] with a plate and you got hot Cheezies. And when you came back,

> you ate the hot Cheezies with your sandwich or your hamburger or your hot dog or whatever you had. And when I was out there [in the plant] just now? I'm eating hot Cheezies. I am a person that eats hot Cheezies. And Mr. Marker said, "You want really good Cheezies, warm, put them on the dash of your car and the sun will heat them."[34]

Cheezies are a "hard bite" snack (unlike the "soft bite" of the better known Cheetos[35] by Frito-Lay) and are made with real Canadian cheddar cheese. They are manufactured at only one small factory, located in Belleville, 190 kilometres east of Toronto, on the northern shore of Lake Ontario. The original facility, however, was in Tweed, Ontario (a village of a few thousand people northeast of Toronto).

The Canadian offshoot of Confections Incorporated, W.T. Hawkins Incorporated, was incorporated by Jim Marker and Webb Hawkins (the son of W.T.) on 27 June 1949.[36] In 1947, W.T. learned of an Ohio farmer, Jim Marker, who had designed and built an extruder that allowed him to process and store cornmeal more efficiently for his cattle in winter.[37] It was not the first such extruder. According to Octavian Burtea's chapter in the book *Snack Foods Processing*, the first was developed in the late 1920s by Clair B. Matthews to process animal feed "to increase its digestibility and reduce intestinal injuries."[38] Extruded corn (known in the trade as fried collets) was first marketed as a snack known as Korn Kurls, invented by Edward Wilson.[39] The first successful commercialization of such snacks was in 1946, three years before Marker's invention, by the Adams Corporation, who went on to lease their extruders to other snack manufacturers.[40]

Willard sent his son Webb to meet Marker, and they developed the idea of frying the extruded cornmeal, coating it with cheese, and marketing it as a snack. The *Country Roads* article reported it as "Good-bye cow mush; hello human snack food."[41] The two men became partners and opened a plant in Tweed, Ontario, in 1949 to manufacture Cheezies and a few other snack food products.[42] Tweed was a convenient location, as it was on the rail lines between Toronto and Montreal.[43] By 1960, the Chicago parent company had folded, the victim of the four marriages and divorces of its founder, W.T. Hawkins. With the death of W.T. in 1961, only the Canadian plant remained, under the direction of son Webb Hawkins (as company president),[44] co-founder Jim Marker (as vice-president responsible for production and quality control), Shirley Woodcox (purchasing and human relations), and Webb's wife, H. Lee Hawkins (board chair).[45]

Production

Marker explained that Canada was a practical and economical choice for the location of the Cheezie factory. He said, "For all we know, we might have ended up in Mexico but the main language used at work there is Spanish. Besides, you could instruct or supervise but you couldn't work there because one had to be a Mexican to be employed there. So, we decided against it and began to look closely at Canada."[46]

As has often been the case with manufacturing in North America, this American company was interested in opening a branch plant in Canada because of the lower wages. Marker explained, "We became an employer to many there, just regular folks, you know. The work involved was not high-tech. It did not need highly skilled workers. They worked hard and at the end of the day they earned themselves a wage just like everyone else."[47]

Operating in a building owned by Tweed Steel Works, the Canadian factory had two shifts and 125 workers at its peak, and $1.5 to $2 million in annual sales.[48] From the 1960s through the 1990s, the number of employees ranged from twenty-five to seventy-five—the higher numbers employed during the busy summer seasons.[49] Throughout the company's history, the majority of production workers have been women.

The Cheezie manufacturing process has remained virtually unchanged since its invention in 1948.[50] Plant supervisor Shirley Woodcox claimed, "Although there have been manufacturing improvements, the original tasty formula has not been changed, and, because of the unique extrusion process, every Cheezie is different, like snowflakes—and people."[51] Variables affecting the quality of the product include the corn grade and starch content (which are affected by the corn hybrid and growing conditions). A specific type of cornmeal supplied by Cargill is extruded under pressure and heat, transforming the cornmeal into a gel.[52] The gel is then pushed through dies that expand it to form the varied Cheezie shapes. The extrusion machines used in the factory today are those originally designed by Jim Marker, which produce non-uniform sizes and shapes. The raw Cheezies are fried in oil before being seasoned in a tumbler, where the seasoning is sprayed onto the cooked Cheezies as a "cheese slurry"—that is, a preservative-free mixture of oil, cheese, and salt. As Marker once explained, "I can smell and taste chemicals a mile away, and I don't want anything to do with them."[53] The finished product is collected from the tumbler in large barrels. Once cooled, the Cheezies are packaged for sale—originally by hand and with weigh scales, but now with packing machinery.[54]

What shipping manager Richard Bly appreciates about Hawkins is that they are "doing things exactly the same as when I started . . . the only thing that changes here is the date on the calendar."[55] What has changed is the snack food industry. When Bly began with the company, Hawkins shipped to 2,500 to 3,000 customers (including many independent grocers); now, with the consolidation of grocery stores and distribution centres, they ship to less than 30 customers. Salesmen used to flog the product at individual stores; now grocers' head offices make all purchasing decisions.[56]

All production of Cheezies occurs between Monday and Friday; the plant is closed for the weekend. Director of Finance Tony McGarvey said, "We don't work on weekends. That's sort of a family philosophy thing."[57] In addition, the plant closes early on Friday afternoons. The evening production shift begins at 7:00 p.m., and Cheezies are made until 5:00 a.m. The packing shift and a day production shift begin at 5:00 a.m. Everyone, including cleaning crew, leaves by 5:00 p.m. An additional packing shift works from 3:00 p.m. to 1:00 a.m.[58] The workforce has expanded steadily over the years, from twenty-five employees in 1981 to seventy employees in 2013 (up to 100 in the busy summer months).[59]

The overwhelming majority of production workers at the company have been women, most of them working as packers. There are two explanations for this gender distribution. First, cornmeal is delivered to the plant in twenty-two-kilogram sacks and dumped by hand into the extruders; in earlier years, these sacks weighed forty-five kilograms. The plant is small, and its configuration does not allow the use of either a forklift or vacuum-assisted lifting devices for this task. In addition, working on the packing lines used to be, in the words of Les Sykes, director of operations at Hawkins, "probably considered a more menial job."[60] Therefore, men have tended to apply for work on the process lines and women applied for work on the packing lines. As well, more people are needed to run the packing equipment than to operate the extruders, fryers, and tumblers.[61]

At first glance, this gendered division of labour may seem commonsensical, rooted at least partly in physical difference. Anthropologist Jack Goody has stated, "In human societies generally cooking is seen as part of women's role."[62] In all societies, men's contribution to cooking, he observes, has been largely limited to hunting, butchering, roasting, and cooking outside the house (e.g., barbecuing or factory processing). The "cooking" aspect of Cheezie production, then, conforms to this broad description. And yet, gendered labour is socially and historically contingent. Joy Parr's comparative analysis of the labour force in two Ontario towns, for example, reveals that gendered divisions of labour are not as eternal as Goody suggests. Knitting mill jobs emerged as male occupations in the English midlands, but female ones in Paris, Ontario.[63] In Belleville, lower paid and seasonal packaging jobs at Hawkins were more likely to be held by women. In this town of 50,000 people, according to the city's website, "there is always a large available labour pool"—a fact "not reflected in the published statistics"—due to "the inordinately high level of seasonal or part-time employment."[64] The area "has lower pay rates and lower benefit plan expectations," ostensibly because "housing is more affordable than in major cities."[65] The ideological bias in favour of the male breadwinner model contributes to full-time, permanent, well-paid jobs—factory production rather than packaging—as the domain of men rather than women.

A few women, however, have held key supervisory roles throughout Hawkins's history. Director of Operations Les Sykes said Shirley Woodcox

Figure 24. As it was neither chocolate nor candy, Confections Inc.'s caramel corn was advertised as appropriate for those observing the Lenten fast, c. 1950s.

"was a pioneer in her day. She was our plant supervisor. Shirley did a lot of work in the community—charity work in the community—but she was also a very strong supporter of business women."[66] Woodcox was a charter member and former president of Belleville Business and Professional Women's Club.[67] Barbara Bosiak was responsible for inventory and purchasing at Hawkins for thirty-nine years. When new products were being developed, it was her job to get prototypes made, to size everything, and to assist in putting together the product's look. Bosiak said she was responsible for ensuring that supplies for production were always available: "no oil, no business, no job."[68] She also corresponded with customers, and found that task both interesting and puzzling. Some customers would complain that their Cheezies were too hard: "Well, Cheezies *are* hard."[69] Others would "just write in to say 'Thank you. I love them.' . . . That part was very fun."[70] Some would write asking where they could purchase the product, and her task would be to track down suppliers or wholesalers and write them back. Women like Woodcox and Bosiak were highly visible exceptions at the plant.

Product Variety

While Cheezies are now the company's only product—and have been for more than fifty years—the company used to make other snack foods. These included potato chips, "midget donuts," popping corn, popcorn balls, caramel popcorn, and packaged nuts.[71] Hawkins Gold Star potato chips were sold from coast to coast, and Hawkins was the first to offer barbecue-flavoured chips in Canada.[72] Hawkins designed their own chip-frying equipment, noting that other companies' equipment resulted in chips that were "overcooked, some undercooked, some blistered" and "very uneven in character."[73] Other companies, W.T. claimed, dumped raw chips in cooking oil and used direct heat, with the consequence that chips stuck together to create blisters, clogged the stirrers, and cooked unevenly. Hawkins's machines moved cooking oil at 550 litres per minute to keep all chips separated and heated the oil six metres away from the chips themselves. The results were chips that cooked evenly and oil that did not become rancid from direct heat.

Figure 25. Hawkins potato chip can, n.d.

Figure 26. Hawkins "Small Frys" midget donuts, n.d.

Figure 27. NHL hockey star Bobby Hull and Shirley Woodcox, with a giant Hawkins potato chip bag, c. 1950s. This photo was never used for promotions due to Hull's licensing agreements. It was produced solely because Woodcox was a hockey fan.

Other companies packaged their chips in glassine or foil bags that were not airtight; Hawkins used double-walled cellophane bags, which not only kept out air but also allowed consumers to see the chips before purchasing them.[74]

Hawkins's caramel corn took two years for the company to develop. "Even 'Du Pont' said we could never manufacture and package such a product for a shelf life of 30 to 45 days," W.T. declared, but the company succeeded. The superiority of their product over that of competitors was explained to Hawkins salesmen: Western Biscuit Limited in Canada had tried to make a similar product in 1948, but, according to a Hawkins company memo, it "stuck together, stuck to one's teeth, didn't have the proper flavour . . . and in time the line became such a failure, they discontinued the department, sold out what equipment they had (which was the wrong kind) and quit with a heavy loss." Cracker Jack, W.T. claimed, had tried unsuccessfully to copy Hawkins's product. The key differences were that Hawkins used only a particular sugar, an exact mix "to the fraction of an ounce," cooked the coating to "within 3 degrees" of the necessary temperature, used a "special butter" that was added "at just the right point," and sold the product in an airtight bag.[75]

One of the more distinctive products offered by Hawkins was Magic Pop, a dual-chambered package containing popping corn and cooking oil. Magic Pop was offered as a solution to the "challenge" of making popcorn at home. According to a memo from Armand Turpin to sales representatives, "You understand that even a slight variation, as little as 3% in shortening and corn will result in small popped kernels, hard centres, many unpopped grains, etc. Here is a ready mixed package, balanced to the fraction of an ounce. What housewife knows such a balance or even by guessing could do it if she tried. Plus all this, see how simple and easy it is to prepare hot, thrifty popcorn with MAGIC POP."[76] Magic Pop was considered a complement to the "frozen foods, prepared cake mixes," and other products that a postwar world had "made so simple and easy for the housewife to prepare."[77] Magic Pop had been in development for nine months. Turpin's memo explained, "At times we almost gave it up. It seemed impossible. We found, however, through hundreds of test

Figure 28. Hawkins Cheezies and Magic Pop, n.d.

Figure 29. An early advertisement for Cheezies, n.d.

poppings at Tweed, how we could do it. It takes a *very special* shortening . . . just the right balance of everything. It was a long, hard job, but we did it!"[78]

Not only was Magic Pop a boon to the housewife, it was so easy to use that, as another memo from Turpin claimed, "any person, in fact, any child can make two quarts of excellent popcorn with our Magic Pop. There is no trick at all: just SQUEEZE, HEAT and EAT."[79] Studies had shown, Turpin asserted, that only one in ten families popped corn at home in the mid-1950s. Others refrained from doing so perhaps "because they don't know how or don't want to buy a popper or don't want to mess up the kitchen doing it the old fashion[ed] way."[80] Magic Pop could be made in any pot and required no skill: a memo from W.T. told employees to simply "cut the end, pour it in the pan and pop it."[81]

Magic Pop is an example of the convenience foods that became popular in this period. Harvey Levenstein notes that convenience foods emerged in the postwar era of working women (though Alice Kessler-Harris shows that poor women have always had to work outside the home).[82] Food industry leaders in the 1950s received the sexist instruction that "the large proportion of the convenience food market made up by working women made it particularly important to have simple recipes on their packages." Such instructions then would enable wives to prepare meals quickly on their arrival home from work but before their husbands returned for dinner.[83] The notion that a task as simple as popping corn would require detailed instructions for housewives flows from such ideological views. According to Levenstein, convenience foods like cake mixes and pre-measured Magic Pop, it was argued, would give women "the gift of *time*," which they could "reinvest in bridge, canasta, garden club, and other perhaps more soul-satisfying pursuits"[84]—a particularly class-based judgement. Not only time would be saved, the United States Department of Agriculture claimed, but also money.[85]

The wide array of Hawkins products that included Magic Pop was subsequently reduced to just the Cheezie, in part because of the fire on 6 January 1956 that burned the Tweed factory to the ground. The factory was a victim of its proximity to the railway. Jim Marker explained, "The sparks fell on the burlap that was used for insulating up near the eaves. There was this water station [for the trains] nearby and when the trains start up again to go, they generated sparks, which fell on our building."[86] Shirley Woodcox recalled bags of popcorn "breaking open and popping when the kernels hit the hot concrete floor days after the fire."[87] Fortunately, none of the company's seventy-five employees were on site at the time, though other losses totalled $250,000 in 1956 dollars (the equivalent of $2.2 million today).[88] Marker declared at the time, "The fire in Tweed was bad; everything buckled. We lost a lot of tools. These have been replaced and we are now building new equipment."[89] Current company owner Kent Hawkins recalled that the

Figure 30. Workers outside the Hawkins Cheezies factory, Tweed, Ontario, 1956.

fire occurred when he was five: "I told my father (Webb) not to worry, that I was going to help him someday. He was almost in tears."[90]

The company recovered from the fire quickly, relocating to Belleville. According to an article in the *Belleville Intelligencer,* the reeve of the village of Tweed "held a special meeting of council" shortly after the fire "with a view to keeping the plant in Tweed,"[91] but was unsuccessful, as the mayor of the neighbouring city of Belleville took advantage of the situation. The same day the plant burned, Belleville's mayor contacted the company; the following day, she and the chair of Belleville's Industrial Commission met with Webb Hawkins. Webb was given a choice of sites in Belleville, and he chose what was known as the Graham Building at 105 South Pinnacle Street.[92] The building had housed the Belleville Canning Company from 1899 to 1960 (which made cans from tin imported from Wales); during the Great War, the building had been used as a military barracks.[93] Unfortunately, unbeknownst to the company, the property was adjacent to land that had been contaminated by the city's nineteenth-century coal gasification plant.[94] Environmental studies performed by Hawkins in the early twenty-first century revealed that coal tar had seeped down to the bedrock and leaked into Hawkins's property.[95]

The company saw the 1956 fire and subsequent relocation of the factory to Belleville as an opportunity. The Tweed plant, Marker declared, had been "terribly congested. . . . We not only have more space here [in Belleville], but it is better laid out and will make for great efficiency."[96] The company's expectations were high: they hoped to employ 150 people at a $5,000 weekly payroll in their new 1,860-square-metre facility in Belleville (557 square metres larger than their Tweed plant had been).[97] Fifteen days after the fire, they signed a lease on the building and began moving seven train carloads of machinery.[98] Workers from Tweed commuted to the new plant, less than forty kilometres away. Management intended to produce Cheezies within seven days at their new facility (a feat they were able to accomplish), and planned to produce Magic Pop and Gold Star potato chips "as machinery became available,"[99] according to the *Belleville Intelligencer.* An article in *What's*

Happening Magazine explained, "If they had been out of production for an extended period, they may have lost their place on store shelves."[100]

The Myths of Cheezies

As in all businesses, corporate myths have developed over time at Hawkins. These myths serve both to create a particular workplace culture and to market the product. Management scholar Georges Lewi explains that such myths are "(often unusual) *stories* that people tell and consider to be true. They explain the situation of an individual within a group, of a business in its economic context, and the reason why things are as they are. Myths enable us to shape the future since they provide an *overall explanation,* give meaning to what exists and (re)define identities, the raison d'être for each individual in a group."[101] The corporate mythology of Hawkins Cheezies contains a few key stories: Cheezies as sole product, the absence of advertising, Hawkins as a family company, and Hawkins as part of Canadian identity.

Such mythology may be seen as a type of "fakelore"—a term created by folklorist Richard Dorson to deride the sanitization and commercial exploitation of folklore by those he dismissively called "money-writers."[102] Sociologist William Fox argues that fakelore exists to "serve societal-wide economic and political interests of dominant social groups."[103] Fakelore thus "reflect[s] . . . and reinforc[es] salient values of the dominant culture" and "contributes to social coordination and ideological and cultural hegemony."[104] Andrew F. Smith has studied fakelore in the domain of food studies. He argues that food fakelore emerges only under a set of specific conditions: the story must "ring true" and be impossible to disprove; it must "explain a real problem"; it must be simple; it must give a group "visibility"; and it must be "attractive."[105]

At Hawkins, mythology recasts the reason why Cheezies have been their only product since the 1980s.[106] The non-business-related decline of the American parent company, Confections Incorporated, limited Hawkins's product range. Cheezies were more popular sellers than other Hawkins products. Potato chip manufacturing was abandoned by the company in the late 1970s, since it was difficult to compete with Hostess and Frito-Lay: very few area farmers raised chipping potatoes, potatoes had to be processed rapidly and Hawkins had limited storage facilities, and potato chips (unlike Cheezies) were fragile and could not be shipped cross-country.[107] Hawkins management, however, explains their specialization in Cheezies as a deliberate choice tied to quality control and tradition. Current president and owner Kent Hawkins notes that the one small factory and single product line mean that "we can make a decision quickly and easily without being constrained by the bureaucracy that characterizes many other companies. . . . It started as a sideline but we've been at it ever since and today, I get to make a living from it. I'm very proud of my family heritage and of all that we've created."[108]

Cheezie inventor Jim Marker asserted, "If you're doing something well, you should continue to do it. Cheezies has been our forte and Cheezies will remain our forte."[109] Even the distinctive variety of shapes of Cheezies is explained not as a consequence of the manufacturing process but as a deliberate marketing decision. Willard Hawkins explained to salesmen in 1955 that Cheezies are "made in odd sized pieces, some larger than others, because we found that the public preferred it that way. Some folks like the smaller pieces and others prefer the larger ones. Plus this, it has a home-made appearance. In other words, it doesn't look like a molded manufactured piece where every piece is exactly the same form and size."[110] Manufacturing only Cheezies, and manufacturing them in non-uniform shapes, are here presented as logical choices as much as they are the result of circumstances.

The company, however, did experiment with different flavours of Cheezies, though these were never marketed.[111] White cheese, peanut butter, pizza, and chicken were tested locally. Nacho-flavoured Cheezies were well received, but it was decided that there was not a large enough market for the product. Instead, the decision was made to market Cheezies in only one flavour but in several sizes of packaging.[112] Shipping manager Richard Bly explained: "They still manufacture the Cheezies the same way. Nothing's different. Everything's exactly the same. . . . Nothing's changed. And that's good. . . . Give the people what they want. . . . We are probably—and this is only my assumption—we are probably one of the only companies I know in the world—and I mean *the world*—who sell the same product in over ten different sizes of bag. . . . You give the public what they want. . . . That's what they want. So we do it."[113]

Confections Incorporated had been aggressive promoters of their products; W.T. Hawkins, by contrast, eschews advertising. This avoidance extends to a refusal to display signage on the Belleville factory. McGarvey explained, "Jim Marker didn't like to encourage visitors."[114] Factory tours are not provided, and descriptions to the press—never mind photos—of Marker's famous extruder are not provided.[115] Advertising, Hawkins management believes, would only encourage further sales. As the company already sells all they can make, more sales would necessitate a plant expansion or longer working hours—neither of which management sees as desirable. Jim Marker explained, "With production, you need to keep an eyeball on it all of the time. That's the only way you can determine if the quality standards are what they should be. If you expand, it becomes really difficult to oversee all of that."[116] Owner Kent Hawkins declared, "My business mantra: Big is not always better. . . . My dad used to say, 'Don't get greedy.'"[117] Hawkins makes occasional promotional exceptions, as when they acquiesced to requests to feature Cheezies on the CBC television show *Corner Gas* and when they allowed Stuart McLean to tour the plant prior to the recording of his *Vinyl Café* CBC radio show in Kingston, Ontario.[118] And, in the early days, when Hawkins was making potato chips, they produced a television ad (featuring a young Kent Hawkins and his siblings) promoting the "Wonder Mouse" toy that was included in the chip bag.[119]

The company's reluctance to advertise—they do not even have a Facebook or Twitter account—is interpreted by some as a laudable consequence of Hawkins's Canadian identity. According to a blog post, "Unlike Jelly Bellies [jelly bean manufacturers] in California who have turned their factory into a carnival of color and celebration, the Hawkins Cheezies factory in Belleville is just a factory. Very Canadian."[120] Other customers express disappointment: "Just last week, Warren and I made a point of driving to their plant. I wanted to check it out and hopefully visit their on-site store. I had visions of picking up a whole carton to share among family and friends.

Who doesn't love Cheezies? . . . To our great disappointment there was no store. Actually the old white building did not even have a sign (what's with that?). . . . I went away quite disappointed. It seemed like low hanging fruit to improve their marketing and consequent sales. Start with a sign. Geesh."[121]

The familial nature of the factory and the product is another aspect of the corporate mythology of Hawkins. Situated in a city of 50,000 people, shop-floor relationships are reminiscent of those in a small town. This familial atmosphere was shaped in part by the hiring of family members of factory workers; it was not unusual for two or three generations of a family to be employed at Hawkins.[122] For example, at least one of Doris and Albert Short's ten children worked at Hawkins every year for fifteen years. Shirley Woodcox, plant manager for fifty-six years, explained, "You always remember the real good ones and the family name registers the next time you're going through a batch of job applications."[123] Oriol Short, the youngest of the Short children, told the local newspaper in 1978, "It's like one big family here."[124]

The friendly atmosphere of the plant was described by Les Sykes as he told the story of his hiring and his promotion to director of operations.[125] Sykes was employed in construction and farm machinery repair when he was hired by Shirley Woodcox to repair her husband's riding lawn mower. She was impressed by the work and offered him a job at Hawkins. "In typical Shirley fashion, you really didn't get a job [description]. . . . She wasn't very explicit about details like that," Sykes said.[126] He started in shipping before moving through all the production jobs and returning to shipping. He "didn't particularly care for that job . . . so I just started doing things around the factory that I saw needed to be done . . . quickly worked myself into the maintenance part. After a few years, I became maintenance supervisor. . . . Eventually you're the person who's done it all and seen it all."[127] The casual family atmosphere at Hawkins could be somewhat off-putting, from his perspective:

> I thought Hawkins was a little backward when I came here. I couldn't believe some of the stuff, the way they did it. The way people acted, the things that they got away with. It was—to me, in a lot of cases, they behaved very unprofessionally. I know that

> in previous jobs, their behaviour wouldn't have been tolerated. Fired. So it was kind of a shock to see the way things operated. But as you work in that environment, things kind of morph and you get to know the personalities of the people that are here. You learn to adapt to the system and you realize that, as with almost any organization, there are a lot of really good people.[128]

Historically, familial labour relations have been used in a paternalistic way by some businesses to generate corporate loyalty in the face of low wages. At Hawkins, Sykes said, wages for production workers were, for a time, too low: "People would leave to go almost anywhere else because we were just not paying enough."[129] Pay was eventually increased, and, in recent years, Hawkins has not had difficulty competing for workers against the Sears warehouse and the call centres located in Belleville. Director of Operations Les Sykes observed: "W.T. Hawkins I think fulfils maybe a niche in the city of Belleville, in that we hire people who maybe could not be employed anywhere else. . . . We do not require grade twelve education to work on the floor, so that there are a lot of our employees who are absolutely intelligent but, for one reason or another, have simply not finished high school. That doesn't preclude them from working at W.T. Hawkins."[130]

Hawkins also hires employees who have intellectual disabilities or limited literacy. Human resources manager Cathy McAllister observed, "I've never seen a company that works so hard in order to make these individuals feel like they are very important contributors to society."[131] Owner Kent Hawkins explained: "They're all part of my family here. If they're working hard for me, I'm going to try and do what I can for them; it goes both ways. . . . [I've got] sixty to seventy families relying on me, and I'm relying on them. If we work together, it's all good. That's how I look at it. They are like part of my family out there. They don't realize it, but I think of them a lot, that way. And I know the work they put in, and I know they work hard."[132]

In addition to what Finance Director Tony Garvey called "all the Cheezies you can eat,"[133] Hawkins offers some employee benefits. Cathy McAllister operates Manpower, a private franchise of a multinational company that has worked with Hawkins since 1967. Manpower was hired by Hawkins to handle human resources at the company, as Hawkins was "in the business to produce Cheezies, and not to do the administration that came with their people," McAllister said.[134] Employees hired through Manpower (those in packaging at Hawkins) have had an optional extended health and dental plan since 1994; Hawkins employees in supervisory roles or in shipping have a defined benefit pension plan. The two businesses have a long history together: McAllister's father was a graphic artist who had helped design the Hawkins logo and who took the photographs that were printed on the commemorative cans of Cheezies for Hawkins's anniversary.[135]

Production line manager Geraldine Fobert worked at the company for more than half a century, and her twin sister, Joyce Brady, worked for many years as supervisor of the "Dirt Patrol" (the nickname for the cleaning crew).[136] They began work at the company at age sixteen when they accompanied their mother to her job at Hawkins.[137] Fobert's first job was with the women on the packaging line; she claimed that one co-worker was so good, "she could *sleep* and bag—and never miss a cup!"[138] Fobert stated that past and present employees often stopped her in the street to inform her of their family members' health concerns. She and her sister "went to every wake" because they "cared about the people." Women in the plant, she said, "would tell you stories of their lives while you were doing laundry," washing the rags that the "Dirt Patrol" used to clean the equipment. "That's what makes people united in many ways. You don't forget, because you carry them here all the time," Fobert declared, pointing to her heart. Throughout her interview, Fobert (who has never married and has no children) referred to the workers as her "kids."[139] Her retirement celebration was attended by the company president and the mayor of Belleville.[140]

McGarvey explained that the familial atmosphere at the plant derived in part from the fact that, like Fobert, Jim Marker was unmarried and neither he nor Shirley Woodcox had children, "so they made the workers their family."[141] McGarvey himself was hired at Hawkins when he was a student in 1981; later employed as an accountant at KPMG in Toronto, he returned to Hawkins because he missed its familial atmosphere and Belleville's small-town life.[142]

Marker's birthday and Hawkins's incorporation date were the same, and so his birthday and the company's anniversary were celebrated simultaneously. For many decades, a huge barbecue and party have been held on 27 June, shortly before the long weekend to celebrate Canada Day on July 1.[143] The company's thirty-fifth anniversary was celebrated with a dinner and dance, with mementos for all and service awards for long-time employees. Truck driver John Freeman was honoured for eighteen years of service; Bob Speck, similarly honoured, had been an employee since the original plant in Tweed.[144] The forty-fourth anniversary included a roast beef dinner hosted at the plant. Employees honoured were the twins Gerry Fobert and Joyce Brady (thirty-five years of service), office manager Joe Calberry (twenty-five years), and shipping supervisor Rick Bly (eighteen years).[145] Shirley Woodcox worked at Hawkins for fifty-six years before retiring.

Marker's death in 2012 was mourned well beyond Belleville, where the Hawkins plant was closed for a day in his honour.[146] Kent Hawkins described him to the *Globe and Mail* as "kind of a rough, tough creampuff. He could be hard, but deep down, he really cared about the people who worked for him."[147] Though Kent Hawkins was company president, Marker "was the decision-maker here in Belleville."[148] Tony McGarvey recalled, "Jim was a very intense guy. As a student, you were almost afraid of him in the beginning. But once he saw you were hard-working, he would be patient and teach you. That first impression was just respect."[149] Marker remained involved with the company until shortly before his death, having "Cheezies sent out to his house every week so he could test them," according to an article in the *Belleville Intelligencer*.[150] He also returned his ownership stake in the company to the Hawkins family. As McGarvey said, "That's just the kind of relationship this family was. It was more than just making money."[151] This investment in workers meant that there were never layoffs at the company during what used to be the slow season of January through March. McGarvey noted, "We've got a lot of long-term employees—we're talking thirty or forty years—and these are the people who knew him. Our plant supervisor just retired after fifty-three years and if it was someone you didn't want to work for you certainly wouldn't have stuck around for fifty-three years."[152]

Richard Bly, shipping manager, has been employed at Hawkins for more than forty years.[153] His first job was as a summer student at Hawkins, unloading bags of cornmeal from railway boxcars by hand. He has done virtually every job at the factory—shipping, maintenance, fryer, and assistant supervisor—and he met his wife at the plant. He believes and regrets that federal privacy legislation, which restricts access to information about employees' joys and griefs, has made socializing on the job more difficult: "There are so many rules and regulations now, that do not permit the family atmosphere to take place. . . . We have all become human machines . . . and that's sad."[154] Family businesses like Hawkins are a dying breed, he believes.

The familial nature of the Hawkins product is evidenced by the way consumers have embraced it as part of their social rituals. A bulletin board in one of the Hawkins factory offices is pinned with photos mailed to the company by Canadian consumers. One group of photos is of unusually shaped or surprisingly large individual Cheezies. Another group is of men in recliners, holding bags of Cheezies, celebrating their recent retirement. Curiously, this last group is not of Hawkins employees. Rather, these are Canadians who equate the end of their working days with the relaxation implied by La-Z-Boy chairs and their favourite snack food.

Hawkins Cheezies are depicted by the company, and are perceived by consumers, as distinctly Canadian. The American origins of the now-defunct parent company are neither promoted nor hidden by Hawkins, and neither are they unusual in a country like Canada whose manufacturing firms often have been branch plants of U.S. firms.[155] In an advertisement, the company has described Cheezies as "a staple of the Canadian diet,"[156] and invokes nationalism with its packaging: "Little red maple leaves adorn each packet, right above the words 'A Canadian Company.'"[157] The *Canadian Oxford Dictionary* even has a listing for the product: "Cheezies *plural noun, Cdn proprietary* a snack food consisting of finger-sized pieces of extruded cornmeal coated with powdered cheese."[158] The cheese used is Canadian, but the corn comes from the American Midwest, as Canadian corn is unavailable in the quantities needed.[159] Local newspapers, noting its production and some of its ingredients, declared Cheezies were "the all-Canadian snack food."[160] Ontario provincial parliament member Todd Smith observed, "Jim Marker used to call the cheezie the greatest snack food on earth, and many kids all over Canada have pulled the familiar red, white, and blue bag of Hawkins out of their treat bag every year at Halloween."[161] Many consumers cite the independent Canadian identity of the product as part of its appeal:

> I love that they taste better than any other cheese snack, they have no preservatives, they are gluten free, and it helps they are Canadian![162]
>
> All of those puffed, American-style inflated tube cheezies are not even in the same universe as Hawkins.[163]
>
> Its [*sic*] a Canadian thing![164]
>
> Hawkins are one of the last truly Canadian junk foods out there for us to enjoy—along with ketchup chips![165]
>
> Best memory of eating Cheezies . . . Saturday nights watching Hockey Night in Canada with my dad and having hot dogs and Cheezies for dinner.[166]
>
> These cheezies destroy Cheetos ☺ Canadian Pride![167]

Canadian pride in Hawkins Cheezies versus Frito-Lay Cheetos is not limited to production and taste, however. Combustion properties are also valued by some consumers. Becky Bravi, in an article in the *Science Creative Quarterly*, reported: "I held a match to the Cheezie and sure enough it ignited and began to burn and then it began to burn brighter and bigger until a flame twice the size of the Cheezie itself was achieved . . . [O]ur crunchy, all Canadian, real cheese contender [Hawkins] burned brighter and bigger and longer than the American competitor, the Cheetos Puff."[168]

Whether consumed as snack food or as fire starter, the Canadian-ness of Hawkins Cheezies is seemingly one of its key features.

—— • ——

Hawkins Cheezies are, at least in some ways, then, the antithesis of the stereotypical "junk food" condemned by today's popular media. This stereotype portrays snack food manufacturers as global multinationals with little interest in local or charitable matters except insofar as they promote business, and as corporate masterminds making business decisions that favour the financial bottom line over people, and who make products that are continually tweaked by research and development staff to maximize consumer interest if not actual "addiction." While Hawkins is subject to the same rules of capitalist competition as others in their industry, their history suggests that there have been other forces at play as well, including historical accident, family relationships, and a sense of humility.

From their origins as Chicago-based Confections Incorporated—a company so large that Lay's once asked to be bought out by them[169]—W.T. Hawkins has shrunk to a tiny factory in a small Ontario town. They are content with their small size and single product, using the power of myth to turn circumstance into design. They are not alone in their rejection of capitalist growth imperatives: Durkee-Mower, manufacturers of marshmallow "fluff," takes a similar approach to business. Using equipment that dates back a half century, largely rejecting computer automation, limiting their product lines, avoiding advertising, and (like Hawkins) refusing to remodel their 1950s-era wood-panelled offices, Durkee-Mower is evidence that Hawkins is not unique, though unusual.[170] Despite their distant American origins, for many Canadian snack food consumers, Hawkins Cheezies are "a Canadian thing!"[171] For these people, eating these oddly shaped, cheese-covered, deep-fried bits of extruded cornmeal remains an affordable and enjoyable "socio-historical experience."[172]

5

THE "ROMANCE" OF CHOCOLATE

Paulins, Moirs, and Ganong

"The making of candy has now become a science rather than an art; the romance has gone out of it."

— R. WHIDDEN GANONG, SAINT CROIX COURIER, MARCH 1973 —

Paulins, Moirs, and Ganong are three of the oldest chocolate manufacturers in Canada, all dating back to the nineteenth century. Of the three, only the last is still in business. Paulins, maker of the popular Cuban Lunch, was the first confectionery manufacturer in western Canada. Moirs created one of the best-known boxes of Canadian chocolates: Pot of Gold. Ganong was the first chocolatier to ship across Canada and invented the tradition of giving heart-shaped boxes of chocolates on Valentine's Day.

These three companies' stories offer some important insights into change over time in the confectionery industry. Paulins's story reveals the general public's lack of knowledge regarding the production of some of their favourite snack foods. Their story also suggests that management can make an important difference in the quality of the daily work life of employees, but that managers are no match for owners who are more committed to profit than to their workers. Moirs's story uncovers the central role played by women workers in the confectionery industry, the paternalist work environment in which they found themselves, and the negative consequences for them when investors make poor business decisions. Ganong is a survivor—and (atypically) is now headed by a female chief executive officer. Ganong's endurance demonstrates that paternalist practices may evolve rather than disappear over time, as employee boarding houses whose matrons regulated workers' behaviour were replaced with a mutual identification of town and business.

Class and gender are key components of the history of chocolate. Sidney Mintz has revealed the importance of chocolate in the provision of fast and cheap calories for early industrial workers.[1] Examining the sensory history of chocolates like the Cuban Lunch, however, reveals that people reminisce about these snacks not out of ignorance or addiction—and not only because of their physiological taste—but because of the nostalgic collective taste that unbounded community groups like Facebook's "Bring Back the Cuban Lunch" embody. The labour process hidden in the product is touched on by these group members when they discuss recipes. But neither food activists like Michael Pollan, Mark Bittman, and Michael Moss, nor snack enthusiasts like these Facebook group members, give voice to the significant—and gendered—labour issues involved in the production of these snacks. Workers at chocolate factories had physically taxing jobs. The loss of those jobs due to the consolidation of the snack food industry was a serious blow. Demands to end junk food consumption, on the one hand, or to revive nostalgic brands, on the other, ignore these important issues. "Taste is a social fact," the editors of a special issue of *Food and Foodways* on sensory history remind us, "and sensory experiences instil and reinforce social and cultural values."[2] At work is more than just Pierre Bourdieu's emphasis on social distinction and cultural capital.[3] Bourdieu says the "work of memory, the notion of quality, individualized obsession, political economy, the politics of recognition, and even indigestion"[4] all play a role. Unfortunately, but perhaps not surprisingly, what is still too often ignored is the role of the worker—particularly when that worker is a woman.

Paulins

Until their closure in 1991, Paulins was one of the oldest companies—and the first biscuit maker and confectioner—in western Canada.[5] They trace their origins to 1876, when they were founded as the Chambers Steam Biscuit Factory at 158 Main Street in Winnipeg.[6] Four years later, W.H. Paulin opened a competing bakery just down the street at 254 Main Street. The Chambers factory moved to 11 Ross Avenue in 1882, Paulin moved to 47 William Avenue, and by 1884, the two businesses had merged, employing twenty-five workers. In 1899, the merged business was incorporated as the Paulin-Chambers Company (and was referred to in the local area simply as "Paulins"). A four-storey factory was constructed (later expanded to six floors), and manufacturing developed beyond biscuits and into chocolates and confectionery.[7] The factory was expanded in 1909, and in the 1920s, warehouses were added in Fort William, Ontario; Regina and Saskatoon in Saskatchewan; Calgary and Edmonton in Alberta; and Vancouver, British Columbia. By the 1930s, Paulins was making seventy different types of biscuits and 200 kinds of confectionery, employing 200 people.[8]

In 1902, management locked out the (mostly female) employees of Paulins after they expressed interest in joining a union. Worker unrest was blamed at the time on changes in labour legislation mandating shorter working hours, according to the *Manitoba Free Press*, "as the management had decided that the shortened hours would have to be met with a reduction in wages."[9] As a consequence, the women had contacted the Canadian Bakery Workers Union. Management must have been able to reach an agreement with the women, as the factory was never unionized.

A second dalliance with the Canadian Bakery Workers Union occurred in 1945, when union representatives met with Paulins employees (then grown to 380 in number) "to discuss plans regarding union certification by the war labor board," said an article in the *Winnipeg Free Press*—plans that never came to fruition.[10] Again, management responded to the threat from labour: a pension plan was created in December 1946 for all those employed a minimum of two years at Paulins (employees who had served in the military during the war were credited for such service).[11]

The closest the workers came to union certification was in 1967, when Winnipeg Local 389 of the Bakery and Confectionery Workers' International Union of Manitoba appealed to the Manitoba Court of Queen's Bench to overturn a decision by the Manitoba Labour Board not to order a certification vote at the company.[12] Paulins workers remained non-unionized, though an article in the *Winnipeg Free Press* stated they "had a collective agreement and were represented by a bargaining committee"—in essence, a company union.[13] A *Winnipeg Free Press* reporter observed in a different article, "Paulins was always a non-unionized shop. But a plant committee representing the workers, mutual respect and an open-door policy kept everyone happy by all accounts. Wages were above the industrial average, ranging from $10–$14 an hour."[14]

On 1 February 1991, after 115 years of operation, Paulin-Chambers was terminated, putting 290 people out of work.[15] Though Montreal's Culinar Incorporated[16] were responsible for closing the factory after they purchased it from George Weston Limited,[17] the company's end had actually begun when the latter bought Paulin-Chambers in the early 1980s. As an industry expert interviewed for this research observed, "That Paulin-Chambers was a big deal. . . . They owned McCormick's in Ontario (that was a big confectionery manufacturer) and that was all vertically integrated with Loblaw's, Western Grocers, and National Grocers. . . . And you have to talk about the confection industry in conjunction with the retailers."[18]

Vertical integration was achieved when food retailers purchased existing manufacturing firms (such as Paulins) in the 1980s to produce brands for their grocery stores. Weston, for example, purchased manufacturing facilities to produce their President's Choice label products. During the same time period, these national grocery retail chains—like Weston's Superstore and Loblaws—opened new stores and introduced computerized cash registers and scanners. In his book *The Chocolate Ganongs of St. Stephen*, David Folster comments, "The chain stores were only interested in national buying. They wanted to buy a product for all their stores across the country from a single supplier. . . . They wanted to buy out of a central office; they wanted one vendor number to put in their computers for one product; and they wanted the price to be the same coast to coast."[19]

These national retail chains' purchasing model was ultimately responsible for the death of Paulin-Chambers. An anonymous industry expert explained that retailers justified these decisions in light of their major investments in "stores and technology and land acquisitions... because every store that they opened was 60, 70, 80 million dollars . . . big investments. Not for the faint of heart."[20] This capital-intensive investment by retailers led to their decision to end investment in manufacturing and vertical integration. The same industry expert stated, "They started selling off their McCormick's, closed down Paulin-Chambers, because with their newly acquired retail volumes, they could extract *huge* concessions from all the manufacturers."[21] The profit margins in retail were better than in manufacturing, and there was not the same need for continuous investment in technological improvement. Shelf space was sold to the highest bidder, and "that was part of the demise of all these smaller companies. You had to be big, you had to have [national] standards, and you had to supply [retailers] nationally because they went to central buying. . . . [The] retailers control that shelf space and they will come to you and say, 'You'll pay us whatever we want for your product to be on that shelf, or you will not be on our shelves.' They have unlimited power. They're omnipotent."[22] Cost-saving measures, as grocery retailers moved into real estate and away from vertically integrated manufacturing, thus were responsible for the closure of Paulins.

Some were convinced that the death of Paulins was due not to the move to centralized purchasing by retail chains, but to fallout in Quebec from the failure of the Meech Lake Accord.[23] Local newspapers reported that Paulins workers saw "the end of the line for Paulins in Winnipeg as part of some bigger political game, one where Quebec again bests the West. . . . Culinar, which is partly owned by the Quebec government, is viewed as the force behind a carefully orchestrated conspiracy that began when it took over in February 1988."[24] These conspiracy theories were reinforced by the fact that the Winnipeg factory was the most profitable of the plants owned by Culinar. The anonymous industry expert commented, "But, for political reasons because Loblaw's and Weston is headquartered in Toronto, they would, of course, keep the Ontario plant first. And the Montreal plant was bigger, so the Winnipeg plant became the expended one. It's true."[25]

Workers also expressed frustration, according to the industry expert, that Culinar ignored their request to "buy the equipment and take over the building's lease and keep the jobs in Winnipeg."[26] The industry expert sympathized with their disappointment, calling Paulins's owners "really not nice people."[27] He asserted that the Loblaw's and Weston "empire" that owned Paulins was "very closed-minded about any competition." They refused to sell their equipment to competitors when they closed the Winnipeg factory. Instead, whatever wasn't moved to their other manufacturing plants in Ontario and Quebec was sold for scrap metal or else "they smashed it to pieces."[28] Scott-Bathgate's Nutty Club, a Winnipeg confectioner of equally long provenance, made a similarly unsuccessful effort to purchase the company. In addition to making and branding their own candy, Paulins made candy that was packaged and sold by Nutty Club. Jim Burt, Nutty Club's owner, contacted Paulins's director of manufacturing when the factory closed, offering to invest if he and other former employees decided to start another candy business. "But," he said, "it never got off the ground. We tried and tried. We had so many meetings, but couldn't do it."[29]

Though Culinar offered some assistance with job searches and transitions for former Paulins employees, it was inadequate. "In a tightfisted economy that seems to have little room for the unskilled, where do people go after years of making jelly beans, banana cream cookies, graham wafers and scotch mints?" the *Winnipeg Free Press* asked, observing, "Only about 20 former employees at Paulin Culinar have found jobs."[30]

Working on the Cookie Line

Lynda Howdle was a Paulins employee, working on the main floor as a cookie packer.[31] Born and raised in Winnipeg by a stay-at-home mother and a father employed at Modern Dairies, she worked a variety of jobs until 1979 when, as a twenty-seven-year-old mother, she was hired at Paulins. She worked there until the factory closed twelve years later. Prior to the 1970s, Paulins refused to hire married women; single women were attracted to the company's wages and limited benefits. Howdle recalled, "I have never worked in a place where there were so many single older ladies."[32] Her Paulins wage helped her supplement her young family's low income and, when she divorced her husband, allowed her to purchase her house. She said, "It was a great place to work. The [local news]paper said we were like a family, and we were."[33] Indeed, many literal families worked at the plant: Howdle's own mother worked in the office, and her son and daughter were employed at the plant as teenagers during summer months.

Production was organized so that each floor of the factory made different products. Cuban Lunches were produced on the fourth floor of the factory, together with Easter bunnies and other chocolates. Christmas candy was made on the fifth floor (by male workers, as the task was considered skilled work), and jujubes and toasted marshmallows were manufactured on the sixth floor. The third floor was shared by hard candy and by the Ruffles and Puffs chocolate cookie lines, which were produced around the clock. Howdle said, "Puffs and Ruffles never stopped. They ran the full day unless the machine broke."[34] Puffs were a chocolate-covered marshmallow with a jam centre and a cookie base. Ruffles were a chocolate-covered coconut cookie.[35] Howdle described the complicated process of packing them by hand: "They would come down the belt, and you wore gloves, especially with the chocolates. You would grab three and kind of squish them together. First you'd take the box off the belt, and then you would put twelve in. Then you had to turn the box around. We would do two boxes at a time. So you'd have a little ledge, and you'd grab three, put them in, turn the boxes around, put in another piece of corrugated paper, and then do those."[36] The chocolate cookies were not always a consistent size, which made for further challenges. Workers would have to either push the cookies together to pack them into the boxes, or remove some to ensure that the final packaged weight would be correct.

Workers at Paulins were a tight-knit group, who socialized at events organized by the company or by fellow employees. They invited each other to cotillions for their daughters' eighteenth birthdays, for example. The company provided Christmas and Thanksgiving dinners, fishing trips for male employees and restaurant meals for women employees, and gifts of a fresh turkey and a five-pound (2.2-kilogram) box of Paulins cookies at Christmas.

Figure 31. Paulins Puffs packaging, n.d.

"They treated their staff really, really well," Lynda Howdle recalled.[37] The company was not unionized, but had a worker grievance committee, of which she was a member. At her former job as a sewing factory worker, Howdle "used to come [to work] crying," and management metaphorically "chained you to [the machine] and watched every move. . . . You had to eat your lunch at the machine. It was terrible." Not so at Paulins, she reflected nostalgically.

When the plant was slated for closure, Howdle was appointed a member of the Labour Adjustment Committee tasked with assisting Paulins workers with finding other employment. This job was difficult, despite the four to six months' notice that was given workers, as many of the women at the plant could not write in English. Their employment prospects were therefore limited.[38] Some went on to find work at Pic-a-Pop (a local soft drink manufacturer), Grannie's Poultry, and Canada Packers (a meat-packing plant). Howdle herself received further education that helped her transition into new work.

Paulins's director of manufacturing, Tom Yasumatsu, attempted to prevent the closure of the plant.[39] His parents were Japanese Canadians who were interned in Manitoba during the Second World War; they had to give up their twelve-hectare fruit farm and instead harvest sugar beets. He began work at Paulins as a sixteen-year-old office boy in 1954, as it was one of the few companies that would hire Japanese Canadians:

> I used to answer all of the ads in the paper, but the minute I would walk through the door and they saw me, "Oh sorry, the job is filled." I knew why. . . . So, it's been a tough life in that sense. Yeah, I started around sixteen and even then when I was interviewed [at Paulins], he gave me the job as office boy and he did say: "You are the first of your kind that we have ever hired, so you better do a good job." I am glad to say that it took about fourteen years and then he reported to me. I felt pretty good about that.[40]

Yasumatsu was promoted to file clerk and treasurer, working his way through all the departments at Paulins. When he was promoted to manufacturing director, he said that he made a point of treating his employees differently from the way other managers did at the company. Rather than sitting with management during coffee breaks, he would sit with his workers, "and we would laugh and joke. I got to know nearly every employee in that place."[41]

Yasumatsu was responsible for the shift from piecework to hourly wages at Paulins. Though he was in management, he made an effort to assist his workers with negotiating their salaries: "We had piecework when we first took over. I thought, 'This is nonsense.' I said, 'I think you people are getting a pretty decent wage. I am gonna raise that decent wage, so we are not going to be having any squabbles.'"[42] Whether employees themselves actually thought the wage was decent is, of course, another question. Replacing piecework with hourly wages did solve one significant problem at Paulins: competition among workers for placement on the production line. Yasumatsu said that workers "wanted to be at the front of the line because at the front of the line, the product comes through, and they would gather everything up that comes through so that people at the end of the line have nothing left to package."[43] The result of the move to hourly wages, according to Yasumatsu, was "less arguments and fighting about who was supposed to be at the front and who was supposed to be at the back [of the production line]."[44]

In his interview, Yasumatsu identified more strongly with his employees than with upper management. This identification was as much a function of his regional nativism (rooted in western Canadian alienation) as cross-class alliance. Yasumatsu recalled an instance where he met with his Winnipeg plant workers and the head office representatives from Toronto to negotiate wages. He "kept slipping slips of paper under the table" to his employees' chief negotiator, suggesting counters to the head office representatives' offer. After the meeting, when he was questioned about what had happened by the head office representatives, Yaumatsu justified his behaviour to them: "I am in charge of that building. I know what's going on in that building and I know what I can afford. It's as simple as that. Are you telling me that if they don't ask for something that I don't give it to them? That's not the way I work." He then refused to accompany the head office representatives to dinner, telling them: "I'm taking the [employee negotiating] committee out for dinner. And you are not welcome."[45]

Though the Winnipeg plant was the only profitable plant owned by Culinar, it was sacrificed to support the other plants in Ontario, British Columbia, and Quebec. (By contrast, Lynda Howdle had heard rumours that the plant's closing was due to the Quebec "separatists" who had purchased the company, who closed it in retaliation for Manitoba's rejection of the Meech Lake Accord.) When Yasumatsu was informed about the plant closure, he demanded several thousand dollars to take his management team to Las Vegas, saying, "'We are going to go to Vegas and have a ball for three days because we have a lot of pain coming up.' . . . We had a heck of a good time. Then we came back to shut the place down. Such a sad day."[46] Though he had the opportunity to be transferred to another Culinar plant, Yasumatsu decided to leave the company when the Winnipeg plant was closed:

> The thing that was interesting about that time was that you couldn't shut down [Culinar's plants in] Ontario or Vancouver because they were such big areas. They figured it was important to have our face out there, but who gives a shit about Winnipeg. That's why we got shut down. It was pretty sad because I could have went and worked at the other plants. Moved my family and basically take over as the boss but I just couldn't do that. I have 500 employees and I am going to lay everyone off and say "See you guys. I have my job"? I couldn't do it.[47]

Yasumatsu ensured that the head office representatives were not present on the last day of work at the Paulins factory in Winnipeg, so that workers could say goodbye to each other privately. He said, "I got there extra early. Knew all the employees were in the building. I locked the door. [Representatives from the head office] showed up in a cab. They were pounding on the door, pounding on the door, and finally walked away."[48] Yasumatsu left Paulins at age fifty-one and did not find comparable work until five years later, when he was hired as production supervisor at the Melrose Coffee

Company. He commented, "Those were five very lean years."[49] He said he continued to meet with former Paulins employees for a weekly lunch: "A lot of people were still in their sixties and fifties. Those were the people dying ten to fifteen years later, so I went to a lot of funerals. I used to meet with a group of [former] employees at the Garden City Mall where they have lunch. I'd meet them every Wednesday until I was the only one left."[50]

Near the end of his interview, Yasumatsu retrieved and opened the briefcase he had used while he was at Paulins. He had not opened it since his last day on the job in 1991. He then read aloud letters and cards of thanks and sympathy that he received that day from former employees:

> I just wanted to let you know that I was not lying when I told you that I was a good boss.
>
> *[Interviewer] It sounds like you changed things there.*
>
> I sure as hell did.[51]

Steve May and Laura Morrison note that such nostalgic reflections are a demonstration of agency. They are evidence that "family and social ties matter, regardless of whether they occur at work or at home. . . . [T]he distinctions between work and family, public and private, labor and leisure are blurred by social, affiliative networks that transcend these dichotomies."[52] Yasumatsu could not prevent the plant closure, but he could control, to some extent, the way in which that closure happened. His comments reveal what Christopher Wright, in an article for *Labour History*, calls the "contradictory location of managers as both controllers of subordinate employees, as well as being subject to control themselves in terms of their performance and work intensity."[53]

Collective Memory and the Cuban Lunch

With the closure of the company in 1991, Paulins products have not been made for a quarter century.[54] Yet, the memory of their taste remains—and is memorialized in a public Facebook group called "Bring Back the Cuban

Lunch." The Cuban Lunch was a slab of chocolate that contained peanuts, and that was formed and packaged in the shallow, rectangular equivalent of a cupcake liner, complete with fluted edges. The "Bring Back the Cuban Lunch" Facebook group describes their mandate as an effort to revive "the best chocolate/peanut combination ever invented," in much the same way that a consumer campaign led to the return of the discontinued Mexican Chili flavour of Old Dutch potato chips.[55] The group also functions as a social community, as the invited membership extends beyond nostalgic former consumers. One post suggests, "Even if you don't remember them or have never had the pleasure of tasting one . . . just join the group, invite all your friends and see what happens!!!"[56] As of 2016, the group's membership was 380. Members participate in the Facebook group by posting photos, debating the merits of various recipes and alternative products, and sharing their memories of eating Cuban Lunch.

As is evident from the group's name, the group discusses efforts to revive the brand. One member suggested that the group contact confectioners to ask them to include the Cuban Lunch in their product line: "We should all put a consumer request together and send it to any and all candy companies to see if they would undertake producing the Cuban Lunch again."[57] Trademark ownership was identified as a potential setback for such a plan, however. Member Daniel Gilchrist caused some brief excitement within the group when he posted that, after a two- or three-year effort, he had succeeded in tracking down the current owner of the Cuban Lunch trademark.[58] The owner's lawyer, he asserts, responded that he should make a financial offer for it. Some group members have suggested crowd funding to revive the product: one post asks, "Who wants to go in with me and start a company to re-make the Cuban Lunch again? Email me and I will set up a kickstarter[59] plan."[60] Another asks, "Has anyone bought the rights and recipe yet? surely someone wants to become Cuban Lunch King!"[61] These efforts to revive the brand are not the main focus of the group, however, despite the group's name.

More of the group's time is spent debating existing alternatives to the Cuban Lunch. Whittaker's Peanut Slab is often promoted within the group as the closest, currently available, taste substitute for the Cuban Lunch (comments include: "close but not quite as it is a little bit sweeter and not quite the right consistency,"[62] and "too thin and not enough crunch").[63] Members discuss with each other how to arrange shipping of this product from New Zealand, its point of origin. Hershey's Mr. Goodbar is sometimes also suggested as an inadequate alternative. Occasionally, a one-off suggestion is made:

> David Dunster: The closest I can get to a Cuban Lunch is the 'Fruit & Nut' from Cadbury. [This despite the fact that the Cuban Lunch never contained fruit.]
>
> Chris Neufeld: That is the opposite of 'close.'[64]

The taste of these alternative chocolate bars is seen as inferior to that of group members' collective memory of the original Cuban Lunch. Some attribute this taste difference to the conditions of production or to nationalism: according to one post, "Hard to duplicate the original Winnipeg treat by mass producing in [the United States of] America."[65]

Since revival and alternatives are both disappointing, the majority of the discussion within the group is centred on replication. Despite group agreement that the Cuban Lunch consisted exclusively of chocolate and peanuts, a wide variety of potential recipes are proposed and debated, incorporating butterscotch, potato chips, and other additives. This debate is assisted by the fact that the Internet does not contain any images of the original Paulins Cuban Lunch packaging (and thus its ingredient listing). Pronouncements are made on the degree to which these recipes reproduce the group members' memories of the taste of Cuban Lunch. Thus, for example, Duff MacDonald posted a Cuban Lunch recipe sourced from Donna Peck-Harland of "Kirkfield Park United [Church], Winnipeg (She worked on the line making them every day!)."[66] By naming the recipe's author and her church affiliation, by asserting that she was a former Paulins worker who had made Cuban Lunches, and by not providing the original date or place of publication, MacDonald gives this recipe a timeless authority. The recipe is the duplicate of one printed in the *Winnipeg Free Press* in 2002,[67] but includes variations such as adding coconut. Peck-Harland's Cuban Lunch recipe ingredients are peanut butter chips, butterscotch chips, chocolate chips, crushed ripple potato chips, and unsalted peanuts. The recipe calls for the ingredients to be melted and poured into cupcake liners and then refrigerated.[68] Further research reveals that this recipe was submitted originally by Ms Peck-Harland to the Fort Qu'Appelle Prairie Christian Training Centre's *A Cookbook of Memories,* first published in 2001.[69] Nowhere does this cookbook claim that Peck-Harland was a Paulins worker.

"Bring Back the Cuban Lunch" group members who tried the Peck-Harland recipe deemed it inauthentic, despite not knowing its provenance. Some asserted that this recipe was "not the Cuban Lunch I remember," as they didn't "remember any potato products in it." Duff MacDonald, who had posted the recipe to the Facebook page, responded: "[Cuban Lunch didn't contain any potato products] that you know of . . . maybe the one I like did too." In other words, there may have been other ingredients in the Cuban Lunch, ones that were less identifiable to the average eater than chocolate and peanuts but which nonetheless contributed to its distinctive taste. As sociologist Priscilla Parkhurst Ferguson reminds us, "Taste is notoriously untrustworthy."[70]

The taste of a Cuban Lunch, then, is about more than its acknowledged ingredients; there must be some additional component that made the product more than simply chocolate and peanuts. The inclusion of crushed Old Dutch[71] ripple chips in purported Cuban Lunch recipes, for example, is an attempt to reproduce an historical and nostalgic taste that cannot be accessed through the acknowledged simple ingredients (chocolate and Spanish peanuts) of the no-longer-available original product. Some group members hint at the impossibility of reproducing the original taste. One post commented, "I'm not really sure if it was that they were that good or if it's more a childhood memory thing, taking me back to a simpler time. In any event I would love to try one again and find out."[72] Others acknowledge that the point of the recipes is not to replicate the taste but to replicate *memories through* taste:

> Alice Cristofoli: I found a recipe on the internet and made them a couple years ago. They were almost the same as the original Cuban lunch.
>
> Dallas Patterson Jr.: I've tried one of the recipes too, but it's been so long since I've had the original it's hard to say if it's close. Was still very good though.
>
> Patti Garner: If you taste a recipe that brings back the memories of the Cuban Lunch, that's all you need! lol [laugh out loud].[73]

Some suggest that the taste was determined not only by the content but the form of the product: the thickness of the bar and its distinctive crimped edges. One member commented, "Sure, anyone can put peanuts in chocolate, that's child's play. For me, it was more about the shape/presentation."[74] There are those, however, who persist in their quest for the "one true" recipe, despite seemingly knowing the Cuban Lunch's two-ingredient identity. Chris Neufeld commented, "Ok, look . . . is it SERIOUSLY that hard in this interconnected world, to find someone that worked at the damn place, and can give us the basic REAL recipe? I mean really, I'm not asking for the nuclear codes . . . it's chocolate and peanuts for sh*t sake!"[75]

The appearance of a former Paulins employee on the Facebook page led to excited speculation within the group that the debate over the chocolate-and-peanuts confection's composition might finally end. David Ingram worked at the Paulin-Chambers factory in Winnipeg for one summer in 1981, making marshmallows, throwing sugar on spearmint gummy leaves, pulling taffy, and stirring chocolate for the popular Cuban Lunch. He asserted: "There were no peanut butter or butterscotch chips in the chocolate—just that magical sweet chocolate with peanuts!"[76] He recalled that the man who made the chocolate at that time was Doug Riach, and suggested that the group locate and contact him for the recipe: "I really believe that the true secret is in the chocolate recipe. I believe Doug still lives in Winnipeg and is still a fine curler. Find Doug Riach and pump him for information. Good luck!"[77]

David Ingram is seemingly the only group member who speaks of having worked at the former factory. Given the history of the plant (and particularly its closing), it is not surprising that former workers are less nostalgic than former consumers. A blogger identified only as Joan recalled that her first job was on the Cuban Lunch line at Paulins: "This was the job of my dreams coming out of high school. . . . I could just see my parents crying, clapping and yelling, telling all the neighbor's [*sic*] about their daughter who had moved to Winnipeg, got a job, and was now in charge of CUBAN LUNCHES."[78]

Her initial enthusiasm was dampened by the stresses of working in mass production. Grabbing the chocolate confections from the production line, placing each into "a brown paper 'crinkly' cup," sending them to packaging, all while also sorting for broken pieces, was a stressful operation, She said, "If you don't keep up, you are fired." When she was promoted to packaging, the stress did not abate: "The machine would package them, and then you had to box them up, as fast as they were coming down off the machine. It was faster than a speeding bullet, I shit you not." Boxes then were lifted manually onto shipping pallets. Joan recalled, "There was no let up. . . . It was hell. But I [was] determined, all because of those Cuban Lunches." The stress of the work took a physical toll on her after a few months. She strained her neck while working on the packing line: "It was so sore, I could hardly move my head. I applied way to[o] much liniment on my neck and burned it. I had a red mark on it for months. The dream was starting to fade." She quit shortly thereafter: "If this was what work was going to be about, I wanted no part of it."[79] However, for many women workers at Paulins with limited education or for whom English was not their first language, such a choice was simply not possible.

Moirs

Paulins is not the only major Canadian chocolate maker that has disappeared: Moirs was a chocolatier that traced their origins to 1816. Pot of Gold, one of the best-known brands of Canadian chocolates, was the invention of Moirs, which began in 1816 when Benjamin Moir opened a bakery in Halifax, Nova Scotia. Moirs was a source of pride for Maritimers, as it was the only business in Halifax with a national product. By 1862, the company had expanded to occupy a five-storey building, and Moir's son, William C. Moir, took over the company (then named Moirs, Son & Company). The business recovered from a terrible fire in 1867,[80] and grandson James W. Moir established a confectionery branch in 1873. The company shifted their focus from baking to confectionery, historian Ian McKay explains, because Prime Minister John A. Macdonald's National Policy for Canada's economic development "was more favourable to confectionery than flour milling or bread baking."[81] When another fire destroyed the plant in 1903, James Moir incorporated the business as Moirs Limited.[82] He went on to open a paper box factory, a chocolate mill, and a wooden box mill. With his retirement in 1925, the company went public to raise capital for expansion. Ownership transferred from the third generation of the Moir family to a group of Halifax businessmen: James McGregor Stewart QC, Colonel John Crerar MacKeen, and W.B. Proctor.[83]

Fires were a common hazard in the confectionery industry in the nineteenth and early twentieth centuries. Firefighting was a difficult task in conditions where poorly equipped volunteers had to use low-pressure hydrants to deliver water to burning buildings constructed to minimal fire codes.[84] Many chocolate factories produced not only chocolate but also candy—including candy centres for their chocolates. Candy fires were particular problematic, as these fires burned at very high temperatures. And candy factories were particularly prone to fires, as two of their most common ingredients—cornstarch (used in making candy forms) and sugar—are explosion hazards.[85]

Moirs opened their new factory in 1929, which newspapers dubbed "the House of 8000 Window Panes."[86] The new plant was a nine-storey building of 14,490 square metres—a tribute to the huge expansion that the business underwent after James Moir's retirement. A conveyor system saved labour, and a Carrier air-conditioning system kept even the hottest production room at a consistent eighteen degrees Celsius. In addition to the factory, Moirs operated a 1,580-square-metre office, a 3,440-square-metre bakery, a 3,065-square-metre paper box factory, an additional 3,065-square-metre factory, a chocolate refining plant, a warehouse, a box mill, and a hydroelectric power plant.

The company made their own shredded coconut, chocolate coatings, and chocolate shavings, and employed 1,126 workers (not including salesmen).[87]

Much like at Paulins, the Moirs factory's nine floors were each dedicated to a specific form of manufacturing or packaging.[88] The ninth floor was the nut- and fruit-cleaning room. The eighth and seventh floors were for hard candy production. The sixth floor was dedicated to fancy packaging. Enrobing (coating with chocolate by machine) and hand dipping of chocolates occurred on the fifth floor. Standard packaging was carried out on the fourth floor. The bakery and packing were located on the third floor. Offices, a nurse's station, and a maintenance shop occupied the second floor, while the first floor served as a warehouse. Centres for various chocolates were made in the plant itself, as was the chocolate coating for them. The starch room was where cream and jelly centres for chocolates were formed: a Baker Clay Continuous machine dropped liquid cream or jelly into impressions made in trays of starch that acted as moulds (known as moguls).[89] These starch trays were then dried at eighty-two degrees Celsius, and the starch screened for reuse by Allis-Chalmers sieves. Some 545 to 680 kilograms of fondant per hour could be produced in this way.[90] In the hard candy room, candy was boiled in copper kettles before being cooled and cut into shapes. The bonbon room was where fruit centres were coated in chocolate. Workers in the dipping room (exclusively women) dipped chocolate by hand. Here, electric heaters kept pans of chocolate in a liquid state. Women would carefully dip individual pieces of fruit or nuts in chocolate, swirl them dextrously to create a pattern on top, then place them on trays covered in embossed paper that would transfer the words "Moirs xxx" to the bottom of each chocolate. The women were paid a piece rate, but had to redip the confections without pay if the coating was uneven.[91] Cheaper-quality chocolates were coated by machine in the enrober room.[92] Here, according to an article in the *Atlantic Advocate*, chocolate cherries "passed like a parade of pink ookpiks on the way to their chocolate shower."[93]

"Moirs xxx" was the name of the chocolate coating developed by James W. Moir and L.E. Covey. Covey was superintendent of the chocolate-making department, and had joined the company in 1878 at age fifteen. While

Figure 32. Corn starch forms for candy making, 2013.

women were tasked with shelling the cocoa beans needed, Moir and Covey supervised the cooking of the xxx coating.[94] Moir named the coating xxx because, as reported in "Making Chocolates" from the Moirs Clippings archive, "it conveyed to him, from pleasant association one hopes, the hall mark of excellence of a dissimilar product."[95] The xxx formula remained unchanged over the years.[96]

The Pot of Gold chocolate box, Moirs's biggest seller, was developed in 1928. It was the first "mixed assortment box" of chocolates offered for sale by a confectioner.[97] The box design featured a rainbow with an attractive young woman sitting at its end; eleven different models were featured on the Pot of Gold box during its first thirty-five years. An article in the *Halifax Chronicle-Herald* reported, "The designs have varied considerably, with the emphasis in recent years on the conservative. Both the girl and the rainbow were more subdued. . . . But this Christmas [1969] a beautiful girl again is the centre of attraction, and the rainbow is back in all its splendour."[98] The year 1974 was the last in which the box featured a "Pot of Gold girl," but the rainbow continued to be used, and was promoted in a television jingle: "We all know where the rainbow goes. . . . We are told it's a pot of gold."[99] Liberace was featured in advertisements for Pot of Gold in 1975—his first commercial work.[100]

The majority of workers at Moirs were women, and (for a time) the majority of women employed in Halifax were employed at Moirs. Three of every five women working outside the home in Halifax in 1891 were Moirs workers.[101] In her MA thesis for Dalhousie University, Margaret Anne Mulrooney explains that work at Moirs was organized along gender lines: candy making was "considered men's work," while women "sorted, packed, wrapped, shined, weighed, or inspected the finished products."[102] Women also did hand dipping of chocolates, and were paid a piece rate; this work was not considered as skilled as that performed by the male candy workers who operated the machinery.[103] Ian Sclanders wrote in an article for *Maclean's*, "A sugar man, boiling hard candy, can't depend on his thermometer. He has to judge when it is cooked by how the bubbles break on the surface. And he has to adjust the temperature of his steam-heated copper pan to changes in the weather, raising it on damp days and lowering it on dry days. He constantly glances through the window at the sky. Among the things he has to know is which batch should be cooled on stainless steel, which should be cooled on marble and which should be cooled on wood."[104] Women took two years to learn to hand dip chocolate, and as much as six years to reach peak speed at the task.[105] Few women were employed in administration at the company.[106] Mulrooney claims that low wages at Moirs in the 1950s contributed to "a reputation as being an undesirable employer in Halifax: parents reportedly warned daughters against leaving school by threatening, 'If you quit we'll send you to Moir's to work!'"[107]

Line speed was determined to some extent by the Moirs workers themselves. Women working on piece rate found that pressure to speed up their work came from their co-workers rather than supervisors. A Moirs employee recalled working on a line, placing individual candies into boxes: "I remember them hollerin', 'Hey put your candy in.' Wouldn't be the chargehand or the supervisor, it would be your next door neighbour. 'Hey come on, get your candy in, that's my money going down the line.'"[108] Workers who were not paid piece rates would slow down the assembly line by jamming belts with jelly candies or pressing against belts with their knees.[109] Despite the poor wages, some women preferred factory work at Moirs to secretarial work elsewhere: as one former Moirs worker explained, "[T]here ain't no man I'm going to carry coffee for."[110] In addition to gender divisions, a hierarchy of labour within the Moirs factory was established in part by the cleanliness of a particular job: those who worked in fancy packing were superior to those in the messier chocolate room.[111] With increased mechanization in a newly constructed plant in 1975, work speed increased at Moirs and the gendered labour division diminished.[112]

The Second World War and immediate aftermath, with the rationing of sugar and limited access to foreign inputs like cocoa, hampered production of chocolate for Moirs and other confectioners.[113] Moirs took pains to explain that they did not condone, and neither were they responsible for, a black market in chocolate bars in 1946: bars were not available over the counter in some stores; yet, in others, merchants displayed punchboards with chocolate bars as prizes. An article in the *Hants Journal* reported, "Moirs, as other reputable firms, do their best to give their retailers a quota of their pre-war supply. They can exercise no control over that dealer as to the ultimate disposal of that quota, whether he sells it over his counter or from under his counter to regular customers or disposes of it en bloc as is suspected in some cases, to the operators of these punchboards."[114] Moirs explained the 1947 price increase of chocolate bars from five cents to eight cents in detail to their customers. The price of cocoa beans had rise from 10 to 23.5 cents per pound, and sugar prices had also risen. A Federal War Excise Tax of one cent had been added to chocolate bars. American chocolate bars had shrunk in size during the war, while Moirs bars remained the same size. British chocolate bars had doubled in price, but the cost of Moirs bars had not. In short, Canadian chocolate bars were the "best value in North America" and customers "will not have the least cause to feel that the confectionery manufacturers have taken advantage of decontrol to exact unfair prices from the public."[115]

In justifying the price increase, Moirs was responding to a long-held belief by the North American public that chocolate bars should be priced at five cents. The first wrapped chocolate bar in North America was produced by Ganong in 1910.[116] Chocolate bars were unpopular, at first, because children had only pennies to spend rather than nickels, and adults preferred to give presents of boxed chocolates rather than bars. Chocolate bars became popular with the First World War, as, according to an article in *Printers Ink*, they were the "least compromising to masculine dignity"[117] of candies available for soldiers wanting a quick-energy food. They were also easier to display than bulk candy in tobacconist shops. By the early 1930s, chocolate bars were the most popular item of confectionery in North America. Moirs introduced their five-cent bar in 1930.[118] When chocolate bar prices rose from five cents to eight cents in 1947, Canadian children protested across the country. In Edmonton, 200 children marched and picketed confectionery stores; the number was 3,000 in Ottawa. In Vancouver, children "raced through the corridors" of the provincial legislature, "shouting and whistling" and chanting "We want five-cent chocolate bars," according to the *Edmonton Journal*.[119] Similar protests were held in Winnipeg, Montreal, and Regina.[120] Winnipeg's YWCA teen canteen boycotted eight-cent bars, and the Coordinating Board of Youth Centres formed an investigating committee to examine the situation.[121]

The 1950s brought significant changes to Moirs, both in ownership and in the workforce. Rumours of the sale of Moirs to central Canadians emerged in the 1950s. With the death of James McGregor Stewart, the remaining partners decided to transfer control of the company to younger men—but they preferred that Moirs remained in the hands of Maritimers. In 1956, Benjamin Moir's great-grandson—the last Moir family member associated with the company—retired from management. John Crerar MacKeen, Frank Manning Covert, and E. Leroy Otto became the owners of Moirs.[122] The company made Canadian labour history a year later when the company unionized.[123] For the first time in Canada, two unions signed a joint contract. Joint certification by Teamsters Local 927 and the Bakery and Confectionery

Workers International Union Local 446 affected some 1,000 workers at the plant. Wages at the plant improved somewhat as a result of unionization.

Moirs made a point of their significance to the local economy in 1958, when management decided to issue their payroll solely in silver dollars for one week. Local businesses, seeing the silver dollars in their cash registers, would realize the impact of Moirs on their own success. Moirs noted in an explanatory advertisement, "**The same payroll goes out 52 times a year.** We won't pay it in Silver Dollars, but we do want you to see its effect just this once! WE SOLICIT YOUR SUPPORT FOR ALL MARITIME INDUSTRY."[124] Employees also received an explanation: a message from E. Leroy Otto said the silver dollars would be recognized by "the citizens and business people" of the area so that they would "feel the impact of your earning and what you spend each week." The souvenir pouch in which they were presented would "help you remember the day you helped everyone to realize how important your earnings are to them."[125] Moirs bakery superintendent James Monaghan observed that "it was fun today to see the men & girls getting paid carrying their little cotton bag [of] silver . . . (a job well done)."[126]

Many Moirs employees worked long term for the company, and many Halifax families had multiple generations working at the plant. Lily Wasson, lead hand in the hand-dipped chocolate department, received her fifty-year service pin in 1961. She was one of 108 employees with twenty-five years of service or more who were honoured by the company at a banquet that year.[127] Eden Longard was the first to receive a gold watch for fifty years of service with Moirs in 1976.[128] He had been hired at age seventeen, and by age twenty-one had been promoted to shipping foreman. Longard received a tour of the newly constructed Moirs factory in Dartmouth, and "was impressed with the modern equipment and the better working conditions."[129] Other employees with twenty-five, forty, and fifty years of service were honoured with lapel pins featuring the initial "M" for Moirs and one, two, or three diamonds.

Moirs employees held their own celebrations, whether of holidays, birthdays, or no occasion at all. Moirs salesmen composed a poem to simultaneously mock themselves and highlight their importance to the success of the business:[130]

Moirs Mighty Moffat threw a party at the rink
To thank the boys who keep the show from toppling
They curled and sang and ate and smoked and p'rhaps they had a drink
At any rate there was a lot of bottling. . . .

Harry Dunn and Gorgeous George (They're really two of a kind)
Muscled in, and not a smoke nor drink did muff
They think it's easy "On the road" to sell the Moirs Line
But all they do is make the blinkin' stuff

It seems that all the salesmen do is beef, complain and spend
The Credit man keeps losing the best account
And Moffat with his tight wad ways! These ways he won't A mend [sic]
But the profits mount and mount and mount and mount.

Though Moirs had record sales in the late 1950s, by the next decade, they were struggling.[131] The company appealed to the Supreme Court of Nova Scotia after the provincial government expropriated some of their land for highway construction. They hoped to develop a chocolate bar that would gain them the same national recognition as had their Pot of Gold chocolate box. They received some tax assistance from Halifax city council, but claimed to pay higher taxes than other confectioners in Canada. And, according to their annual report for 1960, they were in the midst of labour negotiations that might require them to introduce a pension plan as "something long overdue in our industry."[132] Their biggest concern, however, was the federal tax on confectionery.

Moirs, Halifax newspapers, and the Confectionery Association of Canada all fought for the tax exemption of chocolate and candy in the 1950s and 1960s. Arguing that "candy is a food,"[133] the *Halifax Chronicle-Herald* claimed that high taxes on chocolate and candy were lowering their consumption. Children, "who have the least money," were the most affected by these taxes: "Reduced consumption, therefore, is not a sacrifice shared by all," another

Figure 33. Boxing Easter eggs, Moirs Ltd., c. 1962.

Figure 34. Luxury Package, Moirs XXX Chocolates, newspaper advertisement. n.d.

newspaper article reported.[134] Moirs vice-president E. Leroy Otto led a delegation of the Confectionery Association to Ottawa in 1960; they met with Prime Minister John Diefenbaker to ask for the removal of the 11 percent tax on confectionery.[135] In their 1962 annual report, the company reported on their ongoing efforts to change government policy. Moirs management questioned "both the logic and the equity in a tax law which says that you take a group of ingredients and bake or freeze them and they are not subject to sales tax, but when you cook them in a pot, they are subject to sales tax."[136] Also illogical was that chocolate-coated biscuits and some desserts were tax-exempt.[137] According to their annual report, Moirs believed that their industry was "not being treated as an important industry supplying a great many people with employment and providing a valuable energy food to the public, but rather as an instrument to collect taxes."[138] Moirs (and their competitor Ganong, another Maritime confectioner) were most affected by the tax because of ready access from overseas markets and their distance from central Canada.[139] The subsequent loss of $13.5 million in revenue would not be significant to the federal government, a Halifax newspaper argued, but "for firms like Moirs in Halifax and Ganong's in New Brunswick it could mean the difference between survival and extinction."[140]

Moirs's survival was assured—at least for the time being—when it was sold to Standard Brands Limited in 1967.[141] Standard Brands had been formed in 1929 with the merger of Fleischmann (makers of yeast), Royal Baking Powder, E.W. Gillett (makers of Magic Baking Powder), and Chase and Sanborn (coffee).[142] The Nova Scotia businessmen who had owned Moirs explained that the sale was necessary: an article in the *Atlantic Advocate* reported that it "was a matter of watch it die or sell it to a company which could afford to revive it and which would let it grow on its native soil."[143] The decision was a risky one: only five years after the sale, Standard Brands threatened to close the factory.[144] A year after this threat, in 1973, Standard Brands bought Lowney (an American chocolate company with a branch plant in Canada) and combined them with Moirs; their merged head office was located in Montreal. That same year, Standard decided to move the Moirs plant from downtown Halifax to a new facility across the harbour in Dartmouth.[145] It was an effort to address the aging and sprawling nine-storey factory, as well as the financial losses the company had sustained in the 1960s.[146] Moirs's chocolate bar production moved to the Lowney plant in Quebec; Lowney's boxed chocolate production moved to the Moirs plant.

The new Dartmouth plant opened in 1975. The *Globe and Mail* reported that the Nova Scotia government's industrial development agency provided "nearly $2.4 million in loan financing covering a 20-year land and building lease."[147] The new facility had 10,915 square metres of production space and 350 full-time workers—a steep decline from the company's heyday of more than 1,000 employees in the early 1950s.[148] Sales increased by almost 11 percent that year, however, and the company made a profit of $10 million, prompting one newspaper reporter to conclude that "Nova Scotia's first candy industry might stay in the neighborhood another 103 years."[149] It was not to be: Standard Brands sold the business in 1987 to Hershey, which closed the plant in 2007. Moirs, Ian McKay observes, was "a flagship of indigenous capital" that "survived the initial onslaught of the merger movement" of the late nineteenth century.[150] It was not able to survive that of the early twenty-first century, however. Hershey closed its other Canadian plant and reduced its workforce at its American factories by 10 percent, while opening production facilities in Mexico.[151] Moirs employee Christina (Missy) Fuller mourned the end of an era: "I thought I was going to retire there. . . . There were sons and daughters working alongside their parents who had worked there for most of their lives, and then not after too long, sons- and daughters-in-law, too."[152]

The iconic Pot of Gold chocolates continue to be produced, but not in Canada, and not by Moirs. For many Canadian families, they were a Christmas tradition. Archivist and oral historian Sarah Story recalls waiting for her turn "to look at the insert containing the list of chocolate fillings" and then take her "sweet time picking out that one special chocolate for the day. That was our limit for the day when we were kids, so we had to make it count!" Her personal favourites were "the plain square of chocolate marked 'Pot of Gold' in the centre of the package" or the chocolate containing three whole hazelnuts: "I also remember the commercials in the 1980s/90s for Pot of Gold, and have not forgotten that old jingle, 'We all know where the rainbow goes.'"[153] The rainbow now goes to Hershey, North America's largest chocolate producer, and maker of Pot of Gold.[154]

Ganong

Moirs's rival, Ganong, was the other major Maritime Canadian confectioner. Unlike Moirs and Paulins, Ganong is still in operation and its ownership remains in the hands of the descendants of those family members who founded the company. Ganong was established in St. Stephen, New Brunswick, by brothers James Harvey Ganong and Gilbert White Ganong in 1873. The company began as a grocery, confectionery, and soapery.[155] In 1884, the brothers split the company, with Gilbert Ganong retaining ownership over the confectionery business. Ganong became Canada's "first national confectioner in 1888 when it began shipping its products to British Columbia"[156] at the opposite end of the country, and, by 1891, produced 7 percent of Canada's confectionery.[157] The company survived a devastating fire in 1903 that saw firefighters from the adjoining American state of Maine crossing the Canada–U.S. border to assist. Insurance covered only half the family's losses, which were extensive, since they lived in quarters above the retail store in front of the factory. The entire building and all the family's belongings were destroyed.[158]

Gilbert Ganong was succeeded by his nephew, Arthur Deinstadt Ganong, on his death in 1917. The fact that Gilbert had no children made the succession complicated. The New Brunswick Museum states, "Financial difficulties and challenges to the control of the company within the family during the mid to late 1930s eventually were settled by the courts."[159] David Ganong, two generations later, recalled "his father's generation had bitter arguments, especially between those who held shares but did not work in the business and those who did. He remembers many combative evenings at the dinner table over dividends, and who received what for their efforts. The family wound up in court over the value of shares."[160] Gilbert Ganong's widow, Maria, died in 1934; her estate was not settled until 1942.[161] Ganong historian Margaret McCallum explained, "For some years in the thirties, the business wasn't making money. They were buying supplies, paying salaries, selling their product and just breaking even or running a loss. . . . But they were supporting all those people who were working in the business, and maintaining the brand presence so that when things improved they'd still be there."[162]

Arthur Ganong served on the executive of the Confectionery, Biscuit, and Chocolate Industries of Canada. He became known for eating roughly a kilogram of chocolate daily,[163] claiming "in his later years [that] the only thing which kept him alive was the box of chocolates he ate every day."[164]

Ganong produced an extensive variety of confectionery in the 1940s. Production included boxed chocolates (Ganong's Best, Delecto, Lagoon, True Value assortment, and Goodwill), bulk candies (Almontinos, Assorted, Caramels, Cream Drops, Cream Peppermints, Maple Walnuts, Milk Caramels, Nougatines, Bordeaux, Chips), and bars (Assorted, Clover Milk, Crystal Cream Peppermints, Diamond Mints, Evangeline Cream, Fudge Assorted/Chocolate/Vanilla, Jelly Rolls, Nut Milk, Pal-o-Mine, Peppermints, Rainbow Nougat, Rich Crisp, Service, Snow Pudding, Three Bears, Wafer Rolls).[165] During the Second World War, Ganong shipped chocolates bars to the Canadian Armed Forces (154,268 boxes in 1943, almost twice as many as were shipped for domestic consumption).[166] Total monthly production during the war ranged from 181,435 to 199,580 kilograms of chocolate.[167]

Arthur's son, Randol Whidden Ganong, became company president in 1957 after having served two years as mayor of St. Stephen.[168] Similar to his predecessor, he ate up to a kilogram of chocolate daily.[169] Newspapers claimed that Ganong family members ate the chocolate they manufactured "as a staple food rather than as a between-meal extra, without any noticeable effect on teeth, health or weight."[170] By the 1950s, the company employed one of every eight people living in St. Stephen.[171] In 1955 and 1960, Randol Ganong resisted two unionization drives by the Bakery and Confectionery Workers International Union (BCWIU),[172] and, the *Times Globe* reported, "was quoted in the *Financial Post* as saying he would lock up, sell or move the plant if the union moved in. He later denied the quote."[173] The BCWIU responded by calling for a boycott of Ganong. The BCWIU vice-president, John H. Reid, remarked, "This company has, by every conceivable method, resisted our organizing attempts and their products continue to be manufactured under working conditions inferior to those in plants under contract with our union."[174] In response to Ganong's threat to shut down the plant if unionized, he observed, "Theirs being the only major industry in St. Stephen's, N.B., it's not hard to understand the impact that threats of this kind have on the employees."[175] A decade after this failed attempt, Randol asserted that the company was committed to remaining local:

> I've seen the factories slowly disappear—soap, textile, shoe and fertilizer. We're the only ones left. I saw families ruined in 1956–7 when the textile mill closed down. I'll have no part of that. This is my life. We Ganongs have gone to school with our employees and meet them after hours everywhere. One of my foremen used to be my skip on the curling team. They work with us, not for us. We haven't had a strike in our 100 years. Our management group is tops. We hunt and fish and dig clams together. It's all a low-pressure operation, a relaxed kind of living.[176]

The New Brunswick government agreed with this assessment, noting that absenteeism at the company was low and staff turnover was less than 10 percent annually.[177] The company faced only one strike in their history: in April 1911, twenty women walked out for a few days in protest of their new supervisor.[178]

Randol Whidden Ganong presided over the company's centennial anniversary in 1972. It was a difficult time for the company on the family front, as his sister Joan Ganong fought with him in the boardroom, but there was nonetheless much to celebrate.[179] Ganong sold some 350 different types of candy nationwide, manufactured at their sole plant in New Brunswick.[180] Randol received the "Candy Man Award" from the Confectionery Manufacturers Association of Canada a few years later as "the individual who has made the most significant contribution to the confectionery industry."[181] He was succeeded in 1977 by his nephew, David Ganong.[182]

David Ganong inherited a business that faced significant challenges. The *National Post* reported that problems included "low margins and behind-the-times marketing. The return to profitability came by slashing the number of product lines, cancelling many historic products that were part of life in Atlantic Canada."[183] David left Ganong in 2008, and the first non-family number (Doug Ettinger) was appointed as chief executive officer. David returned to the role in 2012 when Ettinger left to become chief executive officer of Scotsburn Dairy in Nova Scotia, where his family lived.[184] The Ganongs later considered the brief leadership by a non-family member to be a mistake. David Ganong stated, "We reached out to an outsider to lead the company. It didn't work out as well as I thought it would, so I stepped in for a while."[185] David's daughter, Bryana Ganong, succeeded him as president in 2014.[186] While still manufacturing such classics as Pal-o-Mine bars and "chicken bones," the company also engages in private-label manufacturing (making products for another company's brand) for businesses such as Sunkist and Laura Secord; private labels accounted for 60 percent of Ganong's business in 2014.[187]

Ganong claims credit for several innovations in Canadian confectionery: the chocolate-nut bar, the heart-shaped box of Valentine chocolates, and the Maritime favourite "chicken bones." Ganong employee Frank Sparhawk invented the latter, a cinnamon-flavoured candy with a chocolate centre, in 1885. The heart-shaped Valentine candy box was invented in 1906 by the Home Paper Box Company, which had been established by Ganong. The chocolate-nut bar was the 1910 creation of Arthur Ganong and expert confectioner George Ensor of Baltimore.[188] According to the *Saint Croix Courier*, Ensor was invited for "two weeks to teach [Ganong] employees how to make gumdrops and . . . stayed for 40 years."[189] Ensor and Arthur Ganong developed these bars for their fishing and hunting trips, and decided to sell them for five cents to compete with flat milk chocolate bars imported from Switzerland.[190] Another expert confectioner from Baltimore, Edward Bosein, worked at Ganong from 1887 to 1941 and invented the Pal-o-Mine chocolate bar (a two-piece chocolate bar with peanuts and fudge) in 1920.[191]

The chicken bone is one of Ganong's most popular chocolate candies. Cinnamon candy is cooked in a copper kettle, then kneaded at a hot table. Two strips of candy are cut off with scissors; one is set aside, while the other is mixed with red colouring and returned to the batch to dye it translucent red. The candy is then pulled by machine to turn it opaque pink. The reserved strip of candy is kneaded back into this mixture to add a sheen to the final product. The candy is flattened, and bittersweet chocolate is folded into the centre. The candy is described by The Chocolate Museum as "like a hot dog on a bun—albeit a 40 kg hot dog!" The ends of the candy are sealed to keep the chocolate inside, then it is taken to a heated rolling conveyor and fed by hand into a cutting machine. Once cut, the chicken bones travel through a cooler to harden before being sent to packaging.[192]

The manufacturing of centres for Ganong chocolates is a complex process involving specialized machinery. Centres are formed in a machine known as a starch mogul. First, cornstarch, sugar, and other ingredients are cooked in copper kettles. Moulds (carved by hand) are loaded into the starch mogul, and trays of cornstarch are then pressed by a mould board to form impressions of the mould. Liquid candy is poured into these impressions and is left to set. The trays of candy centres are emptied by machine onto a conveyor, which removes the cornstarch for reuse.[193]

Centres made in the starch mogul are transferred to a wire mesh conveyor, beneath which is a drum covered in melted chocolate that coats the bottoms of the centres. These "bottomed" centres travel over a cooled table, then under a curtain of melted chocolate to coat the tops of the centres. The decorative swirl patterns on top of each chocolate are unique to each type of centre, and help identify the chocolate. The chocolates are cooled and then returned to room temperature. Workers place trays into boxes (which are machine-folded) and then place chocolates into each tray; they cover these with a protective pad and the box lid. An additional chocolate is added to any boxes that are underweight, before the boxes are wrapped in cellophane.[194]

Ganong, like most confectioners, has long relied on women and immigrant workers.[195] Women workers at Ganong, said an article in the *New Brunswick Beacon*, "would show up around May with their suitcases bursting at the seams, and they'd move in to a bright yellow building on the corner of Main Street."[196] The bright yellow building was Elm Hall, purchased in 1906 as a boarding house for female workers.[197] An article for *Labour/Travail* by historian Margaret McCallum reported that Elm Hall "was intended to attract young female workers to St. Stephen, and to ensure that their cost of living would not exceed their wages."[198] The boarding house, a symbol of the company's paternalist attitude to their female employees who "followed a strict set of rules under the care of a house matron," was sold in the 1930s.[199] The low wages limited the number of local workers the company was able to attract, so Ganong imported workers from the United Kingdom between 1905 and 1907, and chartered schooners to bring 600 young women from Newfoundland between 1911 and 1913.[200] A century later, still faced with difficulties attracting local workers, Ganong invited thirty Romanian workers to immigrate to Canada to work in their plant for two years.[201] Worker shortages continued to be a challenge, and the company was forced to respond in a number of ways: turning down orders, offering more flexible shifts, and increasing wages.[202] These combined efforts resulted in a doubling of the workforce to 350 employees in the period from 2011 to 2013.[203]

The majority of workers at Ganong have always been women. Margaret McCallum notes that the gendered labour division ("men made the candy and women added the finishing touches") was established years earlier when the factory was smaller.[204] Then, too, there was the "assumption that women's participation in the paid labour force was secondary to their domestic role, and that jobs promising higher earnings and better opportunities for advancement should go to men."[205] The work was seasonal, and so thought to be better suited to supplementary income earned by married women. As well, there was "the firm's conservative and paternalistic style of management." Finally, "shared community notions about what was appropriate" contributed to a belief that hand dipping and packing chocolates was "women's work."[206] This, despite the fact that, as the *Toronto Star* reported, hand dipping chocolate was a skilled job, requiring five years of training to "recognize by touch the chocolate's ideal dipping temperature of 88C within a two-degree margin."[207] McCallum's five explanations for the gender division at Ganong may really be reduced to one: the company's paternalist attitudes.

Ganong's paternalism evolved in the late twentieth century, as the company and the town in which they operated increasingly identified with each other in new—and very public—ways. Ganong collaborated with the town

Figure 35. A 1942 advertisement on display in The Chocolate Museum, St. Stephen, New Brunswick.

of St. Stephen to establish a chocolate museum in their former factory and to hold a chocolate festival each summer. Chocolate Fest was created in 1984, and The Chocolate Museum was opened in 1999 (nine years after Ganong moved into a newly built factory).[208] The annual festival is sponsored primarily by Ganong, together with St. Stephen's city council, the regional tourism association, the local chamber of commerce, and various local businesses. It includes a variety of events and is presided over by two mascots, described by the festival brochure as "the Great Chocolate Mousse and his lovely wife Tiffany."[209] Restaurants promote chocolate items; a day spa features "chocolate facial, chocolate and chicken bone gel nail manicure or a chocolate cream hair mask!"[210] Typical events include "Chocolate Mania," with games, activities, live entertainment, and vendors; "Chocolate Lovers Celebration," in which "we name our Chocolate Lover of the Year and induct three new people into the Chocolate Lovers Society"; a chocolate brunch; community picnics, barbecues, and suppers; "Chocolate Tea Party & Hunt with Lucy the Ladybug"; truck mud racing; food tastings; three- and five-kilometre runs; treasure hunts; a "Taste of Chocolate," featuring a tour of The Chocolate Museum followed by a visit to "meet real Ganong employees, discover how they make the candies and chocolates, enjoy fun competitions and live entertainment, and sample lots of delicious chocolate treats"; hand dipping chocolates with Ganong employees; walking tours; a chocolate pudding-eating contest; and yard sales, dances, and parades.[211]

The Chocolate Museum exhibits elide many of the challenges faced by the workers, casting a paternalist veneer over their efforts. "Ganong paid good wages and offered employees opportunity for advancement," one display reads. "Young factory helpers could work their way up to candy makers, hand-dippers, salesmen and even managers. As a result, many employees stayed with Ganong for the remainder of their working lives."[212] It is unlikely that women employed as candy makers would make the transition to sales or management. And the lifelong employment of many at the factory was a testament to the lack of opportunities for those with limited educations in small-town New Brunswick.

Figure 36. Former Ganong factory, now The Chocolate Museum, 2013.

Figure 37. Promotion of the Taste of Chocolate exhibit at St. Stephen's Chocolate Fest, featuring the Great Chocolate Mousse, 2013.

North American free trade and the consolidation of the confectionery industry were challenges that company president David Ganong faced in the late twentieth century.[213] In order to compete with American companies, Ganong had to modernize and expand their factory.[214] They worked to standardize Canadian nutritional labelling requirements in line with those of the United States.[215] They toyed with the idea of opening a multi-million-dollar chocolate theme park.[216] They entered into a joint venture with a manufacturer in Bangkok to supply candy to Asia, and they moved from their downtown location in St. Stephen to a new factory on the outskirts of town.[217] As did his ancestors before him, David Ganong lobbied government on behalf of his industry—asking for removal of the tariff on imported sugar.[218] And Ganong expanded into private-label production for Laura Secord, a chocolate company that traces its origins to Toronto in 1913.[219] Ganong has been contracted to make products for Laura Secord since 2004; such private-label manufacturing has been the core of Ganong's business since then.[220] Specialization, modern marketing, computer-controlled distribution, and an emphasis on export improved the profitability of Ganong.[221] A *Toronto Star* article reported that Ganong "supplies at least 40 per cent of the Canadian market for heart-shaped boxes and they are the company's biggest selling item nationally."[222] Ideological views of gender persist in curious ways: the company introduced a "masculinised" version of the heart-shaped chocolate box—the "tuxedo box"—for women to give Valentine's chocolates to men.[223]

———— • ————

In the 1970s, R. Whidden Ganong asserted that the "romance" of chocolate making had vanished; confectionery production had become "a science rather than an art."[224] Moirs's Pot of Gold, Paulins's Cuban Lunch, and the heart-shaped boxes of Valentine's chocolates invented by Ganong were products that gained strong followings, though few outside the industry understood the conditions under which they were produced. The primarily female workforce of Paulins, Moirs, and Ganong may have enjoyed the camaraderie of their co-workers both on and off the job, but they also had to cope with low wages and a gendered division of labour. Moirs workers were unionized and Paulins workers were not, yet neither was able to forestall the closure of the companies that employed them. Of the three, only Ganong has persisted—despite family conflicts, the challenges of their situation in a small town, and the demands of international competition.

The romantic myths of the chocolate industry are tied to consumption rather than production. The heart-shaped boxes and the invention of the tradition of gifts of chocolates to one's female loved ones are romantic symbols that mask the historical realities of female labour in these chocolate factories. Ganong's past difficulty in attracting employees, and their paternalist attitudes toward their women workers for much of their history, are evidence of the fact that chocolate making has always been more business than art form. Profit making took precedence over emotional connections. The familial ties that were so carefully cultivated on the shop floor helped stave off the unionization of the largely female, comparatively uneducated workforces at two of these companies. Though managers like Yasumatsu may have tried to resist, they too were subordinate to the demands of capital, and so their effectiveness was seriously limited. Yasumatsu may have been able to make the closing day of the Paulins factory an in-house affair, successfully excluding representatives from the head office, but he could do nothing to prevent the plant closure itself. Moirs's owners were similarly more concerned with profit than with the relationships they claimed to have cultivated within their workplaces. The art of these businesses was in their use of romantic myth to sell their products; business decisions, however, were always guided by the science of economics.

6

CANDY MANUFACTURERS

Surviving in an Anti-Sugar World

"It's a kid's dream. . . . You want to make candy."

—— WILLIAM ARTHUR BURBINE, INTERVIEW, 2013 ——

The main ingredients of many snack foods are problematic. Cocoa, the key component in chocolate, has connections, in some cases, to child labour. Manufacturers of cheaper chocolate have been faced with the ethical problems of palm oil.[1] Cheezies' main ingredient is corn, which has been criticized for its distortion of the American agricultural system.[2] But worst of all, perhaps, is candy. Candy, at base, is primarily sugar, a substance that has come in for increasing condemnation.[3]

Anthropologist Sidney Mintz, in his classic book *Sweetness and Power,* explains how sugar became the cheap fuel and "drug food"[4] of European workers: by 1900, sugar comprised almost a fifth of dietary calories for the average English person.[5] As "the first mass-produced exotic necessity of a proletarian working class,"[6] sugar (together with tobacco and tea) became a "low-cost food substitute . . . for the metropolitan laboring classes."[7] Sugar, Mintz argues, "made it possible to raise the caloric content of the proletarian diet without increasing proportionately the quantities of meat, fish, poultry, and dairy products."[8]

Candy manufacturing is a challenging business, requiring both skill and strength to work with kilograms of molten sugar. Skilled labour can be replaced with automated equipment, but the equipment itself is expensive and the end product considered by some to be inferior. The small profit margins in candy production mean that it is difficult for smaller, independent firms to compete with larger bulk manufacturers. Robertson's Candy in Nova Scotia has continued a family tradition of handmade candy production that began in 1928. Cavalier Candies in Manitoba has survived by specializing in kosher jelly slices and by engaging in private-label manufacturing for other firms. The candy made by Purity Factories is just one of the many product lines that keeps this Newfoundland firm in business. Browning Harvey could not compete and so abandoned their bakery and confectionery production to become Newfoundland's Pepsi bottler. Scott-Bathgate's future in Winnipeg is debatable, though the company has been in existence for over a century. Candy manufacturing, then, is perhaps the most risky type of snack manufacturing.

Robertson's Candy

Roy Robertson is a second-generation candy manufacturer in Truro, Nova Scotia. He has been making candy since 1977, continuing a business begun by his father, William Christie Robertson, in 1928. Robertson's Candy makes their products using the original equipment purchased by the founder. It's very much a family business: employees in the 1980s included Roy, his wife, Alice, and their six sons.[9] Roy Robertson explains, "I grew up down on King Street and the candy shop was always in the backyard and it's been the same for my children."[10] Lately, the business has been run by three or four employees, with an additional half dozen hired for the run-up to the Christmas season. The company is known for two things: one of the largest candy-mould collections in the world and the production of toy candy (also known as barley candy, a popular Christmas tradition in the Maritimes).[11]

Robertson began his candy-mould collection when he was a young teenager. He visited "Mr. [J.D.] Fraser, who ran Moirs," the chocolate factory in Halifax.[12] Fraser showed him the candy moulds, and Robertson begged his father to buy them. Over the years, he acquired more from small, independent producers like Caroline Candy, Hawkesbury TP Company, Springhill Candy, Yarmouth Candy, and others. He now has thousands of moulds, many of them collectors' items, which are "likely worth more than the business" he owns.[13] Most sit unused on shelves, as their complicated designs result in candy that is too fragile to make affordably. "For example," he says, "certain ones you have to make five to get one good one. Some are two pounds, so it's a real waste." He uses some to make displays for his wife's craft shows.

The Robertson's Candy factory was established in the backyard of the Truro home in which Roy Robertson was born.[14] Roy's father, William Robertson, had started work in the Eaton candy factory in 1912. The day after the 1917 Halifax explosion, he purchased the equipment from the destroyed Eaton factory to launch his own business. In addition to candy, he manufactured Minard's Liniment[15] and syrups (to which water could be added to make non-alcoholic beverages). Today, the factory is still in a Truro backyard, albeit two blocks away from its original location. Roy Robertson worked in his father's candy business as a child, then established a career working for Truro Electric and Nova Scotia Power before a back injury forced him to leave this work. Roy's brother, who had been the family's main candy maker, left for a job in the Thompson, Manitoba, mines. The departure of his brother, together with the high humidity in summer that interfered with candy production, restricted the operation of the business to production solely for the Christmas season.[16] Roy's father was preparing to sell the family business to someone in Springhill, Nova Scotia, in 1977, when Roy decided to purchase the business instead.[17]

One of Robertson's most popular candies is their Big Uglee Mints. When first formed, these mints are soft and so become misshapen: as Robertson said, "They're not like a nice oval."[18] He originally described them as ugly, and the name stuck: "I said, [let's call them] big uglee mints. . . . Everybody gets a kick out of it and loves them because they'll melt in your mouth."[19] Other products include ribbon candy and toy candy (also known as clear toys, animal toys, barley candy, or shapes). Toy candy, Robertson explained, was a traditional candy in Germany. In Philadelphia, where much American candy was made in the past, Thomas Mills made candy moulds to produce candy in shapes to hang on Christmas trees (in much the same way that the hooks of candy canes and the curves of ribbon candy were designed for

Figure 38. Robertson's candy mould collection, 2013.

hanging). Clove candy is a specialty of Robertson's, one not common among other confectioners. Sticks for suckers (or lollipops) used to be placed by hand at the company. Robertson damaged his hand doing this task, and now they instead make large pops of 170 to 198 grams in a candy press. Chocolate used to be manufactured, as well, before it was deemed too expensive to produce, except as a centre for "chicken bones."[20]

Much of the candy at Robertson's is produced by hand rather than machine. Equipment includes propane stoves, copper kettles, and a sizing and wrapping machine dating back to 1924. All the company's equipment is old, said employee William Burbine, "which is kind of cool because they're still running better than something probably you'd buy new today."[21] Copper kettles are used for open candy processes. Stainless steel can produce hot spots and burn the candy; copper conducts heat more evenly. Open kettles are used so that water can be boiled away as the candy is processed. A vacuum cooker may be used instead (and produces candy more quickly), but

Figure 39. Candy making at Robertson's Candy, 2013.

Roy Robertson prefers the taste of candy made the old-fashioned way in an open copper kettle. He said, "It depends on what you want: a great volume business with little profit or a little business with a decent margin."[22] A local magazine described the labour process: "It's labour intensive work because everything, from the weighing of ingredients to the packaging, is done by hand. Even the pulling to incorporate air into what will become the satin mix hard candies, is hand-done. A large piece of the cooling mixture is spun into a rope, and hung on a large hook on the wall to be pulled and pulled some more, until the mixture turns opaque and is cool enough to handle. Colour is then applied before it goes into a roller machine to be shaped and cut."[23]

Humidity is the bane of the candy maker. It has been a challenge at Robertson's for the production of ribbon candy in particular. Prior to the installation of heat pumps, if humidity was above 55 percent, ribbon candy could not be made, as the candy would stick to the production table.[24] Fifty-five percent humidity is optimal for running candy-making equipment; above that threshold, the hydroscopic maltose makes the machinery too sticky to function properly. The addition of heat pumps to the factory in 2013 resulted in the lowest humidity levels ever at Robertson's. Robertson said, "So we're very, very hopeful that we've found an answer. . . . It costs the same amount to run the business on a day when you don't make candy as on days you do."[25]

Most of the few employees at Robertson's are seasonal and part-time workers. Robertson said they are "housewives or . . . their families have grown and left. They do it to supplement their income. . . . A girl was in here yesterday, and she told me that last year she was thirty-six hours short of getting her time to get her unemployment. What do you do? I would have hired her another week if had known that, because she's a good worker."[26] Robertson declares, "I guess I'm soft or something because I try to treat the people the way I would want to be treated. . . . Or they wouldn't be here, I guess, if they didn't like it."[27] He says that, for many of his employees, money is less important than their enjoyment of the work.[28]

William Burbine, one of Robertson's employees, expressed this sentiment himself in his interview.[29] Burbine is committed to the business, seeing himself as more than an employee. He said, "You learn to do it and you do it. That's why Roy tries to keep me working, because he knows that I paid attention. I know how to do things. And I'll do the extra to get things done. To me, I'm not working for a paycheque, I'm working for a job."[30] He earns minimum wage, and explains the trade-off between income and stress: "I'd rather be happy, working, than stressed. I mean, I go home, I'm not stressed about anything. Not like some people who go home and are like, 'I wanna kill my boss.' Happiness is better. And money's not happiness."[31] Burbine had been employed elsewhere, but did not care for the management at his former workplace. Looking to leave, he heard about Robertson's, applied for a job, and has been working there ever since. "Like I say, I enjoy it. It's fun. It's interesting. . . . I've done a bit of everything," Burbine said, summarizing his working experience at a lumber mill, in the army, as a Tim Hortons baker, in the construction industry, and as a shipper and receiver. His work philosophy is: "Take what work you can find, where you can find it, when you can find it."[32] His mother had been a Moirs chocolate worker, and he recalls his home had plenty of candy in it when he was a child. He began working at Robertson's in 2008 as a seasonal employee, making clear toys.

The rush before the Christmas season "can get quite hectic," as Burbine makes 500 cases of clear toys in three weeks: "That's a lot of candy. A lot of cooking." When candy production is slow, Burbine does other work for the company owner, including construction: "Whatever the boss needs done. Doesn't all have to do with candy. Helping build a bathroom in the basement. There's just a lot of little things that need to be done, and Roy likes to keep me working. . . . Actually, I drive him crazy. Actually, I think I almost work him to death. . . . I love working here . . . Roy, you know, he's a good boss."[33]

The company expanded to year-round production with the purchase of Thomas N. Poulter Natural Foods of Hawkesbury, Ontario.[34] Poulter was founded by a British candy maker who worked for Montreal's Penny Jane candy, and bought their equipment when Penny Jane was bought by Trebor (and ultimately by Hershey).[35] They made brewers' high-maltose candy, which is less sweet than candy produced from high-fructose corn syrup. When Poulter was unable to continue, Roy Robertson purchased their equipment and moved it from Ontario to Nova Scotia. The product line is known as "Naturaltreats," and are gluten-free and peanut-free, and use maltose instead of cane sugar.[36]

This business growth has resulted in an increase in Burbine's seasonal employment at Robertson's. Instead of making candy from September to December, he now starts production in May. He is experimenting with introducing new candies to the company's product line, such as caramel corn, and Big Uglee Mints coated in chocolate. Burbine says, "Trying to branch out a little more, because it is a small business, and it's harder now-a-days because of all the different taxes, and let's just say the government, so we've got to branch out more to keep things going."[37] In the summer of 2014, FOG mints ("For Our Guests") were introduced; these are in wintergreen and spearmint flavours in addition to the Big Uglee Mints' peppermint flavour.[38] Borrowing an east-coast trope, the packaging features a picture of a Nova Scotia lighthouse.

Competition in the candy trade is fierce. Robertson said, "We need to produce the most candy in the shortest period of time now, and either it's profitable or it's not."[39] From September to December is the company's busiest season: without Christmas business, there is no business. Preparation for Christmas begins in August: candy moulds are prepared, extra sugar is purchased, and seasonal workers are hired.[40] Confectionery trade shows are held in Tampa, Atlantic City, and Chicago; the biggest in the world is held in Cologne, Germany. Robertson commented, "They literally give you a map. . . . It's just a maze. . . . And it's hard to believe that there are so, so many people in the industry."[41] He explained that retailer control of the market is an additional challenge: "You either play by their rules or you're out of the game."[42] Robertson cited the example of Florida representative Jerry Rehm, who owned a candy company that supplied Disney. When Rehm died, Disney changed their supplier; the fifteen toffee makers at Rehm's business were reduced to three part-time employees as a consequence.

Cheaper products from foreign competitors are Robertson's main business challenge. According to Robertson, "It doesn't seem to matter what you have. You have the best quality in the whole wide world. And the buyer's there, and he picks up a beautiful can from China: the candy's all stuck together in it, you don't know what it's made with." This inferior product is cheaper, however. "You just have to say, 'We cannot compete.' We make the best quality candy that we can make. . . . It's a much finer made [product], same as a bakery cookie and a homemade cookie. To me, there's no comparison. And that's how I like to compare our candy to [that of] a big volume candy factory."[43] Large-volume candy factories can make as much in one batch as Robertson's is able to make in an entire day. Robertson says he would "like to pay everybody $50 an hour," but it is not possible. Heating costs are high, and at times he has to spend more money on packaging than he does on the product. "Last year [2012], I could buy sugar from the wholesale clubs cheaper than I could buy it from the distributor. You go figure that! . . . And that's the only way you stay in business: nickel and diming it."[44]

Robertson employee Sidney Hollett was responsible for establishing an Internet presence for the company. Prior to the existence of the company's website, advertising was limited. Robertson said, "I guess just word of mouth . . . CBC, CTV . . . and a lot of the newspapers would do our articles . . . but mostly, calling on stores is how we promoted our product at that time."[45] At one time, the business had three salesmen on the road; they have been replaced by commissioned salespeople. According to Robertson, "They're calling on the stores anyhow. So they call on these stores, and they pick up a few extra bucks to pay for their stuff along with their other lines that they have."[46] Despite the nostalgic affection Maritimers have for Robertson's Candy, keeping the business afloat remains a challenge. But, as the owner observes, "If it was easy, everybody would be doing it."[47]

Cavalier Candies

George Bond and Ronald Samuel founded Cavalier Candies as Bond and Ronald in Winnipeg, Manitoba, in 1922. Bond was the owner and manager; Samuel was the candy maker.[48] One of their most popular products was (and continues to be) agar jelly fruit slices, made by soaking strips of agar seaweed overnight, then cooking them into flavoured jelly, thirty-six kilograms at a time. Charles Spencer Fletcher, owner of Edmonton's Pavey Candy, purchased the company in 1957;[49] he expanded their market from the province to the nation.[50] Fletcher divided the business into two: Cavalier Candies (which manufactures confectionery) and Cavalier Foods (which imports confectionery). Individually wrapped jelly fruit slices (marketed as the "Pizazz" brand) were launched in the 1970s. Fletcher's son, Walter, joined the business in 1986, and Cavalier Candies is now the largest confectioner in western Canada, and the largest agar fruit slice manufacturer in North America.[51]

While best known for their fruit slices, Cavalier manufactures a variety of candies. The company brochure indicates that these include candy canes; "satin baby pillows: a popular mixture of tiny hard candy pillows in a 'cocktail' of traditional flavours"; "assorted cut rock: traditional 'design in the centre' hard candies"; Christmas ribbon candy; chocolate- or mint-filled straws; mint humbugs; red- or green-striped mint pillows; raspberry, lemon, and fruit drops; toasted marshmallows; "toasted peanut butter logs: golden coconut toasted hard candy with a smooth and creamy peanut butter filling"; and Turkish delight.[52] In the 1930s, the business also produced chocolate and fudge, but they now solely produce hard candies and fruit slices.[53]

The original factory, a two-storey brick plant with 100 employees, was located at 690 McGee Street in Winnipeg's West End. A fire seriously damaged the business in 1947.[54] In addition to the fire (whose traces lingered into the 1950s), the Second World War provided challenges for the company in the 1940s. Sugar rationing limited the company's daily production; once the day's quota was used up, workers were sent home for the rest of the day.[55] In 1961 or 1962, the company moved from McGee Street to King Edward Street. In 1971, Cavalier Candies moved again, this time into the McClary Building at 185 Bannatyne Avenue in Winnipeg's Exchange District. The plant now employs fifty or sixty people. Initially, they used only three floors in the McClary Building; by 2015, they occupied all six floors. The fifth floor warehouses Christmas candy, stored in airtight eighteen-litre pails. The fourth floor is where jelly fruit slices and toasted marshmallows are made. Most of the hard candy production occurs on the third floor. The second floor is where the jellies are placed in trays.[56]

One of the longest-serving employees at Cavalier was Clarence Gould, who worked there from age nineteen to seventy-nine. He was hired in 1954 as "a gopher" at Bond and Ronald on McGee Street, and retired as general manager of Cavalier in 2014.[57] Gould was educated in a rural one-room school until eighth grade. He completed his high school equivalency at Red River College. Later, he obtained a food-handling certificate, and trained in power engineering to operate the factory's steam unit.[58]

Gould recalled the gendered division of labour that used to characterize the candy factory. Men worked as candy makers and their helpers, jobs that required them to lift forty-five-kilogram bags of sugar. Women did the jobs that required more detail or less strength: they toasted coconut, cut jelly slices, and made chocolates.[59] After Easter, the women would start making roses for the next year. Gould said, "They'd take a big gumdrop and they'd put a sucker stick in it. They'd dip them in wax, and then they'd hold them up like this and just go around, turn it. And they'd make all the roses, different sizes, small, big."[60] Once the roses had dried, they would be packed in boxes for the next Easter, ready to decorate chocolate eggs.

Candy makers were skilled workers who had to carefully monitor production. Experienced workers would evaluate candy during various stages by sight and by touch, such as by dipping one's hand in cold water before reaching into a vat of hot caramel to test its texture.[61] Jelly consistency would be tested between two fingers, and temperature could be assessed on one's wrist. Jelly production used to be a more complicated process, resulting in only two batches of 180 kilograms per day. Today, Cavalier is able to produce 2,270 kilograms per day.

Candy helpers did the open-fire cooking. They weighed the corn syrup or glucose, placing it on a scale to ensure it would not ruin the kettle. This sugar was then added to water on a copper kettle on a stove. The helper stirred the mixture until it dissolved. Gould explained, "If the candy maker didn't want to lose you and have you wander off, he'd make you stir it longer than you needed, just to make sure you were there."[62] It was hot and heavy work: two men were needed to lift the handled copper pots off the stove. The hot, liquid candy was poured onto a steel slab that was cooled by water so that the candy could be worked. The modern process is somewhat different, and much faster: once removed from the kettle, the batch is vacuumed to remove moisture and cool it.

Like Robertson's, Cavalier used to employ travelling salesmen, but that ended when independent shops closed and larger companies shifted to mass purchasing. At one time, Gould made deliveries to an independent drugstore in Winnipeg. Each week, he delivered one dozen toasted marshmallows, from which the company made only $2.25 profit. Negotiating contracts with individual stores thus was not profitable for the manufacturer, either. What has been profitable is private-label manufacturing. Cavalier sells products under their name at Superstore and through Publishers Clearing House under the name "Fiji." Cavalier also makes candy for Scott-Bathgate's Nutty Club. Gould said, "A lot of people don't know that Nutty Club does not make candy. They buy from other people."[63]

Much of Cavalier's continued success is credited by Gould to president Walter Fletcher's investment in new machinery. "If you want to stay in business," Gould says, "you've got to keep making more and making it faster, trying to keep your cost down."[64] Cavalier plans to make use of German technology to improve jelly-slice production, preventing colours from running into each other. The assistance of a $50,000 grant in 2014 allowed Cavalier to install new machines to individually wrap fruit slices and to shrink-seal gift boxes. The grant was provided by the Government of Manitoba, Agriculture, Food and Rural Development's Growing Forward 2, "a five-year agricultural policy framework agreement among federal-provincial-territorial governments."[65] The machinery allows the company to pack 1,000 candies per minute. Vice-President James Fletcher explained, "We're a large supplier of Passover confections. . . . With the new machines we were able to increase our output by 40 percent for December, and January sales were the highest in the history of the company."[66] Shipping times were cut almost in half as a result, and ten additional workers were hired.[67]

Over the years, Cavalier has experimented with products other than candy. The Easter department made hollow chocolate animals from moulds until the early 1960s. The process was abandoned as simply too time consuming: six groups of women took an entire day to make the moulded chocolates, after which they had to be hand decorated and packaged.[68] At one point, Cavalier sold and serviced ice cream machines to stores. These contracts did not generate much profit, and the machines required too much maintenance. Smaller stores did not benefit from the high-volume ice cream machines, as they required many sales or the ice cream they held would get too old. Other unsuccessful machine sales and service ventures included slushy drink machines by Stoelting, and popcorn machines. Ultimately, Cavalier decided to persevere with just candy.

Purity Factories

Purity Factories produces candy, cookies, crackers, and flavoured syrup at their plant in St. John's, Newfoundland. The company traces its origins to Wood's Candy Store, founded by Frederick Barnes Wood in the 1890s.[69] The business was purchased by Calvert Coates Pratt, Albert Edgar Hickman, and Wallace R. Goobie in 1924; they added peppermint knobs (or nobs) and hard bread, both Newfoundland favourites, to the product line.[70] New manufacturing facilities were built in the 1950s. In addition to producing their own lines, Purity does private-label manufacturing for Mrs. Alison's, Royal Pilot, and Heritage Mills, and functions as distributors for Jade mushrooms and mandarin oranges, Barbour's peanut butter, King Cole tea, and Lees snowballs. The owners sold the company to Doug Spurrell and Gerry Power in 2004.[71]

Purity Factories occupies two buildings on the same plot of land in St. John's. Candy and jam production occur in one end of a building, with the baking department in an adjacent alcove; the two areas are connected by a shipping corridor, above which are offices. In a separate building, syrup production (beverage concentrates) takes place. The syrup department is seasonal, with production primarily for Christmas. The baking line is long, beginning at the far end of the main building. Much of the packaging in the bakery is done by hand; trays for biscuit packages are filled in this way, for example. Most of the candy manufacturing is also done by hand, though in this department, packaging is largely automated.[72]

In Purity's candy department, peppermint knobs are cooked in a closed copper kettle. Each batch requires forty-four kilograms of sugar. Once the candy has cooked, it is poured out onto flour. Broken pieces of peppermint knobs from previous batches are mixed in, along with peppermint flavouring. A portion of the candy is then cut off and set aside: colouring is added to it, and it is later returned to the candy batch to create a striping effect. Portions of approximately six kilograms are transferred to an enclosed vertical mixer on a water-cooled table. The candy is then moved onto a water-heated table, and pieces of it are stretched and pressed by hand against the coloured portion that had been reserved for striping. The candy is stretched, cut, and pressed back together repeatedly to create multiple stripes. The goal is four to five stripes per peppermint knob, achieved solely through the skill of hand and eye. Two men are set to this task, which requires considerable strength. Speed is also needed, as the candy cools quickly.[73]

Once the multiple striping effect has been achieved, the batch is fed into a machine that stamps out the knobs. The candy exits the machine as a lumpy sheet, and two women are employed to break the knobs from the sheet by smashing them with the flat of their hands. They pick out misshapen knobs, to be returned to later batches for reprocessing. The finished knobs are shaken with sugar to prevent them from sticking together in packaging. The entire process is negatively affected by humidity: on humid days, more women are employed on the line to speed the process. Automated bagging machines are used, which weigh the correct amounts for packaging and screen for metal fragments that might have been introduced by the machinery.[74]

Purity was not able to sustain themselves purely as a confectioner, and so added a baking department in the 1930s.[75] In the baking department, a long production line runs the length of one of Purity's two buildings. From a dough mixer, dough is sent to a proofing room. Male workers operate the dough mixer and feed the proofed dough through rollers. Automated machinery and a conveyor system carry the rolled dough through to a cutter and on through the bake ovens. Trimmed dough left over when the cookies are cut is recombined with dough at the start of the line; thus, the only wasted dough is that produced at the end of the day.[76] From the ovens, cookies

Figure 40. Purity Factories gift box, 2013.

Figure 41. Purity Factories mural on syrup plant, 2013.

move along an overhead conveyor to the packing line. Women workers stand on either side of the packaging conveyor and pack by hand. Five to twenty women work on the packing line, depending on what is being made. Sixteen women, for example, are needed to pack the round milk lunch biscuits. Most of these workers are middle-aged or older, and are so familiar with the work that they are able by sight to pick up just enough off the conveyor at one time to fill a row in a package, minimizing their movements.[77] A business student, viewing this same process on a tour of the Purity factory in 1933, stated that "it appears that they have to learn how to pack the biscuits in, how many of each kind, and the arrangement of them. Quite a feat of memory, I should call it!"[78]

Several of the items produced by Purity are Newfoundland specialities. Jam jams (soft cookies sandwiched with jam) are one of their most popular cookies, for which Purity makes their own jam.[79] Hard bread (also known as hard tack or pilot biscuits, whose sole ingredients are flour, water, and salt) is a key ingredient in the Newfoundland dish known as fish and brewis (hard bread boiled with codfish and salt pork).[80] Hard bread is also ground by Purity and sold to locals who use it to make moose sausages. Flaky pilot biscuits are popular with northern Canadian communities; it is soaked in water and then fried with butter and onions.[81]

Purity Factories workers are unionized. Members of the Newfoundland and Labrador Association of Public and Private Employees (NAPE/NUPGE) Local 7013, they were locked out in August 2010, after contract negotiations broke off and a strike vote was taken. Co-owner Doug Spurrell claimed the lockout was for the safety of the product, but employee Susan Reid offered a different explanation: "There's the kings, the lord and the peasants."[82] The *CBC News* reported that the employers' final offer was "a raise of between 25 cents and 35 cents per hour over five years" (on an average wage of sixteen dollars an hour) plus "a crackdown on sick days and more company control over annual leave."[83] Half of the fifty-two workers at the plant had been employed there for over thirty years, and an additional five had worked there for more than twenty years.[84] One female employee, featured in a CBC news report, had worked at Purity for forty-seven years without either benefits or a pension plan.[85] Working conditions, which included factory temperatures of close to forty degrees Celsius in summer, were also an issue.[86] The four-month lockout ended in January 2011, when workers accepted a contract that provided for a three-dollar increase per hour over five years.[87] A month later, however, a number of layoffs were initiated.[88]

Bunn Cooze is one of the unionized workers at Purity. Since her hiring in 1974, she has participated in three strikes (in 1986, 1997, and 2010). "We had a grand old time" on the picket line, she recalled. Reflecting on the 2010 lock-out, she observed, "They were set in their ways and we knew what we wanted . . . we did get what we wanted, but we got layoffs to go with it." The main issue, she said, was money.[89] Though Purity's workforce has been willing to strike for improvements in wages and working conditions, management has been able to use the seasonal nature of the work to limit worker gains.

Cooze began working at Purity Factories in 1974, as a seventeen-year-old high school graduate.[90] It was a difficult place to get a job, she said, as it paid well compared with McDonald's. Her first two months on the job involved standing in one spot, packing hard bread. She then moved up on the line to packing jam jams. For sixteen years, she worked in Purity's bakery department, then became a syrup mixer in 1992. Syrup making is a seasonal job, as most sales are at Christmas: "Everyone buys it for Christmas with a piece of fruit cake," she said. To make syrup, she drives a forklift, hangs a 910-kilogram bag of sugar, brings it upstairs, and mixes it with water and flavouring. It is then delivered to the women workers downstairs, who bottle it, making nine batches a day. She unloads the bottles in the shipping department during the off-season. On occasion, she works in the candy department or wherever else she is needed. On the day of our interview, she was packing hard bread. When she began working in the syrup department, two women would produce 200 bottles per day. Now three women produce 500 cases a day. This improvement in efficiency is why she works in other departments during the off-season for syrup production. Everything used to be bagged by hand, but now packaging is largely automated.

The workforce at Purity consists primarily of women.[91] Cooze stated that the bakery department employed approximately twenty-two women and fifteen men. Two men and two women worked in the candy department.

One woman and two men produced jam. Syrup production employed four women, and packing had two to four men (and, occasionally, Cooze herself). All workers are employed full time, but during the slow season, they are laid off. Before holidays, Purity increases production in the bakery department. If not as much is sold as was expected, workers could be laid off for a week until the product sells again. They are given two weeks' notice that they will be laid off for one week. She notes that for the younger workers with mortgages, this can be difficult, but it is not a big problem for those who have been employed at Purity for a long time. The majority of Purity workers, she says, have been there for more than thirty years. In a provincial economy with few options for women with limited education, Purity is able to retain workers for decades.

Browning Harvey

For years, Purity's main Newfoundland competitor was Browning Harvey, a firm that produced many of the same products as Purity: confectionery, hard bread, and biscuits. Browning Harvey also made "aerated waters" (carbonated soft drinks).[92] The company began in 1931, the result of the merger of A. Harvey & Company Limited (founded in 1865; shippers and manufacturers of hard bread) and G. Browning & Son (founded in 1860; a bakery and biscuit factory). After the merger, the business expanded to include two factories and added candies and soft drinks to their product list; since 1944, they have been the exclusive Pepsi bottler in Newfoundland and Labrador, and soft drinks are now their sole product.[93] In the 1940s, however, Browning Harvey confectionery products included all-day suckers, marshmallow squares, "coco bits," "monty bars," chocolate all sorts, licorice mint whirls, jumbo cubes, "refreshers," licorice all sorts, cough drops, "milky licks," caramels, assorted kisses, peppermint knobs, and "XL mixture."[94] Purity produced a greater selection of candy than did Browning Harvey; Purity also distributed candy for Lowney and McCormick, while Browning Harvey distributed for the less popular David & Frere and Adler's.[95]

The Browning Harvey candy department received some upgrades in the late 1940s. A new chimney and oil-fired furnace were installed. Dressing and rest rooms, as well as additional toilets, were added for the female workers.[96] The plant manager recommended replacing some machinery parts on the firm's eight cutting and wrapping machines, installing ductwork and a blower over the department's oil fires, and installing new equipment and washing facilities in the marshmallow room.[97] By 1951, however, the candy department had been eliminated, replaced by a bakery plant expansion.[98]

Browning Harvey often looked to its competitor, Purity, for ideas for improvement. Browning Harvey's general manager, Eric Ellis, toured the Purity Factories bakery in 1952 and again in 1953, and concluded that Purity had the competitive advantage in that department as well as in confectionery. Ellis noted that Browning Harvey was "trying to produce biscuits at a profit with old fashioned equipment," and could not succeed. With their advanced equipment, Purity needed only "two men, one girl" to produce the equivalent number of lemon cream biscuits that could be made at Browning Harvey by nine men and one woman working a twelve-hour shift. Ellis concluded, "A few years ago they [Purity] were in the same position as we find ourselves, today, and it is now common knowledge what they have done to meet Mainland competition and reduce production costs as low as it is possible."[99] Browning Harvey biscuits could not compete in an overseas market, Ellis suggested, as they were "packed in wooden boxes with open seams, where and how they are stored after leaving the factory and the consumers rarely receiving the biscuits tasting the same as when they left the oven."[100]

The 1950s were a decade of serious financial challenges at Browning Harvey. In 1951, they reported significant losses due to their English biscuit and jam departments.[101] Having lost $50,000 in six months, the board concluded that it "would be necessary to cease operating" if these departments continued in this way.[102] Despite the introduction of new sandwiching and biscuit-stacking machines earlier that year, profitability had not improved.[103] The financial challenges of these departments had implications for the remainder of the business: workers at the company's West End plant had their request rejected for a wage increase of ten cents per hour for a fifty-hour work week, due to the losses at the English biscuit plant.[104] Wage increases of 7 percent for office and sales staff were approved, however. Workers at the West End plant responded by joining the BCWIU; the board responded by contesting the application for certification with the Labour Relations Board.[105] Increased efficiencies in the English biscuit department—primarily through the introduction of new machinery—resulted in hiring three more men and releasing thirty-one women.[106] By the end of the year, company profitability had returned: Christmas bonuses were paid, though less was spent on cash gifts and Christmas poultry than in the previous year.[107] Financial challenges persisted, particularly in the face of competition with Purity Factories, and one of Browning Harvey's two bakery plants was closed in 1958 (despite management's doubts that doing so would prevent further losses).[108]

Browning Harvey attempted to resist unionization. The board argued, not surprisingly, that "the best interests of both the employees and ourselves" would be served by the formation of a company union instead.[109] Certification proceeded despite their objections, and the board's attention shifted to negotiating the first contract. The union wanted a closed-shop clause and job classifications resulting in wage increases totalling $20,000; a draft agreement was approved in conciliation.[110] Four years later, BCWIU continued to push for the closed shop.[111]

Manager Eric Ellis was not surprised that the company's workforce had unionized. Referring to the West End plant, he told the board of directors: "I have no hesitation in stating that the unrest among the employees over wages has worked to the disadvantage of the Company for many months. Including the Overseers they have not been inclined to take special interest in their work."[112] He observed that, having joined the BCWIU, "it cannot be expected that [workers] are going to be satisfied in the future, as in the past, working forty-eight hours a week without a half holiday and working nearly every other night."[113]

Survivors of deceased Browning Harvey employees had their own reasons for dissatisfaction with the company. When a retired employee who had been receiving a pension[114] of thirty dollars per week died and his pension was terminated, his sixty-year-old widow asked Browning Harvey for financial assistance. The board opted to cover the funeral expenses for her husband and pay her an annuity of forty-five dollars per month (seventy-five dollars per month less than her husband had been receiving). Four years later, they reduced that survivor benefit still further, to only twenty-five dollars per month.[115] In 1958, six years after her survivor benefit reduction, the widow contacted the company again, asking for confirmation that the twenty-five dollars per month was to be in perpetuity. She was informed that the amount was to have been paid only for one year, and that her financial assistance was terminated.[116]

Browning Harvey has survived to the present by becoming the bottler for Pepsi on the island in 1944.[117] With postwar advances in refrigeration and the decline of the Maritime shipping industry, there is no longer as much need for hard bread. Newfoundland joined Confederation in 1949, and so Canadian foreign confectionery firms suddenly became domestic. Browning Harvey's list of competitors thus expanded from Purity to include mainland Canadian companies. Confectionery had been eliminated earlier, due to competition from Purity. Baking was soon terminated, and so the bottling contract became the company's sole business.

Scott-Bathgate

Scott-Bathgate is one of the oldest confectioners in western Canada. In 1903, A.E. Scott and James Loughrin Bathgate began the business in Winnipeg, Manitoba, building their own facility at 149 Notre Dame Avenue in 1906. They doubled their square footage in 1910, but a fire in 1917 destroyed everything.[118] In 1920, Joseph K. May joined the staff, becoming a director five years later and vice-president in 1932. In 1937, he bought a controlling interest in the company.[119]

By 1953, Scott-Bathgate had expanded considerably. The company had branches in eight cities: Fort William, Calgary, Edmonton, Vancouver, Regina, Saskatoon, and Victoria. The company proudly boasted in a special section of the *Winnipeg Tribune*: "The venture into the western branch policy satisfied the promise that Scott-Bathgate Ltd. would grow with the country, and help the country grow by its policy of service to its customers."[120] Scott-Bathgate owned four buildings in Winnipeg in the 1950s. The company's divisions included the head office; the seed division; and a soda fountain, fruit, and syrup division. Products included Nutty Club brand candies, nuts, fountain fruits and syrups, popcorn, mustard, and Dan Dee seeds. Scott-Bathgate celebrated their fiftieth anniversary in 1953, at which time forty-nine of their employees (including some secretaries, supervisors, managers, accountants, nut processors, warehousemen, chemists, carpenters, and salesmen) were also shareholders.[121]

The 1950s were the heyday of Scott-Bathgate. The firm owned their own fleet of cars and trucks (Austins, Fords, and Pontiacs), which were housed and serviced in their own 2,090-square-metre, two-storey, ninety-stall garage at 131 Portage Avenue.[122] The company owned three other buildings in Winnipeg, totalling an additional 9,290 square metres. The head office and the facilities for production of nuts, popcorn, peanut butter, and cellophane bags were at 149 Notre Dame Avenue. The Dan Dee seed division had been created in 1943, and a building at 80 Lombard Avenue was purchased to house it.[123] A dedicated carpentry shop in the Lombard building also produced sales racks for Nutty Club displays in retail outlets.[124] The factory at 149 Pioneer Avenue made candy, mustard, food colouring, sunflower seeds, and nuts. The company's fourth building was the former Eaton's warehouse on Alexander Avenue.[125]

Much of the success of Nutty Club in the 1950s was due to its president, Joseph K. May. It was under his leadership that the expansion of the company occurred, transforming the business from distribution to production. The company's famous Can-d-man mascot was instituted in this era. In the 1930s, red and white stripes replaced the original Nutty Club colours of orange and black created in 1928.[126] These colours were carried over to the new Can-d-man mascot: red-and-white-striped candy cane pieces served as the top-hatted mascot's body and limbs.[127] Celebrating the company's fiftieth anniversary, May credited the youth and enthusiasm of his staff for the company's success. Fred Dodds, appointed senior vice-president in 1944, had joined the company as a fifteen-year-old bicycle messenger in 1925.[128] Most of Scott-Bathgate's

Figure 42. Scott-Bathgate factory signage, Winnipeg, 2013.

executives and salesmen were young men in their twenties. But, in the special section of the *Winnipeg Tribune*, mention was also made of a "Miss M. Ross, who is a trained seed analyst, and is in charge of the [seed division] laboratory and is responsible for maintaining quality checks."[129]

Salesmen played a key role in the success of the company in the 1950s. These eighty-two men, the *Tribune* section reported, were "extremely important. . . . In [the salesmen's] strength is the company's strength and growth."[130] Scott-Bathgate salesmen went to extreme lengths, at times, to secure sales. According to the *Tribune*, Bob Frizzell, for example, sailed a specially equipped boat to cover his territory "from Vancouver to the Alaskan border and over to the Queen Charlotte Islands and the northern tip of Vancouver Island."[131] His boat was outfitted with Scott-Bathgate goods on panels that folded away during sailing. Jack T. Speirs serviced his territory of northern Manitoba, Saskatchewan, and Ontario by plane. Speirs explained his sales technique: "The travelling salesman is consulted by every storekeeper in the north on new merchandising ideas, on new merchandise and transportation. He helps each solve his problems and he becomes a sort of clearing house on merchandising and transportation ideas—a valued visitor where he goes. He helps his customers save time, money and effort by giving to each the knowledge of all in deciding on what to buy and how to sell it."[132] In the *Tribune* article, Scott-Bathgate management endorsed this approach and linked it to nationalism: "There you have it—in that last paragraph. The value of a salesman: A man helping develop a country's economy."[133]

Scott-Bathgate produced some products themselves, contracted other manufacturers to produce items that they then packaged as their own, and distributed other companies' brands. Though they were perhaps best known for Nutty Club candies, they did not manufacture these themselves. Paulins and Cavalier made these products for Nutty Club.[134] The former director of manufacturing at Paulins, Tom Yasumatsu, explained, "Back in those days, it was like Paulins and Scott-Bathgate Ltd. fighting with each other, but the candy was all coming from the same place. . . . [Scott-Bathgate] had the facility but the equipment would cost a heck of a lot, so why do that if we were willing to sell them our products? I had no problems with that. They got it dirt cheap. We maybe just made a nickel over cost price. But, it kept our people employed. . . . They just got the candy, put into onto their packaging equipment, and banged it out."[135]

Other confectioners in Winnipeg at the time included Progress Candy, but, Yasumatsu explained, "they did ten pounds to our [Paulins] million. . . . Progress Candy is gone now.[136] Scott-Bathgate (Nutty Club) never made their own candies. We were really the only big candy manufacturer here."[137] Scott-Bathgate was the exclusive distributor in western Canada of Dare's cookies.[138] Like Purity, they manufactured "fruit cordials" which, the *Winnipeg Tribune* reported, were "sold to general stores for housewives to make their own cold drinks."[139] They were the first in western Canada to retail nuts in cellophane packaging.[140] Under their own brand name, they also sold candies, marshmallow crème, peanut butter, popcorn, hot chocolate, pancake syrup, cake decorations, food colouring, mustard, and cellophane bags. They were the exclusive distributors in western Canada for a variety of international foodstuffs and household goods.[141]

Mustard production and nut processing were two major components of Scott-Bathgate's business. They were the only company in Canada to grow, grind, process, and sell their own mustard.[142] Every year, they contracted farmers to plant 610 hectares in Manitoba, using their own seed from Dan Dee, Scott-Bathgate's registered and pedigreed seed division. At their Winnipeg plant, they would grind the harvested mustard seed, transfer it to a 1,515-litre vat filled with vinegar, and stir it for twenty-four hours. It would then receive a final grinding before being packaged for sale.[143] Scott-Bathgate purchased peanuts and other nuts, and kept them in cold storage before roasting them. The *Tribune* described a process whereby a hopper sent the nuts into "a revolving, gas-heated drum. The chaff is drawn away from the roasted nuts. They are then cooled."[144] Sandpaper rollers removed the nuts' skins. Women working at a conveyor belt would hand pick the defects. The conveyor ended in "a revolving perforated drum" that allowed small or broken nuts to fall through the holes for removal prior to packaging.[145]

May was succeeded as company president by Jim Burt, who joined Scott-Bathgate in 1959. Burt had been a pilot for Trans Canada Airlines. He later married Joseph K. May's daughter, and became company president in 1972. The majority shareholders of Scott-Bathgate have been members of the May family since 1933.[146] Jim Burt has not had as much success with Scott-Bathgate as with another company he owns, Gravure International. Burt, David McMillan (then president of Dad's Cookies, Toronto) and Robert May (son of Joseph K. May) became partners in Gravure International, a flexible packing company, in 1973. After RJR Nabisco acquired Dad's Cookies, Burt and May bought out McMillan to become sole owners. Gravure has plants in Toronto, Vancouver, Winnipeg, North Carolina, and Italy.[147] They make printed packaging for Nabisco, Beatrice Foods, Paulin-Chambers (before it closed), Dad's Cookies, Weston Foods, Scott-Bathgate, and Dare Foods.[148]

Scott-Bathgate, unlike Gravure International, has had difficulty competing in the marketplace. The company changes 200 of the 2,000 items it produces and 2,000 items it distributes every year. Burt explained, "The food business has become a tough, tough business. It has become a lot more competitive and it's falling into fewer and fewer hands. There aren't nearly the number of small corner stores and independent stores that there used to be, so it's become a lot more difficult for us to grow.... Mr. May used to say, 'We live in the cracks that the big boys can't fill,' and he was right."[149]

In January 2007, the company moved most of their production from their buildings at Pioneer and Lombard to the former Eaton warehouse on Alexander. Burt described the emptying Pioneer building: "We moved so much through here—this used to be chock-a-block full of product."[150] The aging building is inadequate for contemporary manufacturing: its loading dock is too small for modern trucks. "We had to turn away orders because we had no space. It was madness," Burt said. The plan is eventually to move the company's entire operation to Alexander Avenue, leaving the Pioneer building vacant. Scott-Bathgate no longer owns a fleet of vehicles, and its parking garage has been turned into a surface parking lot managed by Impark.[151] Advertising has also declined over the years. Scott-Bathgate used to be a major sponsor of Kiddies Day at Salisbury House in the 1940s, providing free candies and free rides "in Nutty Club's Fleet of Austins," advertised by Salisbury House in the *Winnipeg Free Press*.[152] Under Burt's leadership, promotion has focused on supermarket displays rather than on sponsorships or television and newspaper ads. Burt explained that their confectionery was "an impulse item.... How often are you persuaded to buy a candy item after watching a television commercial?... The candy industry has never held up well.... It is like the rest of the food business. Everybody tells you, 'Get into the grocery business. It is depression-proof.' There has never been a large profit because the merchandising in the business is keen."[153]

Despite its current struggles for survival, Scott-Bathgate's Nutty Club remains iconic for many Winnipeggers. A contemporary art exhibit based on the company was housed at the empty Nutty Club building on Alexander Avenue in 1988.[154] The exhibit featured artistic representations of, and reflections on, Nutty Club, including Eleanor Bond's *Nutty Club Works* and Lorna Mulligan's *Putting Brecht in a Bag* photo essay (which integrated stories from Nutty Club employees with quotations from playwright Bertolt Brecht). A video by Barb Hunt was described by the *Winnipeg Free Press* as a documentary with fantasy elements: the pink candied popcorn produced by

Nutty Club resembled "lava, jewels, fungus, etc." The video concluded with workers "emptying bags of pink popcorn on the factory floor and then treading through it with a mixture of perplexedness, wonder and slightly nervous glee. That may look silly in print, but the effect is cheering. No suggestion of sabotage here, only of workers' playtime, making the factory fun."[155]

Workers may remember the firm somewhat differently, and not necessarily as fun. The local newspaper's obituaries recount the stories of employees who spent formative years—or their entire working careers—at Scott-Bathgate. Dolores Williams's family recalled that her "career as a mustard jar filler was short-lived when the assembly line with the jars she was supposed to fill got ahead of her and ended up all over the floor. She found greater success working at the Red Cross Blood Donor Clinic."[156] According to her obituary in the *Winnipeg Free Press*, Lillian Rouble raised a family while working both at Nutty Club and the Dominion Theatre five days a week "to make ends meet. On Saturday mornings she worked cleaning houses, in the afternoon she would go shopping to the Main Street market, purchasing meats and fresh produce, planning next week's meals."[157] Working conditions and wages at Canadian confectioners—even unionized ones like Purity—were undoubtedly difficult. Yet, many working women relied on these employers to sustain themselves and their families. Whether they can continue to do so in the future is an open question.

When sugar is reviled as "the principal poison in our diets," according to a *New Yorker* article,[158] what are candy makers like Dolores Williams, Lillian Rouble, William Burbine, Clarence Gould, and Bunn Cooze to make of their life's work? Samira Kawash observes that "candy is the one kind of processed food that proclaims its allegiance to the artificial, the processed, the unhealthy. This is something I really like about candy: it's honest. It says what it is. But this honesty also makes candy an easy target."[159] Candy, a product that has been consumed for more than a century, must be understood in light of the business and labour history presented here.

Consumers, rather than producers, have been the focus of much contemporary discourse on candy. In an article in *Environmental History*, Jane Dusselier proposed that popular "images of white middle-class women as indulgent, seductive bonbon consumers" first emerged in the nineteenth century.[160] Cheap sugar in that time period made candy "more accessible to larger groups of younger people, represented freedom and pleasure to children, and the danger of independence to reformers who wanted to control people's intake of sugar, especially in the form of confectionery."[161] Yet, the skilled labour of artisanal candy makers, largely unchanged in over a century, has been rarely examined. In their book *Candy Bites*, Richard and AnnaKate Hartel say these workers "had the 'feel' of the candy and could often tell when a candy was done by their sensory evaluation (visual, feel, smell, etc.)."[162] These skills might not survive another century; we should appreciate them while we can.

Very few Canadian confectioners have been able to survive solely as manufacturers of candy. Purity, Browning Harvey, and Scott-Bathgate, for example, also produced seeds, spices, nuts, condiments, beverages, and baked goods. Candy making could be a family tradition and source of pride, as at Robertson's, or a struggle for financial survival, as with the workers at Purity Factories. In a world in which sugar has been added to so many foodstuffs, and in which mass-produced candy is so cheap, it is difficult for some of these firms to persist, as evidenced by Browning Harvey. Diversification beyond candy has been key to continued endurance for Purity, while specialization has been Cavalier's and Robertson's approach. Whether Scott-Bathgate also can navigate a way forward remains to be seen. Perhaps more so than any other branch of the Canadian snack food industry, confectionery has a wide range of business models. Not all are seemingly destined to survive.

7

KIDS BIDS TELEVISION

Advertising and Child Consumers

"That was our dream! We wanted that bicycle!"

——— ALFRED ADAMS, INTERVIEW, 2013 ———

A children's television show that was designed to increase their families' potato chip consumption would be poorly received in many quarters today. On the Canadian prairies in the 1960s, however, such a program had a tremendous following. Children between the ages of four and twelve would appear on the show, competing for prizes that ranged from dolls that peed on command to lime-green banana-seated bicycles. Their entry ticket to this competition was the physical evidence of past consumption of Old Dutch potato chips. Empty packaging was the currency used to place bids in an auction for prizes.

While, on its surface, *Kids Bids* may be viewed as a classic example of the commercial exploitation of children, there is much more to the story. The children who participated in this program mobilized their communities in a common goal: neighbours, co-workers of their parents, family members, and others were asked to save box tops and bags—not usually by increasing their consumption, but by scouring their neighbourhoods for discards. Children of working-class families used the opportunity to acquire the coveted consumer goods that their parents were financially unable to purchase for them. Children learned lessons in sharing and in handling disappointment.

Perhaps most importantly, children had a treasured opportunity to take the lead, doing something for themselves, without the usual adult supervision.

Old Dutch Kids Bids

Many western Canadians of a certain age share memories of this series of locally produced television shows that aired in the 1960s. Created by Robert Watson of Watson Advertising, the auction-format programs involved children's placing bids on toys, using empty Old Dutch packaging as "points" instead of money. The grand prize was almost always a bicycle. Different versions of the show were produced at various local television stations in northwestern Ontario, Manitoba, Saskatchewan, and Alberta. Each featured a host who interviewed the children to put them at ease, and an auctioneer who supervised the bidding. Some fans of the show also remember attractive young women dressed in Dutch costumes who displayed the prizes to be won. The "Old Dutch girl" in the Winnipeg studio was recalled by one interviewee as particularly eye-catching: "I think every guy in the city was wanting to get into her pants. She was a very nice woman, actually."[1] Program hosts included Cal Dring, Bud Riley, and Jack Masters in Thunder Bay; Gary Gibney, Verne Prior, Reid Brown, Greg Barnsley, Jeff Howard, and Ron McFayden in Saskatoon; Stu MacPherson and Bob Burns in Winnipeg; Ed Kay in Edmonton; and Bob Lang in Lethbridge.[2] Auctioneers included Meyer Steiman in Winnipeg; Maurice Fennell in Thunder Bay; Bill Story and Glen Blacklock in Saskatoon; and the O'Haras in Edmonton.[3] Other television stations that hosted the show included those in Medicine Hat, Regina, and Calgary.[4] The program typically aired on Saturdays at lunch or supper time; it was usually aired live, and occasionally taped for later broadcast.

Verne Prior was one of the many prairie hosts of *Kids Bids,* hosting two versions of the show in Regina and in Saskatoon in the 1960s. He grew up in Winnipeg, attending Glenlawn High School, the University of Manitoba, and the University of Winnipeg, "and never succeeded at anything I did! So I packed it up, went into broadcasting."[5] His broadcasting career began with a job in student radio at the University of Manitoba. He learned that Weyburn,

Saskatchewan, was starting a radio station, and so wrote them, asking for a job, addressing the letter and his audition tape to "New Radio Station, Weyburn, Saskatchewan." They hired him as their news director in 1957. Shortly thereafter, CBC Radio in Regina offered him a job. From there, he made the transition to television. He, his wife, and their children moved to San Jose, California, "on a whim" and then to San Francisco, where he worked as "a detail man [salesman] for a pharmaceutical company." He spent his days calling on doctors, which was "very competitive, very stressful. . . . Made a decent living, but I didn't really enjoy it." The family moved back to Canada, as Prior wanted to get back into broadcasting. He took a job as morning man at a radio station in Regina before moving to Saskatoon and then to Winnipeg. He left broadcasting in Winnipeg, securing a job in public relations with Air Canada, and was transferred to Montreal. He was subsequently invited to become a senior public relations manager at Manitoba Hydro, following which he did a stint at BC Hydro. His final job before retirement was in public relations at BC Gas. He reflected, "Crazy career, but it worked for us!"[6]

Prior recalled that snack foods played a limited but memorable role in his life when he was growing up in the 1940s. He received an allowance of several cents a week, which he would use to buy candy at a local drugstore. His favourite candy was something called "black balls," which were black but changed colour as you sucked on them; at their centre was a caraway seed. He also enjoyed Cracker Jack popcorn and chocolate bars. His uncle Bob, "an aging bachelor who had been in the war," would "get off the streetcar, stop in the store, and pick up a bag of goodies for us" when he would visit Prior and his siblings on Sundays. "We loved him for who he was, but we sure loved him for those treats!" As an adult, Prior likes to eat popcorn, nuts, and raisins as snacks. At Christmas, he regularly receives a can of Poppycock caramel-coated popcorn from his children. When he was raising his own family, they would often have a case of mixed soft drinks from Pic-a-Pop or the Pop Shoppe in the house. "Snacks didn't mean much in our lives," he commented, "because we couldn't afford it."[7]

Despite his not spending much money on snacks in his earlier years, Prior recalled the important role they played in community life. He has vivid memories of Pop Kelly, who made and sold snack foods in Winnipeg in the early twentieth century. Kelly had an old Model T truck: "But he'd taken off the back and put up a plexiglass thing. He sat in there with a chair, and parked on the sidewalk . . . and he sold popcorn sitting in this truck on Portage Avenue!" Prior and other Winnipeggers would buy a box of popcorn "popped right there in the back of his truck. He had a coffee pot that he filled with butter and put on a gas stove there and it melted and he poured the butter on—oh! It was a tradition."[8] Kelly's production and sales methods were a sharp contrast to later twentieth-century manufacturing and promotional systems: *Winnipeg Free Press* reporter Christopher Dafoe recalls, "He was a silent sort of man. He did not grin at you as he took your money. As I recall, his face remained expressionless throughout any transaction. . . . There was no display of emotion."[9]

In the 1960s, Prior hosted two versions of *Kids Bids:* the Regina show and the Saskatoon show. He recalled, "It was just a fun thing to do! Saturday afternoon for, I guess, an hour. It was live."[10] The show had a professional auctioneer, Clarence Brown, from Browns Auction House, Regina. Child contestants ranged from ages four to twelve. Points awarded for use in bidding depended on the size and amount of the empty Old Dutch packaging that the children brought. Prizes included bicycles, baseball bats, games, dolls, and various toys. Prior's job was to act as host, introduce the children, and ask them about themselves. He would ask them about their school, siblings, hobbies, and favourite TV shows: as he said, "They weren't serious questions, like who's going to win the next election, or something."[11]

The show's format was very simple. The set consisted of a couple of portable bleachers on which approximately fifty children would be seated. Prizes available to be won were placed on display in front of the bleachers. Prior would choose a prize at random and the auctioneer would conduct the auction. Prior said a third member of the crew was a "young lady dressed up as the Old Dutch queen on the package, in Dutch regalia" who would assist the other two, and whom Prior would call by an invented Dutch name. Prizes would be bid upon and distributed, and then a commercial break would showcase Old Dutch products, after which the show continued. The ultimate prize was the bicycle. He said, "That was the feature prize of the day. . . . When it was wrapped up, we would say goodbye and congratulations to the kids that won, and come back again next week, save your bags and save your boxes or box tops. See you next week! Yeah, it was a good show. Good show."[12]

Alan Cody was a child contestant on the Saskatoon edition of the show, who had memories of the set and format. He and his siblings appeared on the show so frequently that he identified with the production crew, using the pronoun "we" during his interview: "I think we taped on Tuesdays. 'We'—ha! I think we taped on Tuesdays and it aired on Saturday."[13] The auctioneer, he recalled, was usually Glen Blacklock, whose family owned Blacklock Auctions. Cody said, "I don't know if they paid him anything or not, or they just took him for a beer after. . . . It would be like a real auction. You put up your hand to bid." Prizes were typically toys, though, he recalled, the "odd time there were other things, like whatever some store was trying to get rid of, basically, like an electric drill." Toy prizes included "guns that made noise and 'Johnny Seven One Man Army' type things, a lot of board games, dolls, and sewing baskets, stuff like that." After a child won a prize, Cody said, "they'd do a little interview like on the Oscars: 'I'd like to thank my mom and my dad and my dog Trixie.'"[14]

Those appearing on the show were not child actors, but children from the local community in which the show was produced. Some children—like the Cody siblings—would appear on the show more than once, somewhat to the frustration of hosts like Prior, who said, "Kind of gets under my skin a little bit, but we did have some repeats, although not always." Many of these "repeat" children had big bags full of empty packaging, and kept winning. Prior asked one child how they had collected so much packaging, and was told that his father was a garbage collector and would bring it home. "I kind of thought that was unfair," Prior commented. Prior contacted Regina City Hall to complain and was told there was nothing they could do about it: "When that garbage is out, it's out." He said he thought that was "not quite right somehow. . . . I really feel sorry for some of the kids who came out [and couldn't compete]. But they had fun, I think, basically, too, just being on TV and being there." He didn't approve of those who obtained empty packaging from others; he would have preferred that the children used only packaging that they had purchased themselves. Prior explained, "There was no control mechanism; you couldn't regulate it. 'Show me your proof. Show me your purchase receipts.' We couldn't do anything like that so you just had to play on."[15] Prior's son Scott appeared on the show once, but had only about 200 points, whereas children like the garbage collector's son would have 10,000. Scott nonetheless managed to win a small prize once.

Like Scott Prior, Ken Lang was the son of a *Kids Bids* host, who watched the show avidly. Lang, son of Lethbridge *Kids Bids* host Bob Lang, lived for the end of the show, hoping that the winning child would be unable to cope with the moment. In a comment on a blog post about the program, Lang asked, "Do you remember my dad loading 'the winning kid's' arms up with chip bags at the end of the show? I do! It was live TV and the Lang kids, 7 of us, watched the Sears black & white rabbit-ears TV, cheering against chip bag boy. Why? Because the more he dropped the more came home in a big cardboard box to feed us Lang kids. . . . Good memories."[16] Lang's father was surprised by a child contestant on at least one occasion. Karen McAuley recalled that she appeared on the Lethbridge *Kids Bids* show, and was greeted by host Bob Lang, who was "pleased to see that I had a bag of Old Dutch potato chips"—not the empty packaging that children used to place bids, but a bag that appeared to be full. McAuley said, "He commented that I had brought chips to eat in the show and as I dumped the contents onto the large stool on the contestant floor, I said, 'no, just a dead bat I found outside the station!'" McAuley was gratified by the reaction she received: "The show immediately went to commercial while everyone got themselves back under control. It was awesome."[17]

Moments of excitement like McAuley's, and the regular thrill of seeing who would win the bicycle, meant that hosts like Lang and Prior became minor celebrities in their communities. They were often recognized by children outside the TV station as a consequence of their hosting of *Kids Bids*. Prior preferred the recognition of these children to that of adults who knew he hosted televised bingo games and who subsequently asked him why he never chose their numbers. *Kids Bids* was not Prior's favourite hosting job, however. He preferred his time with *Reach for the Top*, a quiz show in which teams of students representing their high schools competed against each other. He commented, "That was probably the most delightful and pleasurable thing I did in my whole career." *Reach for the Top* was more rewarding for him than *Kids Bids* because, with the latter, "the whole objective was to sell Old Dutch potato chips."[18]

Empty Packaging for Prizes

Much like Verne Prior, *Kids Bids* creator Robert Watson was a man with a varied career history. Born in Scotland, he left school at age fourteen to enter radio college in Edinburgh and then entered the Merchant Navy.[19] After the Second World War ended, he abandoned plans to become an architect and instead moved to Venezuela to work on a cattle ranch. From Venezuela, he moved to a cattle ranch in Brazil, and then took a job with Shell Oil in Curaçao. He immigrated to Canada in 1952, eventually settling into work in an advertising agency in Calgary in 1960. He formed his own agency, Watson Advertising, in 1966; Old Dutch Foods became one of his largest clients.[20]

There was no American equivalent of the *Kids Bids* television programs. This, despite the fact that Old Dutch Foods had a plant in Minnesota that predated the first Canadian Old Dutch plant in Winnipeg—and despite the hosting of such "kiddie auction" programs by other chip companies in the United States.[21] Old Dutch in the United States did employ the advertising strategy of redeeming empty packaging for prizes, however. Old Dutch founder Vernon Aanenson met entertainer Bob Hope in the 1950s, and created a promotion that allowed consumers to exchange packaging for a free ticket to see Bob Hope.[22] His son, Steven Aanenson, said it was a "huge promotion and a very successful one."[23] The first such promotion was for tickets to see musician and bandleader Fred Waring in the twin cities of Minneapolis and St. Paul: an empty thirty-nine-cent chip bag was worth twenty-five cents toward the one-dollar to three-dollar cost of a ticket. This promotion resulted in a 61 percent sales increase for Old Dutch. The company decided to offer a similar promotion for two Bob Hope shows they booked for the

Minneapolis auditorium.[24] Old Dutch management discussed the possibility of booking shows featuring the entertainers Ed Sullivan, Julius LaRosa, Jimmy Durante, Eddie Fisher, Martha Raye, and Liberace. Vernon Aanenson declared, "We consider it [the Fred Waring show] an experimental though highly promising promotion. We feel there's a good chance that something entirely new in the way of food merchandising may have its successful 'first night' right here in the Twin Cities."[25] *Kids Bids* in Canada was similarly "a great success" and "really started us developing brand loyalty,"[26] Steven Aaenson said. An American version of *Kids Bids* was never considered, according to Steve, "probably because we were doing well enough. The United States market at that time was extremely fragmented, you know. There was probably 400 regional snack food companies back in the '50s and '60s. That has really come down to quite a few less than that now. It's probably less than sixty at this point. . . . [They've been] bought out or gone into bankruptcy. Quite a few have gone into bankruptcy."[27]

Kids Bids was Old Dutch's most significant advertising campaign in Canada. Former Old Dutch plant manager Martial Boulet recalled, "Oh, yeah. We made good when we had *Kids Bids*. It was good. But we had to go pick up all these bags and we had to count them to make sure they were right. Because we didn't want anyone to cheat on bidding. . . . You could not find an Old Dutch bag on the street, no place, along the fence when the wind had blown. None. Anybody saw a bag of Old Dutch, when *Kids Bids* were on, they were picked up."[28] *Kids Bids* was so popular that there was actually a secondary market for empty Old Dutch packaging. Classified advertisements in the *Winnipeg Free Press* offered potential buyers the opportunity to accumulate Old Dutch points quickly. "Old Dutch Wrappers (Total 5,865) Best Offer," read one such ad in 1962.[29] Other sellers offered empty packaging worth 20,000 or 25,000 points.[30] The show's popularity also meant that Old Dutch had to take steps to ensure that there was no cheating. Staff in Calgary had to pick up and count the bags that children carted to the television shows to confirm their point value (though in Winnipeg, Saskatoon, and Regina, there apparently was no such confirmation process). In one instance, a bunch of chip bags that had never been used were taken from the garbage at the Old Dutch plant in Calgary and used on the local *Kids Bids* show. Children who won bicycles on the program using these stolen bags were tracked down by the Old Dutch sales department and had their bikes taken away from them.[31] The Old Dutch plant in Winnipeg had their own challenges related to the show. Cascades, who made the cardboard boxes for Old Dutch chips, noticed that someone at their plant was removing the box tops to redeem them for points on *Kids Bids* before the boxes were filled with chips. An Old Dutch employee said, "It was a little bit of funny business going on."[32]

Advertising to Children

Perhaps the first promotional advertising targeting children and offering a bicycle as the ultimate prize was the "Bicycle Bar"—a chocolate bar manufactured in the late 1920s by Manitoba confectioners Hyde-Robertson.[33] Children who purchased sufficient bars could redeem inserts in the packaging for a CCM bicycle. To receive a bike, as explained in a Hyde-Robertson advertisement in the *Winnipeg Tribune*, children had to collect "the green numbers, 1 to 48." Collecting the "red numbers, 1 to 24" would earn a "CCM joy-cycle."[34] Other lesser prizes from Spalding's Athletic Goods could also be obtained. For fifteen inserts, children could receive a "Babe Ruth Home Run Special Baseball," a "playground ball," or a baseball bat. Twenty inserts were needed for various baseball mitts, and twenty-five for a tennis racket. "Save all your cards: They are valuable," children were exhorted in another advertisement. "More big prizes to be announced later."[35] No other big prizes were announced; however, the public's "misunderstanding" of the process for winning a bicycle was clarified. Another Hyde-Robertson advertisement in the *Winnipeg Tribune* explained: "There seems to be some misunderstanding as to what is required to entitle a boy or girl to one of these prizes. Obviously it is easy to collect cards 1 to 48 in green, or cards 1 to 24 in red, but these collections must include one card which bears the signature of Hyde-Robertson Limited, otherwise there would be a prize for every 48 or 24 bars sold, and this, of course, is not contemplated and would obviously be a financial impossibility."[36]

In light of advertising errors by merchants and "the disappointment expressed by some of the boys and girls who thought they were entitled to prizes," the company decided to award bikes to all those with the correct card sequence despite the absence of a signature—at least until noon on 25 April 1929.[37] Two weeks later, the company ran an advertisement with a photo depicting the bicycle winners.[38] Children again were encouraged to save coloured and numbered card sequences, with no mention this time of the need for a card with a company signature. This advertisement said, "Save up the green numbers, 1 to 48, and become the proudest bicycle owner in your district—or the red numbers, 1 to 24, and the CCM joy-cycle is yours upon request."[39] These inconsistent rules for prize redemption may have led to the death of the Bicycle Bar, as this ad was its final mention, though Hyde-Robertson continued to advertise as confectioners a year later.[40]

Advertising that targeted children increased in North America after the 1920s, reaching its zenith in the new medium of television in the 1950s and 1960s.[41] In nineteenth-century North America, purchasing decisions had rested with adults, and advertising was accordingly directed to them. But, by the turn of the century, the idea that children could be consumers, too, began to take hold. Victorian family ideals of patriarchal control began to be replaced by the "middle-class companionate family," whose children received pocket money or an allowance.[42] According to Harvey Levenstein in his book *Paradox of Plenty*, the 1950s saw the emergence of a "child-centered culture," while the 1960s transformed teenagers into "a major engine of the economy and culture."[43] Gary Cross, author of *Kids' Stuff*, explains that radio and movies—and particularly television—cultivated "a separate culture of children."[44] Advertisements for toys "spoke directly to children," bypassing parents.[45] The apotheosis of this process was an American television show created in 1955: the *Mickey Mouse Club*. Cross says it "created a new context for selling toys directly to children. . . . [I]ts central feature was the child performers with whom young viewers could identify."[46] According to Barbara Coleman in an article in *Visual Resources* magazine, the show created an "imagined community" of "white, middle-class suburban preteens" who learned "group lessons about consumerism, appropriate social behavior, and good citizenship."[47]

Coleman says the show promoted "an imagined unity created through technology and based on shared generational values and purchasing power."[48]

Partially in response to the overwhelming popularity of the *Mickey Mouse Club,* moralistic concerns about "protecting children from the market" became a significant issue for many white, middle-class adults by the 1970s.[49] Consumer groups such as Action for Children's Television (ACT) and the Council on Children, Media, and Merchandising were formed to put pressure on industry and regulators. The ACT's original reason for existence was to encourage the production of educational television for children, but, by 1971, "it demanded the banning of ads on kids' TV."[50] These public pressure groups succeeded in 1974 with the introduction of new standards by the Federal Communications Commission that reduced advertising to children. These standards lasted until the Ronald Reagan era.[51] Within Canada, the Children's Code has regulated advertising to children since 1974, making a show like *Kids Bids* impossible to broadcast today.[52]

Scholarly interest in the consumer history of children tends to focus on the perspectives of advertisers and other adults rather than on the children themselves. Children are seen as passive recipients of advertising messages, rather than as active agents who engage with these ads and have their own thoughts, feelings, and responses. The purpose of both the *Mickey Mouse Club* and *Kids Bids* was to market products to children. Where the two differed, however, was in the agency of the children involved. On the *Mickey Mouse Club,* children were hired as actors to participate in choreographed dances, songs, or other performances. On *Kids Bids,* children were unpaid and untrained members of the general public. They gave unscripted answers to the questions asked by the show's hosts, and made their own decisions regarding whether, when, and how much to bid on the offered prizes. No record remains of how children felt at the time about their participation in the *Kids Bids* television shows, but it is possible to interview adults who had been child contestants. The memories of these *Kids Bids* participants—with their insights into economic class, sibling rivalry, and hard-earned winnings—reveal that children's advertising could have positive, albeit unforeseen, consequences.

Working-Class Opportunity

Alfred Adams was one of the many people who watched *Kids Bids* on television as a child.[53] He recalled, "Myself and a good friend, as kids, we spent a couple of summers just madly collecting Old Dutch bags and the tops from Old Dutch boxes in order to get as many points as possible. We would go out on our bicycles and just ride around the neighbourhood for nothing else other than looking for Old Dutch products [*laughs*]!" He recalls that each bag was worth ten points, and each box top was worth twenty-five points. He would tie up bundles of box tops and bags with string, and pack them into cardboard boxes, until he and his friend thought they had enough to bid successfully. The *Kids Bids* show featured prizes of increasing value, with the brand-new bicycle usually as the ultimate prize. He said, "That was our dream! We wanted that bicycle [*laughs*]! Because it was a brand new, three speed bicycle, and that was a lot for them days. That's as many speeds as you got in the sixties, was three." The challenge was to decide if they should bid early on a lower value prize, and ensure that they won something, or hold off to bid on something better, but risk not getting anything.

Adams's father, who helped them carry in all their boxes, dropped him and his friend off at the television studio near Winnipeg's Polo Park shopping centre. When the two saw the other children's stockpiles, they realized they did not have very many boxes. Adams recalled, "As soon as we went in, we realized we were not the leaders of the pack here. We thought we had a lot, but there was other kids coming in with more. And we realized, 'Okay, we're not getting the bicycle. We'll have to make a judgement call on bidding on something else,' because we were out-classed as far as quantity goes. It made us wonder, 'Holy mackerel! Some of these kids, how could they possibly get that much?! Does their dad work at Old Dutch?'"[54]

Partway through the show, Adams and his friend decided they needed to start bidding: "I was a kid. I was so nervous I could barely speak. I was going to be on TV!" His friend was the one who made the bids, and they won a "bowling game. I would describe it as a bowling simulator." It was a

> plastic bowling alley, one lane . . . about a metre long. At one end of it was pins that you set up manually . . . at the other end was a plastic figure of a bowler, about 25 centimetres tall. And he was in the position of a bowler throwing a ball but there was a lever so that you could aim him, back and forth, side to side. And his shoulder and elbow were hinged, and his hand was cupped so that you could take a toy bowling ball and put it in his hand. And then you pull the lever back, aimed him, and let it go. And when you pulled the lever back, his arm went back. And when you let the lever go, it thrust forward and released the bowling ball down in the direction you've aimed it.[55]

Adams had never bowled before, and he had fun learning how to score the game using the cards that were included. He played with it with friends in a bowling league they formed, until the game broke after a few months. He remembered, "It was a really nice experience but it took so long to collect that many points, and it took so many of them to bid for even that, that we didn't continue with it and collect any more."[56]

Adams never saw the broadcast of the show, as it apparently aired live.[57] A few days after it aired, a classmate of his told him, "I saw you on TV last night! On *Kids Bids*!" He had been asked in his interview if the *Kids Bids* show made him consume more Old Dutch chips. He said that any time he or his friends ate chips, "there was no question; it wasn't going to be any other brand. It was going to be Old Dutch." He and his friend encouraged their parents to buy Old Dutch on the rare occasions when they did buy chips. Host Verne Prior's description of the show as a commercial arrangement between Old Dutch and the radio station, designed solely to sell more chips, was clearly accurate. Adams concluded his *Kids Bids* experience was "interesting, if slightly disappointing—because we didn't get the bicycle [*laughs*]. And maybe that's a good thing, because how are two kids going to share a bicycle?"[58]

Sharon Moore watched the Calgary edition of *Kids Bids* on Saturday afternoons, and dreamed of winning the bicycle.[59] As her parents earned only one income at the time, they could not afford to buy her a bike. Her family did not eat snack foods, and her allowance was not enough for her to purchase chips in sufficient quantities to make a successful appearance on *Kids Bids*. But, like many working-class children who were fans of the show, she circumvented the program's objectives to sell chips and employed other strategies to accumulate the necessary packaging. Her grandmother, who lived next door to her, had a renter (an older woman named Johanna who had escaped from East Germany) who volunteered to help collect chip bags. Moore was embarrassed by Johanna's efforts, which included collecting empty bags at bingo and sorting through trash. However, she said, "you had to be not too proud to pick up garbage off the ground."[60] None of Moore's friends or relatives collected Old Dutch points, as there was a stigma associated with garbage picking. Together, however, Moore and Johanna were able to collect enough bags to allow Moore to appear on the show three times—it was only on her third appearance that she placed a successful bid on the bicycle. Johanna accompanied her to the show each time, "calming my nerves when I didn't get the bike the first two times."[61]

It took nearly a year to collect enough bags for Moore's first appearance on *Kids Bids*. The family took pride in her public appearance. Her mother insisted, "You've got to look nice if you're going to be on *Kids Bids*."[62] So she wore a dress that her mother made for her. She did not bid on anything except the ultimate prize, the bicycle, on her three appearances on the show. "I was not going to get sidetracked by some stupid Barbie doll," she stated. Her experience of humiliation in accumulating the packaging used for points meant that she would not waste them. Unsuccessful the first two times, she was able to keep the points she had not used. Thus, she had many points by her third time on the show, when she won the bike. Her persistence had paid off, she said: "*I wanted that bike!* I was getting that bike. If I would have had to go on two more times or six more times, I would have done that." From the day she began collecting to the day she won the bicycle was about a year and a half. The bicycle was a red CCM and she kept it "forever," she said. "Oh, I was just over the moon. I was so excited. Highlight of my life! Listen to me, I am 59, almost 60 years old, and I still remember. . . . Everybody knew that I was on [the show]. Everybody knew that I won the bike. I was a celebrity for five minutes." Her grandmother's renter, Johanna, was equally excited; she had no children of her own, and Moore and her siblings "were kind of like surrogate kids for her."[63]

Moore's appearance on *Kids Bids* allowed her to obtain the bicycle that neither she nor her family could afford to purchase. When Moore was older, her mother found paid employment outside the home. It was only then that the family was able to afford to purchase bicycles for her siblings. Since Moore already had a bicycle, she was given a pair of roller skates instead. Moore believes her *Kids Bids* experience taught her discipline; she learned the value of saving and working toward a goal. She said, "It was very positive for me. It's a highlight of my life. It was a good thing. I got something I wanted. It wasn't that much work, although at the time, eighteen months of saving chip bags seems like a long time. But, if I'd had to try to babysit and earn money at thirty-five cents an hour, I'd have been a long time earning that bike."[64] *Kids Bids* afforded this working-class family an opportunity to obtain a commodity that was then viewed as a necessary part of a middle-class childhood. And the family's ingenuity allowed them to do so without participating in the consumption that the show encouraged.

Gloria (no last name given) and her relatives were similarly pleased to be able to obtain bicycles for themselves on *Kids Bids* that they might not otherwise have been able to afford. Gloria had two nieces and a nephew who were the same age as she was. All four of them won bicycles on *Kids Bids*. She recalled, "My nephew got his bike first (he was the oldest), then down the line. All four of us were riding around on our bikes for years."[65] As the older male, however, the nephew did the bidding for all of them. Gloria said, "I did stick up my hand once (which he promptly smacked down as I bid against him) but we did get my bike. It was so much fun." This deference to patriarchy appears to have persisted, as she noted, "I still like auctions, but I don't bid against my husband. Actually, he lets me do the bidding."[66]

Alan Cody and his siblings also came from straitened circumstances, and were able to take advantage of *Kids Bids* to profit not only themselves but also others in their disadvantaged neighbourhood.[67] As a child, Cody watched the show on television and thought, "That looks like fun."

Like Sharon Moore, he found a strategy other than purchasing Old Dutch products to obtain the needed packaging. His father, who worked as a hotel waiter for thirty-five years, saved chip bags from his workplace for him and his siblings. He said, "My dad had all his customers eating chips. I think he sold more chips than beer. He brought all the bags home and got a lot of his customers—you know, the bar was downtown, so they'd pick up bags on the way home. He had everybody working for him." Cody and his siblings would pick up bags at his neighbourhood's two confectioneries, and would collect them from under bleachers at the local baseball diamond. Cody recalled, "There was more chip bags than we could carry half the time. . . . We scavenged. We were worse than seagulls." While Moore was embarrassed by such scavenging, Cody and his family were not: "We didn't know the meaning of that word 'embarrassment.' No, we were poor and greedy [*laughs*]."[68]

Making an appearance on the show required some careful planning and coordination by the Cody family. Prospective contestants had to phone the television studio to make an appointment, as there was room for only twenty to twenty-five contestants. "It was first come, first served," he said.[69] Cody and his family would go to the TV station for the 7:00 p.m. taping of *Kids Bids*. Their station wagon would be loaded with half a dozen large cases of Corn Flakes cereal boxes, each filled with chip bags. His father would rush home on the nights the show was taping, help load the station wagon, help his children carry in their boxes, watch the taping, then help them carry their winnings home. Cody's recollection is that each bag was worth ten points, twin-pack boxes were worth fifty points, and triple-pack boxes were worth seventy-five points. They would keep just the tops of the boxes, and would bundle them in bunches of 100. It would take only a few weeks to collect enough points for a bike, depending on the time of the year, how many sporting events were happening, and how well business was doing at the bar where his father worked. Autumn was the best time, as there were baseball playoffs, and farmers were finished harvesting and would visit the bar. Cody and his siblings appeared on the show at least three or four times to "watch how it worked" without placing bids. "After that," he remembered, "we kind of got really aggressive."[70]

While Sharon Moore had to appear on the show three times before winning her bicycle, the Cody children were able to win several bikes once they began to bid in earnest. Cody said, "Oh yeah, we pretty much took what we wanted. We were greedy little buggers [*laughs*]."[71] Cody's enormous stockpile of chip bags and box tops, together with his knowledge of the auction game, allowed the family to win multiple prizes. And yet, the "greed" Cody described was used to fairly generous ends. He remembered:

> We got eight bikes. My aunt is a nun. They [the nuns] were always trying to raise money. . . . She sent us a few bags and we won her a bike and they raffled it off. Then my uncle . . . his daughter wanted a bike. . . . They sent us chip bags and we got her a bike. We got six more. We kind of ran out of the need for them, so then we'd go down there and get games and tools [such as a Black & Decker drill] for Dad for Father's Day. And a few times, we went down and we just looked around before the taping started and figured, "Well, we like everything that's here," so we'd clean it up. It is funny we didn't get beat up. But, there was quite a few of us. We weren't that big, but there were lots [of us]. There was about three or four times I think we cleaned the whole show out. I'm surprised they even let us back. It was a lot of fun, a lot of work.[72]

The Cody children appeared on the show several times over two or three years. As the oldest, Alan Cody said he "didn't want to go [on the show] when I went into grade nine because, sure as hell, I would have got beat up for that. There wasn't a lot of humour going on about stuff like that. My brothers and sisters took over. . . . We kind of went on like that until they cancelled it. And I'm not sure what year it was. It was a lot of fun."[73]

Cody said that the inspiration to collect Old Dutch bags and appear on *Kids Bids* came from his family's economic circumstances: "Like I said, we were poor. That was a cheap way for us to get stuff. My dad, he just worked in a hotel, it was just basically a little better than minimum wage. There was eight of us. He didn't make that much money. My mom, she was having babies all the time. Like I said, when I was about twelve, she went working part time. You know, so. . . . That was our only way—other than Christmas—to get anything."[74]

It was his father who insisted that they win prizes for people other than themselves. Cody remembered, "We didn't have much choice. My dad said, 'Well, this is the way it's gonna be.' Basically, 'you guys will be walking down [to the TV station].'"[75] For the family, then, *Kids Bids* appearances were an economic strategy to supplement their inadequate income and assist their relatives.

The significance of these appearances for the family's economic survival made Cody more loyal to Old Dutch: "I still, when I do buy chips, they're always Old Dutch. I don't eat that much anymore because I'm diabetic and potatoes are killer."[76] He also prefers the quality and taste of Old Dutch to that of other brands: "Lays is too much in your face. Their product is too strong. It's got a good taste, but it's just too strong for us. No Name stuff is kind of hit and miss on the quality. Old Dutch is pretty good, and they have new flavours every once in a while just like everybody else. . . . Basically force of habit, mainly." He was a salesman for Humpty Dumpty chips as an eighteen-year-old, but, he said, "I don't think I sold $100 worth in a month. Nobody wanted them."[77]

Doug Krochak was another child of a working-class family who appeared on *Kids Bids,* but, unlike Cody and Moore, he was unsuccessful. Krochak's father was a taxi dispatcher and his mother worked at a sewing factory in Winnipeg.[78] She also washed floors at a department store on Selkirk Avenue in exchange for credit to purchase Christmas presents and treats for the family, like apple turnovers. Krochak and his little sister, Kardene Campbell (née Krochak), did not have sufficient points to win anything, as, he said, "one guy basically won everything. . . . We would bid 100 or 200. He would go 1,000, 5,000, and the bidding would be over. So I think he won all the prizes. He won the big doll at the end. He won everything. So it was really a disappointing experience. Probably more so for my sister than it was for me."[79] His sister was so disappointed that she cried, "so they made sure that she got a doll. So we went home with something." The siblings did not watch

Kids Bids again after this experience. Krochak said, "The same kids seemed to win the bulk of the prizes. That just never seemed fair to me. It didn't seem to jive with kids and participation and having fun. Not that everybody had to win something, but everybody had to be in a situation where they thought they would have a chance to win something. And so it got too Hollywood. Too organized. People were really gunning to get—I would have been happy with a prize. These people were gunning to get a whole bunch of prizes."[80] Kardene Campbell recalls running off the stage, crying, at the end of the program. A few days later, some men visited their home to bring her a doll. She commented, "That's kind of that act of kindness that you remember forever."[81] *Kids Bids* is nonetheless a fond memory for her: "Absolutely. Absolutely. It's all a part of growing up. Yeah, it was good. I wouldn't say I am sorry that I did it. Not at all."[82]

Appearing on the show was a major event in Krochak's childhood. Like Moore's mother did for her, Krochak's mother dressed the children in their best clothing, and his older sister took him and Kardene to the TV station on the bus, which was "a big deal."[83] He saw parts of Winnipeg he had never seen before. His parents' co-workers and neighbours, as well as his aunts and uncles, had helped collect points for them. This community involvement was necessary, as their economic circumstances meant that chips were a rarity in his house, reserved for special events and the occasional Saturday. It was only when he was older and his parents were earning more money that chips appeared in his home on a more regular basis. Krochak commented, "It was kind of a neat experience. Every once in a while you think back about it. Sometimes you are just talking with a group, people in our age group, and [someone would say] 'Sold! For 100 Old Dutch points!' And everybody in our age group would know exactly what you were talking about. My kids don't have a clue."[84]

While he stopped watching *Kids Bids* after his negative experience, Krochak maintains a respect for Old Dutch:

> They were local. They were just part of the community. So, when they did *Kids Bids*, it just kind of made sense because they were

> a part of the community. Even today, Old Dutch are involved, I don't know if you know, but in little kids' football. They've got this age group of football they call "Little Crunchers," and Old Dutch provides all the jerseys. . . . Generally, they're just a good corporate citizen. . . . My first choice when I am going to buy chips was, and still is, Old Dutch. I think it is because they have always maintained a certain amount of this "doing good for the community." Now, I know they are trying to sell their product, and everything else, but they go over and above.[85]

Old Dutch was not the only company that had a gaming component to their advertisements in the 1960s, Krochak recalled. Orange Crush bottles used to have cork lids with a letter printed on the inside of each lid: "You had to spell 'DRINK CRUSH.'"[86] If you collected the correct letters to spell the phrase, you would win twenty-four bottles of Orange Crush. "Then, of course," Krochak said, "you'd get even more letters! I drank a lot of Crush." Red Rose tea offered collector cards printed with birds and flowers that could be used to win items. Jello offered collectible photos of football players; the correct combination of photos and three dollars would get you a jersey. Krochak recalled, "At the hockey rink, everyone would be wearing these same Jello jerseys." Krochak enjoyed these advertising games, though he was undeceived about their real motive: "It was blatant commercialism and advertising, but it was fun too. . . . It gave the same sort of sense of excitement that people have at the casinos today." By contrast, he feels that modern promotional advertising does not offer comparable value: "Now I look at some of the promotions today and I don't see fair value. You have to buy so much more."[87]

Nancy-Ellen McLennan also hoped to win the prizes she could never hope to buy, but she never appeared on the show, though she collected points for others and watched the program. She said, "Eventually we figured out that you could never get on the show unless you had fifty thousand Old Dutch Points, so we'd give whatever we had to anyone we knew who collected. I don't think I ever knew a winner. I think all of those kids' parents owned grocery stores."[88] She lived in the North End, one of Winnipeg's poorer neighbourhoods, and she noted that "the best we ever got was one 16-ounce Pepsi to share among three of us. . . . Snacks were only on babysitter days anyway. Maybe our parents were trying to prove to the sitter that we had discretionary income, which we most certainly did not." When she was a child, snacks in her household typically consisted of garden produce, porridge, and shredded wheat. McLennan said, "This menu was the best thing that could have happened to me in my Shaughnessy Heights childhood, because undoubtedly, unlike all of the River Heights kids, I still have all of my teeth and they are sparkling and white. I have no implants, no caps, and no fillings! So there! Actually, I feel lucky that I never earned enough Old Dutch Points to go on the show."[89]

Bob Babiak was born in the North End and later lived in the Maples, two of Winnipeg's poorer neighbourhoods.[90] His mother worked part-time as a cleaner; his father was not able to work much due to physical challenges. Babiak appeared on *Kids Bids* as a twelve-year-old; his father had collected points without telling him. He said, "I was enthused, but I had no idea what I was getting into." He was excited and so bid poorly on the second prize that was offered: a doll that urinated. Babiak recalled, "I think the bid was like 100, 200, 300. And I bet 1000. So needless to say, I won." He told the host that he wanted the doll for his little sister rather than confessing that he had been carried away with the bidding. "And of course," he said, "it was televised so all my mother's friends were all thrilled with the concept of how nice Bob was and he'd bought his sister a doll. But, in truth, it was simply the fact that I had no concept of proper bidding and I just went for the whole thing." He gave it to his younger sister, who was happy to receive it: "At the time, I got a lot of mileage out of being a great boy and winning a doll for [my] sister. All the neighbours and all my mother's friends thought I was terrific."[91] Babiak's panic may have defeated his opportunity to win prizes for himself, but he was able to make his little sister happy and his family proud.

For the children of working-class families, then, *Kids Bids* offered a hope—and sometimes an opportunity—to exercise economic agency. These children mobilized their communities—family, neighbours, co-workers, church bingo-game participants, and Cub Scout troops—to collect the discarded, empty packaging they could not afford to purchase, filled with product, in any significant quantity in stores.[92] They were aware that the ultimate purpose of the show was to increase sales and consumption, but they were able to subvert that purpose to their own ends. *Kids Bids* gave them a chance to win the commodities that were advertised to them as the necessities of the happy, comfortable middle-class lifestyle to which they aspired. Win or lose, Old Dutch had these children's loyalty.

Life Lessons

For some contestants, *Kids Bids* taught them life lessons in fairness, the importance of sharing, dealing with embarrassment, and coping with disappointment. Danny Hooper had great success on *Kids Bids*, winning all the prizes, but—unlike Moore, Cody, and Krochak—he did not do so as a consequence of economic necessity. He took an entrepreneurial approach to the show, and kept all the prizes for himself. He hired other children to collect chip bags, "paying them 10 cents per hundred."[93] The result was 3,500 Old Dutch points, enough to buy "absolutely everything, including a 'Dante's Magic Show—100 Tricks and Illusions To Amaze Your Friends.'" He then used this prize to put on a magic show in his parents' garage, charging twenty-five cents admission. His selfishness was ultimately punished by his mother: "But this business thrived for one weekend only. Once my mom found out I was charging the neighbour kids she made me refund everybody's money. Was I upset? Yes, wouldn't you be after suffering a financial loss of almost $18? Was I bitter? No, because I learned a valuable lesson. Unexpected outside forces, like your mom, can sometimes cause a business to fail."[94]

Robert Fafara and his brother did not win anything on their *Kids Bids* appearance in Alberta, but they didn't stop dreaming of the prizes. Despite "what felt like a lifetime of collecting Old Dutch potato chip bags and box tops," Fafara said, they did not have enough points compared with those of the other contestants.[95] Fafara was "fixated on the replica of an M16 Marauder rifle and foresaw the hours of battles to be won facing the imaginary enemy that lurked throughout Skyland, an undeveloped stretch of property out behind our family home." Watching the show days later, he and his family were "giggling and laughing, ironically eating Old Dutch potato chips and drinking Pop Shoppe Soda. I grabbed the box top and stashed it away in my pocket as I continued to watch the television dream of that M16 and the enemy that awaited me in the foxholes of Skyland."[96] Together with his family, Fafara was able to enjoy the experience rather than lament the lost prizes.

For some, winning could be as disappointing as losing, as Karen Thomas found when she won the ultimate prize of the bicycle. She appeared on the Calgary edition of *Kids Bids* as a six-year-old in 1963.[97] Later, two of her brothers (Ron and Harold Davidson) were show contestants. Her mother was the one who began collecting chip bags, sending her two older brothers every day to a nearby shopping centre to dumpster dive. Thomas said her mother also increased the family's purchases of Old Dutch chips: "She sure did. As much as all of us six little kids could eat. That's for sure." Once sufficient points had been collected, Thomas appeared on the show. Though another contestant had more points, he chose to bid on an AM/FM radio rather than the coveted bike.[98] Thomas recalled, "All of us were just shocked because we all thought that the biggest prize, the best prize was the bike."[99]

Thomas feared public embarrassment when she was faced with a spelling test as a successful bidder on the show.[100] She described a big, glass chalkboard, similar to a window: "When I walked up to this, I thought 'Wow! This is so cool!' It looked so futuristic to me. Because being in school in grade one, you knew what a chalkboard is, but this was *glass*. It was just *crazy*. And that was so that the camera people could view me as I was spelling out, writing out the words on the board." She had to spell two of three words correctly. She was given a white grease pen. Her first word was "yes." Thomas said, "I am a horrible, horrible speller. I have been since I was tiny. I spelled yes as Y-A-S and I got it wrong." She spelled the second word, "no," correctly. The final word was "ill"; she said her family, who was watching, was "devastated. They're just horrified. They think, 'Okay. There's no way Karen's going to spell it with two Ls. This is just going to be a disaster.'" But she spelled the word correctly, and won the bike: "It was very exciting for me. It was very cool. It was lime green.

It had a banana seat and the high-rise monkey handlebars. And at that time, bringing it home, it was the very, very first bike like it in our whole neighbourhood. Nobody had one like that at all, so it was very cool."[101]

Unfortunately, Thomas never got to enjoy her prize: "I regret it to this day. No—*resent* it." Her brother Ron told their father that, as she did not yet know how to ride a bike, she would likely wreck it. "So," as Thomas said, "the bike that *I won,* that was mine, my brother convinced my dad to give over to him. And his bike [that she got in exchange] had two flat tires. So I spent a lot of time going up and down the sidewalk teaching myself to ride the bike on a bike with two flat tires. And I did it! I was determined, and I did it."[102] Even after learning to ride, she did not get to use the bike that she had won. She said, "No, I don't know why, but Ron still kept it. He wouldn't let me on it. Brothers—boy! He was two years older than me."[103] The triumph of the Thomas women—a mother who organized the collecting of points and a daughter who successfully bid on a bicycle—was ended by the patriarchal control of the Thomas men.

Richard Rosin was able to keep the bicycle he won, though his enjoyment of it was delayed for years. Rosin was only five or six years old when he appeared on *Kids Bids* in Winnipeg.[104] His entire extended family collected chip bags. He recalls his mother's purse containing ants due to the discarded, greasy chip bags she would stuff in there. He was so young when he was on the show, he initially forgot that he had to place bids. Nonetheless, he was able to win a blue CCM bike with monkey-bar handles and a white banana seat, as well as other prizes. The bike "was *way* too big," he said, but it was a two-speed, which was "really quite neat."[105] He had to wait years before he was tall enough to ride it. Every year, he would go to the garage and check to see if he could finally ride it. He was about ten years old when he was finally big enough:

> The bike became important because I did have to wait. Dad would bring the thing off the rack in the garage, and I'd sit on the thing in the spring, and it still wouldn't fit even though the seat was as far down as it could possibly go. There was no bloody way! So I always knew that it was something about patience, and

> something about waiting, and because of me winning the bike, it was something about that bike that was special because it was *won*. Mom and Dad didn't have to buy it. It was the first thing that I *know* that I got *on my own*.[106]

While Thomas learned a lesson in gender relations, Rosin learned a lesson in patience and the satisfaction of self-sufficiency.

By contrast, Doug and Gerilyn (Geri) Peterson found that their agency as children on the show was sublimated to the expectations and demands of adults. Doug was eight and Geri was eleven years old when they appeared on *Kids Bids* on Edmonton's CFRN television, hosted by Ed Kay.[107] Their father worked for Canada Packers, and their mother worked full time at a medical clinic. Their father's co-worker gave 40,000 points' worth of chip bags to him and his sister. Their father said, "This guy has done really good for you. He has collected all these points. He just lost his wife. You better not disappoint me. You have to hold out for the bike." Eager to please their father, the family drove to the television station in a blizzard. Doug recalled that the children were taken into the green room with "all these farm kids . . . who had a hundred million points!" The Peterson siblings "panicked," unable to tell their father—who was sitting in the audience—that they did not have enough points to win the bike. They instead successfully bid on Major Mat Mason's Space Station ("a classic of the time") and a makeup jewellery set that "gave [Geri] third degree burns." Doug said that, not having secured the bike, "we knew Dad was going to kill us. . . . We loved him, but we were scared. We got off the show and Dad said, 'I told you guys to hold out for the God damn bike!' . . . He didn't talk to us the whole trip home." They apologized to him for letting him down. Doug said, "You had to be there . . . oh God, Dad's going to kill us! And our Dad was a sweet man, really, a sweet man."[108]

To this day, every time Doug sees a box of Old Dutch chips, he recalls his adventure on *Kids Bids* and his feeling at the time of being trapped like a "deer in headlights."[109] The memory of that event is a part of his family's oral tradition, he said: "It's fun just talking about it. It makes me laugh. I even told my younger sister about it . . . because, of course, she wasn't a part of

Figure 43. Recordings of *Kids Bids* television programs do not appear to have survived. There is a small collection of photographs of the Saskatoon version of the program, however, taken by television studio CFQC, c. 1960s. In this photo, Saskatoon *Kids Bids* host Ron McFayden stands beside shelves of toys to be won, while a woman in Dutch costume stands before a sign reading "Old Dutch Point System" which lists products and their point values. Regrettably, the point values are not in the photo frame.

this story because she wasn't born then. But she knows the story. We all just laugh, laugh about it." His mother finds the story amusing too, because "she knew what our father was like. 'Got to get that God damn bike.'" His father died not long after their *Kids Bids* appearance, and so Doug remembers the event as "one of my vivid memories of my Dad. He has been gone over forty years. I still miss him a lot." As a child with two parents employed outside the home, Doug recalls that convenience foods were readily available in the house: "We didn't think we were poor. But, you know, times were tough. . . . I can't say my Mom prepared much of anything. She just had stuff in the house for us. . . . She did what [she could] to make things easier." His favourite Old Dutch flavour is "salt and vinegar all the way."[110]

Figure 44. Doug Gibson with CCM bicycle won on *Kids Bids*, Calgary, 1962.

For Geri, however, the event was traumatic.[111] She remembers the experience vividly: "The crucial bit of this is that we were then separated from our Dad [in the studio]. He was shepherded off to where the adults went, and we went into the green room with all the other kids. And we were completely alienated by the process. It seemed like all the kids knew everything that there was to know about everything, and we didn't." Neither does she have fond memories of the auctioneer: "It was real star behaviour, and it seems to me, he was a bit sarcastic with the kids, too." After the show was over, she said, "we saw that our Dad was furious. This guy [their father's co-worker] had spent how many years of his life saving chip bags, and what we had bought was absolute garbage. . . . And for him, you see, he was going to have to go back—and this thing had been live, and the guy [the co-worker] had watched it at home, and we had bought crap. He didn't speak to us all the way home. . . . We'd blown it. It really took the shine out of playing with those toys, too." She felt humiliated at the time, because her father felt humiliated. To her, it was "a complete disaster, but just a funny story forty years later."[112]

Unlike her brother Doug, Geri Peterson expresses somewhat conflicted feelings towards Old Dutch. Local television stations, she asserts, were "in bed with all the big companies, which is clearly the Old Dutch story. [It would be] fascinating if Old Dutch let you into any of their records. . . . Because it would be interesting to know just how well that marketing campaign went."[113] She asserts that the Old Dutch "product is outstanding, having done European travel and been exposed to 'crisps' as they are called here. And their product is outstanding." Old Dutch was the only brand of chips her family ate: "And it isn't because of *Kids Bids*. It was just, if we were only having them once in a while, they were the ones to have." She finds it interesting that the show had a family and rural element, encouraging siblings and small communities to collect points together. She described the show as "not all that exciting for kids to watch." Her experience was "distasteful," as she and her brother "felt kind of bullied. . . . It wasn't a gentle kid's show. You really felt there were sharp elbows. . . . It wasn't a nurturing thing at all. . . . It wasn't a happy thing at all. It was *not* a nice experience. . . . I'm upset, though, because Old Dutch is a good product. And that was a horrible experience."

As the older sibling, her brother blamed her for losing the bike, she believed. She joked, "I think we should form a victim support group [*laughs*]."[114]

Kirk McDougall and his sister were contestants on the Regina edition of the show; their experience was not what they had hoped for, but they made the best of it.[115] Their mother (a stenographer) and her co-workers helped the two of them to collect bags and box tops. McDougall recalls, "Yeah, it was kind of fun. I remember that. I remember the camaraderie with my sister and mom trying to look for all the empty box tops and bags."[116] Their goals were to win the race car set and the Barbie dollhouse. They discovered they had sufficient points for only one toy, and so Kirk sacrificed his interests for those of his sister, bidding only on the Barbie dollhouse. He was twelve or thirteen; his sister was five or six years old. "I am glad I did it," he said. "I would hate to have the story now where I took the race car set and my sister [didn't get anything]. But, at the time, it was kind of tough to give up the race car set. I really wanted the race car set. I did, eventually, get a race car set for Christmas one year. So, I did get one. . . . Quite honestly, it was a real little bit of a life lesson for me to give up the race car set for my sister. I felt really good about that. I really did."[117]

Eating Snacks

A couple of *Kids Bids* contestants reflected during their interviews on the role that snacks had played in their lives as children and later as parents. Richard Rosin recalls that Old Dutch chips were always in his family's house when he was a child, and he associated particular flavours with particular events. Sour cream and onion chips were consumed on Saturday nights. Salt and vinegar chips were eaten during the daytime while he was playing or colouring with friends and cousins. "It was always Old Dutch," he said. "You never brought anything else in the house."[118] For youth group fundraisers or socials,[119] Old Dutch would provide a box of chips and pretzels with cardboard serving trays in the Old Dutch colours. Such donations were a way to advertise and to serve the local community. Rosin still eats Old Dutch chips today. He remembers, "Snack foods—it was always a treat. . . . It was something you looked forward to. It wasn't part of 'I'm running to Sev [the 7-11 convenience store], and I'm going to buy a Big Gulp [a large soft drink] and a bag of chips to tide me over until supper.' That wasn't it. It had its place. And that's how I grew up knowing that snack foods had a place. So, thankfully I was able to bring that forward to my kids. You don't eat this because you are hungry; you eat it because it's a treat."[120]

Grant Wichenko's stance on snack foods is a sharp contrast to that of Rosin's: he is a self-described "junk food freak." His first summer job was at Federated Fine Foods, makers of potato chips in Winnipeg in 1968.[121] When Wichenko turned sixteen years old, his parents told him he had to get a job. He walked down Wellington Avenue, knocking on doors until he found someone willing to hire him. Thus, he was "hired off the street" at Federated. He kept his first paycheque: for thirty-seven hours of work, he made $34.75. He worked the graveyard shift, 10:30 p.m. to 7:00 a.m., cleaning machines. The job involved using an air hose to blow chip particles left behind on the conveyors after the chips left the fryer. He said the job left him "scraping barbecue or onion and garlic off my face. Nobody really cared about health and safety in those days. It was quite the experience. It's probably the single most important reason why I stayed in school. That convinced me: go to school, get a degree, because you don't want to do this for the rest of your life."[122] He was promoted the next summer to the task of cleaning the fryer. This required removing starch: there was "a ton of starch you had to shovel out." Wichenko lost this job when he acquired an infection after potatoes fell on top of him: "I couldn't get my pants on, so I couldn't go to work. So they fired me [*laughs*]." He recalls that he would suggest new flavours to management, including cheese and onion, and salt and pepper (flavours that are now very popular).[123]

Wichenko was displeased when Old Dutch ended the manufacturing of onion and garlic chips in 1996. He went to the Winnipeg factory and bought the last few cases off the production line. He then phoned *Winnipeg Free Press* columnist Gordon Sinclair and asked him to do a story on the chip's demise.[124] Wichenko would drive to Grand Forks, North Dakota, to purchase the American version of the flavour made in the Old Dutch factory in Minnesota. Old Dutch Canada later revived the flavour. Onion and garlic is Wichenko's favourite potato chip. He's been around the country, he said, trying various flavours, including roast chicken in Nova Scotia: they are "horrible but popular." He still misses Mr. Salty pretzels: "There was nothing like them."[125]

Wichenko's interest in becoming a *Kids Bids* participant was his love of junk food; "the idea of winning something struck me as an idea." He thought "what the heck!" but "didn't get very far." He had a paper route in Winnipeg and would collect Old Dutch boxes and bags while delivering papers. He managed to secure enough bags and box tops to have a few thousand points for the *Kids Bids* show in Winnipeg. When he arrived at the TV studio, he was disappointed to see that he had very few points in comparison with those of the other children, who had "shopping bags full of product." He bid on a few things, but was unsuccessful, as the starting bids were often the total number of points he had accumulated. For him, *Kids Bids* was "a frustrating experience." He "didn't put the effort into it that—obviously kids had gone around to their parents and neighbours. Everybody was collecting the stuff for them."[126]

Empowering Children

There were two other aspects of the show that deserve mention: its unintended promotion of conservation, and children's agency. Reflecting on the experience years later, many former contestants and viewers of *Kids Bids* expressed admiration for the environmentalism that the show inadvertently promoted. Thirty years after the show aired, Walter Mrak wrote a letter to the *Winnipeg Free Press,* asking that the program (or one similar) be revived:

> You talk about conservation! You talk about recycling! Who was the beneficiary? The station? The chip company? The kids? Their parents? The manufacturers and retailers of the auctioned items? You bet! All of them were winners and we together as a society were the ultimate beneficiary. Kids became responsible, set goals and solicited help from relatives. The station filled in time with something better than cartoons. The chip manufacturer reaped good will. The suppliers got positive advertising. The parents

> knew where their kids were. What is stopping a similar program today for, let's say, empty milk cartons, once-used paper, cigarette packages? Recycling could be fun, profitable, entertaining, a social event and enriching besides the obvious resource benefits.[127]

Former contestant Bill Brown observed that "when *Kid's Bids* was around you never would see an empty bag of chips littering the city. Occasionally you'd see an empty paper Old Dutch box lying around, but it wouldn't have a lid."[128] Claudia Byczek stated, "I remember picking up chip bags anywhere and everywhere we saw them, it actually was a very environmentally friendly idea because we were picking up other people's litter!!"[129] Ron LeClair "scrounged back alleys and King George school grounds for any empty bags," while LaVerna Wiebe Peters "collected chip bags from ditches and wherever."[130] While it was not the intention of the show's founders, in a time before civic recycling programs, this community cleanup was an undoubted side benefit of the television program. Ironically, a program created to increase product sales had the side benefit of making people aware of the environmental consequences of indiscriminate consumption.

Without intending to do so, *Kids Bids* empowered children. The show elevated children, rather than adults, to the centre of the action. This had been a feature of the *Mickey Mouse Club,* as Gary Cross notes in his book *Kids' Stuff*: "child performers with whom young viewers could identify" were the focus of the show.[131] The children on *Kids Bids*, however, were recognizable as neighbours:

> *Scott Prior*: When's the last time you watched a TV show that had local kids and was locally produced? . . . I guess what I'm getting at is, to me, *Kids Bids* was CFQC as part of Saskatoon, as part of engaging local kids. The closest we get here [in British Columbia] is news once a day from Victoria . . . just about everything else on TV is a network cable—

> *Verne Prior*: Syndicated, or whatever.
>
> *Interviewer*: I think your son has a great point. Those kinds of shows where you could see your neighbourhood kids don't exist anymore.
>
> *Verne*: Yeah, I guess there was that aspect of it, too.[132]

Children of working-class families responded by organizing to collect the points needed to win consumer goods their families otherwise couldn't afford. Children on *Kids Bids* could exercise independence, choosing and securing products themselves. As Richard Rosin observed, participation in *Kids Bids* gave winning children the pride of knowing that they got their rewards "*on their own*."[133]

—— • ——

The stories shared by former *Kids Bids* contestants are not exercises in nostalgia. These are not longings for "a time past" and "a place lost," and neither are they a reaction against the modern world.[134] Sociologist Jyotsna Kapur tells us that nostalgia, "like childhood, is both regressive and progressive. It simultaneously expresses the longing for patriarchal and imperial control while it protests the commercialization of childhood."[135] The design of the *Kids Bids* show allowed child participants, rather than adults, to take the lead. The commercial aspect of the show was manipulated by working-class children, as they made use of the opportunity to acquire otherwise unattainable toys. If there were any traces of nostalgic longing in these stories, we would do well to remember Jennifer Helgren's comments on the function of nostalgia in oral history narratives. Nostalgia "should not be viewed merely as a way that oral history respondents falsify or forget the past. . . . Through nostalgia in oral history, narrators connect the past and the present to criticize social conditions and the process of change."[136] Scott Prior's reflection that television today—even in the face of the rise of "reality" programming—does not offer opportunities for local children in the way that *Kids Bids* did is an example of such critique.

For most *Kids Bids* contestants, the show was a happy childhood memory—but its significance was much greater. For many, it was more than simply an enjoyable game or an opportunity to achieve temporary fame through local television. It was a valued chance to acquire some of the leisure goods of a middle-class lifestyle that their families could not afford. A few participants, though not many, increased their chip consumption in order to achieve their dream. For most, however, collecting Old Dutch points was an exercise in waste recovery and in working toward a goal with family, friends, and community. A *Kids Bids* appearance was a major event for participants, necessitating attention to their appearance and behaviour so that they would maintain the self-respect of their family in their public debut on television. *Kids Bids* gave children the opportunity to make their own decisions, in a very public way. Though they may all have dreamed of winning the bicycle, what they took home from the show was less tangible but perhaps more valuable.

CONCLUSION

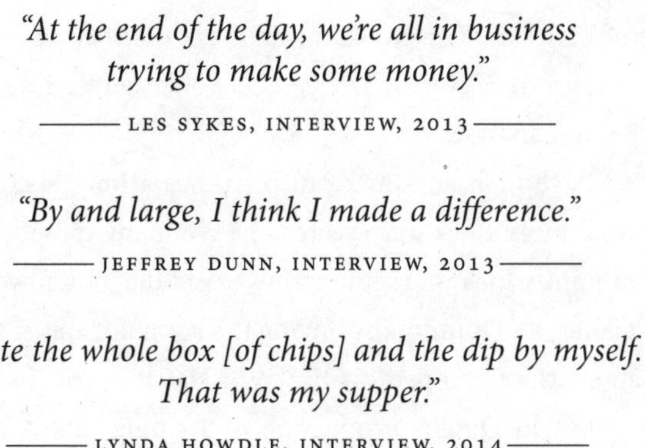

"At the end of the day, we're all in business trying to make some money."

LES SYKES, INTERVIEW, 2013

"By and large, I think I made a difference."

JEFFREY DUNN, INTERVIEW, 2013

"I ate the whole box [of chips] and the dip by myself. That was my supper."

LYNDA HOWDLE, INTERVIEW, 2014

Jeffrey Dunn describes himself as a "blue-collar lifer."[1] He has worked at a series of jobs, but the final twenty years of his career were as a shipper-receiver and union representative at Scott-Bathgate. While he encouraged his younger relatives to get an education so they would have more career opportunities than he has had, he took pride in his work. "I felt it was my job. This is my life. And I'm going to do the best I can for myself and others," he observed. He was pleased to have assisted in the transition to a computerized ordering system at Scott-Bathgate. He took satisfaction, as well, in having helped fellow workers with challenges both on the job and in their domestic lives. Reflecting on his role at Scott-Bathgate, he declared, "By and large, I think I made a difference."

Those who study the food system and its history too rarely share the stories of workers like Dunn. According to Sarah Besky and Sandra Brown in their article "Looking for Work," food scholars still fail to "understand and analyze the role of wage labor within agro-food systems."[2] In his article "Commodity Histories," Bruce Robbins says popular commodity histories of food tend to ignore labour issues, carefully omitting "anything that might make the consumer feel guilty."[3] Yet, ignoring labour is not only about avoiding guilt-inducing information about working conditions, but also about a disrespectful denial of the agency of those employed in this industry. Besky and Brown claim there is a place for "commodity chain studies of global agricultural circulation or ecological interpretations of food production and distribution," but these need to be accompanied by "studies of labor at the microscale of analysis."[4] This book, through its examination of several Canadian firms that produce chips, Cheezies, chocolate, and candy, is a contribution to such microanalyses.

Old Dutch, though an American firm, has a long history in western Canada, dating more than sixty years. The company provided work and a sense of community to young immigrants, saved the jobs of workers at competitors like Humpty Dumpty (by buying the company out at their request), assisted the growth of competitors like W.T. Hawkins (by distributing their product despite Old Dutch's production of a similar line), and supported Manitoba farmers by giving them an alternative when sugar beet production ended in the province. Old Dutch potato chips may be produced by an American-owned company, but many Canadians in western and Atlantic Canada rightly view their purchase as an exercise in buying local and buying Canadian. Manufactured by Canadian workers and made using Canadian potatoes, the nationality of the family who owns the company seems comparatively unimportant. A highly mechanized production process, increasing expansion, and diverse advertising strategies are practices that Old Dutch shares with large food conglomerates. And yet, their flat management structure, limited research and development, and generally positive labour relations mark them as somewhat different from those conglomerates.

Simplistic classification schemes—foreign versus domestic, progressive versus paternalist—are thus not helpful in this case.

The potato chip industry consolidated in the 1980s after a period of growth in the 1950s. Federated Fine Foods, one of hundreds of small chip producers begun by potato growers in the postwar era, was killed by competition. These potato growers found new ways to participate in the snack food economy, however, forming grower associations and working together with government and industry to improve potato production. Kroeker Farms, Haskett Growers, and Southern Potato Company, for example, were able to find a measure of autonomy, cooperating as suppliers for Old Dutch.

The consolidation of chip producers meant that new players entering the market needed unique marketing angles. Boutique chip manufacturers like Covered Bridge and Hardbite have had to make use of their own history to distinguish themselves in the marketplace. Culinary tourism and family farm mythology have been keys to attracting a loyal following for their products. Marketing could take the form of corporate myth, however, as with Hardbite's unclear ownership despite its emphasis on farm origins. And, at Covered Bridge, corporate mythology proved problematic. When Covered Bridge's founder identified too personally with his company, a process encouraged by the company's own marketing campaign, the result was a serious conflict with his newly unionized workers.

The story of Hawkins Cheezies is, on the one hand, the story of the decline of a once mighty giant. A Chicago company formerly so successful that it rivalled Lay's, Hawkins was reduced—in part through the failures of its founder's personal relationships—to manufacturing a single product in small-town Ontario. On the other hand, however, its quirky limitations have been mythologized into strengths. Accidents of history are thus transformed into demonstrations of business acumen.

There are two rival stories of chocolate production in Canada. One is the proud and romantic tale of Canadian invention: the first wrapped chocolate bar, the first heart-shaped Valentine box of chocolates. The other story, not so romantic, is the history of these production companies' primarily female workforces. Low wages and paternalistic monitoring of their female workers' behaviour—both on the job and off—were typical at Moirs and Ganong. At Paulins, unionization may have assisted female workers, but not even a supportive manager like Tom Yasumatsu could save their jobs in the face of global competition. At these chocolate factories, the romantic myth of the product masked the harsh realities of the production process.

Success in candy making is difficult, and always has been. In Newfoundland, Browning Harvey tried to play catch-up to Purity for decades before abandoning the field to them. Cavalier has managed to continue by producing their own specialties and through private-label manufacturing. The future of Scott-Bathgate, one of the oldest firms in Canada, is questionable. The variation in production facilities in this snack category is wide, ranging from the backyard machine shed of Robertson's in small-town Nova Scotia to the large collection of downtown urban buildings of Scott-Bathgate in Winnipeg. In all its variations, candy production remains skilled labour, employing techniques largely unchanged over a century.

The memories of *Kids Bids* contestants, finally, reveal that marketing to children is not always simply the manipulative practice that it appears at face value. *Kids Bids,* a program created to market potato chips to children, had some interesting unintended consequences. The pleasures of competition and the attraction of local fame via television were possibilities. But, for a number of children of working-class background, *Kids Bids* gave them the opportunity to attain some of the trappings of a middle-class existence that otherwise were unavailable to them. In many ways, the program let children, rather than adults, take the lead. In a time before urban recycling programs, children organized family, friends, and community members to assist in collecting discarded packaging. These cooperative efforts, together with seeing fellow neighbourhood children on a locally produced television program, gave many children a sense of pride that outlasted any toys they may have won on the show.

Our current obsession with fat shaming and clean eating is the context in which these snack food manufacturers and workers have to operate. Those interviewed for the research for this book sometimes expressed frustration with the negative attention and blanket condemnation their industry receives. Mike McCartney, production manager at Covered Bridge Potato Chips, explained, "If you don't eat right and exercise, you're not going to be small; you're going to be overweight. I mean, I've worked here five years and I think I've put on ten pounds since I started here. And I don't attribute [that] to eating chips. I'm off the floor more, doing maintenance stuff, and been more in the office. I'm less active, I guess, and my wife's a real good cook."[5] Les Sykes, director of operations at W.T. Hawkins, recalled that scientists' warnings about saturated fats led to the development of hydrogenated oils, which were subsequently discovered to be worse for health than saturated fats.[6] The recommendations of science, he observed, change over time. Smaller companies are at a disadvantage, because they do not have the time, money, or resources to respond as quickly to trends.

In business, there is no place of purity, Sykes cautioned. In his early working life, he was employed in "a great industry"—farm machinery repair—where he "supported farmers and farm machinery. . . . Farmers were seen as these keepers of the earth, and lived very close to the earth." With farming's shift to agribusiness, "that viewpoint of farmers has changed." Factory farming, genetically modified organisms (GMOs), and growth hormones have decreased the general public's respect for farmers. Snack production has undergone a similar shift in the mind of the public. Sykes says:

> In any industry, I think, you have to—I don't know, I'm not really sure what I'm trying to say here, but I guess I'm trying to compare making snack food as compared to what I did before. I really don't see much of a difference between the two. At the end of the day, we're all in business trying to make some money. We're making the very best product that we can make, given the resources and the knowledge that we have at the time. I think that's the very best that you can ask anybody to do, really, in a company.

The function of business, Sykes reminds us, is to generate a profit, first and foremost. There is nonetheless some room to manoeuvre: to produce a valued product, to protect a reputation of quality. He said, "You know, Hawkins has been around for almost sixty-five years now; we certainly hope to be around for many, many more years yet, so all our decisions are made with that viewpoint, in the end. I know that we're slow to make change but we do that consciously because we want to move carefully, because we make only one product—we have to be very careful with that product. I'm proud of it. It's maybe not the best product out there, but we think it's a great product. That's it."[7] Pride in work remains for Sykes and for many others employed in the snacks industry, despite shifts in public opinion.

In the introduction to this book, I recounted the story of my father, who caught gophers during the Depression and used the government money he received in exchange for their tails to buy snacks and soft drinks. The first time he told me this story, I asked him why he didn't use that money instead to assist his struggling parents. His father, like many western Canadian men in the 1930s, snuck into boxcars to ride the rails, looking for work as a farmhand. Surely my father's parents would have benefited from the extra income his gopher snaring produced, however minimal? I don't remember the exact words of my father's response, but I do remember being told that everyone needs some pleasure and enjoyment in their lives, and that no one deserves our moral judgement. Making a point similar to that of my father's, Lynda Howdle, former Paulins employee, recalled her own consumption of snacks at one particular moment in her life.

> When I was separating from my husband, do you know what I used to eat? Everyone would be out. The kids would be out. I would sit and watch [the television soap opera] *Dallas*. I would take—this is terrible—a box of Old Dutch ripple chips and a tub of Philadelphia Dip, and I ate the whole box and the dip by myself. That was my supper. And I would watch *Dallas*, *Knots Landing*, and whatever else was on. That was my Saturday nights for a long time. . . . I ate the whole box and they were bigger than they are now![8]

The wealthy have options for entertainment and therapy that many others simply do not have. And their options are, by and large, free of public shaming.

Enjoyable and therapeutic, snacks play an important symbolic role in celebrating events and maintaining connections between people. In the early twentieth century, Katherine Leonard Turner reminds us in her article "Buying, Not Cooking," convenience foods "offered companionship, status, convenience, or tastier food than was available at home."[9] Snack foods offer many of the same advantages today. A wall in the office at the Hawkins factory, for example, is covered in photos submitted by customers. Many of the photos depict people celebrating their retirement from work with a bag of Cheezies. Scholars would do well to heed sociologist Jennifer Smith Maguire's warning to avoid the "fallacy of the typical divide that privileges either middle-class discerning taste or working-class necessity as the determinants of food practices."[10] Workers may choose snacks out of preference, not merely economic necessity, and their tastes should be respected. Though much needs to be addressed regarding inequality in our present food system, we all have a right, Smith Maguire says, "to engage in food practices in ways and means of [our own] choosing."[11]

Criticism of the food practices of the working class by the middle class has a long history. Katherine Leonard Turner reveals that at the turn of the twentieth century, middle-class reformers disparaged workers for purchasing bread rather than making their own: "Buying bakers' bread represented poor health, a desecration of the wife's traditional role and a scandalous extravagance."[12] Workers themselves may have felt differently, she notes. They "may well have appreciated a cool apartment, a quick, easy meal staple, and the particular delights of certain treats from the bakery. . . . Most critically, the time and resources to bake bread at home were luxuries that many working-class Americans did not enjoy."[13] Bakery bread, delicatessen offerings of ready-cooked foods, and pushcart pies and cakes were convenient and pleasurable purchases for workers. For middle-class critics, however, Turner says, they were "a needless indulgence and a sign of laziness."[14] So much of the language of this period is replicated in ours today. This book may not inspire readers to change their minds about consuming snacks . . . but it is hoped that it may change their minds about unfairly judging those who do and those who work in the industry.

ACKNOWLEDGEMENTS

Writing is often described as a solitary process, yet an author requires a crowd of supporters to accomplish her task. I am thankful for all those who contributed to the production of this book.

A variety of organizations provided the financial and material assistance necessary for my research on the history of Canadian snack foods. I am grateful to the Social Sciences and Humanities Research Council of Canada for an Insight Development Grant, to the University of Winnipeg for an Arts Research Seed Money Award, and to the Oral History Centre at the University of Winnipeg for funding through the James Burns Oral History Pilot Project in Business. The Oral History Centre staff at the University of Winnipeg worked their usual technical and legal magic for me: my thanks to Kent Davies and Kimberley Moore for their practical help, advice, and equipment loans.

This research benefited from the questions and comments of fellow scholars at a number of academic conferences, including: the joint conference of the Association of Business Historians and Gesellschaft für Unternehmensgeschichte, Humboldt University, Berlin, May 2016; A Taste for Feeling: The Affect Project symposium, University of Manitoba, February 2016; the Social Science History Association conference, Toronto, November 2014; the International Oral History Association conference, Barcelona, July 2014; the Canadian Historical Association and Canadian Association of Food Studies conferences, Brock University, May 2014; the Anglo-American Conference of Historians, Institute of Historical Research, University of London, July 2013; the Oral History Society conference, University of Sussex, July 2013; and the Canadian Food History Symposium, University of Winnipeg, October 2013. My food history students at the University of Winnipeg provided helpful critiques as well. Part of the chapter on Cheezies was published earlier in *Oral History,* the journal of the British Oral History Society.

My research assistants were invaluable during this project. Aaron Moseley-Williams spent a week in Ottawa, scanning documents at Library and Archives Canada and at the Canadian Agriculture Library. Sarah Reilly and Elizabeth-Anne Johnson spent two years working with me, interviewing people for this book, processing the interviews for later archival deposit, and scouring libraries, archives, and corporate registry offices across the country. Travelling with Sarah and Elizabeth-Anne on both coasts of Canada, touring plant facilities, and researching companies (and eating snacks, of course) was enjoyable, productive, and memorable work. Sarah Story became involved in this project toward its end, devoting much thoughtful time to some final interviews.

A number of businesses were particularly helpful with my research, offering factory tours, providing access to private documents and arranging interviews. Thank you to Tony McGarvey and Kent Hawkins at W.T. Hawkins; Steven Aanenson, Curt Aanenson, and Iris Treichel at Old Dutch Foods; Ryan Albright at Covered Bridge Potato Chip Company; and Roy Robertson at Robertson's Candy. My thanks as well to Jim Burt of Scott-Bathgate for our conversation.

Colleagues, students, friends, and acquaintances offered suggestions during various stages of the research and writing of this book. Thanks to Royden Loewen, Bob Coutts, Randy Widdis, Chris Dooley, Mike from Los Angeles, Ellen Paulley, Greg Kealey, Steffanie Scott, Jennifer Sygo, Stephen Henderson, Bob Hummelt, Terry Dirks, and Charlotte Cooze. Interest from members of the media in this research resulted in some additional oral histories for this book: my thanks to Robin Summerfield, John Sadoway, Marcy Markusa, Samuel Rancourt, Greg Glatz, Christian Cassidy, Amber Hildebrandt, Thérèse Garceau, and Joel Ralph.

The staff at institutions that provided information to me and my research assistants were extremely helpful: Library and Archives Canada; Agriculture and Agri-Food Canada: Canadian Agriculture Library; Manitoba Companies Office; BC Corporate Registries Office; Belleville Ontario Public Library; Sharon White (Archivist, Community Archives of Belleville and Hastings County); Mac Calhoun (BC Archives); Provincial Archives of New Brunswick; The Chocolate Museum; Nova Scotia Archives; The Rooms

Provincial Archives (Newfoundland and Labrador—perhaps the most beautiful archive in Canada); Newfoundland Historical Society; Sonia Dickin (Saskatoon Public Library); and Trenton Carls (Chicago History Museum).

David Carr, Jill McConkey, and Glenn Bergen of University of Manitoba Press and copyeditor Pat Sanders have been encouraging and enthusiastic throughout the entire process. Such a joy to work with you! And I am grateful to the anonymous reviewers whose detailed advice for revision significantly improved the book.

This book would not have been possible without the assistance of all those who were willing to be interviewed about their experiences with, and memories of, Canadian snack foods. Your sharing of stories, factory tours, photos, and memorabilia was essential to the final product. Thank you.

Finally, thank you to my brother, Tim Thiessen: this book was your idea.

NOTES

Introduction

1. In 2007, more than a quarter of Canadian children were either overweight or obese. Charlene Elliott, "*Taste Rules!* Food Marketing, Food Law, and Childhood Obesity in Canada," *Cuizine: The Journal of Canadian Food Cultures* 1, no. 1 (2008), http://www.erudit.org/revue/cuizine/2008/v1/n1/019371ar.html. For an effective critique of this obesity crisis as a modern-day moral panic that falsely claims to be science based, see Guthman, "Can't Stomach It."
2. Pollan, *In Defense of Food*, 3.
3. Ibid., 1.
4. Michelle Allison, "Food You Like Is Food That Feels Good" (blog post), *The Fat Nutritionist*, 24 January 2011, http://www.fatnutritionist.com/index.php/food-you-like-is-food-that-feels-good/.
5. Pollan, *Food Rules*, 7.
6. Ibid., 8.
7. Rachel Laudan, "A Historian's Take" (blog post), http://www.rachellaudan.com/. Joe Pastry makes this same point in his review of Pollan's *Omnivore's Dilemma*. Joe Pastry, "Omnivore's Dilemma" (blog post), 31 May 2006, http://www.joepastry.com/2006/omnivore_s_dilemma/.
8. Todd Kliman, "How Michael Pollan, Alice Waters, and Slow Food Theorists Got It All Wrong," *Washingtonian Magazine*, 29 May 2015, http://www.washingtonian.com/blogs/bestbites/todd-kliman-otherwise/rachel-lauden-how-michael-pollan-alice-waters-got-everything-wrong.php.
9. Ibid.
10. Ibid.
11. Mintz, *Sweetness and Power*, 145.
12. Ibid., 183.
13. Ibid., 127.
14. Ibid., 145.
15. Ibid., 117.
16. Ibid., 213.
17. Fitzgerald and Petrick, "In Good Taste," 403.

18. Bourdieu, *Distinction*; Mintz, *Sweetness and Power*; Korsmeyer, *Taste Culture Reader.*

19. See Mark Bittman's blog for the *New York Times* at http://bittman.blogs.nytimes.com/; and Pollan, *Food Rules*.

20. Moss, *Salt Sugar Fat;* Michael Moss, "The Extraordinary Science of Addictive Junk Food," *New York Times Magazine,* 20 February 2013, http://www.nytimes.com/2013/02/24/magazine/the-extraordinary-science-of-junk-food.html.

21. Sara Davis, "Framing Junk Food—Again" (blog post), *Scenes of Eating,* 1 March 2013, http://scenesofeating.com/2013/03/01/framing-junk-food-again/.

22. Sara Davis, "Your Junk Food Preference Is Probably Not an Addiction" (blog post), *Scenes of Eating,* 17 January 2013, http://scenesofeating.com/2013/01/17/your-junk-food-preference-is-probably-not-an-addiction/.

23. Turner, "Buying, Not Cooking," 14.

24. Chan, "Snacking in Canada 2008."

25. Joel Gregoire, "Snacking through the Ages," *Canadian Grocer,* 28 January 2011, http://www.canadiangrocer.com/top-stories/nosh-nation-2621.

26. Agriculture and Agri-Food Canada, "Canada's Snack Food Industry," 5 July 2013, http://www.agr.gc.ca/eng/industry-markets-and-trade/statistics-and-market-information/by-product-sector/processed-food-and-beverages/the-canadian-snack-food-manufacturing-industry/?id=1172692863066.

27. Agriculture and Agri-Food Canada, "The Canadian Snack Food Industry," 28 February 2007; Agriculture and Agri-Food Canada, "Canadian Snack Food Industry Statistics, 1997–2010," http://www.agr.gc.ca/eng/industry-markets-and-trade/statistics-and-market-information/by-product-sector/processed-food-and-beverages/the-canadian-snack-food-manufacturing-industry/the-canadian-snack-food-industry-statistics/?id=1336413119576 (accessed 11 October 2015).

28. Agriculture and Agri-Food Canada, "Canada's Snack Food Industry," 5 July 2013, http://www.agr.gc.ca/eng/industry-markets-and-trade/statistics-and-market-information/by-product-sector/processed-food-and-beverages/the-canadian-snack-food-manufacturing-industry/?id=1172692863066.

29. Ibid.

30. von Plato, "Contemporary Witnesses."

31. Carr, *Candymaking in Canada,* 50, 97; Hersheys, "Allan Candy," https://www.hersheys.com/allancandy/en_ca/home.html.

32. Neilson Dairy, "Our History," http://www.neilsondairy.com/Home/History; *Dictionary of Canadian Biography,* "Neilson, William," http://www.biographi.ca/en/bio.php?id_nbr=7618.

33. Virginia Mason, "His Creative Confections Earned Halifax the Title of Toffee Town," *Halifax Courier,* 15 May 2008, http://www.halifaxcourier.co.uk/news/his-creative-confections-earned-halifax-the-title-of-toffee-town-in-the-second-of-a-three-part-series-virginia-mason-recalls-the-toffee-king-john-mackintosh-1-1911589.

34. Scott McCheyne, "Why Old Dutch Canadianized: It Turns out the 49th Parallel Makes Quite a Difference When It Comes to Snack Foods," *Marketing Magazine* 105, no. 9 (6 March 2000): 17; Karen Pinchin, "The Willy Wonka of New Brunswick," *Globe and Mail,* 18 December 2013, L5; Karen Pinchin, "The Story behind a Uniquely Canadian Holiday Treat," *Globe and Mail,* 17 December 2013, http://www.theglobeandmail.com/life/holiday-guide/holiday-survival-guide/the-story-behind-a-uniquely-canadian-holiday-treat/article16002345/.

35. "10 Companies That Control the World's Food," *MarketWatch,* 2 September 2014, https://secure.marketwatch.com/story/10-companies-that-control-the-worlds-food-2014-09-01.

36. This value is calculated using the information that, historically, Old Dutch has spent an amount equivalent to 2 to 4 percent of its sales on marketing, and that sales were $160 million to $250 million at the turn of the millennium. Lee Egerstrom, "In the Chips," *St. Paul Pioneer Press,* 16 December 2001, D1; Kathleen Deveny, "Crunch Time in the Snack Industry," *Wall Street Journal,* 17 November 1990, courtesy of Old Dutch Foods, Roseville, MN.

37. Monod, *Store Wars.*

38. Cooke, *What's to Eat?*

39. Iacovetta, Korinek, and Epp, *Edible Histories,* xiii.

40. Besky and Brown, "Looking for Work," 21.

41. Basok, *Tortillas and Tomatoes.*

42. Mosby, *Food Will Win.*

43. Heron, *Booze;* Penfold, *The Donut.*

44. Roche and McHutchison, *First Fish;* Cho, *Eating Chinese.*

45. Carr, *Candymaking in Canada.*

46. "When food is abundant and cheap, people will eat more of it and get fat." Pollan, *Omnivore's Dilemma,* 102.

47. Ibid., 8.

48. Pollan, *In Defense of Food,* 7.

49. Pollan, *Food Rules,* 5.

50. Ibid., 37.

51. See Chapter 3 for Thomas Broad's story.
52. Levine and Striffler, "From Field to Table," 12.
53. Besky and Brown, "Looking for Work," 20–21.
54. Deutsch, "Memories of Mothers," 168.
55. Ibid.
56. Pollan, *Food Rules*, 85.
57. Ibid., 99. "As technology reduces the time cost of food, we tend to eat more of it. My guess is that the converse still holds true, and that paying more for food—in every sense—will reduce the amount of it we eat. . . . While it is true that many people simply can't afford to pay more for food, either in money or time or both, many more of us can. After all, just in the last decade or two we've somehow found the time in the day to spend several hours on the Internet and the money in the budget not only to pay for broadband service, but to cover a second phone bill and a new monthly bill for television, formerly free." Ibid., 187.
58. Ibid., 105.
59. Ibid., 121.
60. Ibid., 123.
61. Ibid., 131.
62. Laudan, "Plea for Culinary Modernism."
63. Flandrin and Montanari similarly argue, "What history teaches us is that change is inevitable and that there is no point in longing for the past—a past, bear in mind, that was often haunted by hunger." Flandrin and Montanari, "Conclusion: Today and Tomorrow," 553.
64. Laudan, "Plea for Culinary Modernism," 36.
65. Ibid.
66. Ibid., 40–41.
67. Ibid., 42.
68. Ibid.
69. Ibid., 43.
70. Emily Matchar, "Is Michael Pollan a Sexist Pig?," *Salon*, 27 April 2013, http://www.salon.com/2013/04/28/is_michael_pollan_a_sexist_pig/.
71. Tom Philpott, "How Michael Pollan Romanticizes Dinner," *Mother Jones*, 14 May 2013, http://www.motherjones.com/tom-philpott/2013/05/michael-pollan-cooking-gender-and-nostalgia.

72. Sara Davis, "Elsewhere on the Internet—Thinking Links" (blog post), *Scenes of Eating,* 23 April 2013, http://scenesofeating.com/2013/04/23/elsewhere-on-the-internet-thinking-links/.

73. Bowen, Elliott, and Brenton, "Joy of Cooking?," 23.

74. Todd Kliman, "How Michael Pollan, Alice Waters, and Slow Food Theorists Got It All Wrong," *Washingtonian Magazine,* 29 May 2015, http://www.washingtonian.com/blogs/bestbites/todd-kliman-otherwise/rachel-lauden-how-michael-pollan-alice-waters-got-everything-wrong.php.

75. Andersen and Hedegaard Larsen, "'Reflection,'" 293.

76. Joe Garofoli, "Activist at Vanguard of Restaurant Workers' Rights," *San Francisco Chronicle SFGate,* 11 January 2014, http://www.sfgate.com/bayarea/article/Activist-at-vanguard-of-restaurant-workers-rights-5135081.php#page-1.

77. Todd Kliman, "How Michael Pollan, Alice Waters, and Slow Food Theorists Got It All Wrong," *Washingtonian Magazine,* 29 May 2015, http://www.washingtonian.com/blogs/bestbites/todd-kliman-otherwise/rachel-lauden-how-michael-pollan-alice-waters-got-everything-wrong.php#page-1.

78. There are also debates as to whether there is, in fact, an obesity crisis. Gard and Wright argue that the obesity crisis is "primarily a moral and ideological phenomenon, rather than a scientific one." Gard and Wright, *Obesity Epidemic,* 145. Health and life expectancies continue to improve, and there were no significant changes in obesity rates for children or adults from 2003 to 2012, though rates are high (one-third of adults and 17 percent of children). Neither has there been a decline in home-cooked meals in the past twenty years; two-thirds of all calories are eaten at home. Paul Campos, "There Is No Childhood Obesity Epidemic," *New Republic,* 27 February 2014, http://www.newrepublic.com/article/116774/childhood-obesity-rate-declines-dont-give-michelle-obama-credit; Ogden, et al., "Prevalence of Childhood and Adult Obesity," https://jama.jamanetwork.com/article.aspx?articleid=1832542; Rachel Laudan, "The Decline of Home Cooking?" (blog post), 3 October 2014, http://www.rachellaudan.com/2014/10/the-decline-of-home-cooking.html.

79. Levenstein, *Paradox of Plenty,* 259.

80. Ibid., 260.

81. Ibid.

82. Ibid., 262.

83. Boero, "Fat Kids, Working Moms," 113, 118.

84. Guthman, "Neoliberalism," 191.

85. Kathryn Hughes, "Don't Look Down on Those Who Eat Fast Food," *The Guardian,* 8 June 2014, http://www.theguardian.com/commentisfree/2014/jun/08/fast-food-mcdonalds-kfc-jamie-oliver.

86. Ibid.

87. David H. Freedman, "How Junk Food Can End Obesity," *The Atlantic* (July/August 2013), http://www.theatlantic.com/magazine/archive/2013/07/how-junk-food-can-end-obesity/309396/.

88. Ibid.

89. Kathryn Hughes, "Don't Look Down on Those Who Eat Fast Food," *The Guardian,* 8 June 2014, http://www.theguardian.com/commentisfree/2014/jun/08/fast-food-mcdonalds-kfc-jamie-oliver.

90. Zena Olijnyk, "Canadians May Eat Fewer Chips, but We Make Up by Buying Lots of Dill Pickle," *National Post,* 4 May 2000, C10.

91. Centers for Disease Control and Prevention, Division of Nutrition, Physical Activity, and Obesity, "Do Increased Portion Sizes Affect How Much We Eat?," http://www.cdc.gov/nccdphp/dnpa/nutrition/pdf/portion_size_research.pdf; Young and Nestle, "Contribution of Expanding Portion Sizes."

92. Petrick, "Industrial Food," 258–59.

93. Petrick notes that, while industry data is "plentiful and relatively easy to find and use," consumer data is "much more elusive and complicated." Ibid., 266.

94. Alberta Ministry of Agriculture and Forestry, "Consumer Corner—Snacking in Canada," 14 March 2012, http://www1.agric.gov.ab.ca/$department/deptdocs.nsf/all/sis13895; Drew Desilver, "For Most Workers, Real Wages Have Barely Budged for Decades," Pew Research Center *FactTank,* 9 October 2014, http://www.pewresearch.org/fact-tank/2014/10/09/for-most-workers-real-wages-have-barely-budged-for-decades/; René Morissette, Garnett Picot, and Yuqian Lu, "Wage Growth over the Past 30 Years: Changing Wages by Age and Education," 27 November 2015, http://www.statcan.gc.ca/pub/11-626-x/11-626-x2012008-eng.htm.

95. The Nielsen Company, *Snack Attack: What Consumers are Reaching for Around the World,* September 2014, http://www.nielsen.com/content/dam/nielsenglobal/kr/docs/global-report/2014/Nielsen%20Global%20Snacking%20Report%20September%202014.pdf, 4–5.

96. Fresh fruit (383 annual eatings per capita), gum (181), and yogourt (100) are far more popular as snacks than potato chips (88), chocolate (75), or candy (65). Data for the year 2009. Alberta Agriculture and Forestry, "Consumer Corner—Snacking in Canada," 14 March 2012, http://www1.agric.gov.ab.ca/$department/deptdocs.nsf/all/sis13895.

97. Statistics Canada, "Overview of Canadians' Eating Habits," 5 October 2007, http://www.statcan.gc.ca/pub/82-620-m/2006002/4053669-eng.htm.

98. Old Dutch Foods, "Junk Food?," pamphlet, n.d. Courtesy of Old Dutch Foods, Roseville, MN.

99. Martial Boulet interview.

100. Anonymous industry expert interview.

101. Old Dutch Foods, "Junk Food?," pamphlet, n.d. Courtesy of Old Dutch Foods, Roseville, MN.

102. Old Dutch Foods Inc, typescript, n.d. Courtesy of Old Dutch Foods, Roseville, MN. Don Kroeker asserts that potato chips retain more vitamins and minerals than mashed potatoes. Don Kroeker interview.

103. Old Dutch Foods, "Junk Food?," pamphlet, n.d. Courtesy of Old Dutch Foods, Roseville, MN.

104. Old Dutch started using sunflower oil in the 1970s. Other oils that can be used in potato chip manufacturing include cottonseed, soybean, corn, peanut, canola, and palm oil. Kristin Tillotson, "Always Hometown Stars, Old Dutch Chips Hit Movies," *Minneapolis Star Tribune,* 16 February 1997, F1; Letter from Old Dutch Customer Services to Chris Lenfestey, Chippewa Falls, WI, n.d. Courtesy of Old Dutch Foods, Roseville, MN.

105. Old Dutch Foods, "Some People Believe That All Potato Chips Are the Same," pamphlet, n.d. Courtesy of Old Dutch Foods, Roseville, MN.

106. "'Junk' Label Riles Potato Chip Man," *Winnipeg Free Press,* 2 December 1976, 26.

107. Wally Dennison, "Snack Food Firms Relish Tasty Results," *Winnipeg Free Press,* 18 November 1983, 28.

108. "'Junk' Label Riles Potato Chip Man," *Winnipeg Free Press,* 2 December 1976, 26.

109. Shamona Harnett, "Frightening Fat," *Winnipeg Free Press,* 8 September 2003, D1; Shamona Harnett, "What's Your Food IQ?," *Winnipeg Free Press,* 9 March 2009, C7.

110. Winson, *Industrial Diet,* 25.

111. Ibid., 134.

112. Ibid., 167–83.

113. Rick Loewen, "Help the Twinkie-Eaters," letter to the editor, *Winnipeg Free Press,* 11 January 2007, A9.

114. Steven Aanenson interview.

115. Máirtin Mac Con Iomaire, "Culinary Voices," 77.

116. Russell, "Archives, Academy, and Access," 53. The article of mine that she references is "From Faith to Food: Using Oral History to Study Corporate

Mythology at Canadian Manufacturing Firms," *Oral History* 42, no. 2 (Spring 2014): 59–72.

117. Anonymous Old Dutch employee interview.

Chapter 1
OLD DUTCH POTATO CHIPS

1. The epigraph to the chapter is from Ace Burpee, "The Bombers Take Over Old Dutch" (blog post), *Winnipeg Free Press,* 1 September 2009, http://www.winnipegfreepress.com/ace/blogs/The-Bombers-take-over-Old-Dutch-56717502.html. Old Dutch Foods, Inc., homepage, 2015, http://www.olddutchfoods.com/.
2. Old Dutch Foods, Ltd., "Our Story," 2015, http://www.olddutchfoods.ca/about-us/our-story.
3. Naylor, *History of Canadian Business.*
4. Watkins points to Naomi Klein, John Ralston Saul, and Maude Barlow as examples. Watkins, foreword to *The History of Canadian Business,* xix–xx.
5. Hastings, "Branding Canada," 134–58.
6. Carstairs, "Roots Nationalism," 235.
7. Ibid., 236–37. Carstairs states that purchasing consumer goods with "branded symbols of nationalism," such as those made by the clothing company Roots, was "a peculiarly Canadian form of nationalism," as it demonstrated "weary acceptance" of the fact that many of these companies were American owned. Ibid., 237.
8. Cormack and Cosgrave, "'Always Fresh,'" 62. They note, provocatively, "the ability of Tim Hortons to become a site of national narrative and political enactment speaks to this country's ongoing crisis of identity. After all, what kind of community turns to a coffee shop for meaning?" Ibid., 91.
9. Innovation, Science, and Economic Development Canada, "Canadian Industry Statistics (CIS): Glossary of Terms," last updated 22 November 2011, https://www.ic.gc.ca/eic/site/cis-sic.nsf/eng/h_00005.html#employment_size_category (accessed 2 July 2016).
10. See, for example, Bakan, *The Corporation;* Korten, *When Corporations Rule;* Klein, *No Logo.*
11. Peter Carlyle-Gordge, "Creating Fresh New Flavours Is Serious Business at Old Dutch," *Winnipeg Free Press* supplement, 15 December 2001, 16.
12. Old Dutch chips were sold in both bags and one-pound (.45-kilogram) cans as far away as North Dakota in the early 1940s. An ad in the *Bismarck*

Tribune noted the chips "have been very popular in the Minnesota lake region." Advertisement for Logan's grocery, *Bismarck Tribune,* 17 October 1941, 9; advertisement for Beshara's Super Market, *Lead Daily Call,* 30 June 1942, 3.

13. Old Dutch Foods Inc, typescript, n.d., courtesy of Old Dutch Foods, Roseville, MN; Allie Shah, "Obituary: Vernon Aanenson, 82, owners of Old Dutch Foods, Inc.," *Minneapolis Star Tribune,* 12 August 1998, http://www.startribune.com/obituaries/11596796.html; "Top 100 Companies Survey 2001: Plain, Ripple or BBQ," *Manitoba Business* 23, no. 5 (July 2001): 30; letter from Old Dutch Customer Services to Chris Lenfestey, Chippewa Falls, WI, n.d., courtesy of Old Dutch Foods, Roseville, MN; Wally Dennison, "Snack Food Firms Relish Tasty Results," *Winnipeg Free Press,* 18 November 1983, 28; David Neill, "New Flavors to Suit America's Tastes Puts Snack Firm in Chips," *Minneapolis Star,* 29 September 1959, 18A.

14. Bernard Pacyniak, "A Brand for Both Borders," *Snack Food* 85, no. 4 (April 1996): 18.

15. This plant closed in 1983.

16. Steven Aanenson interview; Steven Aanenson, president of Old Dutch Foods, personal communication, 13 May 2015.

17. The 1965 date is given in Old Dutch Foods Inc, typescript, n.d.; a date of 1968 is given in an Old Dutch Foods memo from 1986, but Steven Aanenson states that this date is incorrect. Typescript and memo both courtesy of Old Dutch Foods, Roseville, MN; Steven Aanenson, president of Old Dutch Foods, personal communication, 13 May 2015.

18. Old Dutch Foods was incorporated in Manitoba on 13 October 1955; its initial directors were Barbara J. Palz, Emily Smith, and Vernon Aanenson. Manitoba Companies Office, Old Dutch Foods, file #0108685, 1998. Old Dutch Foods in Minnesota incorporated on 1 July 1967. Notice to lessors, from Vernon Aanenson, 10 July 1967, courtesy of Old Dutch Foods, Roseville, MN. Steven Aanenson expressed doubt that Palz was a director, as she would have been much too young at the time. He recalls that Emily Smith was one of the first (if not the first) employee of the company. Steven Aanenson, president of Old Dutch Foods, personal communication, 10 June 2015.

19. Old Dutch Foods Inc, typescript, n.d., courtesy of Old Dutch Foods, Roseville, MN.

20. Bernard Pacyniak, "A Brand for Both Borders," *Snack Food* 85, no. 4 (April 1996): 18.

21. Scott McCheyne, "Why Old Dutch Canadianized: It Turns Out the 49th Parallel Makes Quite a Difference When It Comes to Snack Foods," *Marketing Magazine* 105, no. 9 (6 March 2000): 17. Scott McCheyne is

marketing and sales coordinator in Calgary. Old Dutch has two marketing managers in Calgary and a director of marketing in St. Paul.

22. "Top 100 Rankings 2005," *Manitoba Business* 27, no. 6 (July/August 2005): 11.

23. Old Dutch Foods (USA), http://www.olddutchfoods.com; Old Dutch Foods (Canada), http://olddutchfoods.ca.

24. A plant in Lachine, QC, was closed in 2013. Steven Aanenson, president of Old Dutch Foods, personal communication, 13 May 2015.

25. David Neill, "New Flavors to Suit America's Tastes Puts Snack Firm in Chips," *Minneapolis Star,* 29 September 1959, 18A.

26. Gail Rockburne, "Crossing the Border: American and Canadian Business in Each Other's Backyards," *Manitoba Business* 15, no. 10 (December 1993): 10.

27. Smith, "Snack Foods," 339.

28. Steven Aanenson interview.

29. David Neill, "New Flavors to Suit America's Tastes Puts Snack Firm in Chips," *Minneapolis Star,* 29 September 1959, 18A.

30. Gwyneth Jones, "Invented in 1855—Potato Chips Boom with New Tastes," *Minneapolis Star,* 4 February 1958, 13A.

31. Bill Gillette, "Old Dutch: Big-Time Business with a Small-Town Flavor," *Snack World* (September–October 1998): 22; email from Janet Brobjorg for Jay Buckingham to Atlas Media Corporation, 26 June 2006, courtesy of Old Dutch Foods, Roseville, MN.

32. Norah Cherry, "American from Paris Gets Credit for Original Potato Chip Order," *Winnipeg Free Press,* 3 April 1970, 19. See also "Potato Chips Snacks Plus," *Winnipeg Free Press,* 27 January 1971, 27.

33. Old Dutch advertisement, *Winnipeg Free Press,* 11 April 1983, 7.

34. Gordon Sinclair Jr., "Filmon Ignores Call of the Moose," *Winnipeg Free Press,* 26 October 1996, A4.

35. Anonymous Old Dutch employee interview.

36. Care2 petition website, "Bring Back the Original Flavor of Old Dutch BBQ Potato Chips," 2009, http://www.thepetitionsite.com/54/bring-back-the-original-flavor-of-old-dutch-bbq-potato-chips/.

37. Ibid.

38. Bill Bashucky interview. Launching new products is a risky and expensive business, however. David Oye interview.

39. The Winnipeg factory can use up to 2,267 kilograms of ketchup seasoning in a week. Anonymous Old Dutch employee interview.

40. Steven Aanenson interview; Curt Aanenson interview.

41. Letter from Old Dutch Customer Services to Chris Lenfestey, Chippewa Falls, WI, n.d., courtesy of Old Dutch Foods, Roseville, MN.

42. "The Perfect Potato Chip," *The Life of Hardip,* 29 April 2012, https://hardiplee.wordpress.com/2012/04/29/the-perfect-potato-chip/.

43. Old Dutch Foods, "Contact Us," http://www.olddutchfoods.com/about-us/contact-us (accessed 23 May 2012). Steven Aanenson notes that green edges are, in fact, undesirable; sun exposure is what causes potatoes to produce a toxin that turns them green. Steven Aanenson, personal communication, 13 May 2015, 10 June 2015.

44. Kristin Tillotson, "Always Hometown Stars, Old Dutch Chips Hit Movies," *Minneapolis Star Tribune,* 16 February 1997, F1.

45. Anonymous industry expert interview.

46. Gwyneth Jones, "Invented in 1855—Potato Chips Boom with New Tastes," *Minneapolis Star,* 4 February 1958, 13A.

47. Martial Boulet interview; anonymous Old Dutch employee interview.

48. Carol Neshevich, "Good, Better, Best!," *Food in Canada* 72, no. 1 (January/February 2012): 43–48; David Oye interview.

49. Gerhard Otto Voth interview; Bill Bashucky interview.

50. Beet powder as a replacement colouring agent resulted in sweetening the taste, for example. Anonymous Old Dutch employee interview; David Oye interview.

51. Doritos, however, are a corn chip rather than a potato chip.

52. Zena Olijnyk, "Canadians May Eat Fewer Chips, but We Make Up by Buying Lots of Dill Pickle," *National Post,* 4 May 2000, C10.

53. Bernard Pacyniak, "Roping in Technology," *Snack Food & Wholesale Bakery* 89, no. 1 (January 2000): 26.

54. Zena Olijnyk, "Canadians May Eat Fewer Chips, but We Make Up by Buying Lots of Dill Pickle," *National Post,* 4 May 2000, C10.

55. Levenstein, *Paradox of Plenty,* 250–51.

56. Cohen, *Consumers' Republic,* 296, 301–8, 315–18, 407.

57. Ibid., 309.

58. See Moss, *Salt, Sugar, Fat.*

59. Steven Aanenson interview.

60. Curt Aanenson interview.

61. David Neill, "New Flavors to Suit America's Tastes Puts Snack Firm in Chips," *Minneapolis Star,* 29 September 1959, 18A.

62. Derek Taylor, "Morning News' Favourite Chips" (Derek Taylor Global News blog), *Morning News*, Global TV, 20 November 2013, http://globalnews.ca/news/976467/morning-news-favourite-chips/.

63. Steven Aanenson, president of Old Dutch Foods, personal communication, 13 May 2015.

64. Geoff Kirbyson, "Old Dutch Plant Marks 50th Year," *Winnipeg Free Press,* 26 August 2004, D9.

65. Stevens Wild, "In the Chips," *Winnipeg Free Press,* 27 September 1989, 21.

66. "While You Were Sleeping: Old Dutch Foods, Winnipeg," *Morning News*, Global TV, broadcast 20 November 2013.

67. Ibid.

68. Derek Taylor, "The MVM (Most Valuable Machine)" (Derek Taylor Global News blog), Global TV, 20 November 2013, http://globalnews.ca/news/959506/the-mvm-most-valuable-machine/.

69. Ibid.; Geoff Kirbyson, "Old Dutch Plant Marks 50th Year," *Winnipeg Free Press,* 26 August 2004, D9.

70. Bill Bashucky interview.

71. Manitoba Starch Products was founded in 1987, and provides potato starch as a gluten-free substitute for wheat flour and cornstarch in baked goods, among other applications. Manitoba Starch Products, "Applications," http://www.manitobastarch.com/applications.html (accessed 31 January 2015). Implementing a starch-reclamation process at Old Dutch reduced their sewer surcharges. Bernard Pacyniak, "Snack Science," *Snack Food* 85, no. 4 (April 1996): 28.

72. Old Dutch in Winnipeg used to use corn oil before switching to cottonseed oil, a blend of cottonseed and corn oils, and then sunflower oil. They now use canola oil processed in Altona, Manitoba. Gerhard Otto Voth interview.

73. Bill Bashucky interview.

74. Bernie Kruchak, "In the Crunch Old Dutch Succeeds," *Western Grocer* (date unknown; circa 1990s), 80–85, courtesy of Old Dutch Foods, Roseville, MN.

75. Manufacturing process observed by the author during a plant tour at Old Dutch, Roseville, MN, 14 October 2013; Keith McArthur, "Hey, You Pig, Quit Hogging All the Chips!," *Winnipeg Free Press,* 25 May 1998, A9.

76. Manufacturing process observed by the author during a plant tour at Old Dutch, Winnipeg, MB, 14 November 2013; Bill Bashucky interview.

77. Joanne Hvala, "Old Dutch Foods Designs 'Dream Plant,'" *Chipper/Snacker* 1977 draft article, courtesy of Old Dutch Foods, Roseville, MN. The published article (January 1978: 67–71) focused instead on the plant's water and heat recovery systems.

78. An industrial washer is used to clean the parts of the tumbler so flavours on a production line can be changed without cross-contamination. Steven Aanenson interview.

79. Gerhard Otto Voth interview. Voth was foreman from 1969 to 2004.

80. Old Dutch was the first snack manufacturer to use x-ray screening in Canada. Bill Bashucky interview.

81. Manufacturing process observed by the author during a plant tour at Old Dutch, Roseville, MN, 14 October 2013; Steven Aanenson interview.

82. David Oye interview.

83. Jean Pierre (J.P.) Petit interview.

84. This facility was Condillo Foods Ltd., which was formed by Curt Aanenson in 1980 and amalgamated with Old Dutch in 2010. Manitoba Companies Office, Old Dutch Foods Ltd., Amalgamation, 1 January 2010; Steven Aanenson interview. Plant manager Derek Walker declared, "When we started, we had 15 employees. Today, we have 124. We're the corn plant [for Old Dutch]—we do the tortillas, the corn chips. We're its only corn processing plant in Canada." Alex Frazer-Harrison, "They Make That Here?," *AirdrieLIFE Magazine* (3 December 2012): http://airdrielife.com/?p=2955 (accessed 11 September 2015).

85. Calgary pollution-control company Aqua Pura Technologies Inc., which was formed in 1984 to develop waste water treatment systems for industrial plants, was purchased by Old Dutch in 1988. Kevin Cox, "Calgary Firm Sees Black Gold in Sludgy Water," *Globe and Mail,* 4 January 1988, B13.

86. Bernard Pacyniak, "Roping in Technology," *Snack Food & Wholesale Bakery* 89, no. 1 (January 2000): 26.

87. A strike by the UFCW was averted in 1979 at the Winnipeg plant when a settlement was reached shortly before the strike deadline. The main issue at that time was wages. "Workers Postpone Call for Strike," *Winnipeg Tribune,* 13 August 1979, 6, University of Manitoba Archives and Special Collections, Winnipeg Tribune Clippings Collection; "Pact Ratified at Old Dutch," *Winnipeg Tribune,* 20 August 1979, 6, University of Manitoba Archives and Special Collections, Winnipeg Tribune Clippings Collection; Steven Aanenson, president of Old Dutch Foods, personal communication, 13 May 2015.

88. "Women's Group Helps Picket Chip Factory," *Winnipeg Free Press,* 9 June 1973, 1; advertisement by labour groups, *Winnipeg Free Press,* 16 June 1973, 5; advertisement by Communist Party, *Winnipeg Free Press,* 26 June 1973, 29.

89. Jeremy Klaszus, "Workers Take Aim at Old Dutch," *Fast Forward Weekly* (2 July 2009), http://www.ffwdweekly.com/news--views/news/workers-take-aim-at-old-dutch-4041/ (accessed 11 September 2015).

90. Tamara Gignac, "Old Dutch Plant Workers Face Lockout," *Calgary Herald*, 27 March 2009, http://www2.canada.com/calgaryherald/news/city/story.html?id=bcf7c630-f23a-4b3b-8305-ee6fd74bb88d.

91. Steven Aanenson interview.

92. Tamara Gignac, "Old Dutch Plant Workers Face Lockout," *Calgary Herald*, 27 March 2009, http://www2.canada.com/calgaryherald/news/city/story.html?id=bcf7c630-f23a-4b3b-8305-ee6fd74bb88d.

93. Supreme Court Justice Ivan Rand established the Rand Formula (or automatic dues check-off) in arbitration that ended the 1945 Ford Motor Company strike in Windsor, Ontario: all workers are required to pay union dues.

94. "Support a Union—Don't Buy Old Dutch," *AUPE News* (8 May 2009), http://www.aupe.org/news/support-a-union-dont-buy-old-dutch/.

95. Canadian Labour Congress, "Labour Council Endorses CLC Boycott of Old Dutch Snack Foods," http://hamiltonlabour.ca/doc.php?did=105.

96. *United Food and Commercial Workers Union, Local 401 v. Old Dutch Foods, 2009*, CanLII 61316 (AB LRB), retrieved on 1 February 2015, http://canlii.ca/t/26h5g; "Old Dutch Members Ratify 4-Year Agreement," *Union: The Membership Magazine for UFCW Local 832* (December 2009): 4.

97. "Victory at Old Dutch Foods!," release by UFCW Local 401, n.d., retrieved 7 January 2013, http://www.gounion.ca/files/dec_15_old_dutch_victory.pdf.

98. Steven Aanenson interview.

99. Steven Aanenson, president of Old Dutch Foods, personal communication, 10 June 2015.

100. Jean Pierre (J.P.) Petit interview.

101. Ibid.

102. Ibid.

103. Martial Boulet interview. At the factory in Roseville, MN, the opposite is the case. Men work on packaging while women are shift supervisors. Unlike in Winnipeg, the Roseville factory uses many automatic case packers. The work is thus not very physical, though it is repetitive. Steven Aanenson interview.

104. Martial Boulet interview.

105. Jean Pierre (J.P.) Petit interview.

106. Bebe Maqsood interview.

107. Ibid.

108. Martial Boulet interview.

109. Shope-Easy and Jewel grocery advertisement, *Winnipeg Free Press*, 9 December 1954, 14.

110. Shop-Easy grocery advertisement, *Winnipeg Free Press,* 21 November 1956, 10.

111. The Bay grocery advertisement, *Winnipeg Free Press,* 11 September 1957, 17; Starland movie listings, *Winnipeg Free Press,* 31 October 1958, 17. The Starland theatre was demolished in 2008. "Winnipeg Starland Theatre Faces Wrecking Ball," *CBC News,* 1 May 2008, http://www.cbc.ca/news/canada/manitoba/winnipeg-s-starland-theatre-faces-wrecking-ball-1.704969.

112. *Old Dutch Foods, Inc., Plaintiff-appellee, v. Dan Dee Pretzel & Potato Chip Co. and Berg's Pretzels, Inc., defendants-appellants, United States Court of Appeals,* Sixth Ciricuit, 477 F.2d 150, argued 28 November 1972, decided 25 April 1973.

113. Paul Levy, "Bob Colburn Wrote Ads for Old Dutch, Fritz," *Minneapolis Star Tribune,* 7 November 2011, http://www.startribune.com/business/133411108.html.

114. "Sing-A-Long with Old Dutch," typescript, n.d., courtesy of Old Dutch Foods, Roseville, MN. See ForgetfulCollector, "1970s Old Dutch Potato Chips Ad," *YouTube,* uploaded 23 September 2009, https://www.youtube.com/watch?v=9UmftgiWXl4&feature=youtube_gdata_player.

115. Bill Farmer, "TV Ads Sterilize Male Libido," *Chicago Tribune,* 16 December 1979, 8. "Miss Old Dutch" also made appearances at store promotions in Winnipeg. Advertisement, *Winnipeg Free Press,* 16 September 1965, 45.

116. Ric Swihart, "Chip Producer Battling Competition" [December 1992], courtesy of Old Dutch Foods, Roseville, MN.

117. Kathleen Deveny, "Crunch Time in the Snack Industry," *Wall Street Journal,* 17 November 1990, courtesy of Old Dutch Foods, Roseville, MN.

118. "Birth, Death Immortalized in Metal," *Winnipeg Free Press,* 20 September 1987, NE/13.

119. RetroWinnipeg, "Old Dutch Commercial (1987)," *YouTube,* uploaded 13 October 2006, https://www.youtube.com/watch?v=2ntNC6bZIuM&feature=youtube_gdata_player. For other Old Dutch ads from this era, see RetroWinnipeg, "Old Dutch Double Dutch Commercial (1990)," *YouTube,* uploaded 20 October 2009, https://www.youtube.com/watch?v=cP6sg0RfSPg&feature=youtube_gdata_player; and robatsea2009, "Old Dutch Potato Chips Potato Wars 1978," *YouTube,* uploaded 17 November 2009, https://www.youtube.com/watch?v=dinQQLjFyIs&feature=youtube_gdata_player (the latter is a quirky parody of *Star Wars*).

120. Bernard Pacyniak, "Roping in Technology," *Snack Food & Wholesale Bakery* 89, no. 1 (January 2000): 26.

121. Kristin Tillotson, "Always Hometown Stars, Old Dutch Chips Hit Movies," *Minneapolis Star Tribune,* 16 February 1997, F1; Chinta Puxley, "Winnipeg: Somewhere between 'Exotic and Obscure,'" *Globe and Mail,* 24 October

2008, http://www.theglobeandmail.com/news/national/winnipeg-somewhere-between-exotic-and-obscure/article20389285/; Randall King, "The Office Plans to Take Us Down a 'Peg," *Winnipeg Free Press,* 8 November 2008, C1.

122. Bill Bashucky interview.

123. Kristin Tillotson, "Always Hometown Stars, Old Dutch Chips Hit Movies," *Minneapolis Star Tribune,* 16 February 1997, F1.

124. An Old Dutch employee notes "the BBQ with the two logs burning is an iconic Old Dutch symbol." Anonymous Old Dutch employee interview.

125. J. Kelly Nestruck, "Uniting the Country, One Tater at a Time," *National Post,* 20 December 2005, AL2.

126. [Maurice] Smith, "Youngsters Need Hockey Equipment," *Winnipeg Free Press,* 12 January 1961, 42.

127. Photo, *Winnipeg Free Press,* 4 July 1961, 1; "Miss Manitoba Must Be Well-Rounded, Talented," *Winnipeg Free Press,* 11 June 1964, 52.

128. Advertisement, *Winnipeg Free Press,* 25 October 1961, 24; advertisement, *Winnipeg Free Press,* 2 February 1966, 26; advertisement, *Winnipeg Free Press,* 2 February 1966, 11; "Hillaby Wins Skeet," *Winnipeg Free Press,* 18 June 1962, 18; Don Osborne, "Jottings from the Business World," *Winnipeg Free Press,* 19 November 1962, 28; "Ex Marks Spot," *Winnipeg Free Press,* 22 June 1964, 3; Ron Campbell, "250,000 Watch Monster Red River Ex Parade," *Winnipeg Free Press,* 27 June 1966, 3; advertisement, *Winnipeg Free Press,* 29 October 1964, 55; "Basketball Teams Getting Trip to Kenora Thursday," *Winnipeg Free Press,* 18 July 1967, 17; Don Blanchard, "'Appreciation Night' Planned for Delveaux," *Winnipeg Free Press,* 19 March 1965, 39; photo, *Winnipeg Free Press,* 30 March 1965, 20.

129. Advertisement, *Winnipeg Free Press,* 7 August 1986, 32; Wanda Chow, "Ex-jailbird Gives Kids Straight Goods," *Winnipeg Free Press,* 28 September 1995, A12.

130. "Here's Activities for Spring Break," *Winnipeg Free Press,* 22 March 1991, 31.

131. "Wirvin Tops Seniors," *Winnipeg Free Press,* 5 February 1960, 26; Maurice Smith, "Perrin Can't See Los Angeles Getting WHL Franchise," *Winnipeg Free Press,* 21 April 1960, 27; "Pin League Winds Up," *Winnipeg Free Press,* 3 May 1965, 26; Gene Telpner, "It Strikes Me," *Winnipeg Free Press,* 26 January 1966, 50; "Cirotzki Wins Trip to Madison," *Winnipeg Free Press,* 23 November 1968, 48; "Dercola, Mousseau in Form," *Winnipeg Free Press,* 12 December 1968, 62; "Pin Sweep," *Winnipeg Free Press,* 22 September 1970, 27; Ted Hart, "It Strikes Me," *Winnipeg Free Press,* 12 March 1971, 43; Al Vickery, "Big Ball and Small in Spotlight," *Winnipeg Free Press,* 20 February 1986, 57; "Classic Standings Unchanged," *Winnipeg Free Press,* 21 January 1971, 50; "St. James Ladies," *Winnipeg Free Press,* 18 June 1970, 62; Ted Hart,

"It Strikes Me," *Winnipeg Free Press,* 27 April 1972, 61; Melissa Martin, "Portage Pitbulls Find Pigskin Heaven," *Winnipeg Free Press,* 28 October 2013, C7.

132. Maurice Smith, "They Welcomed Cold Weather at St. Ambroise," *Winnipeg Free Press,* 19 October 1960, 45; Maurice Smith, "Time Out with Maurice Smith," *Winnipeg Free Press,* 9 June 1961, 19; Maurice Smith, "Time Out with Maurice Smith," *Winnipeg Free Press,* 2 April 1963, 21; Elman Guttormson, "Whips, Spurs and Blinkers," *Winnipeg Free Press,* 21 June 1963, 41; Maurice Smith, "Great Fishing at Great Bear," *Winnipeg Free Press,* 31 August 1963, 45; Stan Bentham, "Outdoors with Stan Bentham," *Winnipeg Free Press,* 6 February 1964, 43; Maurice Smith, "Trout Grow Big in Back River," *Winnipeg Free Press,* 29 August 1964, 51; Elman Guttormson, "'Outsiders' Finally Click," *Winnipeg Free Press,* 21 July 1962, 52; Elman Guttormson, "Sal's Imp Wins Fourth of Year," *Winnipeg Free Press,* 30 July 1963, 19; Elman Guttormson, "Robby-Miles Wins Again for Lew," *Winnipeg Free Press,* 25 June 1964, 47; "Wheat City Purse Tops Card Today," *Winnipeg Free Press,* 25 June 1965, 38; Elman Guttormson, "Filby's Sam's Sam Sets up Season's Biggest Double," *Winnipeg Free Press,* 26 June 1965, 64; Elman Guttormson, "Celeritas Surprises Everyone Including Owners," *Winnipeg Free Press,* 27 April 1972, 60; Bob Armstrong, "A Day or Night at the Downs Now a Year-Round Adventure," Assiniboia Downs advertising supplement, *Winnipeg Free Press,* 5 May 2000.

133. "The Free Press Form Chart," *Winnipeg Free Press,* 30 July 1963, 19; "Eddie Foy Will Visit," *Winnipeg Free Press,* 10 July 1964, 42; "Top Entry at Downs for Ladies' Day Card," *Winnipeg Free Press,* 24 June 1966, 49; Elman Guttormson, "Ruling Lark Osiris Queen," *Winnipeg Free Press,* 3 August 1968, 49.

134. Jimmy Robinson's Famous Duck Lodge, http://jimmyrobinsonsducklodge.com/; Maurice Smith, "Time Out with Maurice Smith," *Winnipeg Free Press,* 29 October 1963, 24; Maurice Smith, "Time Out with Maurice Smith," *Winnipeg Free Press,* 27 October 1964, 23; Maurice Smith, "Twins' Hopes Fading Fast Away," *Winnipeg Free Press,* 13 October 1965, 57; Maurice Smith, "Time Out with Maurice Smith," *Winnipeg Free Press,* 18 October 1966, 25.

135. Mel Dagg, "Outdoors," *Winnipeg Free Press,* 15 June 1979, 78.

136. Thiessen, *Manufacturing Mennonites,* 72.

137. See, for example, Sangster, "Softball Solution"; Sangster, *Earning Respect;* Parr, *Gender of Breadwinners;* Tone, *Business of Benevolence;* Zahavi, *Workers, Managers, and Welfare Capitalism.*

138. Lee Egerstrom, "Snack Food Crunch," *St. Paul Pioneer Press,* 8 February 1993, D1.

139. Ibid.

140. Steven Aanenson interview.

141. "Carl J. Marx, Old Dutch Founder, Dies," *Minneapolis Star,* 7 August 1970, courtesy of Old Dutch Foods, Roseville, MN.

142. Kristin Tillotson, "Always Hometown Stars, Old Dutch Chips Hit Movies," *Minneapolis Star Tribune,* 16 February 1997, F1; Bernard Pacyniak, "A Brand for Both Borders," *Snack Food* 85, no. 4 (April 1996): 18.

143. Lee Egerstrom, "In the Chips," *St. Paul Pioneer Press,* 16 December 2001, D1.

144. David Oye interview.

145. J. Kelly Nestruck, "Can't Dutch This," *National Post,* 8 February 2007, AL5. Old Dutch sales were $450 million in 2012. Sam Black, "Selling Old Dutch for 50 Years," *Minneapolis/St. Paul Business Journal,* 30 March 2012, http://www.bizjournals.com/twincities/print-edition/2012/03/30/for-50-years-selling-old-dutch.html?page=all.

146. Dick McMahon interview.

147. Martin Cash, "Hostess Treats Old Dutch Like Gate Crasher in Toronto," *Winnipeg Free Press,* 6 July 1991, 15; Mark Heinzl, "Hostess on Buying Binge of Rival's Potato Chips," *Globe and Mail,* 3 July 1991, B3.

148. Mark Heinzl, "Hostess on Buying Binge of Rival's Potato Chips," *Globe and Mail,* 3 July 1991, B3.

149. Ibid.

150. Ibid.

151. "When Chips Are Down, Old Dutch Fights Back," *Toronto Star,* 8 July 1991, D2.

152. Heidi Graham, "Toronto Chip War Stirs Ripples in Winkler," *Winnipeg Free Press,* 7 July 1991, 1.

153. "Town Opts out of Spuds Spat," *Winnipeg Free Press,* 10 July 1991, 22.

154. Editorial, "Competition for Chips," *Winnipeg Free Press,* 11 July 1991, 6.

155. Martin Cash, "Federal Officials Looking at Chip War Allegations," *Winnipeg Free Press,* 11 July 1991, 15; Mark Heinzl, "Bureau Checking Chips," *Globe and Mail,* 3 July 1991, B4.

156. Martin Cash, "Niche Player Connects with India Giant," *Winnipeg Free Press,* 16 July 1991, 13.

157. Steven Aanenson notes that Old Dutch would never take away volume discounts for advertising other brands. Old Dutch had established programs to incentivize retailers (for example, if they set up end displays promoting Old Dutch products); if those conditions changed (e.g., if the end display was removed), then the retailer would lose the associated discount. Advertising other brands was never tied to these discounts. Steven Aanenson, president of Old Dutch Foods, personal communication, 10 June 2015.

158. Rey Pagtakhan, "Brave Step," letter to editor, *Winnipeg Free Press,* 9 August 1991, 6.

159. Martin Cash, "Jacks Launches Tax Training School," *Winnipeg Free Press,* 2 February 1993, B11.

160. Lee Egerstrom, "Snack Food Crunch," *St. Paul Pioneer Press,* 8 February 1993, D1; "Happy's to Aanenson," *Snack Food* (December 1982): 7.

161. Bernard Pacyniak, "Roping in Technology," *Snack Food & Wholesale Bakery* 89, no. 1 (January 2000): 26; Old Dutch, special promotional supplement by *Grocer Today* (March 2000), courtesy of Old Dutch Foods, Roseville, MN.

162. Jason Kirby, "Humpty Dumpty Investors Strive to Prevent Crack-Up," *National Post,* 12 February 2005, FP5.

163. Dana Flavelle, "Shareholder Revolt Hits Chip Maker," *Toronto Star,* 4 February 2005, F01; David Oye interview.

164. These smaller companies included Olde Barrel chips in Prince Edward Island and Murphy's chips in Ontario. Sarah Scott, "All the King's Horses . . . ," *National Post,* 1 January 2004, 42.

165. Sean Silcoff, "Old Dutch Buys Humpty Dumpty," *National Post,* 22 March 2006, FP1.

166. Ibid.

167. Richard Blackwell, "Humpty Dumpty Posts Loss," *Globe and Mail,* 20 May 2003, B5.

168. Sarah Scott, "All the King's Horses . . . ," *National Post,* 1 January 2004, 42.

169. Board members included Gerald Schmalz's "company lawyer, a close friend and a local physician." Jacquie McNish, "Shareholders Flex New-Found Muscles," *Globe and Mail,* 26 March 2005, http://www.theglobeandmail.com/report-on-business/shareholders-flex-new-found-muscles/article18219326/?page=all. See also Richard Bloom, "Humpty Dumpty Holders Oppose Old Dutch Deal," *Globe and Mail,* 4 February 2005, B8; Richard Bloom, "Investors Shatter Humpty Dumpty Deal," *Globe and Mail,* 23 February 2005, B4; "Humpty Dumpty Sells Stake to Old Dutch Unit," *Toronto Star,* 2 February 2005, C05.

170. Tavia Grant and Roma Luciw, "Mixed Performance," *Globe and Mail,* 21 March 2006, http://www.theglobeandmail.com/report-on-business/mixed-performance/article1096440/; Romina Maurino, "Old Dutch Buys Humpty Dumpty for $26.7 Million," *Toronto Star,* 22 March 2006, E08; "FP Summary," *National Post,* 22 March 2006, FP2; "Old Dutch Buys Humpty," *Globe and Mail,* 21 March 2006, http://www.theglobeandmail.com/report-on-business/old-dutch-buys-humpty/article20409606/; "Old Dutch to Swallow Competing Chips Brand," *Winnipeg Free Press,* 22 March 2006, B7.

171. "Humpty Dumpty An Easy Sell," *The Record,* 29 March 2006, C4; Ron Deruyter, "Humpty Dumpty Takeover Complete," *The Record,* 18 May 2006, B11; Ron Deruyter, "Humpty Dumpty to Be Sold," *The Record,* 22 March 2006, E4; Romina Maurino, "Old Dutch Gobbles up Humpty Dumpty," *Hamilton Spectator,* 22 March 2006, A18.

172. Andy Hoffman, "Old Dutch to Digest Humpty Dumpty," *Globe and Mail,* 22 March 2006, http://www.theglobeandmail.com/report-on-business/old-dutch-to-digest-humpty-dumpty/article18159046/.

173. "Old Dutch Launching Its Chips in the East," *Winnipeg Free Press,* 27 March 2007, B7.

174. Larry Kusch, "Old Dutch's Full Product Line Goes National," *Winnipeg Free Press,* 10 September 2008, B5; Geoff Kirbyson, "Old Dutch Brand Heads East," *Winnipeg Free Press,* 30 March 2007, B1.

175. Some 180 of those workers were represented by the Bakery, Confectionery, Tobacco Workers and Grain Millers' International Union, Local 550. Jeff Heinrich and Kevin Dougherty, "Quebec Offers Support for Laid-Off Snack-Food Workers," *Montreal Gazette,* 8 May 2013, http://www.montrealgazette.com/business/Parti+Qu%C3%A9b%C3%A9cois+offers+support+laid+Dutch+workers/8355022/story.html.

176. "Quebec Did Not Know Old Dutch Foods Plant Was Closing," *CBC News* Montreal, 8 May 2013, http://www.cbc.ca/news/canada/montreal/quebec-did-not-know-old-dutch-foods-plant-was-closing-1.1380996.

177. "Old Dutch Gets $15-Million Loan from New Brunswick," *Globe and Mail,* 4 August 2010, http://www.theglobeandmail.com/news/national/old-dutch-gets-15-million-loan-from-new-brunswick/article1212765/.

178. Ibid.; Rebecca Penty, "Old Dutch Foods Ltd. Expands in Hartland," *Saint John Telegraph-Journal,* 4 August 2010, B1; "Old Dutch Gets $15-Million Loan from New Brunswick," *Globe and Mail,* 23 August 2012, http://www.theglobeandmail.com/news/national/old-dutch-gets-15-million-loan-from-new-brunswick/article1212765/; Business New Brunswick, Office of the Premier, "Potato chip factory expands, creating 40 additional jobs," news release, 3 August 2010; Quentin Casey, "Potato-Chip Maker's $15-Million Loan to Add Jobs in N.B.," *Saint John Telegraph-Journal,* 3 August 2010, courtesy of Old Dutch Foods, Roseville, MN; Shawn Berry, "Old Dutch to Expand Hartland Plant," *Fredericton Daily Gleaner,* 3 August 2010, courtesy of Old Dutch Foods, Roseville, MN.

179. "Chip vs. Crisp," *National Post,* 28 June 2006, http://www.canada.com/nationalpost/news/story.html?id=d814c148-b15b-4f2e-8468-369537498a9b.

180. Ibid. The comment on the "tasty union" of salt and vinegar is identical phrasing to that used in a *National Post* article published a year earlier. Kelly Nestruck, "Uniting the Country, One Tater at a Time," *National Post,* 20 December 2005, AL2.

181. "Fire Destroys Plant," *Winnipeg Free Press,* 27 September 1965, 11.

182. Randall Hobart, "Old Dutch Will Build Complex in Roseville," *Minneapolis Star* (circa 1960s), courtesy of Old Dutch Foods, Roseville, MN.

183. Photo by Dave Johnson, *Winnipeg Free Press,* 5 May 1972, 1.

184. Paul Roberton, "Fire Guts Building," *Winnipeg Free Press,* 5 May 1972, 1.

185. Ibid.

186. John Hample, "Firemen Fight Second Blaze in Food Plant," *Winnipeg Free Press,* 29 July 1975, 1.

187. Untitled newspaper clipping, *Winnipeg Tribune,* 27 September 1976, University of Manitoba Archives and Special Collections, Winnipeg Tribune Clippings Collection; Maurice Smith, "Time Out with Maurice Smith," *Winnipeg Free Press,* 11 September 1964, 35; Clean Environment Commission advertisement, *Winnipeg Free Press,* 5 June 1985, 15.

188. Anonymous Old Dutch employee interview.

189. "Old Dutch Foods Builds New $3.5 Million Plant," *Winnipeg Tribune,* 12 November 1976, University of Manitoba Archives and Special Collections, Winnipeg Tribune Clippings Collection.

190. Letter to Old Dutch from Mrs. Lois Trast, 5 May 1980, courtesy of Old Dutch Foods, Roseville, MN.

191. Ibid.

192. Susan Sampson, "Doing Crunches with Old Dutch Chips," *Toronto Star,* 18 April 2007, D3.

193. Craig Courtice, "Want Some Vico to Wash Down Those MexiFries?," *National Post,* 28 July 2007, TO11.

194. David Avery, "En-treat-ies: The Great Canadian Confection Election!," *National Post,* 27 June 2006, B2.

195. Others make broader claims: "Old Dutch ketchup chips are a part of the Western Canadian cultural landscape . . . [They are] a standard Western Canadian comfort food." "Food Fight: Old Dutch Ketchup Chips, Baked vs. Fried," *Nearof!* (blog post), 22 November 2010, http://www.nearof.com/?p=74.

196. Salisbury House (often nicknamed Sal's or Sals) is a restaurant chain in Winnipeg. It has been described as "not just a business, but one of the cultural institutions that make this city unique." Bartley Kives, "A Salisbury House Divided," *Winnipeg Free Press,* 20 January 2013, http://www.winnipegfreepress.com/local/A-Salisbury-House-divided-187655271.html.

197. Gordon Sinclair Jr., "Playing Sexual Trivial Pursuit," *Winnipeg Free Press,* 11 October 1985, 27. See also Gordon Sinclair Jr., "Toronto Hearts in Winnipeg," *Winnipeg Free Press,* 22 October 1985, 17.

198. Kielbasa is a type of eastern European sausage, made popular in Winnipeg by the Ukrainian immigrant community.

199. Andrew Maxwell, "More Flood Aid Washes In," *Winnipeg Free Press,* 1 June 1997, A5.

200. Geoff Kirbyson, "Ex- 'Peggers Party It Up in T.O. for Museum," *Winnipeg Free Press,* 8 June 2009, A4.

201. "Your Weekend Weather," *Winnipeg Free Press,* 20 March 2010, A2.

202. Paul Samyn, "Doer Leads Fight for Lab," *Winnipeg Free Press,* 8 March 2004, A1.

203. Paul Pihichyn, "Let Me Be Your Tour Guide to Portugal," *Winnipeg Free Press,* 22 July 2006, E1.

204. "Sweet Home Manitoba," *Winnipeg Free Press,* 4 January 2010, 10. Old Dutch themselves contribute to this tradition—for example, by donating their chips to a fundraising social for a boy who needed a bone marrow transplant. Gordon Sinclair Jr., "Southdale Residents Prove Professionals Wrong," *Winnipeg Free Press,* 16 April 1991, 3.

205. Bothwell Cheese is a Manitoba cheese manufacturer founded in 1936. Bothwell Cheese, "A Brief History," 2013, http://www.bothwellcheese.com/about-us/history.html.

206. "Get Ready for World's Biggest Social," *Winnipeg Free Press,* 2 February 2010, B2. Old Dutch was a sponsor of this event. "Wanna Go to a Social? Everyone Will Be There," *Winnipeg Free Press,* 21 October 2009, B2; notice from organizers of World's Largest Social, *Winnipeg Free Press* advertising flyer, 20 May 2010. See also Morley Walker, "Toronto Digs Festival that Comes Right from the Peg," *Winnipeg Free Press,* 31 July 2006, D3; David Sanderson, "Ain't No Party Like a Manitoba Party," *Winnipeg Free Press,* 15 May 2010, F1; "Saturday Socials Draw Thousands," *Winnipeg Free Press,* 17 May 2010, B2.

207. Bartley Kives, "Long-Distance Longing," *Winnipeg Free Press,* 4 December 2004, F6.

208. Linda Quattrin, "Ontario Glamour Begins to Fade, Jobless Return," *Winnipeg Free Press,* 6 April 1992, C21.

209. Doug Nairne, "Twin Cities Canadian Pines for Old Home, Eh?," *Winnipeg Free Press,* 2 July 1999, A1.

210. Rick Loewen, "Nip Sals Complaints in the Bud," *Winnipeg Free Press,* 26 February 2005, F3.

211. Alison Mayes, "Passing the . . . Flute," *Winnipeg Free Press,* 9 April 2011, G1.

212. Shel Zolkewich, "Reach for the Beach," *Winnipeg Free Press,* 20 January 2007, F5.

213. Bill Redekop, "Seeking a Little Taste of Home," *Winnipeg Free Press,* 3 May 2010, A4.

214. Gordon Sinclair Jr., "Satisfying the Hungry-for-Winnipeg Customer," *Winnipeg Free Press,* 9 June 2009, B1.

215. Geoff Kirbyson, "Old Dutch Plant Marks 50th Year," *Winnipeg Free Press,* 26 August 2004, D9.

216. Kristin Tillotson, "Always Hometown Stars, Old Dutch Chips Hit Movies," *Minneapolis Star Tribune,* 16 February 1997, F18.

217. Bill Redekop, "Hockey Fever," *Winnipeg Free Press,* 10 February 2008, A3.

218. Simon Fuller, "New Business Location Is a Sweet Deal," *Winnipeg Free Press,* 10 February 2013, http://www.winnipegfreepress.com/our-communities/lance/New-business-location-is-a-sweet-deal-226010491.html.

219. Bill Bashucky interview.

220. Old Dutch Foods Ltd., "Arriba Spicy Chopped Salad," http://www.olddutchfoods.ca/recipes/category/28/view/37; Old Dutch Foods Ltd., "Restaurante Pollo Sopa (Chicken Soup)," http://www.olddutchfoods.ca/recipes/category/29/view/38; Old Dutch Foods Ltd., "Old Dutch Restaurante Salmon Appetizer," http://www.olddutchfoods.ca/recipes/category/30/view/39; Old Dutch Foods Ltd., "Old Dutch Dill-licious Salmon Patties with Sun-Dried Tomato Infused Mayonnaise," http://www.olddutchfoods.ca/recipes/category/31/view/41; Old Dutch Foods Inc., "Simplicious Entrees," http://www.olddutchfoods.com/recipes/category/4.

221. Statistics Canada, "Foreign Control in the Canadian Economy: Corporations Return Act (61-220-X)," 2013, http://www.statcan.gc.ca/pub/61-220-x/2013000/aftertoc-aprestdm1-eng.htm.

222. Charlie Angelakos, "Can Your Company Be Foreign Owned—But Still Canadian?," *Globe and Mail,* 27 February 2014, http://www.theglobeandmail.com/report-on-business/careers/leadership-lab/foreign-owned-but-still-canadian/article17137439/.

223. Ace Burpee, "The Bombers Take Over Old Dutch" (blog post), *Winnipeg Free Press,* 1 September 2009, http://www.winnipegfreepress.com/ace/blogs/The-Bombers-take-over-Old-Dutch-56717502.html.

224. Ibid.

Chapter 2
THE CHANGING CHIP INDUSTRY

1. The epigraph to the chapter is from G.H. Fast, quoted in Sheldon Bowles, "Manitoba Potato Chip Firm Set Up in 1960 Now Has Sales Exceeding $2 Million a Year," *Winnipeg Free Press,* 15 June 1968, 13. David Oye interview.
2. Red Dot distributed in Wisconsin, Minnesota, North Dakota, Iowa, Kansas, and Indiana.
3. Nalley's and Williams & Company operated in Washington and Oregon.
4. Blue Bell and Good-ee operated in Oregon.
5. Goodies distributed in Montana.
6. Jackson's distributed in Washington.
7. Scott operated in Minnesota.
8. "Television Snacks Cause Shifts in Potato Marketing," *The Northwest* (September–October 1957): 3–4.
9. "Okay, Some More Job Opportunities," *Phil Are Go!* (blog), 31 July 2012, http://phil-are-go.blogspot.ca/2012/07/okay-some-more-job-opportunities.html.
10. Ibid.
11. Sheldon Bowles, "Manitoba Potato Chip Firm Set Up in 1960 Now Has Sales Exceeding $2 Million a Year," *Winnipeg Free Press,* 15 June 1968, 13.
12. Ibid.
13. Norah Cherry, "American from Paris Gets Credit for Original Potato Chip Order," *Winnipeg Free Press,* 3 April 1970, 19. See also "Potato Chips Snacks Plus," *Winnipeg Free Press,* 27 January 1971, 27.
14. Don Kroeker interview.
15. Ibid.
16. Sheldon Bowles, "Manitoba Potato Chip Firm Set Up in 1960 Now Has Sales Exceeding $2 Million a Year," *Winnipeg Free Press,* 15 June 1968, 13.
17. Don Kroeker interview. Southern Potato Company also provided potatoes to Irish Potato Chips. John Kuhl interview; Marlon Kuhl interview.
18. Don Kroeker interview.
19. Ibid.
20. Ibid.
21. Typescript provided by Don Kroeker, dated 23 January 2015; Don Osborne, "Jottings from the Business World," *Winnipeg Free Press,* 17 February 1962, 62; "Potato Seminar," *Winnipeg Free Press,* 5 March 1969, 12.

22. The Potato Chip Institute International later became the Potato Chip/Snack Food Association.

23. "Potato Chips Defended as High in Food Value," *Winnipeg Tribune*, 19 March 1971, University of Manitoba Archives and Special Collections, Winnipeg Tribune Clippings Collection. This seminar is also mentioned in "Chip Potato Seminar at U of M," *Winnipeg Free Press*, 9 March 1971, 21.

24. Aldo Santin, "Overabundant Water Means Shortage of Spuds," *Winnipeg Free Press*, 29 July 1993, B2.

25. Karen Lerch, "Bigger Potato Means Bigger Potato Chip," *Winnipeg Free Press*, 29 July 1971, 21; "Candy Packaging Can Be Deceptive," *Winnipeg Free Press*, 19 December 1975, 21.

26. Sidorick, *Condensed Capitalism*, 33.

27. Ibid., 31.

28. Ibid., 14, 36.

29. In the early twenty-first century, the CPCA consists of eight chip makers in ten provinces.

30. Joanne Hvala, "CPCA . . . Concerned about Canadian Chippers," *Chipper/Snacker* (October 1977): 26.

31. Ibid.

32. Ibid.

33. Ibid.

34. Ibid., 27.

35. Ibid.

36. Turner and Molyneaux, "Agricultural Science," 45, 50. On wheat, see Varty, "On Protein"; Varty, "Growing Bread."

37. Turner and Molyneaux, "Agricultural Science," 45, 50.

38. Ibid., 44.

39. Ibid., 62–63.

40. Ibid., 63.

41. Thornton, "Retrospectives," 257–58.

42. See Blair and Harrison, *Monopsony in Law.*

43. Ibid., 172.

44. Ibid.

45. Ibid., 187.

46. The Minnesota plant has a more diverse group of potato producers. In April and May, potatoes are purchased from Florida; in May and June, they come from California; in July, the sources are Oregon, Washington, and Colorado; in July and August, potatoes come from Wisconsin and Nebraska; from August through September, the suppliers are in Minnesota and Alberta; throughout the fall and winter, potatoes are obtained from Alberta's Red Deer Valley. This last group "often can cause quality problems" since these potatoes are a storage crop rather than newly harvested. Typescript, n.d., courtesy of Old Dutch Foods, Roseville, MN; Steven Aanenson, president of Old Dutch Foods, personal communication, 13 May 2015.

47. Martin Cash, "Agri-Food Production: From Nowhere to Phenomenal Growth in Just Five Years," *Winnipeg Free Press*, "Manitoba" supplement, 12 April 1997, 24; Manitoba Trade and Investment, "Commodities: Special Crops: Potatoes," last updated c. 2003, http://www.gov.mb.ca/trade/globaltrade/agrifood/commodity/potatoes.html (accessed 1 July 2016).

48. Manitoba Trade and Investment, "Commodities: Special Crops: Potatoes," last updated c. 2003, http://www.gov.mb.ca/trade/globaltrade/agrifood/commodity/potatoes.html (accessed 1 July 2016).

49. Geoff Kirbyson, "Portage Honours McCain Foods," *Winnipeg Free Press,* 9 January 2004, C9; Martin Cash, "Potato Growers Expect Fatter Yield This Year," *Winnipeg Free Press,* 21 July 2007, B9.

50. These companies prefer supplying chipping potatoes to Old Dutch rather than Frito-Lay: the money is better, and Old Dutch does not penalize them if growing or storage conditions make it impossible for them to fulfill their contracts. Anonymous industry expert interview; Don Kroeker interview.

51. Red potatoes, when fried into chips, turn very dark brown. Anonymous industry expert interview.

52. Gerhard Otto Voth interview.

53. Steven Aanenson, president of Old Dutch Foods, personal communication, 10 June 2015.

54. Bernie Kruchak, "In the Crunch Old Dutch Succeeds," *Western Grocer* [date unknown]: 80–85, courtesy of Old Dutch Foods, Roseville, MN.

55. Wayne Rempel interview.

56. The company has 14 non-family members and 165 family members as shareholders.

57. Don Kroeker interview.

58. Ibid.

59. Rogers Sugar closed their plant in Winnipeg in early 1997. Ian Bell, "Manitoba Beet Growers Finally Paid," *The Western Producer,* 21 January

1999, http://www.producer.com/1999/01/manitoba-beet-growers-finally-paid/.

60. Teresa Falk, "Grower Spotlight: Haskett Growers: Grooming Future Farmers," *Spud Smart Media* (3 August 2011), http://www.spudsmart.com/past-issues/summer-2011/183-sum2011growerspotlight.html (accessed 24 August 2016).

61. Peak of the Market is a large, grower-owned vegetable supplier and potato marketing board in Manitoba. Peak of the Market, "About Us," http://www.peakmarket.com/about_us.cfm; Bartley Kives, "Peak of the Market, Potato Farmer Square Off," *Winnipeg Free Press,* 18 September 2009, http://www.winnipegfreepress.com/local/Peak-of-the-Market-potato-farmer-square-off--59724107.html.

62. A hundredweight is 100 pounds or approximately forty-five kilograms.

63. Anonymous industry expert interview.

64. Ibid.

65. John Kuhl interview; Marlon Kuhl interview.

66. The Manitoba Sugar Company was created in 1939, and was purchased by BC Sugar Refinery Co. Ltd. in 1955. Manitoba Sugar was renamed Rogers Sugar in 1995, and the plant was closed in 1997. Administrative history of Manitoba Sugar Company records, Series S15, City of Vancouver Archives, http://searcharchives.vancouver.ca/manitoba-sugar-company.

67. Tom Brodbeck, "MLA Says 'Peg Plant Sacrificed," *Winnipeg Sun,* 25 January 1997, 2.

68. Manitoba Agriculture Hall of Fame, "Peter J. Peters," 2009, http://www.manitobaaghalloffame.com/hall_of_fame.php?ID=146.

69. Southern Potato Company, "History," http://southernpotato.com/history.php.

70. Many of the seasonal workers are Mexican Mennonites, whose ancestors migrated from Manitoba in the 1920s.

71. John Kuhl interview; Marlon Kuhl interview.

72. Marlon Kuhl interview.

73. John Kuhl interview.

74. Ibid.; Marlon Kuhl interview.

75. Ibid.

76. Garth Stone, "A Little Background History," Manitoba Potato Production Days website, http://www.mbpotatodays.ca/history.html; Manitoba Agricultural Hall of Fame, "Anton & Adeline Chorney," 2010, http://www.manitobaaghalloffame.com/ahofmember/chorney-anton-adeline/.

77. John Kuhl interview; Marlon Kuhl interview.

78. Maloni and Benton, "Power Influences," 52.

79. Ibid.

80. Food and Agriculture Organization of the United Nations, "International Year of the Potato, 2008: Global Potato Economy," http://www.fao.org/potato-2008/en/potato/economy.html.

81. Sarah Morrison, "That Beet Is Sweet!" Statistics Canada, 2006, http://www.statcan.gc.ca/pub/96-325-x/2007000/article/10576-eng.htm.

82. Canadian Sugar Institute, "Refined Sugar Production," 2014–15, http://www.sugar.ca/Canadian-Sugar-Industry/Canadian-Sugar-Industry-Statistics/Refined-Sugar-Production.aspx.

83. International Cocoa Organization, "World Map of Production and Net Exports of Cocoa Beans in 2005/2006," http://www.icco.org/statistics/other-statistical-data.html.

84. Marie-Andrée Hamel and Erik Dorff, "Corn: Canada's Third Most Valuable Crop," Statistics Canada, March 2014, http://www.statcan.gc.ca/pub/96-325-x/2014001/article/11913-eng.htm.

85. Marlon Kuhl interview.

86. Don Kroeker interview; Wayne Rempel interview.

87. Anonymous industry expert interview.

88. Don Kroeker interview.

89. Preibisch, "Pick-Your-Own Labor"; Read, Zell, and Fernandez, *Migrant Voices*, 6.

90. The North-South Institute, *Migrant Workers in Canada*, 2.

91. Preibisch, "Pick-Your-Own Labor," 413.

92. Two reserves, on either side of the Red River, were created for the settlement of Mennonites from Russia in 1873 (East) and 1876 (West). See Epp, *Mennonites in Canada*, 209–30.

93. Read, Zell, and Fernandez, *Migrant Voices*, 1–2. The classic work on Mexican migrant workers in Canada is Basok, *Tortillas and Tomatoes*. For the history of Mexican Mennonites, see Sawatzky, *They Sought a Country;* and Quiring, *Mennonite Old Colony Vision*.

94. Dick McMahon interview.

95. Anonymous Old Dutch employee interview.

96. Tiling involves burying plastic or clay pipes punctured by holes to drain excess water from fields. Kroeker Farms claims that they were the first to irrigate potatoes in the province. Wayne Rempel interview.

97. Anonymous industry expert interview.

98. They also had a storage facility in Duchess, Alberta. The Taber facility stored 150,000 hundredweights of potatoes; Duchess stored 110,000 hundredweights. These two facilities were sold to the Alberta potato growers around the year 2000. Steven Aanenson, president of Old Dutch Foods, personal communication, 10 June 2015.

99. Anonymous industry expert interview.

100. Ric Swihart, "Old Dutch Spud Storage Finished," *Lethbridge Herald,* 15 September 1979, 23.

101. Beth Anderson, "Industry Pursues Quality Control," *Minneapolis Star,* 4 March 1970, 2C.

102. Don Kroeker interview.

103. Ibid.

104. Ibid.

105. Southern Potato Company, "History," http://southernpotato.com/history.php.

106. John Kuhl interview; Marlon Kuhl interview.

Chapter 3
CORPORATE MYTHOLOGY AND CULINARY TOURISM

1. For a useful introduction to the scholarly field of culinary tourism, see Long, "Culinary Tourism."

2. Certain information was provided by the company pursuant to a Confidentiality Agreement. Subsequently, all such information as had been provided by the company has been removed. All information on the company presented here is obtained from sources other than the company, as documented in the footnotes.

3. Specialty Food Association, "Covered Bridge Potato Chip Company," https://www.specialtyfood.com/organization/41515/covered-bridge-potato-chip-company/.

4. Frito-Lay has a plant in Kentville, Nova Scotia, and Old Dutch has a factory in Hartland, New Brunswick.

5. Joanne Sasvari, "Whetting the Holiday Appetite: Delectable Gifts," *National Post,* 12 December 2012, SR1.

6. Chips & Crisps, "Covered Bridge," http://www.chipsandcrisps.com/covered-bridge.html.

7. Covered Bridge Potato Chips, "The Albright Family," http://coveredbridgechips.com/en/our-story/about-us/.
8. PotatoPro, "Covered Bridge Potato Chip Company Inc.: More Than Just a Chip Maker," 17 February 2009, http://www.potatopro.com/news/2009/covered-bridge-potato-chip-company-inc-more-just-chip-maker.
9. Covered Bridge Potato Chips, "The Albright Family," http://coveredbridgechips.com/en/our-story/about-us/.
10. Jim Romahn, "Covered Bridge Potato Chips Turn Heads," *Farm Focus* (30 October 2008), http://www.atlanticfarmfocus.ca/Canada-World/2008-10-30/article-1055357/Covered-Bridge-Potato-Chips-turn-heads/1.
11. Marc Zienkiewicz, "Crafting a Great Brand," *SpudSmart* (20 July 2015), http://spudsmart.com/crafting-a-great-brand/.
12. "Conservatives Accused of $15B 'Spending Bender,'" *National Post,* 6 September 2008, A6; Atlantic Canada Opportunities Agency, "Covered Bridge Potato Chip Company Celebrates Grand Opening," 25 April 2009, http://www.acoa-apeca.gc.ca/eng/Agency/mediaroom/NewsReleases/Pages/2581.aspx.
13. Atlantic Canada Opportunities Agency, "Federal and Provincial Governments Support Major Expansion to Covered Bridge Potato Chip Company," 16 April 2012, http://www.acoa-apeca.gc.ca/eng/Agency/MediaRoom/NewsReleases/Pages/3582.aspx.
14. Jeff Graham, "5 Questions with Ryan Albright, President and CEO of Covered Bridge Potato Chip Company," *Export Development Canada: ExportWise,* 1 June 2016, http://exportwise.ca/5-questions-ryan-albright-president-ceo-covered-bridge-potato-chip-company/; Covered Bridge Chips, "Covered Bridge Intro," posted 23 December 2014, https://www.youtube.com/watch?v=1nytceHVTo0.
15. Mike McCartney interview.
16. Ibid.
17. Ibid.
18. Ibid.
19. Ibid.
20. Ibid.
21. Ibid.
22. Originally, company president Ryan Albright conducted all tours.
23. Thomas Broad interview.
24. Herr's, "Snack Factory Tour," http://www.herrs.com/SnackFactoryTours.html.

25. Herr's, "About Herr's," http://www.herrs.com/AboutHerrs/History.html.
26. Billy Wharton, "Potato Chip Capitalism or What to Do with a Socialist on Vacation," *Dissident Voice,* 1 April 2013, http://dissidentvoice.org/2013/04/potato-chip-capitalism-or-what-to-do-with-a-socialist-on-vacation/.
27. The Herr family are Mennonites. They offer free copies of the Bible's Proverbs to tourists; these booklets are titled *Chips of Wisdom.* Silverman, *Pennsylvania Snacks*, 6.
28. "Covered Bridge Potato Chip Factory," *Mark & Teri's Travels* (blog post), 6 August 2011, http://markteri.blogspot.ca/2011/08/covered-bridge-potato-chip-factory.html; Covered Bridge Potato Chips, "The Process," http://coveredbridgechips.com/en/the-process.
29. Anonymous Covered Bridge employee interview.
30. Thomas Broad interview.
31. Ibid.
32. Ibid.
33. Ibid.
34. Ibid.
35. Heron and Storey, *On the Job*, 14.
36. Ibid., 14–15.
37. Ibid., 15.
38. Ibid., 29.
39. Ibid., 30.
40. Ibid.
41. Thomas Broad interview.
42. Ibid.
43. Ibid.
44. "Covered Bridge Chips Boycott Call Will Be Escalated, Union Says," *CBC News* New Brunswick, 6 January 2016, http://www.cbc.ca/news/canada/new-brunswick/covered-bridge-strike-reaction-1.3391286.
45. "STUdents boycott Covered Bridge Chips," *The Aquinian,* 26 January 2016, http://theaquinian.net/students-boycott-covered-bridge-chips/.
46. Ibid.
47. Jeremy Keefe, "Potato Chip Factory Workers Picket over Labour Dispute with Company," *Global News*, 5 January 2016, http://globalnews.ca/news/2435168/potato-chip-factory-workers-picket-over-labour-dispute-with-company/.

48. Covered Bridge Chips, "Covered Bridge Intro," posted 23 December 2014, https://www.youtube.com/watch?v=1nytceHVToO.

49. *United Food and Commercial Workers of Canada, Local 1288P v Covered Bridge Potato Chip Company, 2015,* CanLII 58781 (New Brunswick Labour and Employment Board), http://canlii.ca/t/gl74v (accessed 11 July 2016); Canadian Union of Public Employees, "Take Action: Support Striking Covered Bridge Chips Workers," 16 May 2016, http://cupe.ca/take-action-support-striking-covered-bridge-chips-workers.

50. *United Food and Commercial Workers of Canada, Local 1288P v Covered Bridge Potato Chip Company, 2015,* CanLII 58781 (New Brunswick Labour and Employment Board), http://canlii.ca/t/gl74v (accessed 11 July 2016); Asaf Rashid, "Covered Bridge Potato Chips Workers Take Strike and Boycott Action," NB Media Co-Op, 6 January 2016, http://nbmediacoop.org/2016/01/06/covered-bridge-potato-chips-workers-take-strike-and-boycott-action/.

51. *United Food and Commercial Workers of Canada, Local 1288P v Covered Bridge Potato Chip Company, 2015,* CanLII 58781 (New Brunswick Labour and Employment Board), http://canlii.ca/t/gl74v (accessed 11 July 2016).

52. Ibid.

53. Ibid.

54. Asaf Rashid, "Covered Bridge Potato Chips Workers Take Strike and Boycott Action," NB Media Co-Op, 6 January 2016, http://nbmediacoop.org/2016/01/06/covered-bridge-potato-chips-workers-take-strike-and-boycott-action/.

55. Jacques Poitras, "Covered Bridge Owners Should Be Pulled from TV Ad, Labour Group Say," *CBC News* New Brunswick, 7 January 2016, http://www.cbc.ca/news/canada/new-brunswick/chips-covered-bridge-strike-1.3392767.

56. "Union Takes on Chipmaker at Grocers' Doorsteps," *Canadian Grocer* (19 May 2016), http://www.canadiangrocer.com/top-stories/union-takes-on-chipmaker-at-grocers-doorsteps-64848.

57. Daniel McHardie, "Covered Bridge Potato Chips Strike Ends after 5 Months," *CBC News* New Brunswick, 25 May 2016, http://www.cbc.ca/news/canada/new-brunswick/covered-bridge-chips-strike-over-1.3599049.

58. First contract legislation provides binding arbitration in a newly unionized workplace where the employees and employer are unable to successfully negotiate a first collective agreement. New Brunswick New Democrats, "Covered Bridge Situation Shows Need for First Contract Legislation, Cardy Says," 8 January 2016, http://www.nbndp.ca/news/page/2/; "Covered Bridge Chips Strike Concerns Green Party's David Coon," *CBC News* New Brunswick, 9 March 2016, http://www.cbc.ca/news/canada/new-brunswick/covered-bridge-chips-coon-1.3484171.

59. "Covered Bridge Chips Faces Strike," *Huddle*, 5 January 2016, http://huddle.today/covered-bridge-chips-strike/.

60. Monod, *Store Wars*, 57.

61. Ibid., 61.

62. Ibid.

63. Ibid., 62–63.

64. Marc Zienkiewicz, "Crafting a Great Brand," *SpudSmart* (20 July 2015), http://spudsmart.com/crafting-a-great-brand/.

65. "Company News: Nalley's Canada," *Globe and Mail*, 4 April 1995, B16.

66. "Nalley's Selling Chips Division to Utah Firm," *Kitsap Sun*, 11 September 1994, http://www.kitsapsun.com/news/1994/sep/11/nalleys-selling-chips-division-to-utah-firm/?print=1.

67. Rice, "Lower Mainland Food System," 37.

68. Ibid., 37–38.

69. Jenny Lee, "B.C. Potato Chip Company Finds Identity in 'new and Edgy' Parsnips," *Vancouver Sun*, 31 March 2016, http://www.vancouversun.com/mobile/business/vs-business/parsnips+rescue/11821625/story.html.

70. CTV interview with Sepp Amsler of Naturally Homegrown Foods, 4 May 2007, https://www.youtube.com/watch?v=nQ_cxzWosTs&feature=youtube_gdata_player; Sepp Amsler, LinkedIn profile, https://www.linkedin.com/pub/sepp-amsler/13/b31/191.

71. Rice, "Lower Mainland Food System," 39.

72. "B.C. Health-Food Company Takes a Hardbite out of Asian Markets," *Vancouver Sun*, 28 November 2005, http://www.canada.com/story_print.html?id=10bfb3ba-0de8-4325-952b-7b23f1af4c79&sponsor (accessed 25 August 2016).

73. Mary Teresa Bitti, "Deal or No Deal," *National Post*, 12 January 2009, FP6; CBC Television, "Dragon's Den Pitches: Hardbite Chips," http://www.cbc.ca/dragonsden/pitches/hardbite-chips; Kerry Gold, "Dragon's Den Success Stories: Hardbite Potato Chips," *MSN Money* (17 May 2011): http://money.ca.msn.com/small-business/gallery/gallery.aspx?cp-documentid=22789615; Taryn Mcelheren, "Local Chip Company to Take a Bite out of National Market," *Metro Vancouver*, 11 March 2009, http://metronews.ca/news/vancouver/83684/local-chip-company-to-take-a-bite-out-of-national-market/.

74. Hardbite Potato Chips promotional flyer, circa 2013.

75. Geoff Peters, "Pete Schouten and Braden Douglas—Co-owners of Hardbite Potato Chips—Food Talks Vancouver Vol 4" (blog post), 23 January 2013, http://geoffmobile.com/blog/pete-schouten-and-braden-douglas-co-

owners-of-hardbite-potato-chips-food-talks-vancouver-vol-4; "Food Talks Volume 4, October 23," *Vancouver Foodster* (18 September 2012), http://vancouverfoodster.com/tag/ok-crush-pad/.

76. Heppell's Potato Corp., "About," 2015, http://heppells.ca/about/.

77. Heppell's Potato Corp., 2015, http://heppells.ca.

78. Hardbite used to send their chip and oil waste to landfills. "Canada: Hardbite Potato Chips Works to 'Close the Loop,'" *Fresh Plaza* (24 January 2014), http://www.freshplaza.com/article/117271/Canada-Hardbite-potato-chips-works-to-Close-the-Loop; Kacey Culliney, "The Circle of Snacks: Chip Waste to Biogas Is Viable, Says Naturally Homegrown," *Bakery and Snacks* (28 January 2014), http://mobile.bakeryandsnacks.com/Processing-Packaging/The-circle-of-snacks-Chip-waste-to-biogas-is-viable-says-Naturally-Homegrown-Foods#.VAdXsEuaLwJ.

79. Crew Marketing Partners, "Confessions of a Serial Entrepreneur" (blog post), 15 April 2015, http://www.crewmarketingpartners.com/pete-schouten/.

80. Geoff Peters, "Pete Schouten and Braden Douglas—Co-owners of Hardbite Potato Chips—Food Talks Vancouver Vol 4" (blog post), 23 January 2013, http://geoffmobile.com/blog/pete-schouten-and-braden-douglas-co-owners-of-hardbite-potato-chips-food-talks-vancouver-vol-4.

81. Braden Douglas, http://www.bradendouglas.com/.

82. Braden Douglas, "Fame Sells" (blog post), 13 May 2014, http://www.bradendouglas.com/fame-sells/.

83. British Columbia Ministry of Agriculture and Lands, "'Buy Local' Funding Supports Hardbite from Seed to Chip," 15 April 2013, http://www.newsroom.gov.bc.ca/2013/04/buy-local-funding-supports-hardbite-from-seed-to-chip.html.

84. Deanna Rosolen, "Top 10 Innovators," *Food in Canada* (2 June 2014), http://www.foodincanada.com/features/top-10-innovators/.

85. The Corporate Registry in British Columbia does not require corporations to file shareholder information, and Naturally Home Grown Foods did not provide names when requested.

86. Hardbite Potato Chips promotional flyer, circa 2013; Hardbite Potato Chips home page, http://hardbitechips.com/.

87. Homenick is president, Leroux is chair, and Schouten is secretary-treasurer. Leroux has been chair of the British Columbia Vegetable Marketing Commission and of the British Columbia Hog Marketing Commission. BC Registry Services, "BC Company Summary for Naturally Home Grown Foods Ltd.," 31 March 2015; British Columbia Ministry of Agriculture and Lands, "British Columbia Agri-Food Trade Council," http://www.agf.gov.bc.ca/trade/bcaftc.htm; Government of British Columbia, "Resume of

Orders in Council," 38, no. 13 (9 June 2011), http://www.qp.gov.bc.ca/statreg/oic/2011/resume13.htm.

88. Mary Teresa Bitti, "Healthy Potato Chip Whets Dragons' Appetites," *National Post,* 27 October 2008, FP6.

89. Kristi Ferguson, "Spotlight: Home Grown Foods," *Fraser Valley Pulse,* 21 February 2011, http://fraservalleypulse.com/lowermainland/pulse-spotlight/spotlight-home-grown-foods-02-21-11/.

90. Jennifer Bain, "10 New Tastes to Try," *National Post,* 20 February 2008, L5.

91. "Democracy Never Tasted So Delicious," *National Post,* 30 June 2006, B6.

92. Yum Yum, "Our Story," http://www.yum-yum.com/en/Our+story (accessed 25 August 2016).

93. Steve Brandon, "Yum Yum!" (flickr post), 6 March 2008, https://www.flickr.com/photos/steve-brandon/2318325272/.

94. From July through September 1990, Mohawk people from Kanehsatake, Quebec police, and the Canadian army were involved in an armed standoff over land rights near Oka, Quebec. See Alanis Obomsawin's documentary *Kanehsatake: 270 Years of Resistance* (National Film Board, 1993), http://www.nfb.ca/film/kanehsatake_270_years_of_resistance/; Begin, Moss, and Niemczak, *Land Claim Dispute;* Ladner and Simpson, *This Is an Honour Song;* MacLaine, Baxendale, and Galbraith, *This Land Is Our Land;* Winegard, *Oka.*

95. Tina Tenneriello, "Yum Yum's Re-introduction of Its Indian logo Is Tasteless," *CJAD News,* 8 November 2013, http://www.cjad.com/cjad-news/2013/11/08/yum-yums-reintroduction-of-its-indian-logo-is-tasteless.

96. "Krispy Kernels Snacks Slammed over 'Little Indian' Logo," *CBC News*, 8 November 2013, http://www.cbc.ca/news/canada/montreal/krispy-kernels-snacks-slammed-over-little-indian-logo-1.2419920; Tina Tenneriello, "Yum Yum's Re-introduction of Its Indian Logo Is Tasteless," *CJAD News*, 8 November 2013, http://www.cjad.com/cjad-news/2013/11/08/yum-yums-reintroduction-of-its-indian-logo-is-tasteless. Dick Burhans argues that it was not Crum, but his sister Katie Wicks, who was the inventor of the potato chip. Burhans, *Crunch!,* 19–20.

97. Karlee Weinmann and Kim Bhasin, "12 Uncomfortably Racist Vintage Brand Mascots," *Business Insider* (8 September 2011), http://www.businessinsider.com/racist-company-mascots-2011-9?op=1.

98. Ibid.; "Eating Crow: Transcript," *On the Media* (27 April 2007), http://www.onthemedia.org/story/129403-eating-crow/transcript/; "Ethnic Stereotypes: A Look at Speedy Gonzales and the Frito Bandito," *Speedy Gonzales and the Frito Bandito: Latino Stereotypes in Popular Culture* (blog post), 7 April 2013, https://diversitygroup16.wordpress.com/2013/04/07/ethnic-stereotypes-a-look-at-speedy-gonzales-and-the-frito-bandito/; Westerman, "Death of the

Frito Bandito"; Walker and Gratton, "Mexican American History Online," 51; Lewald, "Hispanic World."

99. Lewald, "Hispanic World."

100. "'Buy Local' Funding Supports Hardbite from Seed to Chip," BC Government News, 15 April 2013, https://news.gov.bc.ca/stories/buy-local-funding-supports-hardbite-from-seed-to-chip.

101. Marcie Good, "How the Hardbite Makers Repurpose Imperfect Potatoes," *BCBusiness* (21 July 2016), http://www.bcbusiness.ca/tech-science/how-the-hardbite-makers-repurpose-imperfect-potatoes.

102. Paula Forbes, "Dan Barber on Why the Farm-to-Table Movement Doesn't Go Far Enough," *Eater* (12 June 2014), http://www.eater.com/2014/6/12/6208269/dan-barber-on-why-the-farm-to-table-movement-doesnt-go-far-enough; Valli Herman, "The Farm-to-Table Backlash Is Here," *Fortune* (28 September 2015), http://fortune.com/2015/09/28/farm-table-local-food/.

103. Rickey Yada interview.

104. Martial Boulet interview.

105. Kacey Culliney, "Small Snack Makers Create Better Personal Connections, Says Packaged Facts," *Bakery and Snacks* (18 September 2013), http://www.bakeryandsnacks.com/Markets/Small-snack-makers-create-better-personal-connections-says-Packaged-Facts.

106. Ibid.

107. Barthes, "Myth Today," *Mythologies,* 133.

108. Mark Ibold, "Profile in Obsession: Nick Leggin," *Lucky Peach* (4 March 2015), http://luckypeach.com/profile-in-obsession-nick-leggin-founder-of-potato-chip-world/.

Chapter 4
CHEEZIES

1. Parts of this chapter were published earlier in Thiessen, "From Faith to Food."The epigraph to the chapter is from Kent Hawkins, "Out of Office, Kent Hawkins," *Air Canada enRoute* (31 October 2013), http://enroute.aircanada.com/en/articles/out-of-office-kent-hawkins. "That's Cheezies with a Zed!," *CBC News Storify* (2012), https://storify.com/cbccommunity/canadian-inventor-of-cheezies-snacks-dies.

2. Kent Hawkins interview; "Popcorn Meet Schedules Vending Exhibs, Topics," *The Billboard,* 24 November 1951, 123. A sales bulletin from 1937 noted that

they had sold 30,000 cases of chocolate-covered cherries in only four days. Bulletin no. 3 to salesmen, 23 April 1937, courtesy of W.T. Hawkins Ltd.

3. "Candy Makers Strive to Fill Holiday Orders," *Chicago Daily Tribune,* 17 October 1942, 23; Genevieve Flavin, "40 Pct. of All Nation's Candy Made in Chicago," *Chicago Daily Tribune,* 29 September 1949, 4.

4. "Town of West Chicago, District 36, Corporations," *Suburbanite Economist* (4 March 1959): 26; "Quadrennial Real Estate Assessment—1959," *Suburbanite Economist* (10 August 1960): 65.

5. "Hawkins Heads Association of Popcorn Makers," *The Billboard,* 5 January 1946, 87. The National Popcorn Association was formed in 1943, and W.T. delivered one of the keynote speeches at their inaugural meeting. The group organized in response to their worry that the popcorn industry would be destroyed by government decisions during wartime that would reduce the size of the corn crop. Their goal was to have popcorn "declared an essential food item and its production continued." "Popcorn Men Form Group," *The Billboard,* 23 January 1943, 64.

6. Kent Hawkins interview. Dick Burhans notes, "In 1949 a weary Herman Lay, diagnosed with ulcers and exhausted from the nonstop hustle of business, almost sold Lay's but was talked out of it." Burhans, *Crunch!,* 45.

7. W.T. Hawkins, "Loyalty Begets Loyalty!," *Snacks Distributors' News* 2, no. 5 (April 1946): 1, courtesy of W.T. Hawkins Ltd.

8. Ibid.

9. Ibid.

10. W.T. Hawkins, "Division Manager's Manual," 21 November 1955, 1, courtesy of W.T. Hawkins Ltd.

11. Ibid., 3.

12. Ibid., 4.

13. Memo to distributors from Armand Turpin, General Manager, Confections Inc., 9 May 1955, courtesy of W.T. Hawkins Ltd.

14. W.T. Hawkins, "Division Manager's Manual," 21 November 1955, 6, courtesy of W.T. Hawkins Ltd.

15. Ibid., 9.

16. Ibid.

17. Memo to sales representatives from Armand Turpin, General Manager, Confections Inc., 30 April 1955; 1950s sales flyers. All courtesy of W.T. Hawkins Ltd.

18. Advertisement for distributors and salesmen, c. 1947, courtesy of W.T. Hawkins Ltd.

19. Memo to buyers and sales managers from Armand Turpin, General Manager, Confections Inc., 30 April 1955, courtesy of W.T. Hawkins Ltd.

20. Memo to supervisors from W.T. Hawkins, 12 April 1955, courtesy of W.T. Hawkins Ltd.

21. "Wife of Popcorn King Sues His Kin, Charging Alienation," *Chicago Daily Tribune,* 21 August 1953, B10.

22. Ibid.

23. Ibid.

24. Ibid.

25. "Deserted Wife Demands Share of Property," *Freeport Journal-Standard,* 29 October 1953, 15; "Popcorn King's Wife Sues to Tie up Assets," *Chicago Daily Tribune,* 29 October 1953, B8.

26. "Popcorn Man's Wife Gives up Keys to Farm," *Chicago Daily Tribune,* 25 November 1953, 15.

27. "Gets Divorce, $105,000 from 'Popcorn King,'" *Chicago Daily Tribune,* 30 June 1954, C11. Sadly, this third divorce—with its possible hiding of assets—was not the last marital difficulty for W.T. Hawkins. He returned to Chicago and remarried a young woman named Lanie in 1956, with whom he had a son. She, too, made it into the Chicago newspapers when she was charged with assault with a deadly weapon in a domestic dispute at their home one evening. W.T. "claimed she hit him with an ash tray and threatened him with a butcher knife and dagger." "Popcorn King Charges Wife with Assault," *Chicago Daily Tribune,* 5 May 1960, D11.

28. Angela Hawn, "Say Cheez!," *Country Roads* (Spring 2013): 24; Kent Hawkins interview.

29. Angela Hawn, "Say Cheez!," *Country Roads* (Spring 2013): 24.

30. Adrian Morrow, "Jim Marker Moulded Cheezies into a Canadian Icon," *Globe and Mail,* 2 May 2012, http://www.theglobeandmail.com/incoming/jim-marker-moulded-cheezies-into-a-canadian-icon/article4104357/.

31. 'Balbulican,' comment on 'RkBall,' "Are You Better Than a Cheezie?" (blog post), *The way the Ball bounces,* 18 July 2008, http://thewaytheballbounces.blogspot.ca/2008/07/are-you-better-than-cheezie_18.html (accessed 20 May 2013).

32. "Yolkobsens Cheezies and Champagne Frenzy" (blog post), *Guatemala Social Media News Blog,* 10 March 2011, https://socialmediasnews.wordpress.com/2011/03/10/yolkobsens-cheezies-and-champagne-frenzy-top-5-canadian-news-reports/ (accessed 26 August 2016).

33. Lauri Cunningham, post on "Hawkins Cheezies Fan Club—Food of the Gods," Facebook group page, 23 April 2009.

34. Geraldine (Gerry) Fobert interview.

35. Cheetos were invented by Charles Elmer Doolin in 1948; his company was purchased by H.W. Lay & Co. in 1961. David Simmonds, "But It Tastes like Cardboard," *Wellington Times,* 16 January 2013, 8.

36. Tom Gavey, "Snack-Food Formula Called Key to Hawkins's Success," *Belleville Intelligencer,* 26 June 1993, 1.

37. Marker's uncle was a corn miller. Angela Hawn, "Say Cheez!," *Country Roads* (Spring 2013): 28; Jo Anne Lewis, "The World's Greatest Cheezies," *What's Happening Magazine* (February/March 1994): 31; Senator Nancy Green Raine in Hansard, Senate of Canada, 1st session, volume 148, number 79, 15 May 2012.

38. Burtea, "Snack Foods," 287.

39. Smith, "Snack Foods," 340.

40. Burtea, "Snack Foods," 287–88; Huber, "Snack Foods," 353.

41. Angela Hawn, "Say Cheez!," *Country Roads* (Spring 2013): 24.

42. Jack Evans, "Our 50th Year: Hawkins Cheezies," *Belleville Intelligencer,* 7 June 1998, 20; Adrian Morrow, "Jim Marker Moulded Cheezies into a Canadian Icon," *Globe and Mail,* 2 May 2012, http://www.theglobeandmail.com/incoming/jim-marker-moulded-cheezies-into-a-canadian-icon/article4104357/.

43. Jo Anne Lewis, "The World's Greatest Cheezies," *What's Happening Magazine* (February/March 1994): 38.

44. Webb Hawkins died in 1990; his son Kent is company president. Careless, *CANADA*, 434.

45. Ibid.; Kent Hawkins interview.

46. Benzie Sangma, "Hawkins Cheezies: Belleville's Snack to the World," *Belleville Intelligencer,* 3 May 2003, D2.

47. Ibid.

48. "W.T Hawkins Co. Has Established Plant in City," *Belleville Intelligencer,* 23 January 1956, 1.

49. "Industries at a Glance," *Belleville Intelligencer,* 31 March 1981; Belleville Industrial Development Department, "List of Belleville Industries" (1983, 1986–89, 1991, 1993–94), *Belleville Intelligencer* clippings file; City of Belleville Department of Economic and Business Development, Industrial Investment brochure, January 1989; *Scott's Ontario Industrial Directory,* 3rd to 5th and 9th to 11th eds. (Oakville: Penstock Publications, 1962–67, 1972–79).

50. Loblaws spokesperson Dave Nichol claimed that Jim Marker "assured me that the Hawkins Cheezies that are made today are identical to the ones he

first turned out in 1948. Identical." "The Best Cheezies in the World: Bless You Belleville!," Dave Nichol's "Insider's Report" advertisement, *Globe and Mail,* 9 June 1984, D14.

51. Careless, *CANADA*, 434.

52. Les Sykes interview.

53. Jo Anne Lewis, "The World's Greatest Cheezies," *What's Happening Magazine* (February/March 1994): 38. On another occasion, Marker said, "I fought off a lot of people's attempts to put in various flavouring and inferior ingredients over the years." "The Best Cheezies in the World: Bless You Belleville!," Dave Nichol's "Insider's Report" advertisement, *Globe and Mail,* 9 June 1984, D14.

54. Les Sykes interview.

55. Richard Bly interview.

56. Ibid.

57. Tony McGarvey interview.

58. Ibid.

59. "Industries at a Glance," *Belleville Intelligencer,* 31 March 1981; Belleville Industrial Development Department, "List of Belleville Industries," April 1993 (also April 1994, March 1991, 1989, 1988, 1987, 1986, 1983), *Belleville Intelligencer* clippings file; City of Belleville Department of Economic and Business Development, Industrial Investment brochure, January 1989; *Scott's Ontario Industrial Directory,* 3rd through 12th eds. (Oakville: Penstock Publications, 1962 through 1979), 2–20; Ontario Department of Trade & Development, Industrial Development Branch, Ontario Development Corporation, 1971 Industrial Survey for Belleville as of June 1971; Hawkins 40th anniversary flyer; Angela Hawn, "Say Cheez!," *Country Roads* (Spring 2013): 26.

60. Les Sykes interview.

61. Ibid.

62. Goody, *Cooking, Cuisine and Class,* 71.

63. Parr, *Gender of Breadwinners,* 59–76.

64. City of Belleville, Ontario, "Industry and Labour," http://belleville.ca/business/page/industry-and-labour.

65. Quinte Economic Development Commission, "Labour," http://www.quintedevelopment.com/labour/.

66. Les Sykes interview.

67. Jack Evans, "Our 50th Year: Hawkins Cheezies," *Belleville Intelligencer,* 7 June 1998, 20.

68. Barbara Bosiak interview.

69. Ibid.

70. Ibid.

71. W.T. Hawkins, "Heading into the 90's . . . Hawkins Snack-Food Success," company brochure, c. 1992, courtesy of W.T. Hawkins Ltd.

72. Memo from Armand Turpin, General Manager, Confections Inc., 9 August 1955; Memo from W.T. Hawkins Ltd., 24 March 1955. Salesmen were told, "We know that you'll grasp this occasion to greatly increase your volume with this entirely new product, *with no competition as yet to contend with.* No competition YET—that is true—but don't count on it for too long. Others will try to imitate us." Memo from Armand Turpin, General Manager, Confections Inc., 24 March 1955. All courtesy of W.T. Hawkins Ltd.

73. Memo to distributors from W.T. Hawkins, President, Confections Inc., 14 July 1955, courtesy of W.T. Hawkins Ltd.

74. Ibid.

75. Memo to distributors from W.T. Hawkins, President, Confections Inc., 7 July 1955, courtesy of W.T. Hawkins Ltd.

76. Memo to sales representatives from Armand Turpin, General Manager, Confections Inc., 16 June 1955, courtesy of W.T. Hawkins Ltd.

77. Ibid.

78. Ibid.

79. Memo from Armand Turpin, General Manager, Confections Inc., 4 August 1955, courtesy of W.T. Hawkins Ltd.

80. Ibid.

81. Memo to distributors from W.T. Hawkins, President, Confections Inc., 9 June 1955. Magic Pop's competition was TV Time popcorn, which W.T. described as "a messing deal where they have to get out the shortening first, melt it and then cut the bag that contains the corn and add it at a certain point," unlike Magic Pop where you "cut the end, pour it in the pan and pop it." Further, Magic Pop was the better deal at thirteen cents versus TV Time's cost of nineteen cents or more. Memo to distributors from W.T. Hawkins, 9 June 1955. All courtesy of W.T. Hawkins Ltd.

82. Levenstein, *Paradox of Plenty,* 101–2, 210; Kessler-Harris, *Women Have Always Worked.*

83. Levenstein, *Paradox of Plenty,* 105.

84. Ibid., 106, citing the chairman of the board of the Corn Products Company in 1969.

85. Ibid., 113.

86. Benzie Sangma, “Hawkins Cheezies: Belleville’s Snack to the World,” *Belleville Intelligencer*, 3 May 2003, D2.

87. Jo Anne Lewis, “The World’s Greatest Cheezies,” *What’s Happening Magazine* (February/March 1994): 37–38.

88. “W.T. Hawkins Co. Has Established Plant in City,” *Belleville Intelligencer*, 23 January 1956, 1; Bank of Canada, “Inflation Calculator,” http://www.bankofcanada.ca/rates/related/inflation-calculator/ (accessed 22 May 2013).

89. Ibid.

90. Kent Hawkins, “Out of Office, Kent Hawkins,” *Air Canada enRoute* (31 October 2013), http://enroute.aircanada.com/en/articles/out-of-office-kent-hawkins.

91. “W.T. Hawkins Co. Has Established Plant in City,” *Belleville Intelligencer*, 23 January 1956, 1.

92. Ibid.

93. American Can of Canada, “The Canadian Heritage Label Collection,” pamphlet, n.d., Belleville Public Library, *Belleville Intelligencer* clippings files, Business and Industry.

94. “Property Near Cheezies Plant Contaminated,” *Quinte News*, 27 April 2013, http://www.quintenews.com/2013/04/property-near-cheezies-plant-contaminated/44514/.

95. Tony McGarvey interview.

96. “W.T. Hawkins Co. Has Established Plant in City,” *Belleville Intelligencer*, 23 January 1956, 1.

97. Ibid.

98. Ibid.

99. Ibid.

100. Jo Anne Lewis, “The World’s Greatest Cheezies,” *What’s Happening Magazine* (February/March 1994): 37–38.

101. Georges Lewi, “The Mythical Approach,” *Georges LEWI*, http://www.georges-lewi.com/EN/ (accessed 11 August 2015).

102. Dorson, “Folklore and Fake Lore,” 335.

103. Fox, “Folklore and Fakelore,” 252.

104. Ibid. See also, on the fakelore of potato chips, Fox and Banner, “Social and Economic Contexts,” 114–26.

105. Smith, “False Memories,” 254.

106. Adrian Morrow, "Jim Marker Moulded Cheezies into a Canadian Icon," *Globe and Mail*, 2 May 2012, http://www.theglobeandmail.com/incoming/jim-marker-moulded-cheezies-into-a-canadian-icon/article4104357/.

107. Barbara Bosiak interview.

108. "Hawkins Cheezies" advertisement, *Belleville Intelligencer*, 27 March 2002, B12.

109. Jack Evans, "Our 50th Year: Hawkins Cheezies," *Belleville Intelligencer*, 7 June 1998, 20.

110. Memo to distributors from W.T. Hawkins, 22 June 1955, courtesy of W.T. Hawkins Ltd.

111. Richard Bly interview.

112. Ibid.

113. Ibid.

114. Angela Hawn, "Say Cheez!," *Country Roads* (Spring 2013): 26. Some claim that the absence of signage is to discourage unions. This is unlikely, given that the United Food and Commercial Workers have a local in Belleville, and would therefore be aware of the plant's existence. Diane, "Hawkins's Cheezies" (blog post), 3 May 2012, http://westlakemusings.com/2012/05/03/hawkins-cheezies/; UFCW Canada, "UFCW 175 Members Achieve New Contract at Fin-Aire," news release, 29 March 2014, http://www.ufcw.ca/index.php?option=com_content&view=article&id=3946:ufcw-175-members-achieve-new-contract-at-fin-aire&catid=519:directions-14-25&Itemid=6&lang=en; UFCW Canada, "Quinte Humane Society Workers Join the Union—UFCW 175," news release, 20 September 2014, http://www.ufcw.ca/index.php?option=com_content&view=article&id=30249:quinte-humane-society-workers-join-the-union-ufcw-175&catid=9553:directions-14-74&Itemid=6&lang=en; City of Belleville Department of Economic and Business Development, Industrial Investment brochure, January 1989.

115. Angela Hawn, "Say Cheez!," *Country Roads* (Spring 2013): 26.

116. "Hawkins Cheezies" advertisement, *Belleville Intelligencer*, 27 March 2002, B12.

117. Kent Hawkins, "Out of Office, Kent Hawkins," *Air Canada enRoute* (31 October 2013), http://enroute.aircanada.com/en/articles/out-of-office-kent-hawkins.

118. Barbara Bosiak interview. I'm grateful to be one of the few people to be granted a tour of the Hawkins factory.

119. The toy mouse was to be fastened to a shirt button; you could then make it roll over and do tricks. Kent Hawkins interview. Other prizes in Hawkins chip bags over the years included carefully wrapped pennies and balloons. Memo from Armand Turpin, 30 July 1955, courtesy of W.T. Hawkins Ltd.

120. "Are You Better than a Cheezie?" (blog post), *The Way the Ball Bounces,* 18 July 2008, http://thewaytheballbounces.blogspot.ca/2008/07/are-you-better-than-cheezie_18.html.

121. Diane, "Hawkins's Cheezies" (blog post), 3 May 2012, http://westlakemusings.com/2012/05/03/hawkins-cheezies/.

122. Hawkins 40th anniversary flyer; W.T. Hawkins, "Heading into the 90's . . . Hawkins Snack-Food Success," company brochure, c. 1992. All courtesy of W.T. Hawkins Ltd.

123. Alan Parker, "Working at Belleville Plant Considered a Family Affair," *Belleville Intelligencer,* 2 September 1978.

124. Ibid.

125. Les Sykes interview.

126. Ibid.

127. Ibid.

128. Ibid.

129. Ibid.

130. Ibid.

131. Cathy McAllister interview.

132. Kent Hawkins interview.

133. Tony McGarvey interview.

134. Cathy McAllister interview.

135. Ibid.

136. Tom Gavey, "Snack-Food Formula Called Key to Hawkins's Success," *Belleville Intelligencer,* 26 June 1993, 1.

137. Geraldine (Gerry) Fobert interview.

138. Ibid.

139. Ibid.

140. 60th anniversary photo album, 2008, courtesy of W.T. Hawkins Ltd.

141. Tony McGarvey interview.

142. Ibid.; Angela Hawn, "Say Cheez!," *Country Roads* (Spring 2013): 26.

143. Tony McGarvey interview. Canada Day, formerly Dominion Day, is the anniversary of the enactment of the Constitution Act of 1867, which formed the country of Canada.

144. "Hawkins Celebrates Birthday," *Belleville Intelligencer,* 5 October 1983, 9.

145. Tom Gavey, "Snack-Food Formula Called Key to Hawkins's Success," *Belleville Intelligencer,* 26 June 1993, 1.

146. Lesley Ciarula Taylor, "Cheezies Inventor Dies in Belleville, Ont., at 90," *Toronto Star,* 3 May 2012, http://www.thestar.com/news/canada/2012/05/03/cheezies_inventor_dies_in_belleville_ont_at_90.html.

147. Adrian Morrow, "Jim Marker Moulded Cheezies into a Canadian Icon," *Globe and Mail,* 2 May 2012, http://www.theglobeandmail.com/incoming/jim-marker-moulded-cheezies-into-a-canadian-icon/article4104357/.

148. Tony McGarvey interview.

149. Adrian Morrow, "Jim Marker Moulded Cheezies into a Canadian Icon," *Globe and Mail,* 2 May 2012, http://www.theglobeandmail.com/incoming/jim-marker-moulded-cheezies-into-a-canadian-icon/article4104357/.

150. W. Brice McVicar, "Jim Marker: 'Rough, Tough Crème Puff,'" *Belleville Intelligencer,* 3 May 2012, http://www.intelligencer.ca/2012/05/03/jim-marker-rough-tough-creme-puff.

151. Tony McGarvey interview.

152. W. Brice McVicar, "Jim Marker: 'Rough, Tough Crème Puff,'" *Belleville Intelligencer,* 3 May 2012, http://www.intelligencer.ca/2012/05/03/jim-marker-rough-tough-creme-puff.

153. Richard Bly interview.

154. Ibid.

155. For the development of Canada's branch plant economy, see Naylor, *History of Canadian Business.*

156. "Hawkins Cheezies" advertisement, *Belleville Intelligencer,* 27 March 2002, B12.

157. Angela Hawn, "Say Cheez!," *Country Roads* (Spring 2013): 28.

158. Barber, *Canadian Oxford Dictionary.*

159. Angela Hawn, "Say Cheez!," *Country Roads* (Spring 2013): 28.

160. "Hawkins Still the Same after All These Years," *Belleville Intelligencer,* 7 June 1998, 20.

161. Hansard, Legislative Assembly of Ontario, 1st session, 40th parliament, no. 48 (7 May 2012).

162. Samantha Block, post on "Hawkins Cheezies Lovers," Facebook group page, 17 March 2012.

163. Mariah, "The Cross-Continental Cheezie Showdown" (blog post), 5 January 2012, https://theycallthewind.wordpress.com/tag/cheezies/.

164. Brent Alois Johnson, post on "Hawkins Cheezies," Facebook group page, 22 February 2011.

165. Teresa Electro-LadyLux, post on "Hawkins Cheezies," Facebook group page, 22 February 2011.

166. Pam Radbourne-McLauchlan, post on "Hawkins Cheezies," Facebook company page, 21 February 2012.

167. Darryl Miller, post on "Hawkins Cheezies," Facebook company page, 20 September 2011.

168. Becky Bravi, "To Eat Cheezies or Not to (A Cheezie Combustion Paper)," *The Science Creative Quarterly* (11 February 2008): http://www.scq.ubc.ca/to-eat-cheezies-or-not-to-a-cheezie-combustion-paper/.

169. Kent Hawkins interview.

170. Liesener, "Marshmallow Fluff," 52–53.

171. Brent Alois Johnson, post on "Hawkins Cheezies," Facebook group page, 22 February 2011.

172. "The Best Cheezies in the World: Bless You Belleville!," Dave Nichol's "Insider's Report" advertisement, *Globe and Mail,* 9 June 1984, D14.

Chapter 5
THE "ROMANCE" OF CHOCOLATE

1. The epigraph to the chapter is from R. Whidden Ganong, quoted in "Tells History of Industry," *Saint Croix Courier,* 29 March 1973, n.p., New Brunswick Museum Vertical Files, "Ganong family: candy factory," RS 184, Provincial Archives of New Brunswick. Mintz, *Sweetness and Power.*

2. Jung and Cisterna, "Introduction to *Crafting Senses,*" 1.

3. Bourdieu, *Distinction.*

4. Ibid.

5. Canada's first chocolate factory was established in 1809 in Halifax by John F. Ferguson. Macpherson, "Cargo of Cocoa," 89.

6. Edith Paterson, "It Happened Here," *Winnipeg Free Press,* 15 May 1976, 4.

7. "Big Biscuit Concern Observes Its Fifty-fifth Anniversary," *Winnipeg Free Press,* 1 April 1932, 8.

8. Ibid.

9. "Strikers' Mass Meeting," *Manitoba Free Press,* 6 June 1902, 3.

10. "Bakery Union Lays Certification Plans," *Winnipeg Free Press,* 14 March 1945, 22.

11. "Pension Plan Is Announced by Paulin-Chambers," *Winnipeg Free Press,* 17 December 1946, 14. Men aged sixty-five and women aged sixty who retired after a minimum of five years at the company would receive the greater sum of either "a minimum annual pension for Life equal to 30% of their 1946 earnings" or 1.5 percent of their earnings from 1 December 1946 until their retirement. The 30 percent minimum pension was to be paid solely by the employer, with the 1.5 percent pension to be jointly paid by employer and employee. Women who quit their jobs to be married were to have their pension contribution returned to them with interest. Those who quit for other reasons also would have their contribution returned.

12. "Union Bid Decision Reserved," *Winnipeg Free Press,* 4 February 1967, 2.

13. George Nikides, "Plant Closes, Lives Crumble," *Winnipeg Free Press,* 3 March 1991, 3.

14. Paul Samyn, "Death of a Family," *Winnipeg Free Press,* 4 March 1991, 9. Minimum wage in the province at the time was $5.00/hour. Government of Canada, Minimum Wage Database, "Hourly Minimum Wages in CANADA for Adult Workers, 1985-1994," http://srv116.services.gc.ca/dimt-wid/sm-mw/rpt2.aspx?GoCTemplateCulture=en-CA.

15. Nick Martin, "Workers Left with Bitter Taste after Cookie Factory Crumbles," *Winnipeg Free Press,* 2 February 1991, 3; Aldo Santin, "Time Catches Cookie Plant, 290 Losing Jobs," *Winnipeg Free Press,* 18 September 1990, 1; Paul Samyn, "Death of a Family," *Winnipeg Free Press,* 4 March 1991, 9.

16. Montreal dairy giant Saputo bought Culinar in 1999. "With this acquisition, Saputo became the largest manufacturer of snack cakes and fine breads as well as one of the most important cookie manufacturers in Canada." Saputo Inc., "Annual Information Form," 1 June 2002, 4, http://www.saputo.com/uploadedFiles/Saputo/investors-and-medias/financial-documents/NA_2002_EN.pdf. Popular Quebec snack maker Vachon also was purchased by Saputo in 1999; since 2015, it has been owned by Mexican conglomerate Grupo Bimbo. "Canada Bread buys Saputo bakery unit for $120M," *CBC News,* 18 December 2014, http://www.cbc.ca/news/business/canada-bread-buys-saputo-bakery-unit-for-120m-1.2877801; David Kennedy, "Saputo's snack cake business bought up by Mexican-owned Grupo Bimbo," *Financial Post,* 18 December 2014, http://business.financialpost.com/investing/saputos-snack-cake-business-being-bought-up-by-mexican-owned-grupo-bimbo.

17. George Weston Limited owns Loblaw, Shoppers Drug Mart, Choice Properties Real Estate Investment Trust, President's Choice Financial, and Weston Foods. Interbake Foods, a subsidiary of George Weston Ltd., became the owner of Paulin-Chambers. Loblaw is Canada's largest retailer. George Weston Limited, "Our Businesses," http://www.weston.ca/en/Our-Businesses.aspx; Bloomberg Business, "Company Overview of Interbake

Foods LLC," http://www.bloomberg.com/research/stocks/private/snapshot.asp?privcapId=677384.

18. Anonymous industry expert interview.
19. Folster, *Chocolate Ganongs of St. Stephen,* 192.
20. Anonymous industry expert interview.
21. Ibid.
22. Ibid.
23. The Meech Lake Accord was an attempt to have Quebec sign the 1982 Constitution; it was defeated in Manitoba and Newfoundland in 1990.
24. Paul Samyn, "Death of a Family," *Winnipeg Free Press,* 4 March 1991, 9.
25. Anonymous industry expert interview.
26. Ibid.
27. Ibid.
28. Ibid.
29. Tom Yasumatsu interview.
30. George Nikides, "Plant Closes, Lives Crumble," *Winnipeg Free Press,* 3 March 1991, 3.
31. Lynda Howdle interview.
32. Ibid.
33. Ibid.
34. Ibid.
35. Puffs and Ruffles continue to be made by Dare. Dare Foods, "Ruffles Classic," http://www.darefoods.com/ca_en/product/ruffles-classic/167, and "Viva Puffs," http://www.darefoods.com/ca_en/brand/Viva+Puffs/19.
36. Lynda Howdle interview.
37. Ibid.
38. Ibid.
39. Tom Yasumatsu interview.
40. Ibid.
41. Ibid.
42. Ibid.
43. Ibid.
44. Ibid.
45. Ibid.

46. Ibid.
47. Ibid.
48. Ibid.
49. Ibid.
50. Ibid.
51. Ibid.
52. May and Morrison, "Making Sense of Restructuring," 273.
53. Wright, "Historical Interpretations," 26.
54. Exceptions are Puffs and Ruffles, which are made by Dare Foods. See footnote 35.
55. Bring Back the Cuban Lunch, "About," Facebook group.
56. Ibid.
57. Comment by Joanne M. Rizzi, 31 August 2014.
58. Post by Daniel Gilchrist, 24 August 2013; Canadian Intellectual Property Office, Canadian trademark data for "Cuban Lunch," 21 October 2014, http://www.cipo.ic.gc.ca/app/opic-cipo/trdmrks/srch/vwTrdmrk.do?lang=eng&status=OK&fileNumber=0505633&extension=0&startingDocumentIndexOnPage=1.
59. Kickstarter is the world's largest crowd-funding platform, https://www.kickstarter.com/.
60. Comment by Duff MacDonald, 22 March 2013. Alden Gushnowski and J.R. Richardson posted similar comments on 24 August 2013 and 9 September 2013.
61. Post by Daniel Gilchrist, 16 April 2013.
62. Comment by Betty Palen, 22 March 2013.
63. Comment by Duff MacDonald, 1 March 2013.
64. Comments by David Dunster and Chris Neufeld, 18 April 2012.
65. Comment by Neil Batchelor, 15 January 2012.
66. Post by Duff MacDonald, 27 February 2013.
67. Ilana Simon, "Cuban Lunch a No-Bake, No-Fuss Summer Treat," *Winnipeg Free Press*, 17 July 2002, D4.
68. Ibid.
69. "*A Cookbook of Memories:* Cookies, Bars and Candy," Calling Lakes Centre, 2006, http://www.callinglakes.ca/pages/cookbook/cbook07.htm; "*A Cookbook of Memories:* Cookies, Bars and Candy: Cuban Lunch," Calling Lakes Centre, 2006, http://www.callinglakes.ca/pages/cookbook/cbook07b.

htm; "*A Cookbook of Memories,*" Calling Lakes Centre, 2006, http://www.callinglakes.ca/pages/cookbook/cbook01.htm.

70. Ferguson, "Senses of Taste," 371.

71. Specifying Old Dutch chips links the Winnipeg-made Cuban Lunch to another Winnipeg-based snack producer, lending it further authenticity.

72. Post by Kelli Larusic, 24 August 2011.

73. Comments by Alice Critofoli, Dallas Patterson Jr., and Patti Garner, 15 October 2014.

74. Post by Kevlar Shaw, 16 December 2012.

75. Post by Chris Neufeld, 30 January 2012. Censorship in original.

76. Comment by David Ingram, 20 June 2013.

77. Post by David Ingram, 23 May 2012. I have been unable to locate Doug Riach.

78. Joan, "Balonie Goes to the Big City" (blog post), *It's Always Something!,* 16 August 2005, http://fromanywheretoanyone.blogspot.ca/2005/08/balonie-goes-to-big-city.html.

79. Ibid.

80. "Disastrous Fire," *Halifax Acadian Recorder,* 17 April 1867, 2 C6; *Halifax Evening Reporter,* 16 April 1867, 2 C6.

81. McKay, "Capital and Labour," 83n33.

82. The owners at this time were James W. Moir, William C. Moir, Charles B. Moir, and Charles V. Monaghan. Articles of Association of Moir's Limited, 27 April 1903, Nova Scotia Archives, MG 3, Moirs Annual Reports.

83. "Control of Moirs Stays in Maritimes," *Halifax Herald,* 15 September 1956, n.p.; "History of the Company," typescript, 27 August 1931. Both in Monaghan scrapbook, Nova Scotia Archives, MG 3 Vol. 1872.

84. Canadian Fire-Fighters Museum, "Before the Time of Organized Fire Brigades," http://www.firemuseumcanada.com/before-the-time-of-organized-fire-brigades/.

85. Lisa Rose, "Midland Park Confectionery Plant Fire Had Major Impact on '50s Candy Corn Consumption," *NJ.com,* 9 October 2011, http://www.nj.com/news/index.ssf/2011/10/midland_park_confectionary_pla.html; Canadian Centre for Occupational Health and Safety, "OSH Answers Fact Sheets: Combustible Dust," 19 February 2015, https://www.ccohs.ca/oshanswers/chemicals/combustible_dust.html.

86. "The House of 8000 Window Panes," *Maritime Merchant,* 13 June 1929, 27, Nova Scotia Archives, Moirs Clippings, MG 3 Vol. 1868.

87. "Making Chocolates," 8 November 1930, n.p., and "James W. Moir Is Called by Death," 5 August 1941, n.p., Nova Scotia Archives, Moirs Clippings, MG 3 Vol. 1868.

88. Mulrooney, "Femininity and the Factory," 22.

89. The invention of the starch mogul at the turn of the twentieth century transformed the industry: "three men standing at a machine could do the work that previously took twelve or fifteen men, hard at labor." Kawash, *Candy*, 34.

90. "Modernization Leads to Record Years for Moirs," *Candy Industry and Confectioners Journal* (13 September 1960): 5.

91. Mulrooney, "Femininity and the Factory," 45.

92. Untitled manuscript, 21 October 1959, Monaghan scrapbook, Nova Scotia Archives, MG 3 Vol. 1872.

93. Elizabeth Hiscott, "Moirs: A Pot of Gold and a Giant," *Atlantic Advocate* 6, no. 12 (August 1976): 62.

94. "Veteran Employees of Moirs Recall Old Days and Tell of Firm's Remarkable Growth," *Halifax Daily Star*, 2 June 1928, 18.

95. "Making Chocolates," 8 November 1930, n.p., Nova Scotia Archives, Moirs Clippings, MG 3 Vol. 1868.

96. Elizabeth Hiscott, "Moirs: A Pot of Gold and a Giant," *Atlantic Advocate* 6, no. 12 (August 1976): 62.

97. Kirby, *Kitchen Party*, 99.

98. "New Model to Grace Moirs Pot of Gold," *Halifax Chronicle-Herald*, 23 November 1969, 8.

99. Elizabeth Hiscott, "Moirs: A Pot of Gold and a Giant," *Atlantic Advocate* 6, no. 12 (August 1976): 63.

100. Ibid.

101. McKay, "Capital and Labour," 87.

102. Mulrooney, "Femininity and the Factory," 33.

103. Ibid., 37.

104. Ian Sclanders, "Candy Unlimited," *Maclean's* (24 December 1955): 22.

105. Ibid.

106. In the 1970s, a chief accountant and a personnel officer were the only women in administration at Moirs. Elizabeth Hiscott, "Moirs: A Pot of Gold and a Giant," *Atlantic Advocate* 6, no. 12 (August 1976): 63.

107. Mulrooney, "Femininity and the Factory," 23.

108. Ibid., 53.

109. Ibid., 74.

110. Ibid., 105.

111. Ibid., 107–8.

112. Ibid., 177–78.

113. "The Facts: Why Chocolate Bars Are Now 8c," Moirs advertisement [c.1940s], Nova Scotia Archives, Moirs Clippings, MG 3 Vol. 1868.

114. "Stop It Now," *Hants Journal,* 18 September 1946, n.p., Nova Scotia Archives, Moirs Clippings, MG 3 Vol. 1868.

115. "The Facts: Why Chocolate Bars Are Now 8c," Moirs advertisement [1940s], Nova Scotia Archives, Moirs Clippings, MG 3 Vol. 1868.

116. The first American chocolate bar, the "Tango," was produced by Bunte Brothers of Chicago in 1914. "The Rise of the Nickel Bar," *Printers' Ink* (7 July 1932): 72. The world's first chocolate bar was produced by Fry & Son in 1847. Emma Smith and Evan Bower, "Who Invented the Chocolate Bar?," *The New Brunswick Beacon,* 23 March 2011, http://www.newbrunswickbeacon.ca/11808/who-invented-the-chocolate-bar/ (accessed 11 August 2015); Cadbury, "The Story," https://www.cadbury.co.uk/the-story.

117. "The Rise of the Nickel Bar," *Printers' Ink* (7 July 1932): 72.

118. "Making Chocolates," 8 November 1930, n.p., Nova Scotia Archives, Moirs Clippings, MG 3 Vol. 1868.

119. "This Day in *Journal* History: April 29, 1947: Schoolchildren Protest Demise of the Five-Cent Chocolate Bar," *Edmonton Journal,* 29 April 2013, http://www.canada.com/story.html?id=c0c9f055-0632-4323-bcd1-db5f20fa1ac1 (accessed 11 August 2015).

120. Ibid.; Off, "Epilogue," in *Bitter Chocolate;* Ed Coleman, "The Great Chocolate Bar Protest of 1947," *King's County Register/Advertiser,* 2 March 2013, http://www.kingscountynews.ca/section/2013-03-02/article-3187209/The-great-chocolate-bar-protest-of-1947/1 (accessed 11 August 2015).

121. "Manufacturer Raps 8-Cent Filled Bars," *Winnipeg Tribune,* 1 May 1947, 15.

122. "Control of Moirs Stays in Maritimes," *Halifax Herald,* 15 September 1956, n.p.; "History of the Company," typescript, 27 August 1931. Both in Monaghan scrapbook, Nova Scotia Archives, MG 3 Vol. 1872.

123. "Moirs Are Pleased," full page ad, *Halifax Mail Star,* 27 February 1957, n.d., Monaghan scrapbook, Nova Scotia Archives, MG 3 Vol. 1872; Elizabeth Hiscott, "Moirs: A Pot of Gold and a Giant," *Atlantic Advocate* 6, no. 12 (August 1976): 60.

124. E. L[eroy] Otto, vice president and general manager, "Re—Silver Dollar Pay Day," advertisement in *Halifax Mail,* 23 May 1958, in [Colonel] J[ames] D. Monaghan's scrapbook of news stories and advertisements, newspaper

clippings, histories, 1872, Nova Scotia Archives, MG 3 Vol. 1872. Emphasis in original.

125. Message to Moirs employees from E. L[eroy] Otto, 23 May 1958, Monaghan scrapbook, Nova Scotia Archives, MG 3 Vol. 1872.

126. Handwritten note on "Re—Silver Dollar Pay Day," advertisement in *Halifax Mail,* 23 May 1958, Monaghan scrapbook, Nova Scotia Archives, MG 3 Vol. 1872.

127. "Moirs Employees Honored for 3,966 Years of Service," *Halifax Mail-Star,* 7 June 1961, n.p., in [Colonel] J[ames] D. Monaghan's scrapbook of news stories and advertisements, newspaper clippings, histories, 1872, Nova Scotia Archives, MG 3 Vol. 1872.

128. Elizabeth Hiscott, "Moirs: A Pot of Gold and a Giant," *Atlantic Advocate* 6, no. 12 (August 1976): 61.

129. Ibid.

130. [Colonel] J[ames] D. Monaghan's scrapbook of news stories and advertisements, newspaper clippings, histories, 1872, Nova Scotia Archives, MG 3 Vol. 1872.

131. "Modernization Leads to Record Years for Moirs," *Candy Industry and Confectioners Journal* (13 September 1960): 5.

132. Moirs annual report, 31 December 1960, Nova Scotia Archives, MG 3, Moirs Annual Reports.

133. The *Halifax Chronicle-Herald* revisited this argument in 1960, noting that the federal government viewed confectionery as "so important as energy producers that it includes in the basic survival kit for armed service personnel a good-sized package of chocolate and another bag of jellied drops." The newspaper quoted the finance minister as having declared in 1956, "It seems to me that this type of tax is supported, in the mind of the government on the theory that chocolate is a luxury and not a food. To most Canadians I think that chocolate is a food and not merely a luxury." "Unfair and Damaging," *Halifax Chronicle-Herald,* 30 January 1960, 4.

134. "A Highly-Taxed Food," *Halifax Chronicle,* 24 June 1952, in Monaghan scrapbook, Nova Scotia Archives, MG 3 Vol. 1872.

135. "Seek Tax Relief," *Halifax Mail-Star,* 5 February 1960, n.p., in Monaghan scrapbook, Nova Scotia Archives, MG 3 Vol. 1872.

136. Annual Report, 31 December 1962, Nova Scotia Archives, MG 3, Moirs Annual Reports.

137. "Unfair and Damaging," *Halifax Chronicle-Herald,* 30 January 1960, 4.

138. Annual Report, 31 December 1962, Nova Scotia Archives, MG 3, Moirs Annual Reports.

139. "Unfair and Damaging," *Halifax Chronicle-Herald,* 30 January 1960, 4. A resident of St. Stephen, New Brunswick, where Ganong was located, also protested the tax and argued that candy was "a food, not a luxury." Ian Sclanders, "Candy Unlimited," *Maclean's* (24 December 1955): 22.

140. "Unfair and Damaging," *Halifax Chronicle-Herald,* 30 January 1960, 4.

141. "Standard Brands to Take Over N.S. Candy Firm of Moirs," *Globe and Mail,* 24 October 1967, B10.

142. Standard Brands merged with Nabisco in 1982. McGill Digital Archive, Canadian Corporate Reports, "Standard Brands Limited," http://digital.library.mcgill.ca/hrcorpreports/search/detail.php.

143. Elizabeth Hiscott, "Moirs: A Pot of Gold and a Giant," *Atlantic Advocate* 6, no. 12 (August 1976): 59.

144. "2.5 Million Bon-bon Plant for Woodside," *Dartmouth Free Press,* 8 August 1973, 1.

145. Conrad, "Moirs Ltd. Considering Relocation," 1.

146. "Moirs Ltd. Will Move to Dartmouth," *Atlantic Advocate* 64, no. 1 (September 1973): 39.

147. "New and Larger Plant Is Planned for Moirs," *Globe and Mail,* 8 August 1973, B6.

148. Elizabeth Hiscott, "Moirs: A Pot of Gold and a Giant," *Atlantic Advocate* 6, no. 12 (August 1976): 60.

149. Ibid., 63.

150. McKay, "Capital and Labour," 80.

151. Kirby, *Kitchen Party,* 99; Joanie Veitch, "Death of Moirs Factory Has Been a Long One," *Halifax Chronicle-Herald,* 28 December 2007, http://thechronicleherald.ca/community/Business/2007-12-28/article-981108/Death-of-Moirs-factory-has-been-a-long-one/1; "Moir's Closes Factory, 600 Jobs Lost," *Toronto Star,* 21 December 2007, http://www.thestar.com/business/article/287775--moirs-closes-factory-600-jobs-lost; "Hershey to Close N.S. Factory, Last in Canada," *Globe and Mail,* 10 May 2007, B9; "No More Pot of Gold for Factory Workers in Dartmouth," *Globe and Mail,* 22 December 2007, A14.

152. Brenden Sommerhalder, "Once Upon a Halifax: Moirs Chocolate," *Local Connections Halifax* 8 (Winter 2014), http://localconnections.ca/magazineblog/view/40/once-upon-a-halifax-moirs-chocolate (accessed 11 August 2015).

153. Sarah Story, research assistant, personal communication, 22 March 2015.

154. The Hershey Company, "Hershey's History: Growing Globally: Hershey Goes International," http://www.thehersheycompany.com/about-hershey/our-story/hersheys-history.aspx.

155. Surprise Soap Factory was sold to Lever Bros. between 1911 and 1913. "Of Dolls and Dusters and Norfolk Hats," *Saint Croix Courier,* 22 August 1979, C1.

156. Oliver Bertin, "Ganong Acts to End Its Obscurity," *Globe and Mail,* 31 March 1986, B3.

157. McCallum, "Separate Spheres," 72.

158. "The Fire Record," *Globe and Mail,* 17 March 1903, 10.

159. Administrative history, Ganong Bros. Ltd. (St. Stephen) fonds, New Brunswick Museum.

160. Angela Brunschot, "The Big Burden," *National Post,* 22 April 2006, FW7.

161. McCallum, "Separate Spheres," 89–90; Folster, *Chocolate Ganongs,* 117–30.

162. Emma Smith and Evan Bower, "Who Invented the Chocolate Bar?," *New Brunswick Beacon,* 23 March 2011, http://www.newbrunswickbeacon.ca/11808/who-invented-the-chocolate-bar/.

163. "The Dean of Candy Men, R.W. Ganong Honoured," *Saint Croix Courier,* 14 July 1976, n.p., New Brunswick Museum Vertical Files, "Ganong family: candy factory," RS 184, Provincial Archives of New Brunswick; "Confectioners Elect M. Neilson President," *Globe and Mail,* 9 May 1924, 17; "To Stimulate Sales of Candy in Canada," *Globe and Mail,* 4 May 1923, 14.

164. Arthur D. Ganong obituary, *Globe and Mail,* 22 November 1960, 26.

165. Western shipments for 1944, folder MS 1/1, Provincial Archives of New Brunswick, MC 504, Ganong Bros. Ltd. fonds.

166. Newfoundland shipments 1943–44, folder MS 1/2, Provincial Archives of New Brunswick, MC 504, Ganong Bros. Ltd. fonds.

167. Estimated total monthly production, folder MS 1/7, Provincial Archives of New Brunswick, MC 504, Ganong Bros. Ltd. fonds.

168. Philip D. Ganong became vice-president, and former president Arthur D. Ganong became chairman of the board. "Ganong Bros. Announce New Officers," *Globe and Mail,* 21 May 1957, 29; Randol Whidden Ganong obituary, *Toronto Star,* 21 March 2000, 1.

169. "The Dean of Candy Men, R.W. Ganong Honoured," *Saint Croix Courier,* 14 July 1976, n.p., New Brunswick Museum Vertical Files, "Ganong family: candy factory," RS 184, Provincial Archives of New Brunswick; Harry Bruce, "Chocolate—Health Food for the New Millennium," *Toronto Star,* 5 January 1999, 1. Randol Willard's great-niece, Bryana Ganong, the current chief executive officer, observed, "My brother and I, the fifth generation working

in the business, we both eat chocolate and candy every day, but much more moderately." Karen Finchin, "The Story behind a Uniquely Canadian Holiday Treat," *Globe and Mail,* 17 December 2013, http://www.theglobeandmail.com/life/holiday-guide/holiday-survival-guide/the-story-behind-a-uniquely-canadian-holiday-treat/article16002345/.

170. "Invented Candy Bar," *Globe and Mail,* 25 August 1955, 11.

171. Ian Sclanders, "Candy Unlimited," *Maclean's* (24 December 1955): 20.

172. Clive Baxter, "Watch This Case: Small Business Fights Big Union," *Financial Post,* 23 July 1960, n.p., New Brunswick Museum Vertical Files, "Ganong family: candy factory," RS 184, Provincial Archives of New Brunswick.

173. "Ganong's Marks Centennial," *Times Globe,* 10 July 1972, n.p., New Brunswick Museum Vertical Files, "Ganong family: candy factory," RS 184, Provincial Archives of New Brunswick.

174. "Union Asks Boycott on Candy Firm's Products," *St. John's Evening Telegram,* n.d., n.p., in [Colonel] J[ames] D. Monaghan's scrapbook of news stories and advertisements, newspaper clippings, histories, 1872, Nova Scotia Archives, MG 3 Vol. 1872.

175. Ibid.

176. Myron Wilson, "The Sweet Smell of Success," *Globe and Mail,* 10 February 1973, A2.

177. New Brunswick Department of Commerce and Development, advertisement, *Globe and Mail,* 20 September 1979, B3.

178. McCallum, "Separate Spheres," 77.

179. Folster, *Chocolate Ganongs,* 165–70. Joan Ganong, who is described in this book as argumentative and temperamental, sold her shares back to the company in 1975 and "did not again bother company management." Ibid., 170.

180. "Ganong's Marks Centennial," *Times Globe,* 10 July 1972, n.p., New Brunswick Museum Vertical Files, "Ganong family: candy factory," RS 184, Provincial Archives of New Brunswick.

181. "The Dean of Candy Men, R.W. Ganong Honoured," *Saint Croix Courier,* 14 July 1976, n.p., New Brunswick Museum Vertical Files, "Ganong family: candy factory," RS 184, Provincial Archives of New Brunswick.

182. "Dave Ganong Heads Firm," *Saint Croix Courier,* 23 March 1977, n.p., New Brunswick Museum Vertical Files, "Ganong family: candy factory," RS 184, Provincial Archives of New Brunswick.

183. Rick Spence, "Ganong Pivots to Keep with the Times," *National Post,* 3 February 2014, FP4.

184. Gordon Pitts, "Shaken by Chocolate Woes, Ganong Goes Outside for Help," *Globe and Mail,* 19 April 2008, B3; Bertrand Marotte, "Fifth-Generation Ganong to Lead Iconic New Brunswick Chocolate Maker," *Globe and Mail,* 28 April 2014, http://www.theglobeandmail.com/report-on-business/fifth-generation-ganong-to-lead-new-brunswick-chocolate-maker/article18299007/; Alyse Thompson, "Ganong to Return as President of Ganong Bros. Ltd.," *Candy Industry* (20 June 2012), http://www.candyindustry.com/articles/85247-ganong-to-return-as-president-of-ganong-bros-ltd.

185. Rick Spence, "Ganong Pivots to Keep with the Times," *National Post,* 3 February 2014, FP4.

186. Bertrand Marotte, "Fifth-Generation Ganong to Lead Iconic New Brunswick Chocolate Maker," *Globe and Mail,* 28 April 2014, http://www.theglobeandmail.com/report-on-business/fifth-generation-ganong-to-lead-new-brunswick-chocolate-maker/article18299007/.

187. "Ganong Brothers Appoints Bryana Ganong President and CEO," *East Coast Kitchen Party,* 28 April 2014, http://www.eastcoastkitchenparty.net/fooddrink_Bryana_Ganong.php; Rick Spence, "Candy Maker Ganong Pivots to Keep Up with the Times," *Financial Post,* 30 January 2014, http://business.financialpost.com/entrepreneur/ganong-nb-pivot; Rick Spence, "Ganong Pivots to Keep with the Times," *National Post,* 3 February 2014, FP4.

188. "The Dean of Candy Men, R.W. Ganong Honoured," *Saint Croix Courier,* 14 July 1976, n.p., New Brunswick Museum Vertical Files, "Ganong family: candy factory," RS 184, Provincial Archives of New Brunswick; "Ganong's Marks Centennial," *Times Globe,* 10 July 1972, n.p., New Brunswick Museum Vertical Files, "Ganong family: candy factory," RS 184, Provincial Archives of New Brunswick. A 1955 article in *Maclean's* gives the date as 1905. Ian Sclanders, "Candy Unlimited," *Maclean's* (24 December 1955): 20; Terrence Belford and Kira Vermond, "A Day of Fishing Led to Chocolate Bar's Invention," *National Post,* 15 December 1999, E2.

189. "The Dean of Candy Men, R.W. Ganong Honoured," *Saint Croix Courier,* 14 July 1976, n.p., New Brunswick Museum Vertical Files, "Ganong family: candy factory," RS 184, Provincial Archives of New Brunswick.

190. Ian Sclanders, "Candy Unlimited," *Maclean's* (24 December 1955): 32.

191. "Tells History of Industry," *Saint Croix Courier,* 29 March 1973, n.p., New Brunswick Museum Vertical Files, "Ganong family: candy factory," RS 184, Provincial Archives of New Brunswick.

192. The Chocolate Museum CD-ROM, n.d.

193. Ibid.

194. Ibid.

195. McCallum, "Separate Spheres," 77.

196. Emma Smith and Evan Bower, "Who Invented the Chocolate Bar?," *New Brunswick Beacon,* 23 March 2011, http://www.newbrunswickbeacon.ca/11808/who-invented-the-chocolate-bar/ (accessed 11 August 2015).

197. McCallum, "Separate Spheres," 87.

198. Ibid., 88.

199. The Chocolate Museum, "A Home Away From Home" display, St. Stephen, New Brunswick; McCallum, "Separate Spheres," 89–90.

200. Myron Wilson, "The Sweet Smell of Success," *Globe and Mail,* 10 February 1973, A2.

201. Many of these people subsequently applied for Canadian citizenship. John Shmuel, "Labour Pains," *National Post,* 14 February 2001, FP1; Peter O'Neil, "Kenney Plans Job Bank for Skilled Immigrants," *National Post,* 31 March 2012, A8; Neil Reynolds, "Changing New Brunswick's Culture of Dependence," *Globe and Mail,* 7 December 2011, B2.

202. "Worker Shortage Costs Candy Maker Customers," *Toronto Star,* 28 September 2007, B5.

203. Karen Pinchin, "The Willy Wonka of New Brunswick," *Globe and Mail,* 18 December 2013, L5; Karen Pinchin, "The Story behind a Uniquely Canadian Holiday Treat," *Globe and Mail,* 17 December 2013, http://www.theglobeandmail.com/life/holiday-guide/holiday-survival-guide/the-story-behind-a-uniquely-canadian-holiday-treat/article16002345/.

204. McCallum, "Separate Spheres," 78.

205. Ibid., 85.

206. Ibid.

207. Yvonne Butorac, "Get along to Ganong, Maritime Chocolatier," *Toronto Star,* 16 June 2001, L27.

208. Ganong Bros., Limited, "Our Heritage," 2014, https://ganong.com/our-sweet-story/; Rick Spence, "Taking a Page from the Little Guys' Playbook," *National Post,* 22 July 2014, FP7; Folster, *Ganong,* 124–26, 131.

209. Chocolate Fest brochure, 2013.

210. Ibid.

211. Ibid.

212. The Chocolate Museum, "On the Production Front Lines" display, St. Stephen, New Brunswick.

213. Alan Story, "Free Trade Facing Squalls down East," *Toronto Star,* 31 October 1987, D5.

214. Chris Morris, "NB Candy Maker Ganong Bros. Gearing for Free-Trade Challenge," *Globe and Mail,* 29 December 1988, B7.

215. "Jelly Bean Summit," *National Post,* 23 August 2007, A14.

216. Chris Morris, "NB Candy Maker Ganong Bros. Gearing for Free-Trade Challenge," *Globe and Mail,* 29 December 1988, B7.

217. Folster, *Chocolate Ganongs,* 204.

218. Sean Silcoff, "Sweets Makers Take on the Sugar Daddies," *National Post,* 11 September 2000, C01.

219. Ownership of the company changed hands several times, beginning in the 1960s. In 1983, Laura Secord was sold to Britain's Rowntree Macintosh Corporation, which was subsequently bought by Nestlé in 1988. Archibald Candy Corporation (Chicago) bought the business in 1999, and sold it to Canadian and American investment groups in 2004. Laura Secord finally returned to Canadian ownership in 2010. Laura Secord, "About Us," http://www.laurasecord.ca/en/pages/about-us; Laura Secord, "Timeline," http://www.laurasecord.ca/en/pages/timeline.

220. Michelle DaCruz, "Laura Secord to Return Units of Historically Named Firm to Canada," *National Post,* 24 February 2004, FP07; "Ganong Wins Supply Deal for Laura Secord Stores," *Globe and Mail,* 20 January 2004, B11; Marina Strauss, "Laura Secord to Get $10-Million Makeover in Bid to Sweeten Sales," *Globe and Mail,* 23 December 2004, B3; Dana Flavelle, "Deal on Laura Secord Expected Soon," *Toronto Star,* 15 October 2003, E01; "Archibald May Sell Its Candy Businesses," *Toronto Star,* 1 January 2004, C04; Dana Flavelle, "Laura Secord Stores Not Part of Deal as Parent Company Sells U.S. Businesses," *Toronto Star,* 16 January 2004, E01; Dana Flavelle, "Secord Wraps Up Supply Contract," *Toronto Star,* 20 January 2004, D01; Dana Flavelle, "M&M Leads Bids for Laura Secord," *Toronto Star,* 22 June 2004, D01; "Courts Approve Laura Secord Sale," *Toronto Star,* 28 July 2004, E03.

221. Oliver Bertin, "Ganong Acts to End Its Obscurity," *Globe and Mail,* 31 March 1986, B3.

222. Chris Morris, "Canadian Candy Firm Is Sending Chocolate Valentines to Europe," *Toronto Star,* 19 January 1986, B2.

223. Patricia Orwen, "When It Comes to Love Canadian Men Are So . . . Well, Canadian," *Toronto Star,* 12 February 1993, A1.

224. R. Whidden Ganong, quoted in "Tells History of Industry," *Saint Croix Courier,* 29 March 1973, n.p., New Brunswick Museum Vertical Files, "Ganong family: candy factory," RS 184, Provincial Archives of New Brunswick.

Chapter 6
CANDY MANUFACTURERS

1. See, for example, Ryan, *Chocolate Nations;* United Nations International Labour Office, *Rooting Out Child Labour;* Schrage and Ewing, "Cocoa Industry and Child Labour"; Pichler, "Legal Dispossession"; Fred Pearce, "'Green Palm Oil' Claims Land Cadbury's in Sticky Chocolate Mess," *The Guardian,* 20 August 2009, https://www.theguardian.com/environment/cif-green/2009/aug/20/cadburys-palm-oil.
2. See, for example, Pollan, *Omnivore's Dilemma; King Corn,* documentary, ITVS and Mosaic Films, 2007; "For a Healthier Country, Overhaul Farm Subsidies," *Scientific American* (1 May 2012), http://www.scientificamerican.com/article/fresh-fruit-hold-the-insulin/. For a contrary view, see James McWilliams, "The Evils of Corn Syrup: How Food Writers Got It Wrong," *The Atlantic* (21 September 2010), http://www.theatlantic.com/health/archive/2010/09/the-evils-of-corn-syrup-how-food-writers-got-it-wrong/63281/; Marion Nestle, "HFCS Makes Rats Fat?" (blog post), *Food Politics,* 24 March 2010, http://www.foodpolitics.com/2010/03/hfcs-makes-rats-fat/.
3. See, for example, Moss, *Salt Sugar Fat;* Gary Taubes, "Is Sugar Toxic?," *New York Times Magazine,* 13 April 2011, http://www.nytimes.com/2011/04/17/magazine/mag-17Sugar-t.html; Rich Cohen, "Sugar Love," *National Geographic* (August 2013), http://ngm.nationalgeographic.com/2013/08/sugar/cohen-text; Chen, *Taste of Sweet,* 6, 99–117; Gary Taubes and Cristin Kearns Couzens, "Big Sugar's Sweet Little Lies," *Mother Jones* (November/December 2012), http://www.motherjones.com/environment/2012/10/sugar-industry-lies-campaign; Kelly Crowe, "Sugar Industry's Secret Documents Echo Tobacco Tactics," *CBC News,* 8 March 2013, http://www.cbc.ca/news/health/sugar-industry-s-secret-documents-echo-tobacco-tactics-1.1369231. For a contrary view, see John Allemang, "Sugar: The Evolution of a Forbidden Fruit," *Globe and Mail,* 8 August 2014, http://www.theglobeandmail.com/life/health-and-fitness/health/sugar-the-evolution-of-a-forbidden-fruit/article19969475/?click=sf_globe; Samira Kawash, "Is Sugar Toxic? A Reply to Gary Taubes" (blog post), *The Candy Professor,* 27 April 2011, http://candyprofessor.com/2011/04/27/is-sugar-toxic-a-reply-to-gary-taubes/.
4. Mintz, *Sweetness and Power,* 61, 180.
5. Ibid., 6.
6. Ibid., 46.
7. Ibid., 148.
8. Ibid., 193.
9. Ann Semple, "Candies Made by Hand," *Ottawa Journal,* 5 March 1980, 33.

10. Sherry Martell, "Sweet Memories," *Truro Daily News,* 30 November 2012, http://www.trurodaily.com/News/Local/2012-11-30/article-3130918/Sweet-memories/1.

11. "Robertson's Candy Inc.: The Sweetest People in Nova Scotia," flyer from Colchester Museum, Truro, NS, August 2013; Derek McCormack, "Candy: The Lost Chapter to Christmas Days," *Taddle Creek* 15 (Christmas 2005): https://www.taddlecreekmag.com/candy.

12. Roy Robertson interview; "Moirs Carpenter Foreman Ends 37 Years' Service," unnamed newspaper article [c. 1950s], Moirs Clippings, MG 3 Vol. 1868, Nova Scotia Archives.

13. Roy Robertson interview.

14. Ibid.

15. Minard's Liniment is a salve for sore muscles invented in Nova Scotia in the nineteenth century. Minard's Liniment, "A Brief History," http://www.minards.com/history.php.

16. Its weather (as well as its central location and status as a transportation hub) is what made Chicago the "ideal location" for confectioners in the nineteenth and twentieth centuries. "Cool, crisp air is critical for making some particularly weather-fickle candies. A long winter extended the candymaking season in 19th-century Chicago, allowing candymakers to operate for up to seven months per year." Goddard, *Images of America,* 7–8. Nova Scotia's humidity as a Maritime province is a challenge for confectioners.

17. Roy Robertson interview.

18. Ibid.

19. Another source claims that it was employee Bill Fraser who named these mints. "Robertson's Candy Inc.: The Sweetest People in Nova Scotia," flyer from Colchester Museum, Truro, NS, August 2013.

20. Roy Robertson interview.

21. William Arthur Burbine interview.

22. Roy Robertson interview.

23. Marie Nightingale, "The Sweet Taste of Tradition," *Saltscapes* (November/December 2003): http://www.saltscapes.com/index.php?option=com_content&view=article&id=562:the-sweet-taste-of-tradition&catid=22:people-a-culture&Itemid=63.

24. William Arthur Burbine interview.

25. Roy Robertson interview.

26. Ibid.

27. Ibid.

28. Ibid.
29. William Arthur Burbine interview.
30. Ibid.
31. Ibid.
32. Ibid.
33. Ibid.
34. Roy Robertson interview.
35. Carr, *Candymaking in Canada,* 99; Canadian Intellectual Property Office, "Canadian Trade-Mark Data: Penny Jane Candy," http://www.ic.gc.ca/app/opic-cipo/trdmrks/srch/vwTrdmrk.do?lang=eng&status=OK&fileNumber=0441952&extension=0&startingDocumentIndexOnPage=1.
36. "Robertson's Candy Inc.: The Sweetest People in Nova Scotia," flyer from Colchester Museum, Truro, NS, August 2013.
37. William Arthur Burbine interview.
38. Robertson's Candy, Facebook post, 18 June 2014.
39. Roy Robertson interview.
40. William Arthur Burbine interview.
41. Roy Robertson interview.
42. Ibid.
43. Ibid.
44. Ibid.
45. Ibid.
46. Ibid.
47. Ibid.
48. Clarence Gould interview.
49. Pavey Candy was founded in 1921, and closed in 1986. Maurice Tougas, "Mom's Hobby Grew into Sweet Business," *Business Edge News Magazine,* 16 December 2003, http://www.businessedge.ca/archives/article.cfm/moms-hobby-grew-into-sweet-business-4504.
50. Charles Spencer Fletcher obituary, *Winnipeg Free Press,* 31 March 1996, C5.
51. Cavalier Candies Ltd., "About Us," 2011, http://www.cavaliercandies.com/about-us.html (accessed 11 August 2015).
52. Cavalier Candies brochure, 2015, courtesy of Clarence Gould.

53. "A Few of Saturday's Outstanding Offers," *Winnipeg Tribune*, 3 April 1936, 11; Murray McNeill, "Manitoba Is Set to Boom," *Winnipeg Free Press*, 5 March 2003, B5.

54. "Fire Sweeps Candy Plant," *Winnipeg Tribune*, 29 January 1947, 1; "$100,000 Fire Loss in Winnipeg," *Lethbridge Herald*, 29 January 1947, 1; Clarence Gould interview.

55. Clarence Gould interview.

56. City of Winnipeg Historical Buildings Committee, "185–187 Bannatyne Avenue: The Former McClary Building," July 1987, http://www.winnipeg.ca/ppd/historic/pdf-consv/Bannatyne%20185-long.pdf; Clarence Gould interview.

57. Clarence Gould interview.

58. Ibid.

59. Ibid.

60. Ibid.

61. Ibid.

62. Ibid.

63. Ibid. See also Wally Dennison, "Snack Food Firms Relish Tasty Results," *Winnipeg Free Press*, 18 November 1983, 35.

64. Clarence Gould interview.

65. Government of Manitoba, Agriculture, Food and Rural Development, "Growing Forward 2," http://www.manitoba.ca/agriculture/growing-forward-2/index.html; Lorraine Stevenson, "Innovative Food Processors Get Funding Kick-Starts," *Manitoba Cooperator* (7 January 2015), http://www.manitobacooperator.ca/news-opinion/news/local/innovative-food-processors-get-funding-kick-starts-2/.

66. Government of Manitoba, Agriculture, Food and Rural Development, "New Packing Equipment Increases Output and Creates New Jobs," http://www.manitoba.ca/agriculture/food-and-ag-processing/print,new-packing-equipment-increases-output-and-creates-new-jobs.html. As their candies are kosher, Cavalier cannot use corn syrup; instead, they use potato syrup or tapioca. Clarence Gould interview.

67. Government of Manitoba, Agriculture, Food and Rural Development, "New Packing Equipment Increases Output and Creates New Jobs," http://www.manitoba.ca/agriculture/food-and-ag-processing/print,new-packing-equipment-increases-output-and-creates-new-jobs.html.

68. Ibid.

69. Carr, *Candymaking in Canada*, 27.

70. Purity Factories, "About: The History of Purity Factories Ltd.," http://www.purity.nf.ca/about/.

71. Moira Baird, "In the Dough," *St. John's Telegram*, 28 July 2007, http://www.thetelegram.com/Living/2007-07-28/article-1438192/In-the-Dough/1.

72. Tour of Purity Factories, St. John's, NL, 19 August 2013.

73. Ibid.

74. Ibid.

75. Intangible Cultural Heritage, Folklore, and Oral History, "A Christmas Treat!" (blog post), 24 December 2013, http://doodledaddle.blogspot.ca/2012_12_01_archive.html.

76. Broken baked cookies are similarly returned to the dough mix.

77. Tour of Purity Factories, St. John's, NL, 19 August 2013.

78. B.T., "A Visit to the Purity Factory," *The Collegian* (Summer Term, 1933): 26.

79. Tour of Purity Factories, St. John's, NL, 19 August 2013.

80. Ed Smith, "The Double Whammy," *The Telegram*, 4 December 2010, http://www.thetelegram.com/Opinion/Columns/2010-12-04/article-2016984/The-double-whammy/1 (accessed 11 August 2015); James H. Hussey, "Brewis Not So Popular on Island," *Brandon Sun*, 13 April 1963, 11.

81. Tour of Purity Factories, St. John's, NL, 19 August 2013.

82. "Ready for Long Haul, Purity Workers Say," *CBC News*, 19 October 2010, http://www.cbc.ca/news/canada/newfoundland-labrador/ready-for-long-haul-purity-workers-say-1.882292.

83. Ibid.

84. National Union of Public and General Employees, "Purity Factories Ltd. Workers on Strike in St. John's," 6 September 2010, http://nupge.ca/content/3545/purity-factories-ltd-workers-strike-st-johns; "Purity Factory Workers Locked Out Due to Contract Dispute," *Telegram News*, 3 September 2010, http://www.thetelegram.com/News/Local/2010-09-03/article-1723909/Births-1847.

85. "Ready for Long Haul, Purity Workers Say," *CBC News*, 19 October 2010, http://www.cbc.ca/news/canada/newfoundland-labrador/ready-for-long-haul-purity-workers-say-1.882292.

86. Ibid.

87. National Union of Public and General Employees, "NAPE Reaches Agreement with Purity Factories Ltd.," 7 January 2011, http://nupge.ca/content/3893/nape-reaches-agreement-purity-factories-ltd.

88. "Trouble Brewing at Purity Factories," *The Telegram*, 21 February 2011, http://www.nl.dailybusinessbuzz.ca/Provincial-News/2011-02-21/article-2260226/NL%3A-Trouble-brewing-at-Purity-Factories/1.

89. Bunn Cooze interview.

90. Ibid.

91. Ibid.

92. Browning Harvey Limited stationery masthead, 1951, MG 7 Eric Ellis Collection, Box 5, File 18, West End Plant, The Rooms Provincial Archives.

93. Administrative history, Browning Harvey fonds, Provincial Archives of New Brunswick; Browning Harvey, "History," http://www.browningharvey.nf.ca/history.php.

94. Browning Harvey Limited price list, 1 May 1944, MG 7 Eric Ellis Collection, Box 6, File 27, Price Lists, The Rooms Provincial Archives.

95. Purity Confectionery products included penny candies (all-day suckers, strawberry sticks, lemon sticks, union squares, cremola bars, peanut bars, spitfires, banner caramels, C.C. mice, bolly wops, licorice caramels, twin rabbits, pal caramels, M.M. crisps, B.S. caramels, wonder rolls, mill logs, peppermint nobs, brown lumps, peppermint lumps, robins eggs, M.M. bobbers); climax mixture, climax peppermint nobs, climax peppermint lumps, molasses kisses, butterscotch kisses, rum and butter kisses, peanut butter kisses, banana kisses, old-fashioned peppermint nobs, old-fashioned peppermint lumps; bottled sweets such as balls, fruits, black currant drops, butterscotch drops, cherry drops, lemon drops, lime drops, orange drops, pineapple drops, peppermint balls, pear drops, raspberry drops, radio mixture, strawberry drops; fruit slices, jelly beans, black beauty mixture, A.B. gums, French creams; Needlers ten-cent chocolate bars (Kreema Milk, Kreema Milk with fruit, Kreema Orange, Kreema grapefruit); Windsor wafers; Lowney's five-cent chocolate bars (Oh Henry, Cocoanut Lunch, Eat-More, Caravan); McCormick's penny candies (afternoon mints, cream squares, darts, jawbreakers, boomerangs, chocolate novelties, sambos, wild cherries, pops, double thick mints, butter caramels, Stetsons, M.M. strawberries, mello beans, alleys, rainbow wafers). Purity Factories Price List and Order Form, 1 January 1957, Browning Harvey price list, 27 August 1956, and Purity Factories price list, April 1950, MG 7 Eric Ellis Collection, Box 6, File 27, Price Lists, The Rooms Provincial Archives.

96. Letter from Eric Ellis to Browning Harvey Ltd. managing directors, 6 August 1948, MG 7 Eric Ellis Collection, Box 6, File 13, Ellis's Reports and Suggestions to Managing Directors, The Rooms Provincial Archives.

97. "Browning Harvey Limited, West End Branch, Proposal for Programme of Work," 30 July 1948, MG 7 Eric Ellis Collection, Box 6, File 13, Ellis's Reports and Suggestions to Managing Directors, The Rooms Provincial Archives.

98. "Program of Work, New Bottling Building," 10 February 1951, MG 7 Eric Ellis Collection, Box 6, File 13, Ellis's Reports and Suggestions to Managing Directors, The Rooms Provincial Archives.

99. "Manufacturing of Biscuits," report by E. Ellis, General Manager, 20 November 1953, MG 7 Eric Ellis Collection, Box 5, File 18, West End Plant, The Rooms Provincial Archives.

100. "Suggestions for Our Future Policy," 4 July 1952, MG 7 Eric Ellis Collection, Box 6, File 13, Ellis's Reports and Suggestions to Managing Directors, The Rooms Provincial Archives.

101. Browning Harvey Limited Board of Directors minutes, 14 September 1951, MG 7 Eric Ellis Collection, Box 4, File 1, Minutes of Meetings, The Rooms Provincial Archives.

102. Browning Harvey Limited Board of Directors minutes, 7 September 1951, MG 7 Eric Ellis Collection, Box 4, File 1, Minutes of Meetings, The Rooms Provincial Archives.

103. Browning Harvey Limited Board of Directors minutes, 9 June 1951, MG 7 Eric Ellis Collection, Box 4, File 1, Minutes of Meetings, The Rooms Provincial Archives.

104. Browning Harvey Limited Board of Directors minutes, 6 July 1951, MG 7 Eric Ellis Collection, Box 4, File 1, Minutes of Meetings, The Rooms Provincial Archives.

105. Browning Harvey Limited Board of Directors minutes, 21 September 1951, MG 7 Eric Ellis Collection, Box 4, File 1, Minutes of Meetings, The Rooms Provincial Archives.

106. Browning Harvey Limited Board of Directors minutes, 21 September 1951 and 9 November 1951, MG 7 Eric Ellis Collection, Box 4, File 1, Minutes of Meetings, The Rooms Provincial Archives.

107. Browning Harvey Limited Board of Directors minutes, 14 December 1951, MG 7 Eric Ellis Collection, Box 4, File 1, Minutes of Meetings, The Rooms Provincial Archives.

108. Browning Harvey Limited Board of Directors minutes, 11 February and 14 November 1958, MG 7 Eric Ellis Collection, Box 4, File 1, Minutes of Meetings, The Rooms Provincial Archives.

109. Browning Harvey Limited Board of Directors minutes, 24 December 1952, MG 7 Eric Ellis Collection, Box 4, File 1, Minutes of Meetings, The Rooms Provincial Archives.

110. Browning Harvey Limited Board of Directors minutes, 21 May, 30 May, and 4 July 1952, MG 7 Eric Ellis Collection, Box 4, File 1, Minutes of Meetings, The Rooms Provincial Archives.

111. Ibid.

112. "Suggestions for Our Future Policy," 4 July 1952, MG 7 Eric Ellis Collection, Box 6, File 13, Ellis's Reports and Suggestions to Managing Directors, The Rooms Provincial Archives.

113. Ibid.

114. The board of directors considered a group pension plan for all employees in 1958 and again in 1959, but there is no record that they implemented one. Browning Harvey Limited Board of Directors minutes, 14 November 1958 and 21 August 1959, MG 7 Eric Ellis Collection, Box 4, File 1, Minutes of Meetings, The Rooms Provincial Archives.

115. Browning Harvey Limited Board of Directors minutes, 10 October 1956, MG 7 Eric Ellis Collection, Box 4, File 1, Minutes of Meetings, The Rooms Provincial Archives.

116. Browning Harvey Limited Board of Directors minutes, 14 November 1958, MG 7 Eric Ellis Collection, Box 4, File 1, Minutes of Meetings, The Rooms Provincial Archives.

117. Browning Harvey Ltd., "History," http://www.browningharvey.nf.ca/history.php.

118. "Steady Growth Marked," Special section of *Winnipeg Tribune*—"50 Years of Expansion with Scott-Bathgate Ltd.," 24 October 1953, 3.

119. "Dates Show Fifty Years of Progress," Special section of *Winnipeg Tribune*—"50 Years of Expansion with Scott-Bathgate Ltd.," 24 October 1953, 12; "His Hobby Is Watching Men Grow," Special section of *Winnipeg Tribune*—"50 Years of Expansion with Scott-Bathgate Ltd.," 24 October 1953, 5.

120. "Expansion Policy Was Formed in 30's," Special section of *Winnipeg Tribune*—"50 Years of Expansion with Scott-Bathgate Ltd.," 24 October 1953, 22.

121. "Story Tells of Expansion," Special section of *Winnipeg Tribune*—"50 Years of Expansion with Scott-Bathgate Ltd.," 24 October 1953, 3; "Employees Own over $500,000 in Firm's Stock," Special section of *Winnipeg Tribune*—"50 Years of Expansion with Scott-Bathgate Ltd.," 24 October 1953, 3.

122. "Scott-Bathgate Trucks, Cars Always Clean," Special section of *Winnipeg Tribune*—"50 Years of Expansion with Scott-Bathgate Ltd.," 24 October 1953, 3; Dickson Motors advertisement, *Winnipeg Free Press,* 27 November 1950, 7, and 11 April 1953, 8; "Scott-Bathgate Ltd. Has Own Car Fleet," Special section of *Winnipeg Tribune*—"50 Years of Expansion with Scott-Bathgate Ltd.," 24 October 1953, 31; Dave LaChance, "Sweets for Canada" (blog post), *Hemmings Daily,* 30 September 2011, http://blog.hemmings.com/index.php/tag/scott-bathgate/.

123. "Four Winnipeg Buildings Near 'Hub of West,'" Special section of *Winnipeg Tribune*—"50 Years of Expansion with Scott-Bathgate Ltd.," 24 October 1953, 31.

124. "Company Has Own Carpenter Shop," Special section of *Winnipeg Tribune*—"50 Years of Expansion with Scott-Bathgate Ltd.," 24 October 1953, 7.

125. Joan Druxman, "Candy Makes a Child's Dream Come True," *Winnipeg Tribune,* 14 September 1971, University of Manitoba Archives and Special Collections, Winnipeg Tribune Clippings Collection.

126. "'nutty Club' Orange Created for Firm," Special section of *Winnipeg Tribune*—"50 Years of Expansion with Scott-Bathgate Ltd.," 24 October 1953, 28; "Barber Pole Colored Design Aids Sales," Special section of *Winnipeg Tribune*—"50 Years of Expansion with Scott-Bathgate Ltd.," 24 October 1953, 28.

127. Ann Campbell, "Got Junk?," *Western Living* (September 2008): 19.

128. "F.J. Dodds Came up the Ladder Quickly," Special section of *Winnipeg Tribune*—"50 Years of Expansion with Scott-Bathgate Ltd.," 24 October 1953, 7.

129. "Seedmen Are Experts," Special section of *Winnipeg Tribune*—"50 Years of Expansion with Scott-Bathgate Ltd.," 24 October 1953, 29.

130. "Company Salesmen Links in a Chain," Special section of *Winnipeg Tribune*—"50 Years of Expansion with Scott-Bathgate Ltd.," 24 October 1953, 8.

131. "Firm's Nautical Salesman: Bob Frizzell Plies Pacific," Special section of *Winnipeg Tribune*—"50 Years of Expansion with Scott-Bathgate Ltd.," 24 October 1953, 14.

132. "Stories of Firm's Selling in West," Special section of *Winnipeg Tribune*—"50 Years of Expansion with Scott-Bathgate Ltd.," 24 October 1953, 26.

133. Ibid.

134. Tom Yasumatsu interview.

135. Ibid.

136. Progress Candy (1977) Ltd., owned by Ralph Shaff, ceased operation in 2006. Letter from Taylor McCaffrey LLP to Manitoba Companies Office, 12 December 2005, Manitoba Companies Office, Progress Candy (1977) Ltd. files. It was incorporated by Solomon Tapper, Ettie Tapper, Ralph Shaff, and Alexander Victor Chan in 1977. Articles of Incorporation, 9 May 1977.

137. Tom Yasumatsu interview.

138. Dare's advertisement, *Winnipeg Tribune,* 24 October 1953, 4.

139. "Syrups Are Made Here," Special section of *Winnipeg Tribune*—"50 Years of Expansion with Scott-Bathgate Ltd.," 24 October 1953, 8.

140. "Peanut Processing Needs 'Know-How,'" Special section of *Winnipeg Tribune*—"50 Years of Expansion with Scott-Bathgate Ltd.," 24 October 1953, 10.

141. These included Joseph Bellamy & Sons (liquorice, England), Dare Company (biscuits, Ontario), Dyson's (pickles, Winnipeg), G.F. Lovell & Co. (chocolate, England), Wyler & Co. (dehydrated vegetable flakes, Chicago), Riley Brothers (toffee, England), Howe Candy (Hamilton, ON), Beaver Products (floor wax, shoe cleaner, insecticide, Quebec), Britl-Bread Products (rye crisp bread, BC), J.A. Simard & Co. (canned meat spread, Quebec), John Fitton & Co. (fruit-filled candies, England), Harry Horne Co. (custard and gravy powders, Toronto), Habacure (Canada) (ham and bacon cure, Montreal), Ja-Po Products (bleach, Montreal), Krim-Ko Corp. (chocolate fountain syrup, Toronto), Sapoline Company (spot remover, Ontario), Hekman Rusk Co. (tea rusks, Michigan), Marshall & Co. (fish paste, Scotland), O.P. Chocolate Specialties (chocolate wafer bars, Wales), Absorbent Cotton Products (surgical dressings, Montreal), Robert Watson Co. (confectionery, Toronto), Melville Confections (Illinois), Helm Chocolate (England), Plastex (varnish, Moncton), Dr. J.O. Lambert Ltd. (cough syrup, Montreal), B.F. Trappey's Sons (pepper sauce, Louisiana), William Moorhouse & Sons (marmalade, England), Arthur Johnson & Sons (packaged soup, Ontario), Select Food Products (soup bases, maraschino cherries, Toronto), Ripon Foods (cookies, Wisconsin), Venus Foods (dried fruit cookies, Los Angeles), Tecco Products ("liquid wax novelties," Berkeley, CA), O. Gauthier (waffles, melba toast, Montreal), Col-R-Corn (coloured popping corn, Chicago), Coyle Products (chocolate, Ontario), Pulford Drug Co. (cream of olives, Winnipeg), California Olive Packers (olives, California), Fascination Candy (Chicago), Gattuso Olive Oil (Montreal), Kay Brothers (fly coils, England), Batger & Co. (silver dragees, England), Carco (pens, Detroit), C. Kunzle (chocolate, England). Advertisement, Special section of *Winnipeg Tribune*—"50 Years of Expansion with Scott-Bathgate Ltd.," 24 October 1953,16–17.

142. "Nutty Club Brand Mustard Famous," Special section of *Winnipeg Tribune*—"50 Years of Expansion with Scott-Bathgate Ltd.," 24 October 1953, 20.

143. My father recalled that his parents, who were registered seed growers in Manitoba, provided mustard seed to Nutty Club one year in exchange for some spoiled chocolate. They fed the chocolate to their pigs. He claimed that year's ham was the sweetest ever.

144. "Peanut Processing Needs 'Know-How,'" Special section of *Winnipeg Tribune*—"50 Years of Expansion with Scott-Bathgate Ltd.," 24 October 1953, 10.

145. Ibid.

146. Murray McNeill, "Nutty Club Stays Crunchy at 100," *Winnipeg Free Press*, 30 August 2003, 24.

147. Ritchie Gage, "The Cookie Bag Strategist: How Robert May Pursues Business Excellence," *Manitoba Business* (1 May 1992), http://www.thefreelibrary.com/The+cookie+bag+strategist%3A+how+Robert+May+pursues+business+exc

ellence.-a012259122; "One Smart Cookie Wraps Up Honors," *Winnipeg Free Press*, 2 May 1992, 2.

148. Greg Bannister, "Provincial Financing Aids Deal as Local Food Packager Expands," *Winnipeg Free Press*, 9 March 1985, 3.
149. Murray McNeill, "Nutty Club Stays Crunchy at 100," *Winnipeg Free Press*, 30 August 2003, 24.
150. "A Shell of Its Former Self," *Winnipeg Free Press*, 9 June 2007, http://www.winnipegfreepress.com/historic/32262489.html.
151. Ibid.
152. Salisbury House restaurant advertisements, *Winnipeg Free Press*, 17 October 1947, 18; 21 October 1949, 4; 12 October 1951, 36.
153. "Candy Is Dandy, Are Nuts Better?" *Winnipeg Free Press*, 8 December 1969, 15.
154. Donald Campbell, "Lack of Art Criticism Spurs Conference," *Winnipeg Free Press*, 10 June 1988, 32.
155. Randal McIlroy, "Artists Probe Candy Factory," *Winnipeg Free Press*, 11 June 1988, 20.
156. Dolores Terese Blanche Williams (née Radford) obituary, *Winnipeg Free Press*, 2 September 2004, 22.
157. Lillian Rouble (née Maskiw) obituary, *Winnipeg Free Press*, 20 June 2009, 49.
158. Michael Specter, "How Much Harm Can Sugar Do?" *New Yorker* (8 September 2015), http://www.newyorker.com/culture/culture-desk/how-much-harm-can-sugar-do.
159. Kawash, *Candy*, 25.
160. Dusselier, "Understandings of Food," 332.
161. Woloson, *Refined Tastes*, 34.
162. Hartel and Hartel, *Candy Bites*, 10.

Chapter 7
KIDS BIDS TELEVISION

1. Tom Yasumatsu interview. Similarly, a *Winnipeg Free Press* columnist reported in 1962 that his son was "a chip off the old block. When I asked him what prize he liked best on the show he promptly answered Bonnie Davis. But he didn't have enough points to bring her home." Gene Telpner, "Coffee Break," *Winnipeg Free Press*, 19 June 1962, 3.

2. Bud Riley, "CKPR Radio/TV," http://www.budrileyradio.com/ckpr_radio_tv.html; Brian G. Spare, "Kids Bids," *Bayview: Thunder Bay's Magazine of Leisure and Lifestyle* (2013), http://www.bayviewmagazine.com/content/kids-bids (accessed 11 August 2015); Chris Radons, personal communication, 27 May 2013; comments by Jack Neary, Larry Peterson, Kim Surrette, Ken Lang, and Bob Harrington on Janis Thiessen, "Old Dutch Kids Bids: Searching for Past Contestants" (blog post), 7 January 2013, http://janisthiessen.ca/2013/01/07/old-dutch-kids-bids-searching-for-past-contestants/; Alan Cody interview; Doug Krochak interview; Doug Peterson interview.
3. Meyer Steiman obituary, *Winnipeg Free Press,* 14 March 2012, http://passages.winnipegfreepress.com/passage-details/id-189200/name-Meyer_Steiman/; Brian G. Spare, "Kids Bids," *Bayview: Thunder Bay's Magazine of Leisure and Lifestyle* (2013), http://www.bayviewmagazine.com/content/kids-bids; Mauric Tougas, "CFRN at 60: When TV Really Mattered" (blog post), *In This Corner,* 19 October 2014, https://mauricetougas.wordpress.com/tag/eric-neville/; Alan Cody interview.
4. John Ferguson, 10 April 2013 (2:28 p.m.), Beverley Holmes, 14 June 2013 (7:20 a.m.), Bill Brown, 17 June 2013 (9:17 p.m.), Karen Thomas, 21 March 2015 (9:54 a.m.), Gloria, 11 May 2015 (10:03 a.m.), Perry Pachkowski, 11 May 2015 (2:45 p.m.), and Vicki Williams, 9 June 2015 (3:53 a.m.), comments on Janis Thiessen, "Old Dutch Kids Bids: Searching for Past Contestants" (blog post), 7 January 2013, http://janisthiessen.ca/2013/01/07/old-dutch-kids-bids-searching-for-past-contestants/.
5. Verne Prior interview.
6. Ibid.
7. Ibid.
8. Ibid. See also Gordon Sinclair, Jr., "Restoration Unearths Dispute," *Winnipeg Free Press,* 24 August 1993, B1.
9. Christopher Dafoe, "How about Kelly Crescent?" *Winnipeg Free Press,* 28 August 1993, A6.
10. Verne Prior interview.
11. Ibid.
12. Ibid.
13. Alan Cody interview.
14. Verne Prior interview.
15. Ibid.
16. Ken Lang, 21 March 2015 (1:18 p.m.), comment on Janis Thiessen, "Old Dutch Kids Bids: Searching for Past Contestants" (blog post), 7 January 2013, http://janisthiessen.ca/2013/01/07/old-dutch-kids-bids-searching-for-past-contestants/.

17. Karen McAuley, personal communication, 3 July 2015.
18. Verne Prior interview.
19. "Calgary Campaigner Taps Brazilian Ties," *Calgary Herald*, 12 December 2008, http://www.canada.com/story_print.html?id=bc4b24d3-4aee-4b2d-a18c-37d81dfdec25&sponsor.
20. Ibid.
21. Golden Flake (Alabama) and Kitty Clover (Kansas) were two such brands that produced auction shows where children could use chip packaging to bid on prizes. As with *Kids Bids*, the grand prize on these shows was a bicycle. Burhans, *Crunch!*, 52–54.
22. Steven Aanenson interview.
23. Ibid.
24. "Waring Boosts Sales for Old Dutch—Hope to Follow," *St. Paul Dispatch-Pioneer Press* 27, no. 1 (February 1955): 1; "Advertising News," *Minneapolis Sunday Tribune*, 30 January 1955, E5; "Empty Bags Used as Show 'Tickets,'" *Food Field Reporter* (21 March 1955), courtesy of Old Dutch Foods, Roseville, MN.
25. "Old Dutch Promotion," *Minnesota Food Guide* (December 1954): 13.
26. Steven Aanenson interview.
27. Ibid.
28. Martial Boulet interview.
29. Classified advertisement, *Winnipeg Free Press*, 15 December 1962, 39.
30. Classified advertisements, *Winnipeg Free Press*, 4 June 1964, 19; 31 July 1968, 48; 2 August 1968, 28.
31. Martial Boulet interview.
32. Anonymous Old Dutch employee interview.
33. Hyde-Robertson Limited were confectioners in Winnipeg in the late 1920s and early 1930s, located at 170 Isabel Street.
34. "BOYS—GIRLS—Win a Bicycle FREE," Hyde-Robertson Limited advertisement, *Winnipeg Tribune*, 11 May 1929, 2. The joy-cycle was a three-wheeled cycle introduced in 1922. CCM is the Canada Cycle and Motor Company, makers of bicycles and skates. CCM, "CCM Cycle's Past and Present," accessed 12 March 2005, http://www.ccmcycle.com/anglais/pages/pastpresent.html.
35. "Free—100 Bicycles—Buy Bicycle Bars—The New 5c Candy Bar," Hyde-Robertson Limited advertisement, *Winnipeg Tribune*, 27 April 1928, 5.
36. "Bicycle Bars and the Big Parade," Hyde-Robertson Limited advertisement, *Winnipeg Tribune*, 24 April 1929, 5.

37. Ibid.

38. "BOYS—GIRLS—Win a Bicycle FREE," Hyde-Robertson Limited advertisement, *Winnipeg Tribune*, 11 May 1929, 2.

39. Ibid.

40. Hyde-Robertson Limited advertisements, *Winnipeg Tribune*, 19 April 1930, 4; and 14 June 1930, 4.

41. Hutchinson, "Making (Anti)Modern Childhood," 81; Cross, *Cute and the Cool*, 150.

42. Jacobson, *Raising Consumers*, 17–18.

43. Levenstein, *Paradox of Plenty*, 217, 239–40.

44. Cross, *Kids' Stuff*, 148.

45. Ibid., 148, 182.

46. Ibid., 165.

47. Coleman, "Through the Years," 300.

48. Ibid., 305.

49. Cross, *Cute and the Cool*, 180–81.

50. Ibid., 182.

51. Ibid., 183–84; Armstrong and Brucks, "Dealing with Children's Advertising," 98.

52. Canadian Association of Broadcasters, *Advertising to Children in Canada: A Reference Guide* (May 2006), 12, http://www.cab-acr.ca/english/social/advertisingchildren/kids_reference_guide.pdf. For a detailed discussion of broadcasting standards regarding advertising food to Canadian children, see Elliott, "*Taste Rules!*"

53. Alfred Adams interview.

54. Ibid.

55. Ibid.

56. Ibid.

57. Sharon Moore, by contrast, recalls watching a broadcast of one of the *Kids Bids* episodes in which she appeared. "It was very embarrassing," she said. She remembers thinking that she looked "shell shocked." Sharon Moore interview.

58. Alfred Adams interview.

59. Sharon Moore interview.

60. Ibid.

61. Ibid.
62. Ibid.
63. Ibid.
64. Ibid.
65. Gloria, 11 May 2015 (10:03 a.m.), comment on Janis Thiessen, “Old Dutch Kids Bids: Searching for Past Contestants” (blog post), 7 January 2013, http://janisthiessen.ca/2013/01/07/old-dutch-kids-bids-searching-for-past-contestants/.
66. Ibid.
67. Alan Cody interview.
68. Ibid.
69. Ibid.
70. Ibid.
71. Ibid.
72. Ibid.
73. Ibid.
74. Ibid.
75. Ibid.
76. Ibid.
77. Ibid.
78. Doug Krochak interview.
79. Ibid.
80. Ibid.
81. Kardene Campbell (née Krochak) interview.
82. Ibid.
83. Doug Krochak interview.
84. Ibid.
85. Ibid.
86. Ibid.
87. Ibid.
88. Nancy-Ellen McLennan, “TV Front Room” (blog post), *The Wartime House in Shaughnessy Heights*, 14 June 2010, http://shaughnessyheights.blogspot.ca/2010/05/tv-front-room.html.
89. Ibid.

90. Bob Babiak interview.

91. Ibid.

92. Beverley Holmes, 14 June 2013 (7:20 a.m.), Denise Lagace, 30 August 2015 (12:36 p.m.), Larry Peterson, 9 February 2014 (9:50 p.m.), and Joanne Fredericks, 19 May 2016 (3:06 p.m.), comments on Janis Thiessen, "Old Dutch Kids Bids: Searching for Past Contestants" (blog post), 7 January 2013, http://janisthiessen.ca/2013/01/07/old-dutch-kids-bids-searching-for-past-contestants/.

93. Danny Hooper, "Please, Show Me the Dough!" *Edmonton Sun,* 30 April 2011, www.edmontonsun.com/2011/04/30/please-show-me-the-dough.

94. Ibid.

95. Robert Fafara, 7 August 2013 (9:23 p.m.), comment on Janis Thiessen, "Old Dutch Kids Bids: Searching for Past Contestants" (blog post), 7 January 2013, http://janisthiessen.ca/2013/01/07/old-dutch-kids-bids-searching-for-past-contestants/.

96. Ibid.

97. Karen Thomas interview.

98. Her brother Ron won a similar radio when he was on the show as a Grade 3 student.

99. Karen Thomas interview.

100. Here, Thomas's recollection of *Kids Bids* differs from that of other contestants—a fact she herself recognizes. In interviews, no one else mentioned such a test.

101. Karen Thomas interview.

102. Ibid.

103. Ibid.

104. Richard Rosin interview.

105. Ibid.

106. Ibid.

107. Doug Peterson interview.

108. Ibid.

109. Ibid.

110. Ibid.

111. Geri Peterson interview.

112. Ibid.

113. Ibid.

114. Ibid.

115. Kirk McDougall interview.

116. Ibid.

117. Ibid.

118. Ibid.

119. See Chapter 1 for an explanation of prairie socials.

120. Richard Rosin interview.

121. See Chapter 2 for discussion of this company.

122. Grant Wichenko interview.

123. Wichenko also recalled that his manager "was quite the character." His car's dashboard had "two spigots: one for rum and one for Coke, so he could drink while on the highway. That was the '60s: it was perfectly acceptable to do those kind of things." Grant Wichenko interview.

124. Gordon Sinclair, "Filmon Ignores Call of the Moose," *Winnipeg Free Press,* 26 October 1996, 6.

125. Grant Wichenko interview.

126. Ibid.

127. Walter Mrak, "Recycling Fun," letter to editor, *Winnipeg Free Press,* 12 June 1991, 6.

128. Bill Brown, 17 June 2013 (9:17 p.m.), comment on Janis Thiessen, "Old Dutch Kids Bids: Searching for Past Contestants" (blog post), 7 January 2013, http://janisthiessen.ca/2013/01/07/old-dutch-kids-bids-searching-for-past-contestants/.

129. Claudia Byczek, 23 August 2015 (11:12 a.m.), comment on Janis Thiessen, "Old Dutch Kids Bids: Searching for Past Contestants" (blog post), 7 January 2013, http://janisthiessen.ca/2013/01/07/old-dutch-kids-bids-searching-for-past-contestants/.

130. Ron LeClair, 8 September 2015 (4:20 p.m.), and LaVerna Wiebe Peters, 23 December 2015 (8:09 p.m.), comments on Janis Thiessen, "Old Dutch Kids Bids: Searching for Past Contestants" (blog post), 7 January 2013, http://janisthiessen.ca/2013/01/07/old-dutch-kids-bids-searching-for-past-contestants/.

131. Cross, *Kids' Stuff,* 165.

132. Verne Prior interview.

133. Richard Rosin interview.

134. Kapur, *Coining for Capital,* 45.

135. Ibid., 18.

136. Helgren, "'Very Innocent Time,'" 68.

Conclusion

1. Jeffrey Dunn interview.
2. Besky and Brown, "Looking for Work," 21.
3. Robbins, "Commodity Histories," 455.
4. Besky and Brown, "Looking for Work," 21.
5. Mike McCartney interview.
6. Les Sykes interview. Journalist Nina Teicholz's *The Big Fat Surprise* reveals that ditching dietary fats in the 1980s led to increased consumption of carbohydrates. Abandonment of trans fats was accompanied by a return to the use of liquid oils in deep fryers, which generates unhealthy oxidation products—and which had prompted the development of trans fats in the first place. A meta-analysis of seventy-six studies in the March 2014 issue of *Annals of Internal Medicine* concluded, "Current evidence does not clearly support cardiovascular guidelines that encourage high consumption of polyunsaturated fatty acids and low consumption of total saturated fats." Yet, until 2001, the American Heart Association advised the public to eat hard candies as a way to avoid consuming fatty foods. Guthman, citing Gard and Wright, notes that 'common sense' approaches to preventing obesity have been similarly ineffective: there is no "predictable relationship between food intake, exercise, and body size." Teicholz, *Big Fat Surprise;* Nina Teicholz, "The Questionable Link Between Saturated Fat and Heart Disease," *Wall Street Journal,* 6 May 2014, http://online.wsj.com/news/articles/SB10001424052702303678404579533760760481486; Chowdhury et al., "Dietary, Circulating, and Supplement Fatty Acids," 398; Guthman, "Neoliberalism," 189, citing M. Gard and J. Wright, *The Obesity Epidemic: Science, Morality, and Ideology* (London: Routledge, 2005).
7. Les Sykes interview.
8. Lynda Howdle interview.
9. Turner, "Buying, Not Cooking," 34.
10. Smith Maguire, "Introduction," 13.
11. Ibid., 17.
12. Turner, "Buying, Not Cooking," 24. See also Turner's book, *How the Other Half Ate.*
13. Turner, "Buying, Not Cooking," 24.
14. Ibid., 25.

BIBLIOGRAPHY

Primary Sources

GOVERNMENT DOCUMENTS

Bank of Canada
Inflation Calculator

Government of Alberta
Ministry of Agriculture and Forestry

Government of British Columbia
Ministry of Agriculture and Lands
Orders in Council
Registry Services

Government of Canada
Agriculture and Agri-Food Canada
Atlantic Canada Opportunities Agency
Export Development Canada
Intellectual Property Office
Minimum Wage Database

Government of Manitoba
Agriculture, Food, and Community Development
Companies Office
Trade and Investment

Government of New Brunswick
Labour and Employment Board
Office of the Premier, Business New Brunswick

Government of Ontario
Legislative Assembly of Ontario, Hansard

Senate of Canada
Hansard

PUBLIC ARCHIVES

Belleville Public Library (Belleville, ON)
Belleville Intelligencer clippings files
City of Belleville, Industrial Development Department files

City of Vancouver Archives
Manitoba Sugar Company records, Series S15

Colchester Museum (Truro, NS)
Robertson's Candy exhibit

Nova Scotia Archives (Halifax, NS)
Moirs, MG 3

Provincial Archives of New Brunswick (Fredericton, NB)
Ganong Bros. Ltd. fonds, MC 504
New Brunswick Museum Vertical Files

The Rooms Provincial Archives (St. John's, NF)
Eric Ellis Collection, MG 7

University of Manitoba Archives & Special Collections
Winnipeg Tribune Clippings Collection

PRIVATE COLLECTIONS

The Chocolate Museum (St. Stephen, NB)

Old Dutch Foods (Roseville, MN)

W.T. Hawkins (Belleville, ON)

INTERVIEWS

Anonymous interviews are not listed.

Aanenson, Curt. Old Dutch Foods Director, interview by author, Roseville, MN, 14 October 2013.

Aanenson, Steven. President of Old Dutch Foods, interview by author, Roseville, MN, 14 October 2013.

Adams, Alfred. Former *Kids Bids* participant, interview by Elizabeth-Anne Johnson, Winnipeg, MB, 1 November 2013.

Babiak, Bob. Former *Kids Bids* participant, Skype interview by Sarah Story, Montreal, QC, 23 January 2015.

Bashucky, Bill. Old Dutch Winnipeg Plant Manager, interview by Elizabeth-Anne Johnson, Winnipeg, MB, 10 December 2013.

Bly, Richard. Shipping Manager, W.T. Hawkins, interview by author, Belleville, ON, 9 May 2013.

Bosiak, Barbara. Former Inventory and Purchasing employee, W.T. Hawkins Ltd., interview by author, Belleville, ON, 9 May 2013.

Boulet, Martial. Former Old Dutch plant manager in Winnipeg and Calgary, Skype interview by Sarah Story, Calgary, AB, 12 December 2014.

Broad, Thomas. Fryer operator, Covered Bridge Potato Chips, interview by author, Waterville, NB, 10 August 2013.

Burbine, William Arthur. Robertson's Candy employee, interview by Sarah Reilly, Truro, NS, 14 August 2013.

Campbell (née Krochak), Kardene. Former *Kids Bids* participant, interview by Sarah Story, Winnipeg, MB, 25 November 2014.

Cody, Alan. Former *Kids Bids* participant, Skype interview by Sarah Story, Saskatoon, SK, 21 January 2015.

Cooze, Bunn. Purity Factories syrup maker, interview by author, St. John's, NL, 18 August 2013.

Dunn, Jeffrey. Former shipper-receiver and union representative, Scott-Bathgate, interview by Sarah Reilly, Winnipeg, MB, 19 July 2013.

Fobert, Geraldine (Gerry). Former production line manager, W.T. Hawkins Ltd., interview by author, Belleville, ON, 9 May 2013.

Gould, Clarence. Former manager of Cavalier Candies, interview by Sarah Story, Winnipeg, MB, 24 April 2015.

Hawkins, Kent. President, W.T. Hawkins Ltd., interview by author, Belleville, ON, 9 May 2013.

Howdle, Lynda. Former Paulin-Chambers employee, interview by Sarah Story, Winnipeg, MB, 7 December 2014.

Krochak, Doug. Former *Kids Bids* participant, interview by Sarah Story, Winnipeg, MB, 24 November 2014.

Kroeker, Don. Former Chief Executive Officer of Kroeker Farms, interview by Sarah Story, Winnipeg, MB, 29 January 2015.

Kuhl, John. Former President and Chief Executive Officer of Southern Potato Company, interview by Sarah Story, Winkler, MB, 2 February 2015.

Kuhl, Marlon. Vice-President, Southern Potato Company, interview by Sarah Story, Winkler, MB, 2 February 2015.

Maqsood, Bebe. Former worker at Old Dutch Winnipeg plant, interview by Sarah Reilly and Elizabeth-Anne Johnson, Winnipeg, MB, 27 January 2013.

McAllister, Cathy. Director of Operations, Manpower, interview by author, Belleville, ON, 9 May 2013.

McCartney, Mike. Plant Manager, Covered Bridge Potato Chips, interview by Elizabeth-Anne Johnson, Waterville, NB, 9 August 2013.

McDougall, Kirk. Former *Kids Bids* participant, Skype interview by Sarah Story, Nanaimo, BC, 25 November 2014.

McGarvey, Tony. Director of Finance, W.T. Hawkins Ltd., interview by author, Belleville, ON, 9 May 2013.

McMahon, Dick. Old Dutch Foods Distribution Manager, interview by author, Roseville, MN, 15 October 2013.

Moore, Sharon. Former *Kids Bids* participant, Skype interview by Sarah Story, Calgary, AB, 8 December 2014.

Oye, David. Old Dutch Director of Purchasing and Logistics, interview by Sarah Story, Winnipeg, MB, 11 December 2014.

Peterson, Doug. Former *Kids Bids* participant, Skype interview by Sarah Story, St. Albert, AB, 23 November 2014.

Peterson, Geraldine (Geri). Former *Kids Bids* participant, Skype interview by Sarah Story, London, UK, 29 November 2014.

Petit, Jean Pierre (J.P.). United Food and Commercial Workers Union Local 832 representative, and former employee and shop steward at Old Dutch Winnipeg, interview by Sarah Reilly, Winnipeg, MB, 2 May 2013.

Porter, Ken. Former *Kids Bids* participant, interview by Sarah Story, Winnipeg, MB, 27 November 2014.

Prior, Verne. Former host of Old Dutch *Kids Bids*, Regina and Saskatoon, Skype interview by author, Vancouver Island, BC, 14 October 2015.

Rempel, Wayne. Chief Executive Officer of Kroeker Farms, interview by Sarah Story, Winkler, MB, 22 January 2015.

Robertson, Roy. Owner and President of Robertson's Candy, interview by author, Truro, NS, 14 August 2013.

Rosin, Richard. Former *Kids Bids* participant, interview by Sarah Story, Winnipeg, MB, 26 February 2015.

Sykes, Les. Director of Operations, W.T. Hawkins Ltd., interview by author, Belleville, ON, 10 May 2013.

Thomas, Karen. Former *Kids Bids* participant, Skype interview by Sarah Story, Coquitlam, BC, 30 March 2015.

Voth, Gerhard Otto. Former foreman at Old Dutch Winnipeg plant, interview by Elizabeth-Anne Johnson, Winnipeg, MB, 21 November 2013.

Wichenko, Grant. Former *Kids Bids* participant, interview by author, Winnipeg, MB, 15 June 2015.

Yada, Rickey. Dean of the Faculty of Land and Food Systems, University of British Columbia, interview by Sarah Reilly, Guelph, ON, 20 February 2013.

Yasumatsu, Tom. Former Director of Manufacturing, Paulin-Chambers, interview by Sarah Story, Winnipeg, MB, 15 December 2014.

Secondary Sources

Andersen, Boris, and Morten Hedegaard Larsen. "'Reflection': Fighting Five Food Myths About the 'Good Old Days.'" *Food and Foodways* 23, no. 4 (2015): 286–94.

Armstrong, Gary M., and Merrie Brucks. "Dealing with Children's Advertising: Public Policy Issues and Alternatives." *Journal of Public Policy & Marketing* 7 (1988): 98–113.

Bakan, Joel. *The Corporation: The Pathological Pursuit of Profit and Power.* New York: Free Press, 2004.

Barber, Katherine, ed. *Canadian Oxford Dictionary.* 2nd ed. Oxford: Oxford University Press, 2004.

Barthes, Roland. *Mythologies.* Translated by Annette Lavers. New York: Hill and Wang, 1972.

Basok, Tanya. *Tortillas and Tomatoes: Transmigrant Mexican Harvesters in Canada.* Montreal: McGill-Queen's University Press, 2002.

Begin, Patricia, Wendy Moss, and Peter Niemczak. *The Land Claim Dispute at Oka.* Ottawa: Library of Parliament, Research Branch, 1990.

Besky, Sarah, and Sandy Brown. "Looking for Work: Placing Labor in Food Studies." *Labor: Studies in Working-Class History of the Americas* 12, nos. 1–2 (2015): 19–43.

Blair, Roger D., and Jeffrey L. Harrison. *Monopsony in Law and Economics.* New York: Cambridge University Press, 2010.

Boero, Natalie. "Fat Kids, Working Moms, and the 'Epidemic of Obesity': Race, Class, and Mother Blame." In *The Fat Studies Reader,* edited by Esther D. Rothblum and Sondra Solovay, 113–19. New York: New York University Press, 2009.

Bourdieu, Pierre. *Distinction: A Social Critique of the Judgement of Taste.* London and New York: Routledge, 1984.

Bowen, Sarah, Sinikka Elliott, and Joslyn Brenton. "The Joy of Cooking?" *Contexts* 13, no. 3 (2014): 20–25.

Burhans, Dick. *Crunch! A History of the Great American Potato Chip.* Madison: Terrace Books, 2008.

Burtea, Octavian. "Snack Foods from Formers and High-Shear Extruders." In *Snack Foods Processing,* edited by Edmund W. Lusas and Lloyd W. Rooney, 281–314. Boca Raton: CRC Press, 2001.

Canadian Association of Broadcasters. *Advertising to Children in Canada: A Reference Guide.* 2006. http://www.cab-acr.ca/english/social/advertisingchildren/kids_reference_guide.pdf.

Careless, James Maurice Stockford. *CANADA: A Celebration of Our Heritage.* Mississauga: Heritage Publishing House, 1996.

Carr, David. *Candymaking in Canada.* Toronto: Dundurn Press, 2003.

Carstairs, Catherine. "Roots Nationalism: Branding English Canada Cool in the 1980s and 1990s." *Histoire Sociale/Social History* 39, no. 77 (May 2006): 235–55.

Chan, Marion. "Snacking in Canada 2008." Presented at the Conference of the Canadian Snack Food Association, 20 September 2008.

Chen, Joanne. *The Taste of Sweet: Our Complicated Love Affair with Our Favorite Treats.* New York: Three Rivers Press, 2008.

Cho, Lily. *Eating Chinese: Culture on the Menu in Small Town Canada.* Toronto: University of Toronto Press, 2010.

Chowdhury, Rajiv, et al. "Association of Dietary, Circulating, and Supplement Fatty Acids with Coronary Risk: A Systematic Review and Meta-Analysis." *Annals of Internal Medicine* 160, no. 6 (18 March 2014): 398–406.

Cohen, Lizabeth. *A Consumers' Republic: The Politics of Mass Consumption in Postwar America.* New York: Vintage Books, 2004.

Coleman, Barbara. "Through the Years We'll All Be Friends: The 'Mickey Mouse Club,' Consumerism, and the Cultural Consensus." *Visual Resources* 14, no. 3 (January 2011): 297–306.

Conrad, Dulcie. "Moirs Ltd. Considering Relocation." *The 4th Estate* 9, no. 49 (29 March 1973): 1.

Cooke, Nathalie. *What's to Eat? Entrées in Canadian Food History.* Montreal and Kingston: McGill-Queen's University Press, 2009.

Cormack, Patricia, and James F. Cosgrave. "'Always Fresh, Always There': Tim Hortons and the Consumer-Citizen." In *Desiring Canada: CBC Contests, Hockey Violence, and Other Stately Pleasures,* 62–93. Toronto: University of Toronto Press, 2013.

Cross, Gary S. *The Cute and the Cool: Wondrous Innocence and Modern American Children's Culture.* New York: Oxford University Press, 2004.

———. *Kids' Stuff: Toys and the Changing World of American Childhood.* Cambridge: Harvard University Press, 1997.

Deutsch, Tracey. "Memories of Mothers in the Kitchen: Local Foods, History, and Women's Work," *Radical History Review* 110 (Spring 2011): 167–77.

Dorson, Richard M. "Folklore and Fake Lore." *The American Mercury* (March 1950): 335–42.

Dusselier, Jane. "Understandings of Food as Culture." *Environmental History* 14, no. 2 (April 2009): 331–38.

Elliott, Charlene. "*Taste Rules!* Food Marketing, Food Law, and Childhood Obesity in Canada." *Cuizine: The Journal of Canadian Food Cultures* 1, no. 1 (2008). http://www.erudit.org/revue/cuizine/2008/v1/n1/019371ar.html.

Epp, Frank H. *Mennonites in Canada, 1786–1920: The History of a Separate People.* Toronto: Macmillan, 1974.

Ferguson, Priscilla Parkhurst. "The Senses of Taste." *AHR Forum* 116, no. 2 (April 2011): 371–84.

Fitzgerald, Gerald J., and Gabriella M. Petrick. "In Good Taste: Rethinking American History with Our Palates." *The Journal of American History* 95, no. 2 (September 2008): 392–404.

Flandrin, Jean-Louis, and Massimo Montanari. "Conclusion: Today and Tomorrow." In *Food: A Culinary History,* edited by Jean-Louis Flandrin and Massimo Montanari, 548–53. New York: Penguin Books, 2000.

Folster, David. *The Chocolate Ganongs of St. Stephen, New Brunswick.* St. Stephen, NB: Ganong Bros. Ltd., 1990.

———. *Ganong: A Sweet History of Chocolate.* Fredericton, NB: Goose Lane Editions, 2006.

Fox, William S. "Folklore and Fakelore: Some Sociological Considerations." *Journal of the Folklore Institute* 17, no. 2/3 (May–December 1980): 244–61.

———, and Mae G. Banner. "Social and Economic Contexts of Folklore Variants: The Case of Potato Chip Legends." *Western Folklore* 42, no. 2 (April 1983): 114–26.

Gard, Michael, and Jan Wright. *The Obesity Epidemic: Science, Morality, and Ideology.* London: Routledge, 2005.

Goddard, Leslie. *Images of America: Chicago's Sweet Candy History.* Charleston: Arcadia Publishing, 2012.

Goody, Jack. *Cooking, Cuisine and Class: A Study in Comparative Sociology.* Cambridge: Cambridge University Press, 1982.

Guthman, Julie. "Can't Stomach It: How Michael Pollan et al. Made Me Want to Eat Cheetos." *Gastronomica* 7, no. 3 (Summer 2007): 75–79.

———. "Neoliberalism and the Constitution of Contemporary Bodies." In *The Fat Studies Reader,* edited by Esther D. Rothblum and Sondra Solvay, 187–96. New York: New York University Press, 2009.

Hartel, Richard W., and AnnaKate Hartel. *Candy Bites: The Science of Sweets.* New York: Springer, 2014.

Hastings, Paula. "Branding Canada: Consumer Culture and the Development of Popular Nationalism in the Early Twentieth Century." In *Canadas of the Mind: The Making and Unmaking of Canadian Nationalisms in the Twentieth Century,* edited by Norman Hillmer and Adam Chapnick, 134–58. Montreal and Kingston: McGill-Queen's University Press, 2007.

Helgren, Jennifer. "A 'Very Innocent Time': Oral History Narratives, Nostalgia and Girls' Safety in the 1950s and 1960s." *Oral History Review* 42, no. 1 (Winter/Spring 2015): 50–69.

Heron, Craig. *Booze: A Distilled History.* Toronto: Between the Lines, 2003.

———, and Robert Storey. *On the Job: Confronting the Labour Process in Canada.* Kingston: McGill-Queen's University Press, 1986.

Huber, Gordon. "Snack Foods from Cooking Extruders." In *Snack Foods Processing,* edited by Edmund W. Lusas and Lloyd W. Rooney, 315–67. Boca Raton: CRC Press, 2001.

Hutchinson, Braden P.L. "Making (Anti)Modern Childhood: Producing and Consuming Toys in Late Victorian Canada." *Scientia Canadensis: Canadian Journal of the History of Science, Technology and Medicine* 36, no. 1 (2013): 79–110.

Iacovetta, Franca, Valerie J. Korinek, and Marlene Epp, eds. *Edible Histories, Cultural Politics: Towards a Canadian Food History.* Toronto: University of Toronto Press, 2012.

Jacobson, Lisa. *Raising Consumers: Children and the American Mass Market in the Early Twentieth Century.* New York: Columbia University Press, 2004.

Jung, Yuson, and Nicolas Sternsdorff Cisterna. "Introduction to *Crafting Senses: Circulating the Knowledge and Experience of Taste.*" *Food and Foodways* 22 (June 2014): 1–2.

Kanehsatake: 270 Years of Resistance. Director and writer Alanis Obomsawin. Toronto: National Film Board, 1993. Film. http://www.nfb.ca/film/kanehsatake_270_years_of_resistance/.

Kapur, Jyotsna. *Coining for Capital: Movies, Marketing, and the Transformation of Childhood.* New Brunswick, NJ: Rutgers University Press, 2005.

Kawash, Samira. *Candy: A Century of Panic and Pleasure.* New York: Faber and Faber, 2013.

Kessler-Harris, Alice. *Women Have Always Worked: A Historical Overview.* New York: McGraw-Hill, 1981.

King Corn. Director Aaron Woolf. Westport, NY: ITVS and Mosaic Films, 2007. Film.

Kirby, Sheryl. *Kitchen Party: Food Stories from Nova Scotia and Beyond.* Toronto: Stained Pages Press, 2012.

Klein, Naomi. *No Logo: Taking Aim at the Brand Bullies.* New York: Picador, 2000.

Korsmeyer, Carolyn, ed. *The Taste Culture Reader: Experiencing Food and Drink.* Oxford: Berg, 2005.

Korten, David C. *When Corporations Rule the World.* Boulder: Kumarian Press, 1995.

Ladner, Kiera L., and Leanne Simpson. *This Is an Honour Song: Twenty Years since the Blockades, An Anthology of Writing on the "Oka Crisis."* Winnipeg: Arbeiter Ring Publishers, 2010.

Laudan, Rachel. *Cuisine & Empire: Cooking in World History.* Berkeley: University of California Press, 2013.

———. "A Plea for Culinary Modernism: Why We Should Love New, Fast, Processed Food." *Gastronomica* 1, no. 1 (Winter 2001): 36–44.

Levenstein, Harvey. *Paradox of Plenty: A Social History of Eating in Modern America.* Rev. ed. Berkeley: University of California Press, 2003.

Levine, Susan, and Steve Striffler. "From Field to Table in Labor History." *Labor: Studies in Working-Class History of the Americas* 12, nos. 1–2 (2015): 3–12.

Lewald, H. Ernest. "The Hispanic World." *Hispania* 53, no. 2 (May 1970): 309.

Liesener, Katie. "Marshmallow Fluff." *Gastronomica* 9, no. 2 (Spring 2009): 51–56.

Long, Lucy M. "Culinary Tourism." In *The Oxford Handbook of Food History*, edited by Jeffrey Pilcher, 389–406. Oxford: Oxford University Press, 2012.

Mac Con Iomaire, Máirtin. "Culinary Voices: Perspectives from Dublin Restaurants." *Oral History* 39, no. 1 (Spring 2011): 77–90.

MacLaine, Craig, Michael S. Baxendale, and Robert Galbraith. *This Land Is Our Land: The Mohawk Revolt at Oka.* Montreal: Optimum, 1990.

Macpherson, Catherine. "A Cargo of Cocoa: Chocolate's Early History in Canada." In *What's to Eat? Entrées in Canadian Food History,* edited by Nathalie Cooke, 79–86. Montreal and Kingston: McGill-Queen's University Press, 2009.

Maloni, Michael, and W.C. Benton. "Power Influences in the Supply Chain." *Journal of Business Logistics* 21, no. 1 (2000): 49–73.

May, Steve, and Laura Morrison. "Making Sense of Restructuring: Narratives of Accommodation among Downsized Workers." In *Beyond the Ruins: The Meanings of Deindustrialization,* edited by Jefferson Cowie and Joseph Heathcott, 259–83. Ithaca and London: ILR Press, 2003.

McCallum, Margaret E. "Separate Spheres: The Organization of Work in a Confectionery Factory: Ganong Bros., St. Stephen, New Brunswick." *Labour/Le Travail* 24 (Fall 1989): 69–90.

McKay, Ian. "Capital and Labour in the Halifax Baking and Confectionery Industry during the Last Half of the Nineteenth Century." *Labour/Le Travail* 3 (1978): 63–108.

Mintz, Sidney W. *Sweetness and Power: The Place of Sugar in Modern History.* New York: Penguin, 1985.

Monod, David. *Store Wars: Shopkeepers and the Culture of Mass Marketing, 1890–1939.* Toronto: University of Toronto Press, 1996.

Mosby, Ian. *Food Will Win the War: The Politics, Culture and Science of Food on Canada's Home Front.* Vancouver: University of British Columbia Press, 2014.

Moss, Michael. *Salt Sugar Fat: How the Food Giants Hooked Us.* Toronto: McClelland and Stewart, 2013.

Mulrooney, Margaret Anne. "Femininity and the Factory: Women's Labouring Bodies in the Moir's Candy Plant, 1949–1970." MA thesis, Dalhousie University, 2012.

Naylor, R. Thomas. *The History of Canadian Business, 1867–1914.* Toronto: J. Lorimer, 1975.

The North-South Institute. *Migrant Workers in Canada: A Review of the Canadian Seasonal Agricultural Workers Program.* Ottawa: North-South Institute, 2006.

Off, Carol. *Bitter Chocolate: Investigating the Dark Side of the World's Most Seductive Sweet.* Toronto: Random House, 2006.

Ogden, Cynthia L., Margaret D. Carroll, Brian K. Kit, and Katherine M. Flegal. "Prevalence of Childhood and Adult Obesity in the United States, 2011–2012." *Journal of the American Medical Association* 311, no. 8 (26 Feburary 2014). https://jama.jamanetwork.com/article.aspx?articleid=1832542.

Parr, Joy. *The Gender of Breadwinners: Women, Men, and Change in Two Industrial Towns, 1880–1950.* Toronto: University of Toronto Press, 1990.

Penfold, Steve. *The Donut: A Canadian History.* Toronto: University of Toronto Press, 2008.

Petrick, Gabriella M. "Industrial Food." In *The Oxford Handbook of Food History*, edited by Jeffrey Pilcher, 258–78. Oxford: Oxford University Press, 2012.

Pichler, Melanie. "Legal Dispossession: State Strategies and Selectivities in the Expansion of Indonesian Palm Oil and Agrofuel Production." *Development and Change* 46, no. 3 (May 2015): 508–33.

Pollan, Michael. *In Defense of Food: An Eater's Manifesto.* New York: Penguin Books, 2008.

———. *Food Rules: An Eater's Manual.* New York: Penguin Books, 2009.

———. *The Omnivore's Dilemma: A Natural History of Four Meals.* New York: Penguin, 2006.

Preibisch, Kerry. "Pick-Your-Own Labor: Migrant Workers and Flexibility in Canadian Agriculture." *The International Migration Review* 44, no. 2 (Summer 2010): 404–41.

Quiring, David M. *The Mennonite Old Colony Vision: Under Siege in Mexico and the Canadian Connection.* Steinbach, MB: Crossway Publications, 2003.

Read, Jodi, Sarah Zell, and Lynne Fernandez. *Migrant Voices: Stories of Agricultural Migrant Workers in Manitoba.* Winnipeg: Canadian Centre for Policy Alternatives, Manitoba Office, 2013.

Rice, Grant. "The Lower Mainland Food System: The Role of Fruit and Vegetable Processing." Master of Urban Studies thesis, Simon Fraser University, 2014.

Robbins, Bruce. "Commodity Histories." *PMLA* 120, no. 2 (March 2005): 454–63.

Roche, Judith, and Meg McHutchison, eds. *First Fish, First People: Salmon Tales of the North Pacific Rim.* Vancouver: University of British Columbia Press, 1998.

Rothblum, Esther D., and Sondra Solovay, eds. *The Fat Studies Reader.* New York: New York University Press, 2009.

Russell, Polly. "Archives, Academy, and Access: Food Producer Life Stories." *Gastronomica* 15, no. 3 (Fall 2015): 53–58.

Ryan, Orla. *Chocolate Nations: Living and Dying for Cocoa in West Africa.* London and NY: Zed Books, 2011.

Sangster, Joan. *Earning Respect: The Lives of Working Women in Small-Town Ontario, 1920–1960.* Toronto: University of Toronto Press, 1995.

———. "The Softball Solution: Female Workers, Male Managers, and the Operation of Paternalism at Westclox, 1923–60." *Labour/Le Travail* 32 (Fall 1993): 167–99.

Sawatzky, Harry Leonard. *They Sought a Country: Mennonite Colonization in Mexico.* Berkeley: University of California Press, 1971.

Schrage, Elliot J., and Anthony P. Ewing. "The Cocoa Industry and Child Labour." *Journal of Corporate Citizenship* 18 (Summer 2005): 99–112.

Sidorick, Daniel. *Condensed Capitalism: Campbell Soup and the Pursuit of Cheap Production in the Twentieth Century.* New York: ILR Press, 2009.

Silverman, Sharon Hernes. *Pennsylvania Snacks: A Guide to Food Factory Tours.* Mechanicsburg, PA: Stackpole Books, 2001.

Smith, Andrew F. "False Memories: The Invention of Culinary Fakelore and Food Fallacies." In *Food and the Memory: Proceedings of the Oxford Symposium on Food and Cookery 2000,* edited by Harlan Walker, 254–60. London, UK: Prospect Books, 2001.

———. "Snack Foods." In *The Business of Food: Encyclopedia of the Food and Drink Industries,* edited by Gary Allen and Ken Albala, 335–41. Westport, CT: Greenwood Press, 2007.

Smith Maguire, Jennifer. "Introduction: Looking at Food Practices and Taste across the Class Divide." *Food, Culture & Society* 19, no. 1 (March 2016): 11–18.

Teicholz, Nina. *The Big Fat Surprise: Why Butter, Meat, and Cheese Belong in a Healthy Diet.* New York: Simon & Schuster, 2014.

Thiessen, Janis. "From Faith to Food: Using Oral History to Study Corporate Mythology at Canadian Manufacturing Firms." *Oral History* 42, no. 2 (Spring 2014): 59–72.

———. *Manufacturing Mennonites: Work and Religion in Postwar Manitoba.* Toronto: University of Toronto Press, 2013.

Thornton, Robert J. "Retrospectives: How Joan Robinson and B.L. Hallward Named Monopsony." *Journal of Economic Perspectives* 18, no. 2 (Spring 2004): 257–61.

Tone, Andrea. *The Business of Benevolence: Industrial Paternalism in Progressive America.* Ithaca, NY: Cornell University Press, 1997.

Turner, Katherine Leonard. "Buying, Not Cooking: Ready-to-Eat Food in American Urban Working-Class Neighborhoods, 1880–1930." *Food, Culture & Society* 9, no. 1 (Spring 2006): 13–39.

———. *How the Other Half Ate: A History of Working-Class Meals at the Turn of the Century.* Berkeley: University of California Press, 2014.

Turner, Steven, and Heather Molyneaux. "Agricultural Science, Potato Breeding and the Fredericton Experimental Station, 1912–66." *Acadiensis* 33, no. 2 (Spring 2004): 44–67.

United Nations International Labour Office. *Rooting Out Child Labour from Cocoa Farms.* Paper no. 4, *Child Labour Monitoring—A Partnership of Communities and Government*, by Una Murray et al. Geneva: ILO, 2007.

Varty, John F. "Growing Bread: Technoscience, Environment, and Modern Wheat at the Dominion Grain Research Laboratory, Canada, 1912–1960." PhD diss., Queen's University, 2005.

———. "On Protein, Prairie Wheat, and Good Bread: Rationalizing Technologies and the Canadian State, 1912–1935." *The Canadian Historical Review* 85, no. 4 (December 2004): 721–53.

von Plato, Alexander. "Contemporary Witnesses and the Historical Profession: Remembrance, Communicative Transmission, and Collective Memory in Qualitative History." *Oral History Forum d'histoire orale* 29 (2009): 1–27.

Walker, Scott, and Brian Gratton. "Mexican American History Online." *OAH Magazine of History* 23, no. 4 (October 2009): 50–52.

Watkins, Mel. Foreword to R.T. Naylor, *The History of Canadian Business, 1867–1914,* Carleton Library Edition, by R.T. Naylor, xv–xx. Montreal and Kingston: McGill-Queen's University Press, 2006.

Westerman, Marty. "Death of the Frito Bandito." *American Demographics* 11, no. 3 (March 1989): 28–32.

Winegard, Timothy C. *Oka: A Convergence of Cultures and the Canadian Forces.* Kingston: Canadian Defence Academy Press, 2008.

Winson, Anthony. *The Industrial Diet: The Degradation of Food and the Struggle for Healthy Eating.* Vancouver: University of British Columbia Press, 2013.

Woloson, Wendy A. *Refined Tastes: Sugar, Confectionery, and Consumers in Nineteenth-Century America.* Baltimore: Johns Hopkins University Press, 2002.

Wright, Christopher. "Historical Interpretations of the Labour Process: Retrospect and Future Research Directions." *Labour History* 100 (May 2011): 19–32.

Young, Lisa R., and Marion Nestle. "The Contribution of Expanding Portion Sizes to the US Obesity Epidemic." *American Journal of Public Health* 92, no. 2 (February 2002): 246–49.

Zahavi, Gerald. *Workers, Managers, and Welfare Capitalism: The Shoeworkers and Tanners of Endicott Johnson, 1890–1950.* Urbana: University of Illinois Press, 1988.

ILLUSTRATION CREDITS

Figure 1, photo by Janis Thiessen. Figures 2–11, courtesy of Old Dutch Foods, Roseville, Minnesota. Figure 12, Old Dutch Foods Canada Facebook page, 3 July 2014, https://www.facebook.com/photo.php?fbid=879069908787727&set=a.163848356976556.37950.163479673680091&type=1&theater. Figures 13–18, photos by Janis Thiessen. Figure 19, The Canadian Press/Ryan Remiorz. Figures 20–30, courtesy of W.T. Hawkins Ltd. Figure 31, courtesy of Lynda Howdle. Figure 32, photo by Janis Thiessen. Figure 33, courtesy Nova Scotia Archives, Nova Scotia Information Service photo no. 15896. Figure 34, courtesy Nova Scotia Archives Moirs Collection, MG 3 volume 1869. Figure 35, courtesy of Ganong Bros., Ltd. Figures 36–37, photo by Janis Thiessen. Figures 38–39, photos by Elizabeth-Anne Johnson. Figures 40–42, photos by Janis Thiessen. Figure 43, courtesy Saskatoon Public Library, Local History Room, CFQC Photographers Collection, photograph 4212-1. Figure 44, photo by Susan Gibson, courtesy of Doug Gibson.

INDEX

Page numbers in italic indicate illustration.

A

B

H

I

J

K